STARLIGHT ™

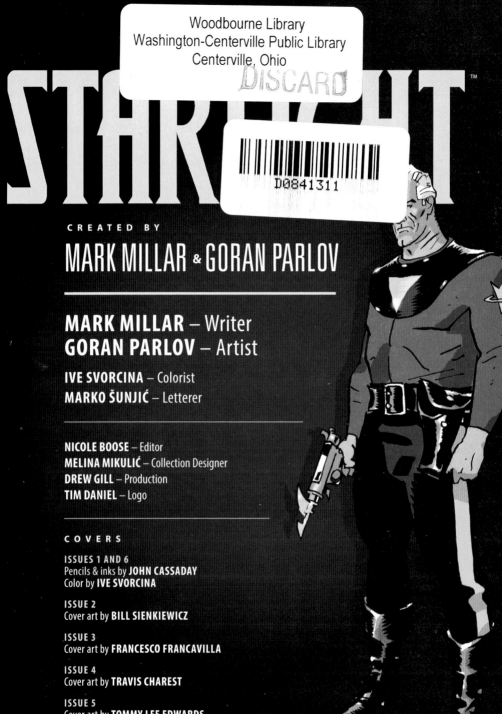

CREATED BY

MARK MILLAR & GORAN PARLOV

MARK MILLAR – Writer
GORAN PARLOV – Artist

IVE SVORCINA – Colorist
MARKO ŠUNJIĆ – Letterer

NICOLE BOOSE – Editor
MELINA MIKULIĆ – Collection Designer
DREW GILL – Production
TIM DANIEL – Logo

COVERS

ISSUES 1 AND 6
Pencils & inks by **JOHN CASSADAY**
Color by **IVE SVORCINA**

ISSUE 2
Cover art by **BILL SIENKIEWICZ**

ISSUE 3
Cover art by **FRANCESCO FRANCAVILLA**

ISSUE 4
Cover art by **TRAVIS CHAREST**

ISSUE 5
Cover art by **TOMMY LEE EDWARDS**

Variant cover artists **GORAN PARLOV, PASQUAL FERRY with DEAN WHITE, ROB LIEFELD with ROMULO FAJARDO, and CLIFF CHIANG**

IMAGE COMICS, INC.
Robert Kirkman – Chief Operating Officer
Erik Larsen – Chief Financial Officer
Todd McFarlane – President
Marc Silvestri – Chief Executive Officer
Jim Valentino – Vice-President

Eric Stephenson – Publisher
Ron Richards – Director of Business Development
Jennifer de Guzman – Director of Trade Book Sales
Kat Salazar – Director of PR & Marketing
Corey Murphy – Director of Retail Sales
Jeremy Sullivan – Director of Digital Sales
Emilio Bautista – Sales Assistant
Branwyn Bigglestone – Senior Accounts Manager
Emily Miller – Accounts Manager
Jessica Ambriz – Administrative Assistant
Tyler Shainline – Events Coordinator
David Brothers – Content Manager
Jonathan Chan – Production Manager
Drew Gill – Art Director
Meredith Wallace – Print Manager
Addison Duke – Production Artist
Vincent Kukua – Production Artist
Tricia Ramos – Production Assistant
IMAGECOMICS.COM

image

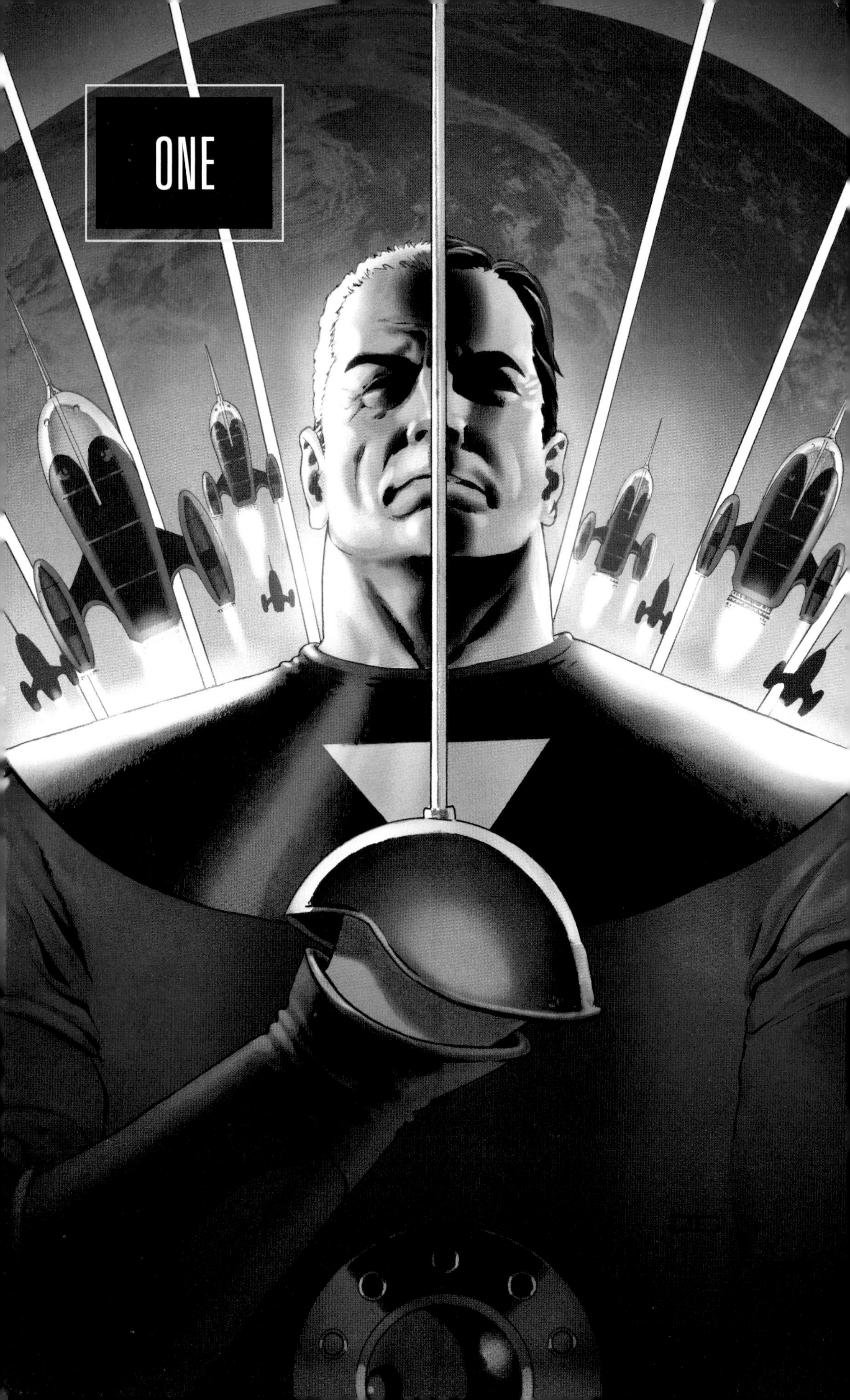
ONE

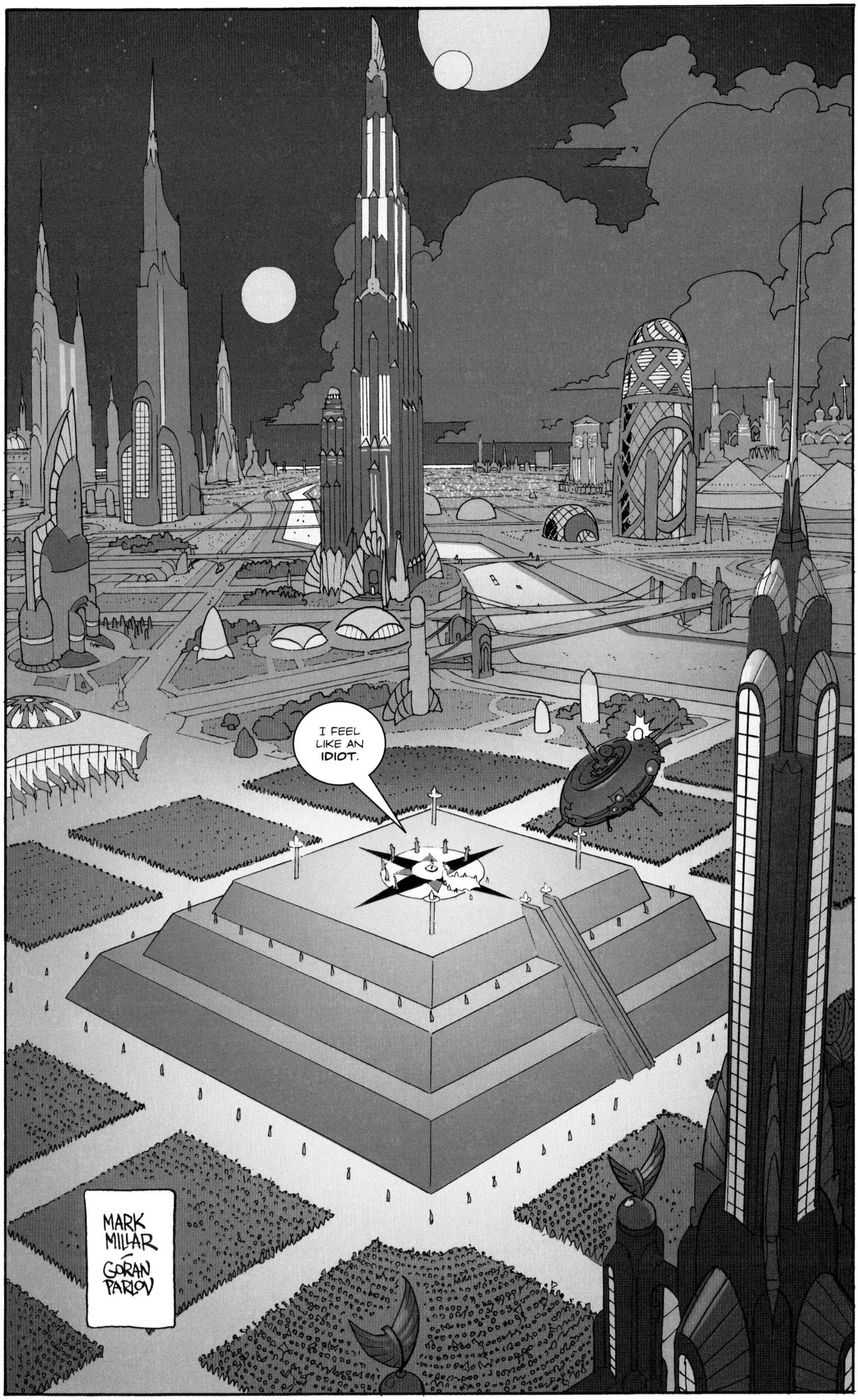

I FEEL LIKE AN IDIOT.
MARK MILLAR
GORAN PARLOV

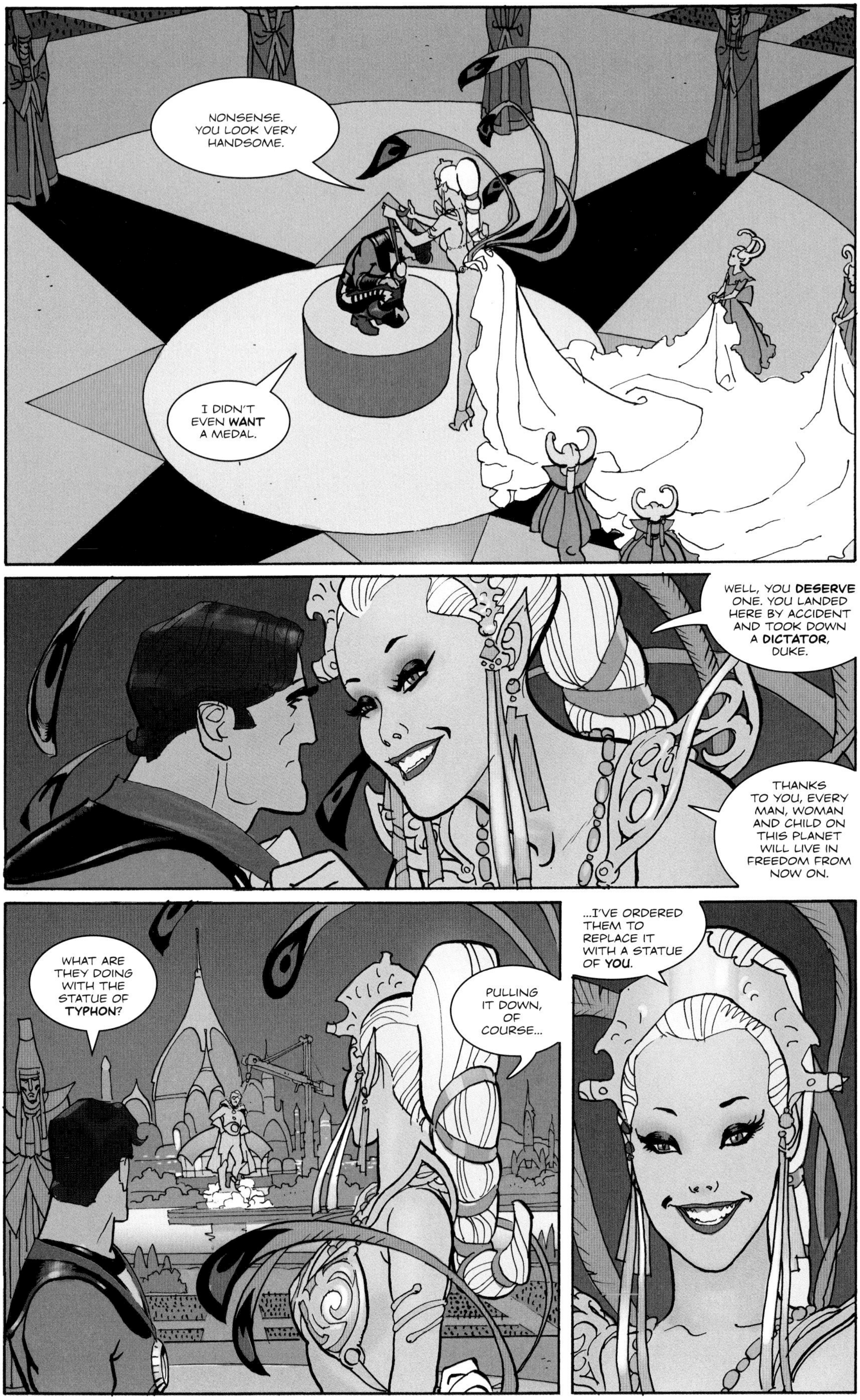
NONSENSE. YOU LOOK VERY HANDSOME.
I DIDN'T EVEN WANT A MEDAL.
WELL, YOU DESERVE ONE. YOU LANDED HERE BY ACCIDENT AND TOOK DOWN A DICTATOR, DUKE.
THANKS TO YOU, EVERY MAN, WOMAN AND CHILD ON THIS PLANET WILL LIVE IN FREEDOM FROM NOW ON.
WHAT ARE THEY DOING WITH THE STATUE OF TYPHON?
PULLING IT DOWN, OF COURSE...
...I'VE ORDERED THEM TO REPLACE IT WITH A STATUE OF YOU.

DEET DEET DEET DEET

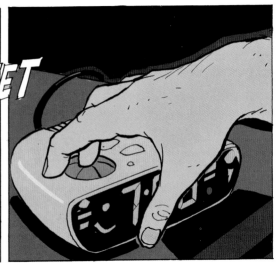

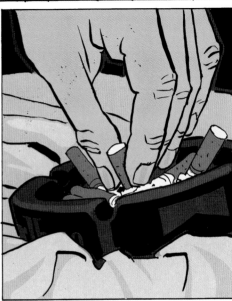

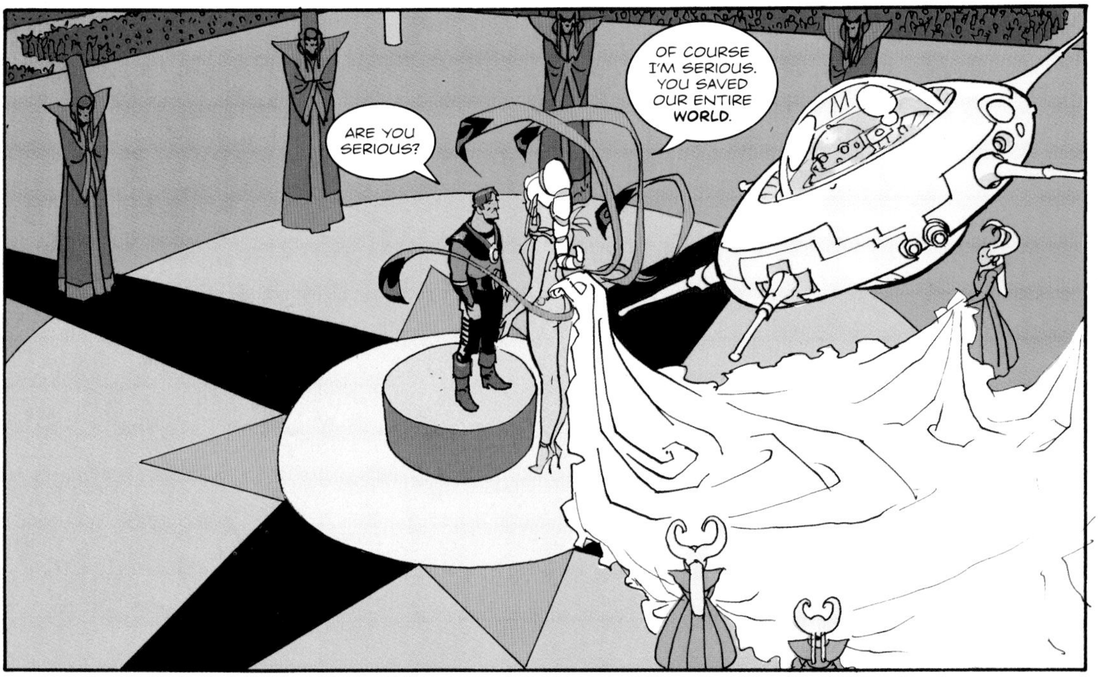
ARE YOU SERIOUS?
OF COURSE I'M SERIOUS. YOU SAVED OUR ENTIRE **WORLD**.

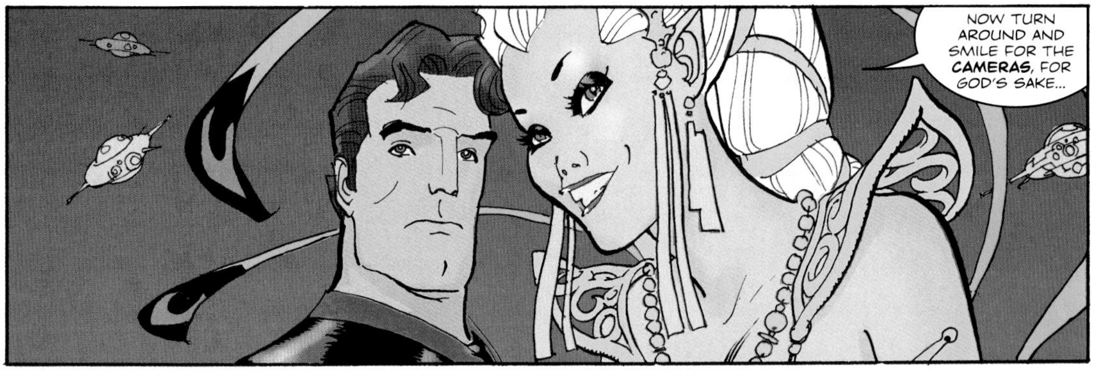
NOW TURN AROUND AND SMILE FOR THE **CAMERAS**, FOR GOD'S SAKE...

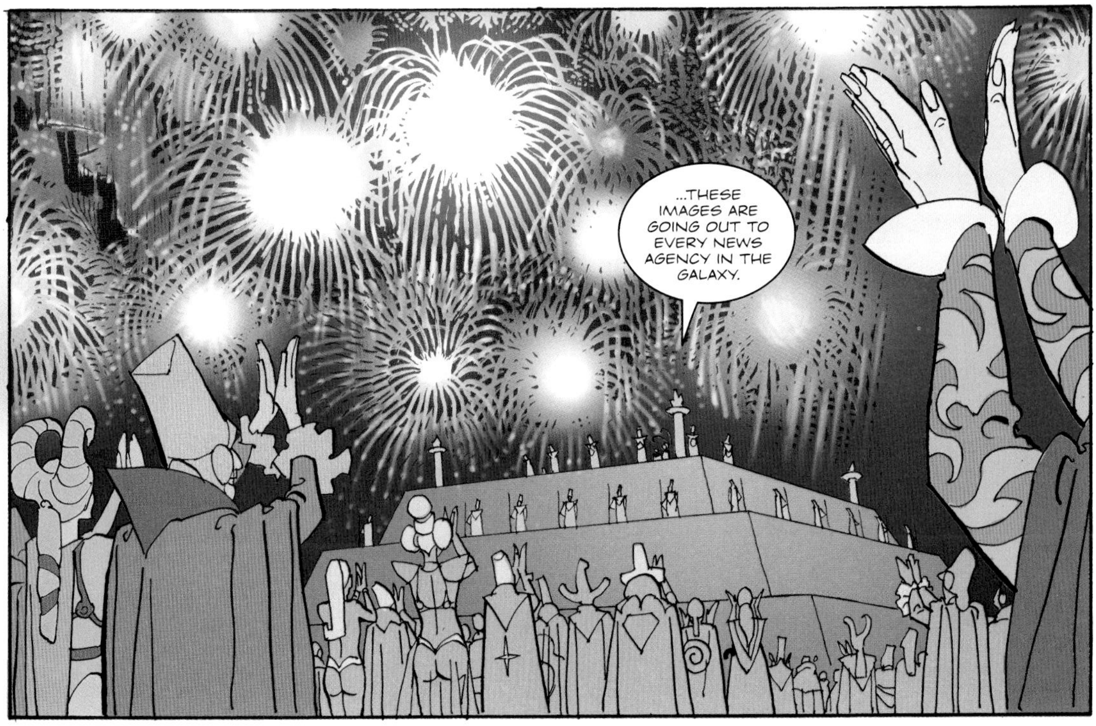
...THESE IMAGES ARE GOING OUT TO EVERY NEWS AGENCY IN THE GALAXY.

DEET DEET DEET DEET

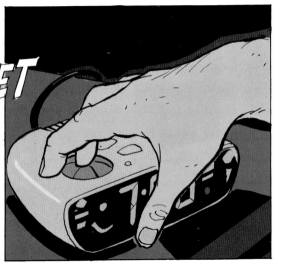

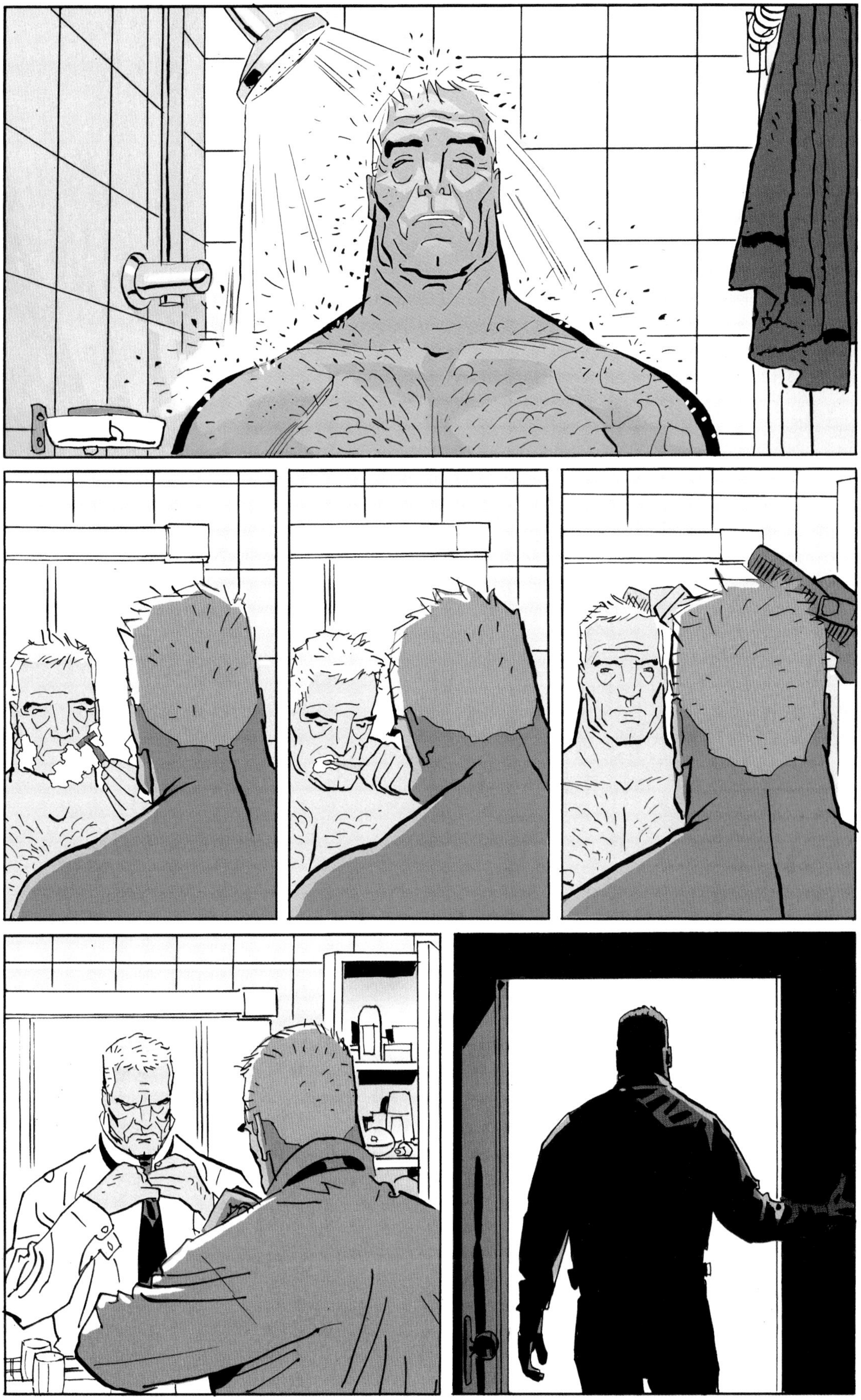

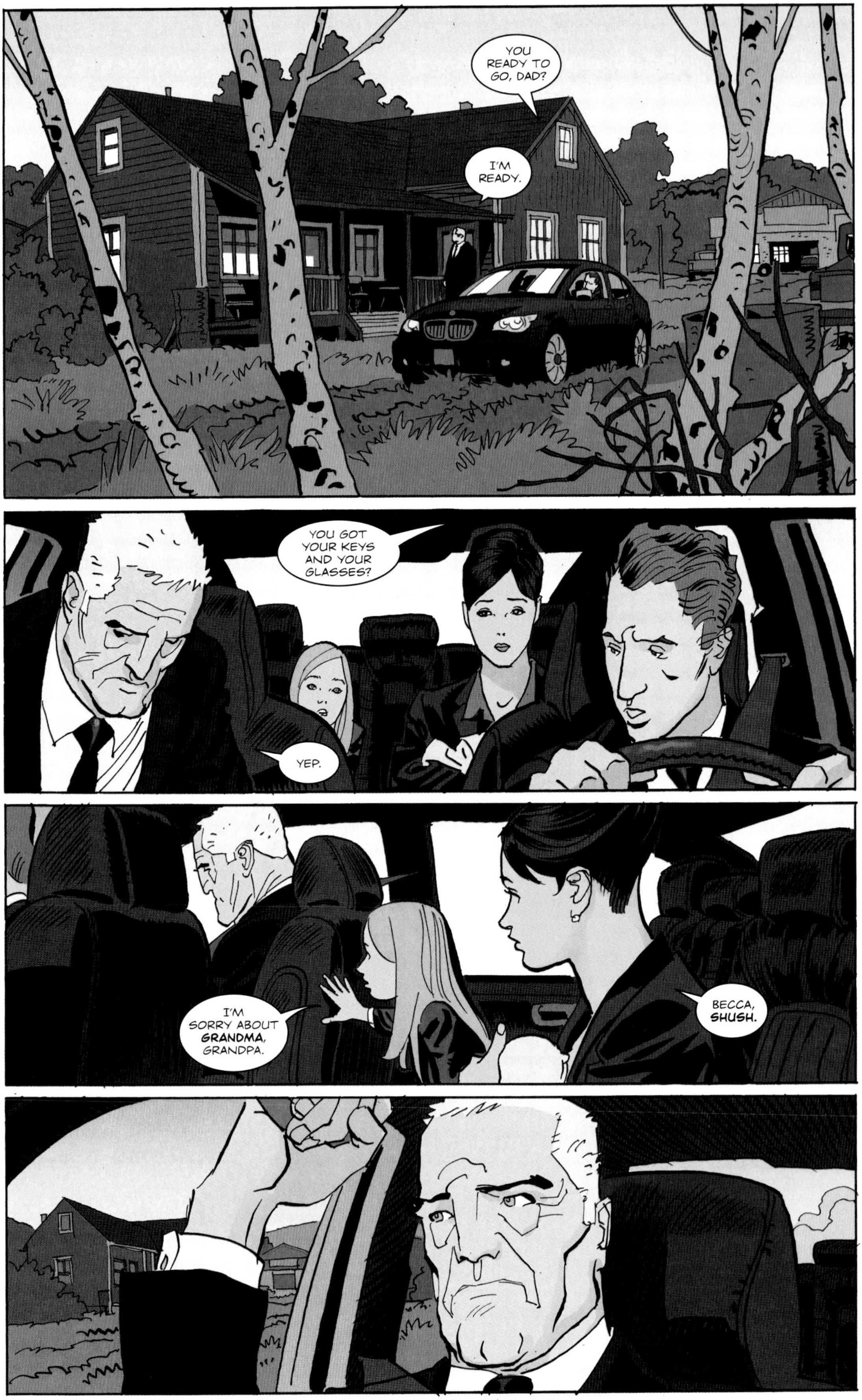
YOU READY TO GO, DAD?
I'M READY.
YOU GOT YOUR KEYS AND YOUR GLASSES?
YEP.
I'M SORRY ABOUT **GRANDMA**, GRANDPA.
BECCA, **SHUSH**.

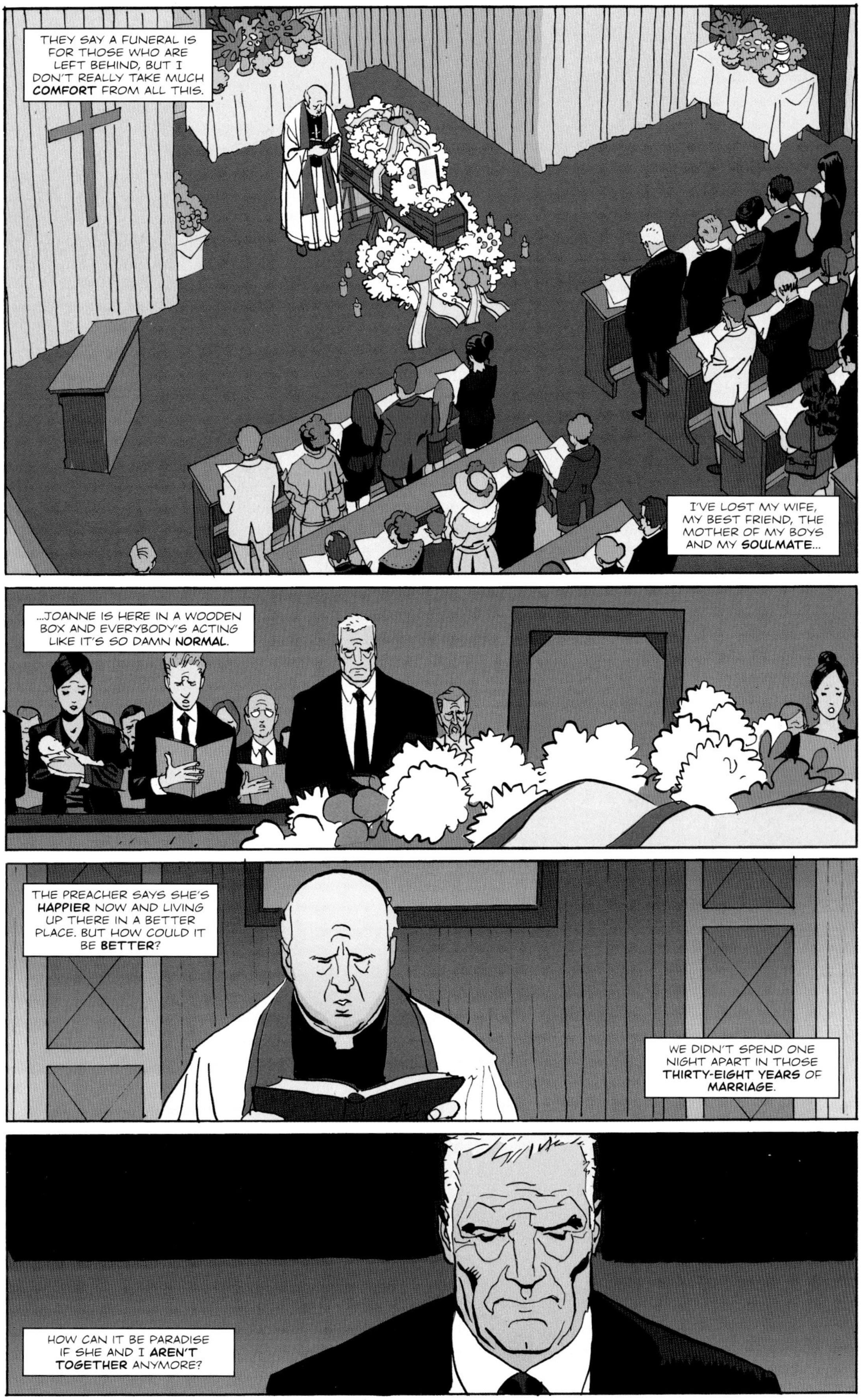
THEY SAY A FUNERAL IS FOR THOSE WHO ARE LEFT BEHIND, BUT I DON'T REALLY TAKE MUCH **COMFORT** FROM ALL THIS.
I'VE LOST MY WIFE, MY BEST FRIEND, THE MOTHER OF MY BOYS AND MY **SOULMATE**...
...JOANNE IS HERE IN A WOODEN BOX AND EVERYBODY'S ACTING LIKE IT'S SO DAMN **NORMAL**.
THE PREACHER SAYS SHE'S **HAPPIER** NOW AND LIVING UP THERE IN A BETTER PLACE. BUT HOW COULD IT BE **BETTER**?
WE DIDN'T SPEND ONE NIGHT APART IN THOSE **THIRTY-EIGHT YEARS** OF **MARRIAGE**.
HOW CAN IT BE PARADISE IF SHE AND I **AREN'T TOGETHER** ANYMORE?

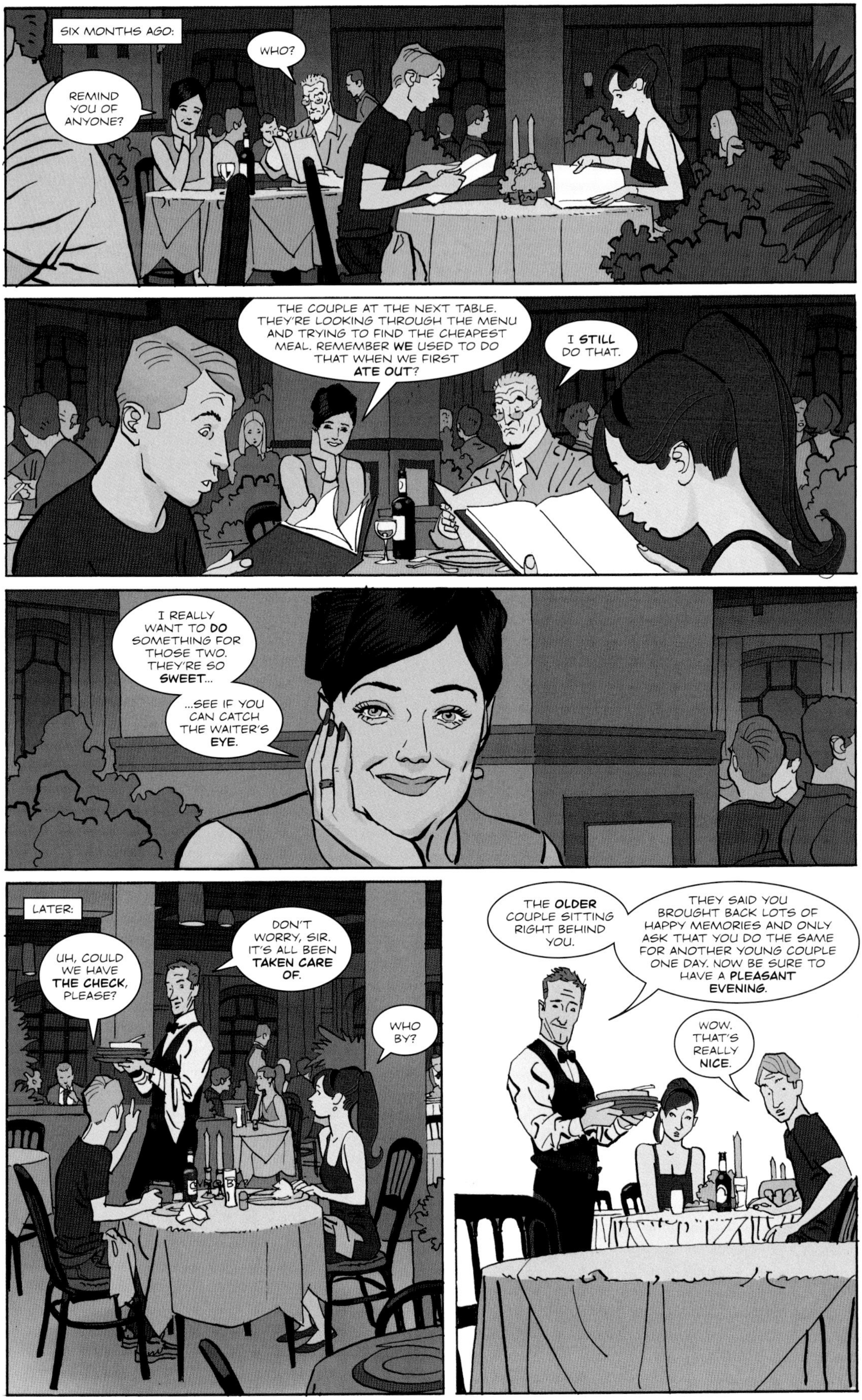
SIX MONTHS AGO:
REMIND YOU OF ANYONE?
WHO?
THE COUPLE AT THE NEXT TABLE. THEY'RE LOOKING THROUGH THE MENU AND TRYING TO FIND THE CHEAPEST MEAL. REMEMBER **WE** USED TO DO THAT WHEN WE FIRST **ATE OUT**?
I **STILL** DO THAT.
I REALLY WANT TO **DO** SOMETHING FOR THOSE TWO. THEY'RE SO **SWEET**...
...SEE IF YOU CAN CATCH THE WAITER'S **EYE**.
LATER:
UH, COULD WE HAVE **THE CHECK**, PLEASE?
DON'T WORRY, SIR. IT'S ALL BEEN **TAKEN CARE OF**.
WHO BY?
THE **OLDER** COUPLE SITTING RIGHT BEHIND YOU.
THEY SAID YOU BROUGHT BACK LOTS OF HAPPY MEMORIES AND ONLY ASK THAT YOU DO THE SAME FOR ANOTHER YOUNG COUPLE ONE DAY. NOW BE SURE TO HAVE A **PLEASANT EVENING**.
WOW. THAT'S REALLY **NICE**.

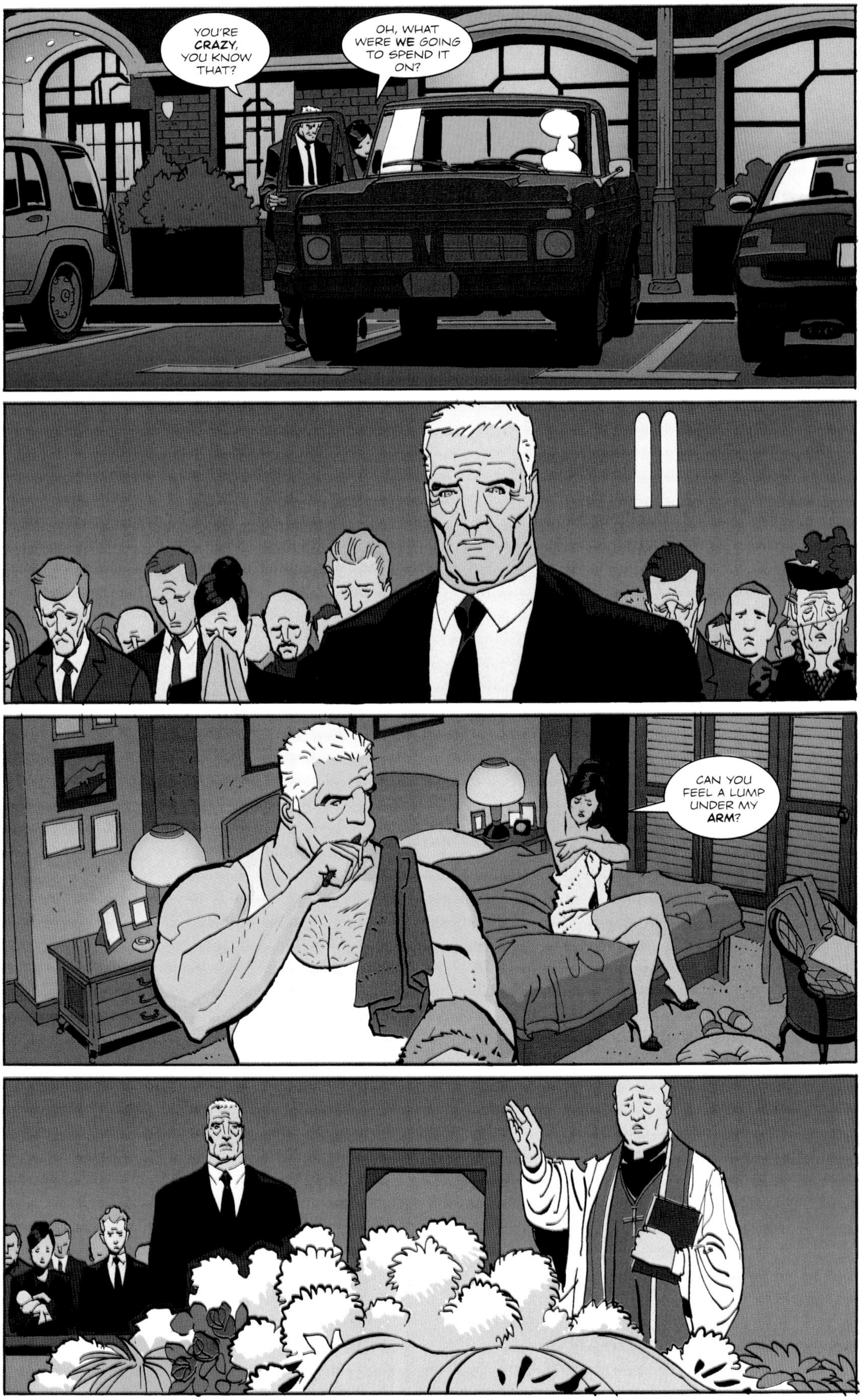
YOU'RE **CRAZY**, YOU KNOW THAT?
OH, WHAT WERE **WE** GOING TO SPEND IT ON?
CAN YOU FEEL A LUMP UNDER MY **ARM**?

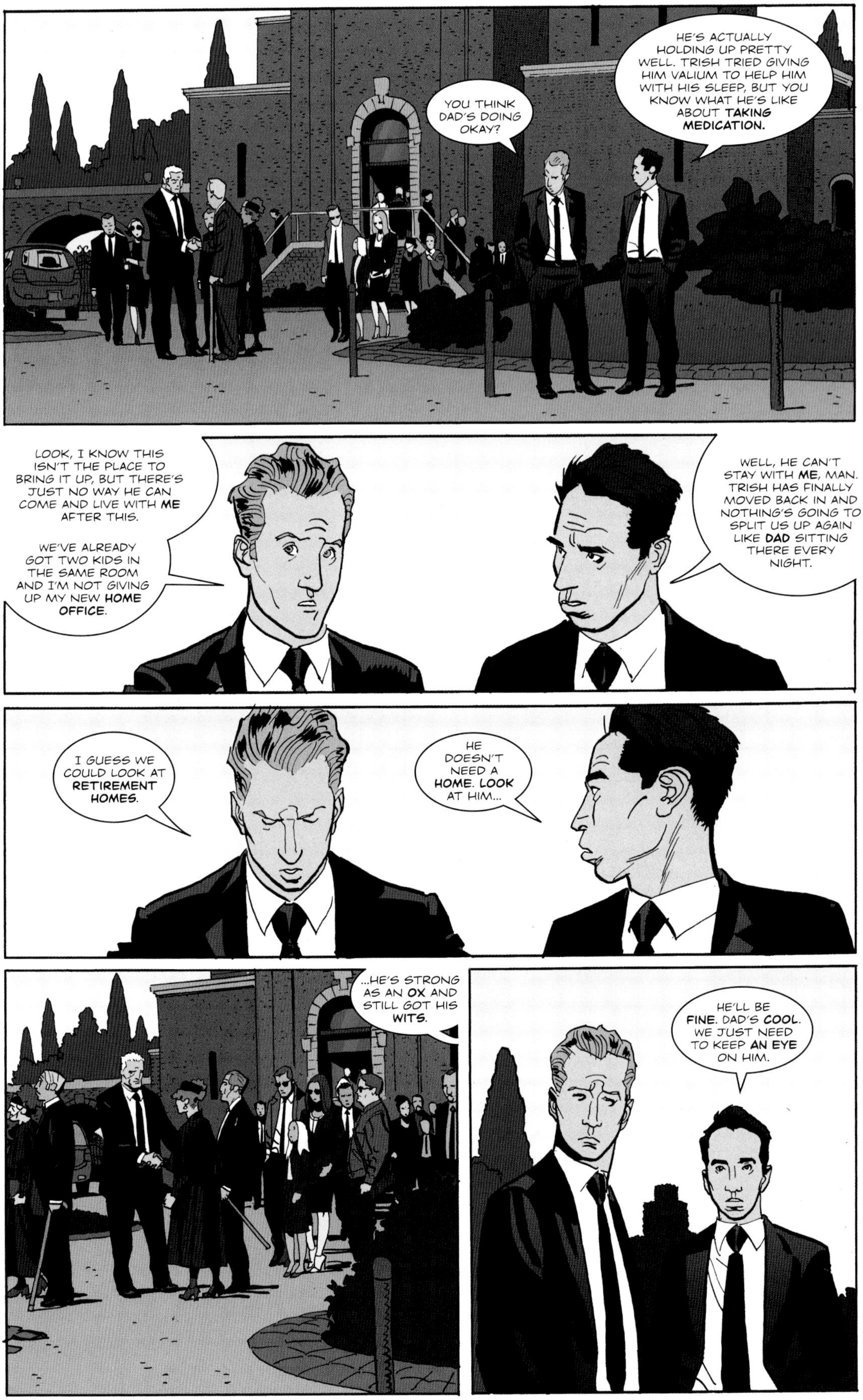
YOU THINK DAD'S DOING OKAY?
HE'S ACTUALLY HOLDING UP PRETTY WELL. TRISH TRIED GIVING HIM VALIUM TO HELP HIM WITH HIS SLEEP, BUT YOU KNOW WHAT HE'S LIKE ABOUT TAKING MEDICATION.
LOOK, I KNOW THIS ISN'T THE PLACE TO BRING IT UP, BUT THERE'S JUST NO WAY HE CAN COME AND LIVE WITH ME AFTER THIS.
WE'VE ALREADY GOT TWO KIDS IN THE SAME ROOM AND I'M NOT GIVING UP MY NEW HOME OFFICE.
WELL, HE CAN'T STAY WITH ME, MAN. TRISH HAS FINALLY MOVED BACK IN AND NOTHING'S GOING TO SPLIT US UP AGAIN LIKE DAD SITTING THERE EVERY NIGHT.
I GUESS WE COULD LOOK AT RETIREMENT HOMES.
HE DOESN'T NEED A HOME. LOOK AT HIM...
...HE'S STRONG AS AN OX AND STILL GOT HIS WITS.
HE'LL BE FINE. DAD'S COOL. WE JUST NEED TO KEEP AN EYE ON HIM.

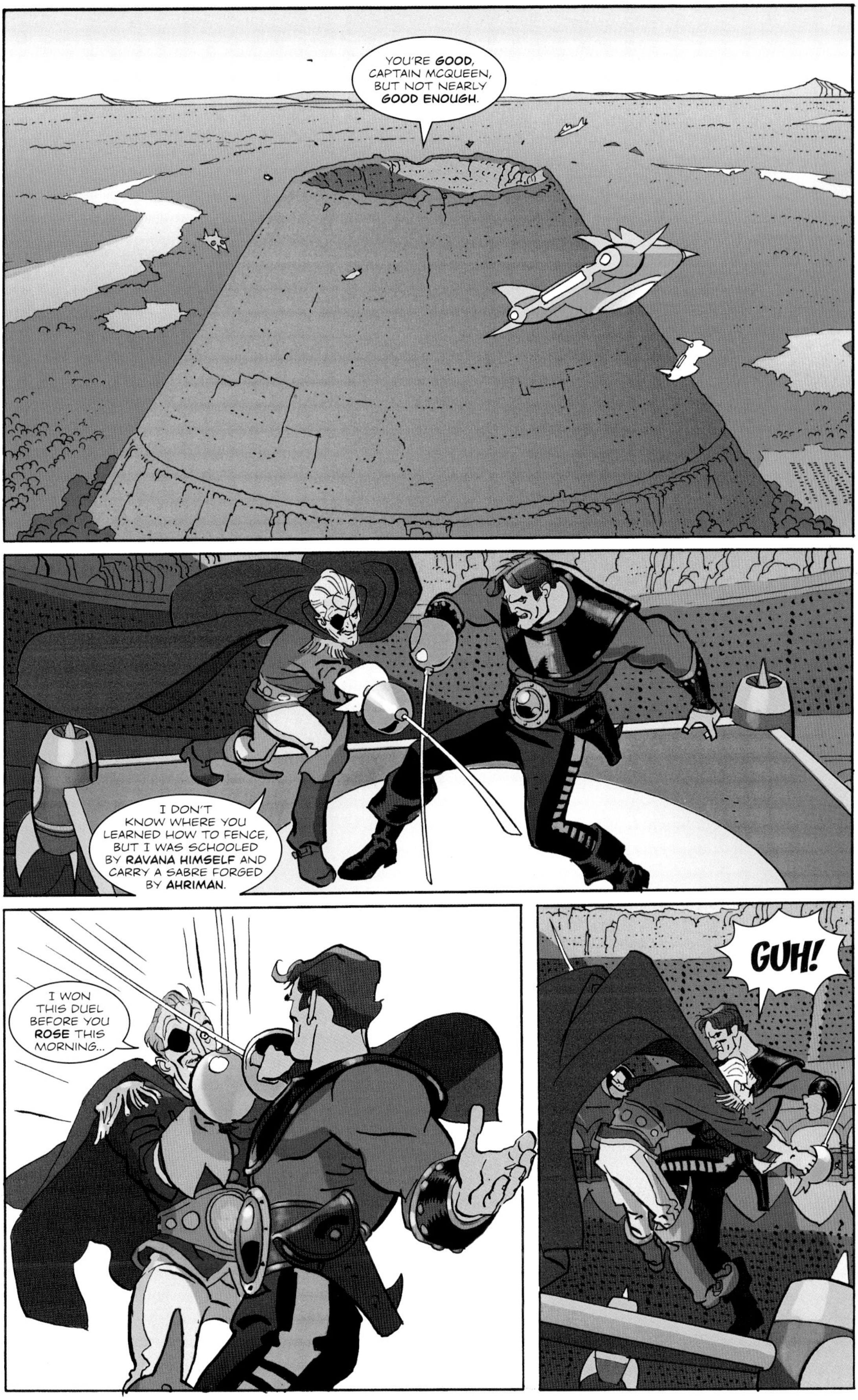
YOU'RE **GOOD**, CAPTAIN MCQUEEN, BUT NOT NEARLY **GOOD ENOUGH**.
I DON'T KNOW WHERE YOU LEARNED HOW TO FENCE, BUT I WAS SCHOOLED BY **RAVANA HIMSELF** AND CARRY A SABRE FORGED BY **AHRIMAN**.
I WON THIS DUEL BEFORE YOU **ROSE** THIS MORNING...
GUH!

A BLOW TO THE **GROIN**?

UNGENTLEMANLY.

NEW YORKER.

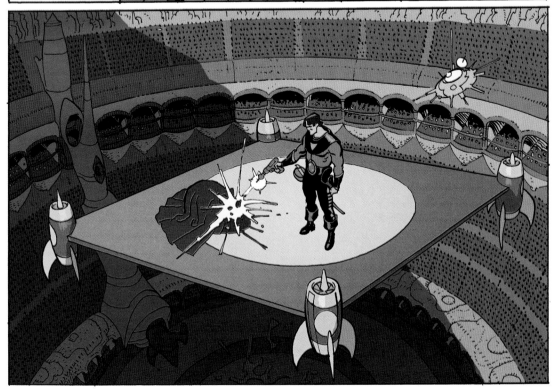

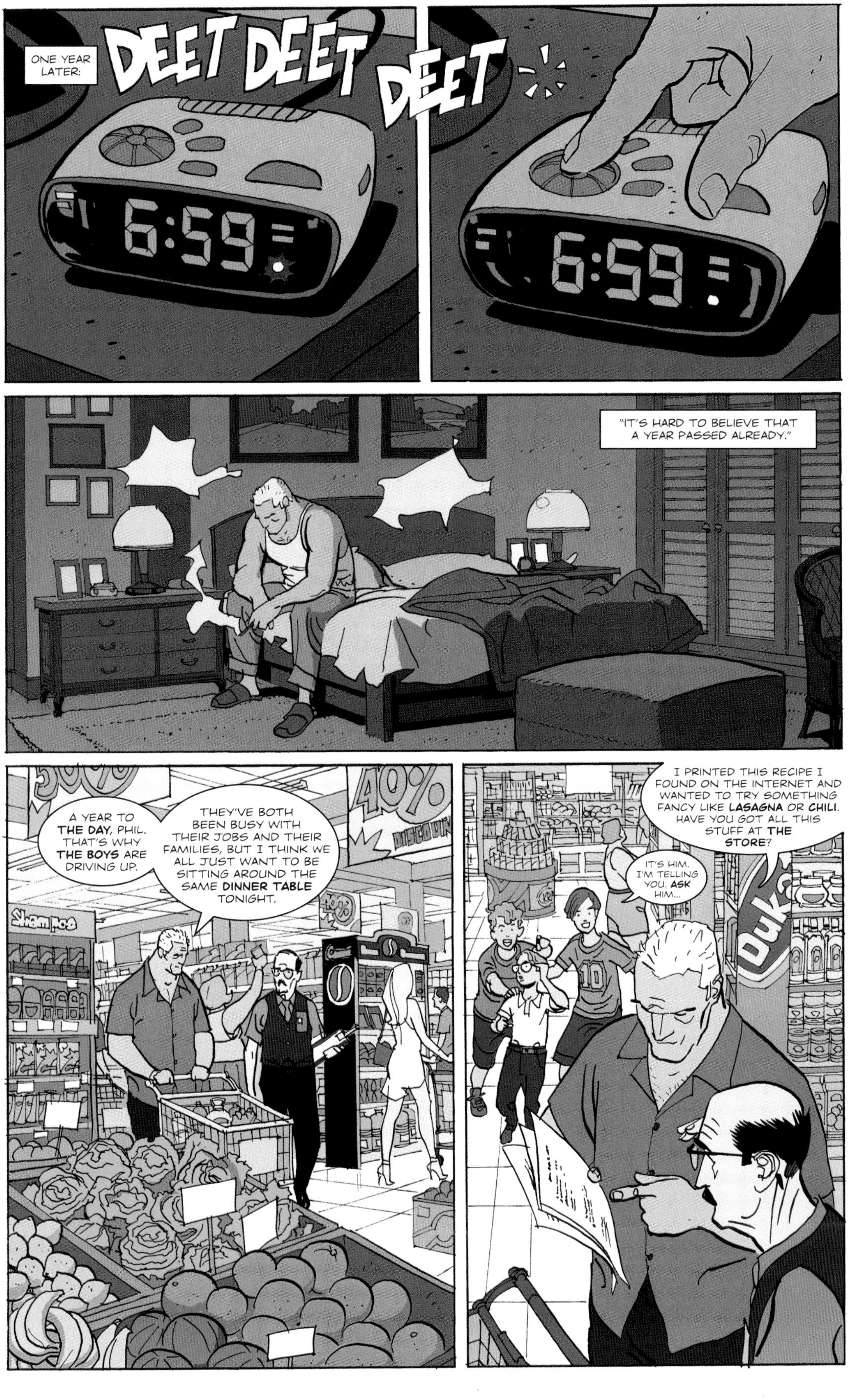

ONE YEAR LATER:
DEET DEET DEET
6:59
6:59
"IT'S HARD TO BELIEVE THAT A YEAR PASSED ALREADY."
40%
A YEAR TO **THE DAY**, PHIL. THAT'S WHY **THE BOYS** ARE DRIVING UP.
THEY'VE BOTH BEEN BUSY WITH THEIR JOBS AND THEIR FAMILIES, BUT I THINK WE ALL JUST WANT TO BE SITTING AROUND THE SAME **DINNER TABLE** TONIGHT.
I PRINTED THIS RECIPE I FOUND ON THE INTERNET AND WANTED TO TRY SOMETHING FANCY LIKE **LASAGNA** OR **CHILI**. HAVE YOU GOT ALL THIS STUFF AT **THE STORE**?
IT'S HIM. I'M TELLING YOU. **ASK** HIM...

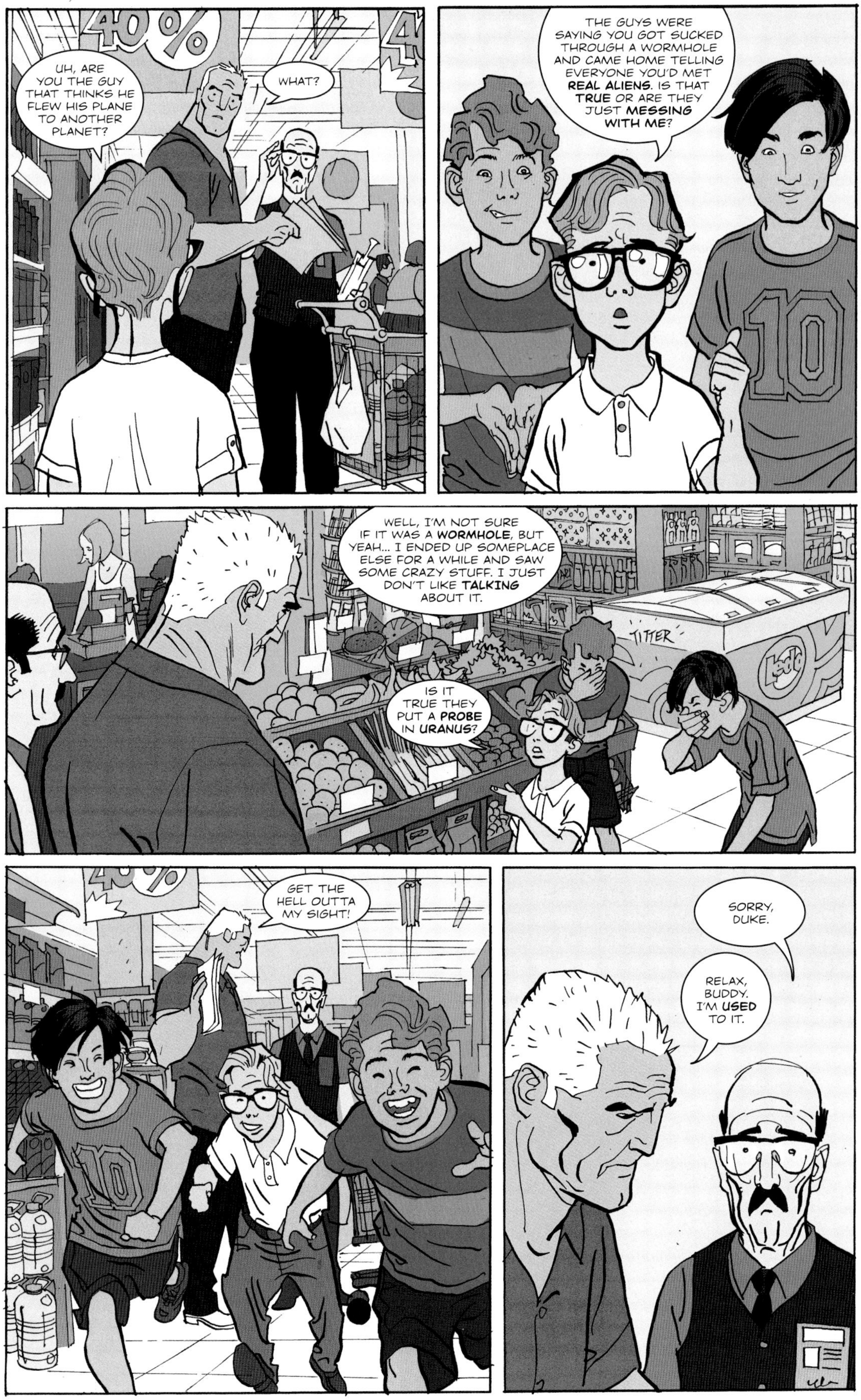
40%
UH, ARE YOU THE GUY THAT THINKS HE FLEW HIS PLANE TO ANOTHER PLANET?
WHAT?
THE GUYS WERE SAYING YOU GOT SUCKED THROUGH A WORMHOLE AND CAME HOME TELLING EVERYONE YOU'D MET **REAL ALIENS**. IS THAT **TRUE** OR ARE THEY JUST **MESSING WITH ME**?
WELL, I'M NOT SURE IF IT WAS A **WORMHOLE**, BUT YEAH... I ENDED UP SOMEPLACE ELSE FOR A WHILE AND SAW SOME CRAZY STUFF. I JUST DON'T LIKE **TALKING** ABOUT IT.
TITTER
IS IT TRUE THEY PUT A **PROBE** IN **URANUS**?
GET THE HELL OUTTA MY SIGHT!
SORRY, DUKE.
RELAX, BUDDY. I'M **USED** TO IT.

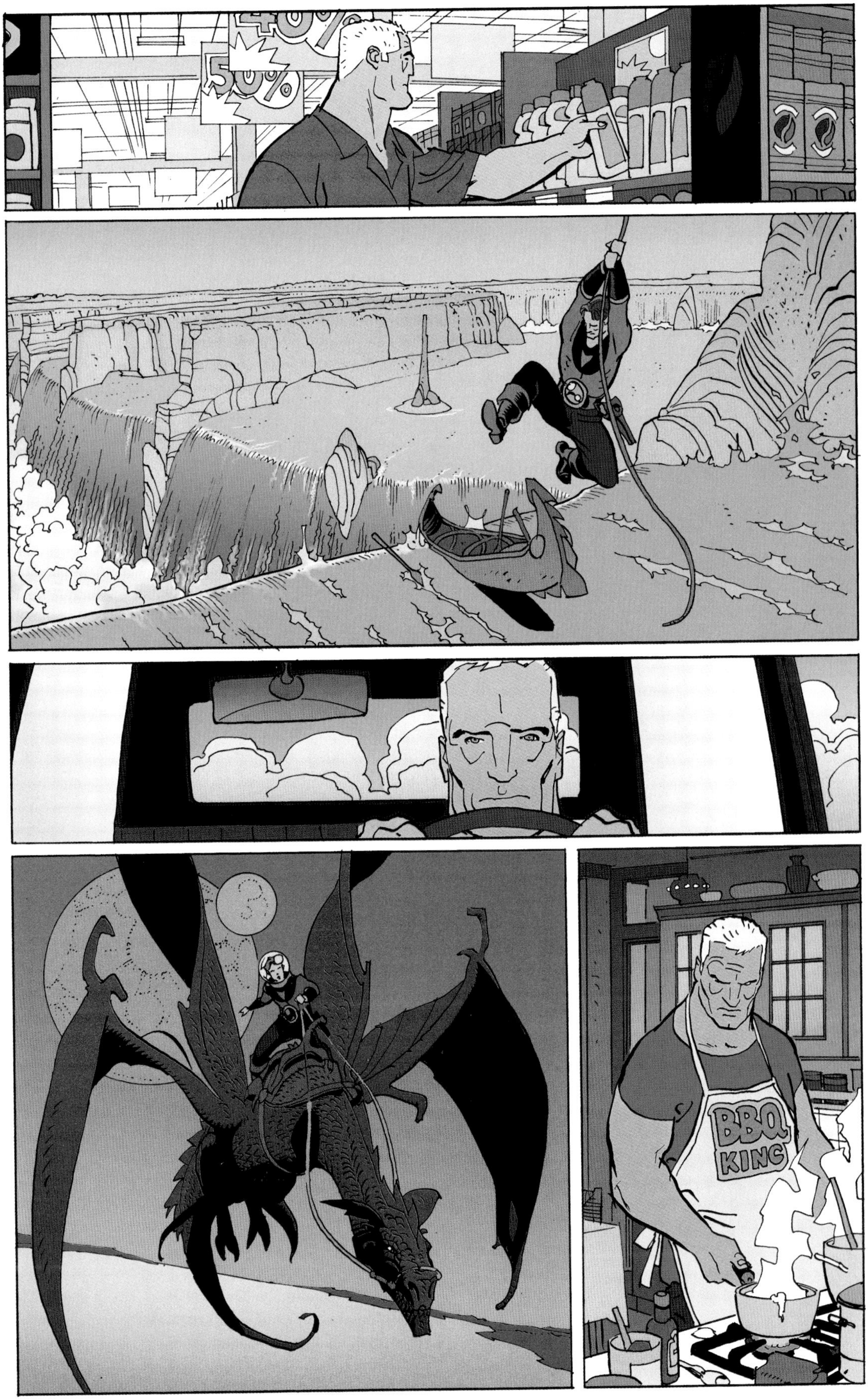

50%
BBQ
KING

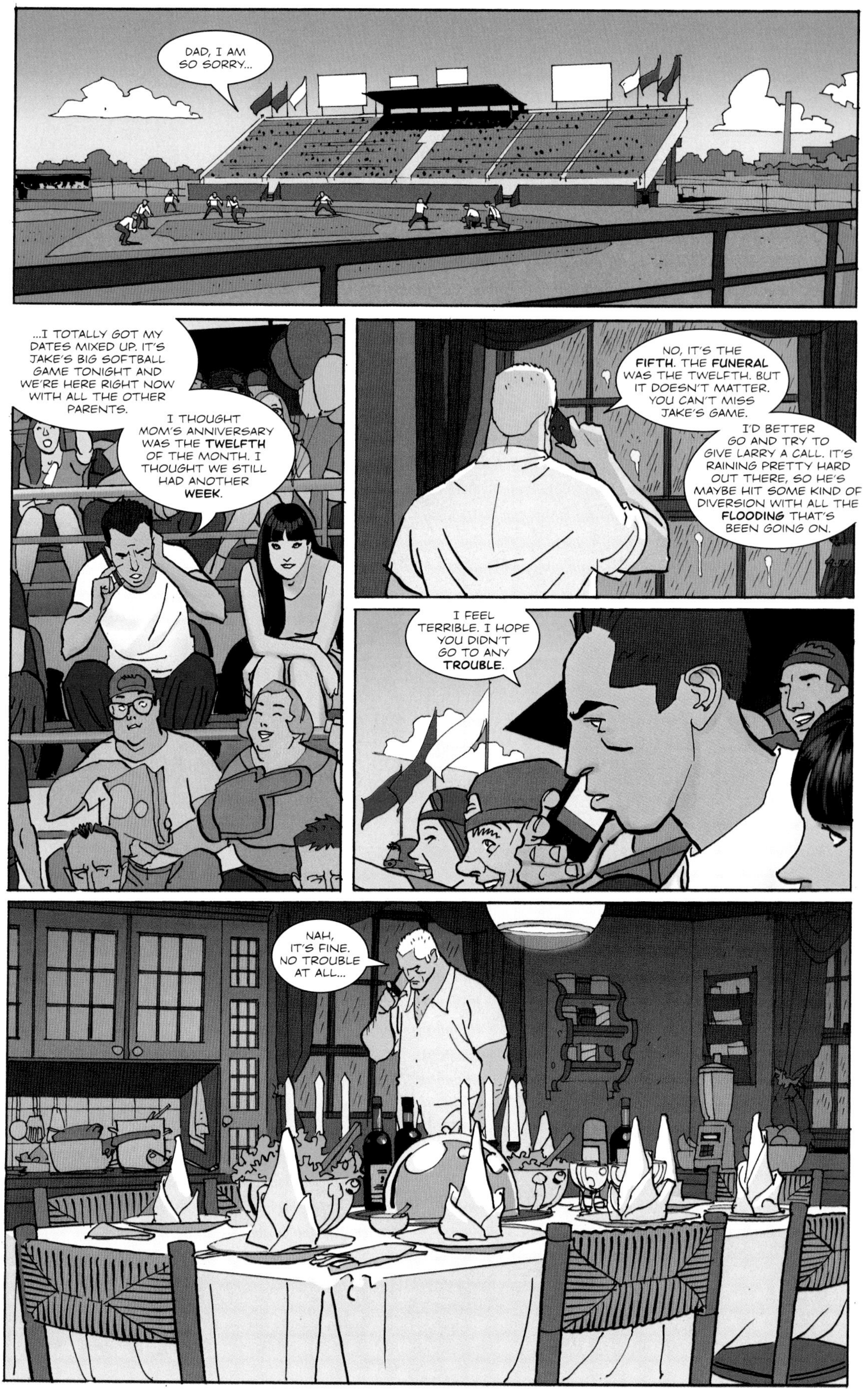
DAD, I AM SO SORRY...
...I TOTALLY GOT MY DATES MIXED UP. IT'S JAKE'S BIG SOFTBALL GAME TONIGHT AND WE'RE HERE RIGHT NOW WITH ALL THE OTHER PARENTS.
I THOUGHT MOM'S ANNIVERSARY WAS THE **TWELFTH** OF THE MONTH. I THOUGHT WE STILL HAD ANOTHER **WEEK**.
NO, IT'S THE **FIFTH**. THE **FUNERAL** WAS THE TWELFTH. BUT IT DOESN'T MATTER. YOU CAN'T MISS JAKE'S GAME.
I'D BETTER GO AND TRY TO GIVE LARRY A CALL. IT'S RAINING PRETTY HARD OUT THERE, SO HE'S MAYBE HIT SOME KIND OF DIVERSION WITH ALL THE **FLOODING** THAT'S BEEN GOING ON.
I FEEL TERRIBLE. I HOPE YOU DIDN'T GO TO ANY **TROUBLE**.
NAH, IT'S FINE. NO TROUBLE AT ALL...

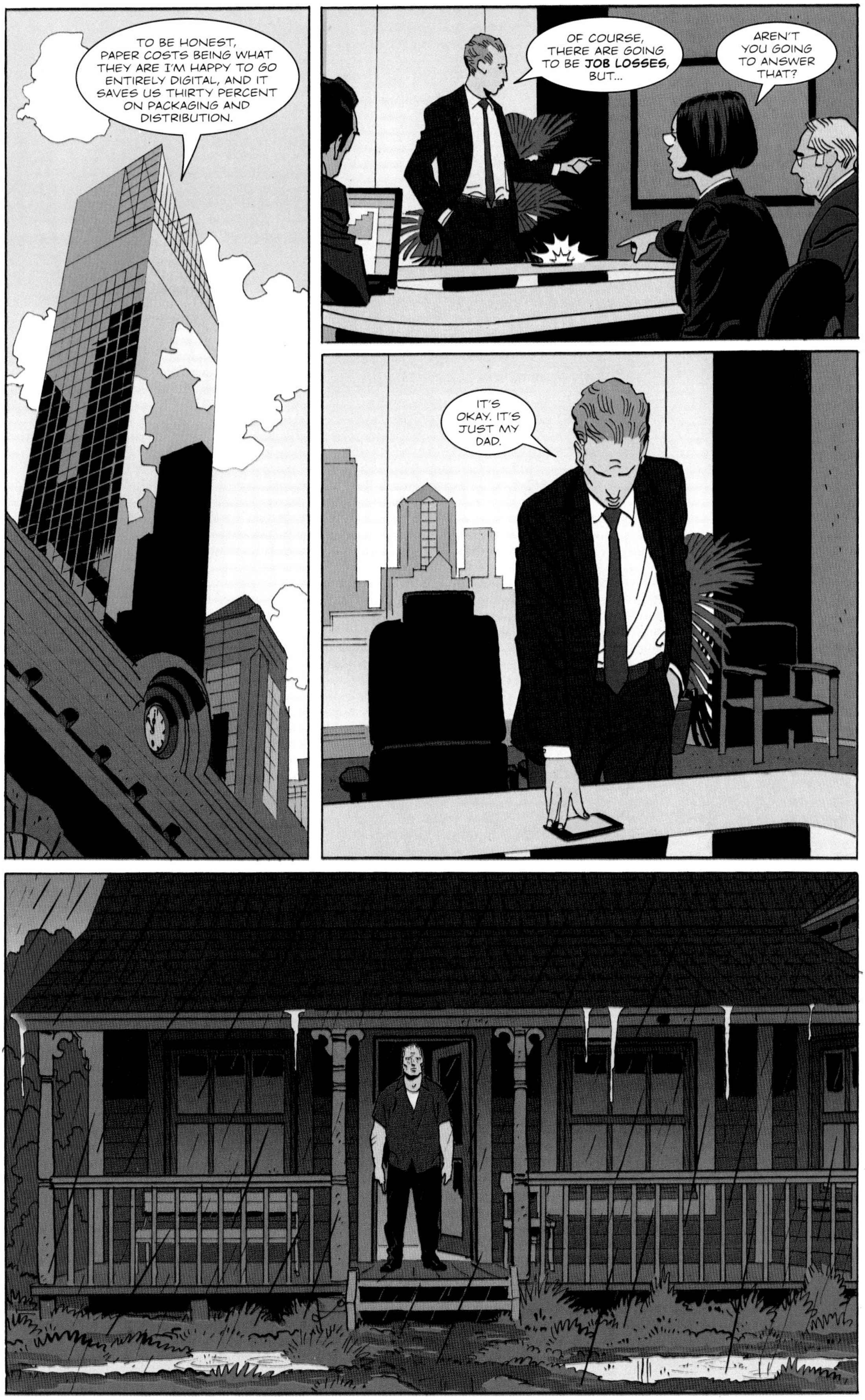
TO BE HONEST, PAPER COSTS BEING WHAT THEY ARE I'M HAPPY TO GO ENTIRELY DIGITAL, AND IT SAVES US THIRTY PERCENT ON PACKAGING AND DISTRIBUTION.
OF COURSE, THERE ARE GOING TO BE **JOB LOSSES**, BUT...
AREN'T YOU GOING TO ANSWER THAT?
IT'S OKAY. IT'S JUST MY DAD.

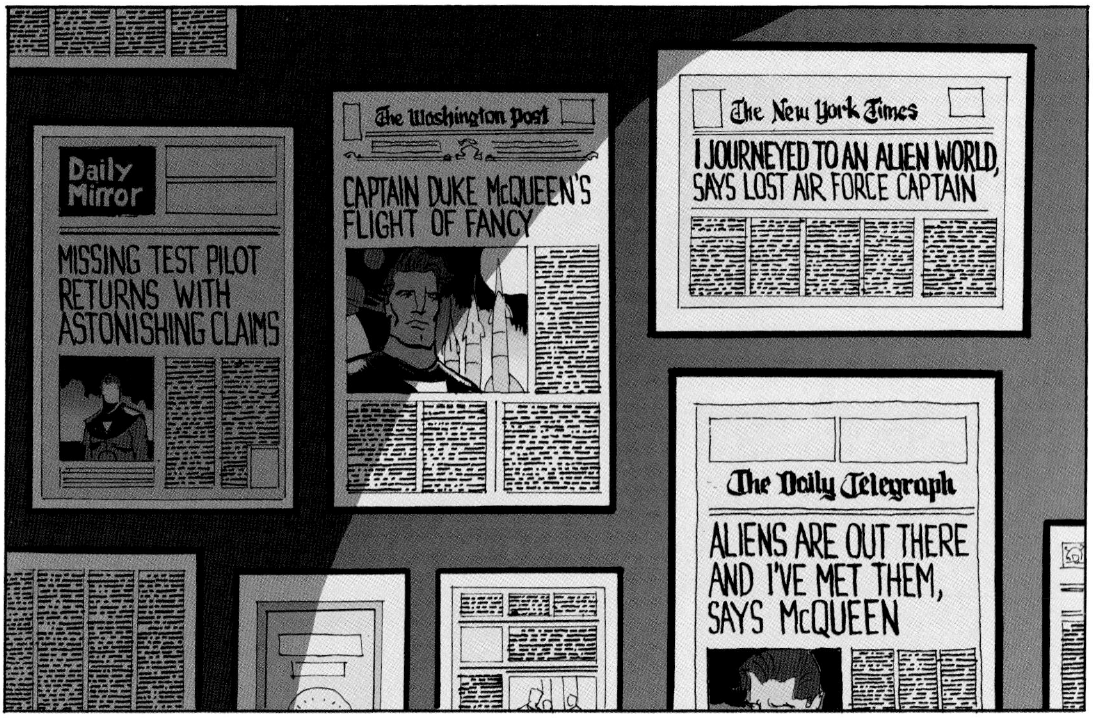
Daily Mirror
MISSING TEST PILOT RETURNS WITH ASTONISHING CLAIMS
The Washington Post
CAPTAIN DUKE McQUEEN'S FLIGHT OF FANCY
The New York Times
I JOURNEYED TO AN ALIEN WORLD, SAYS LOST AIR FORCE CAPTAIN
The Daily Telegraph
ALIENS ARE OUT THERE AND I'VE MET THEM, SAYS McQUEEN

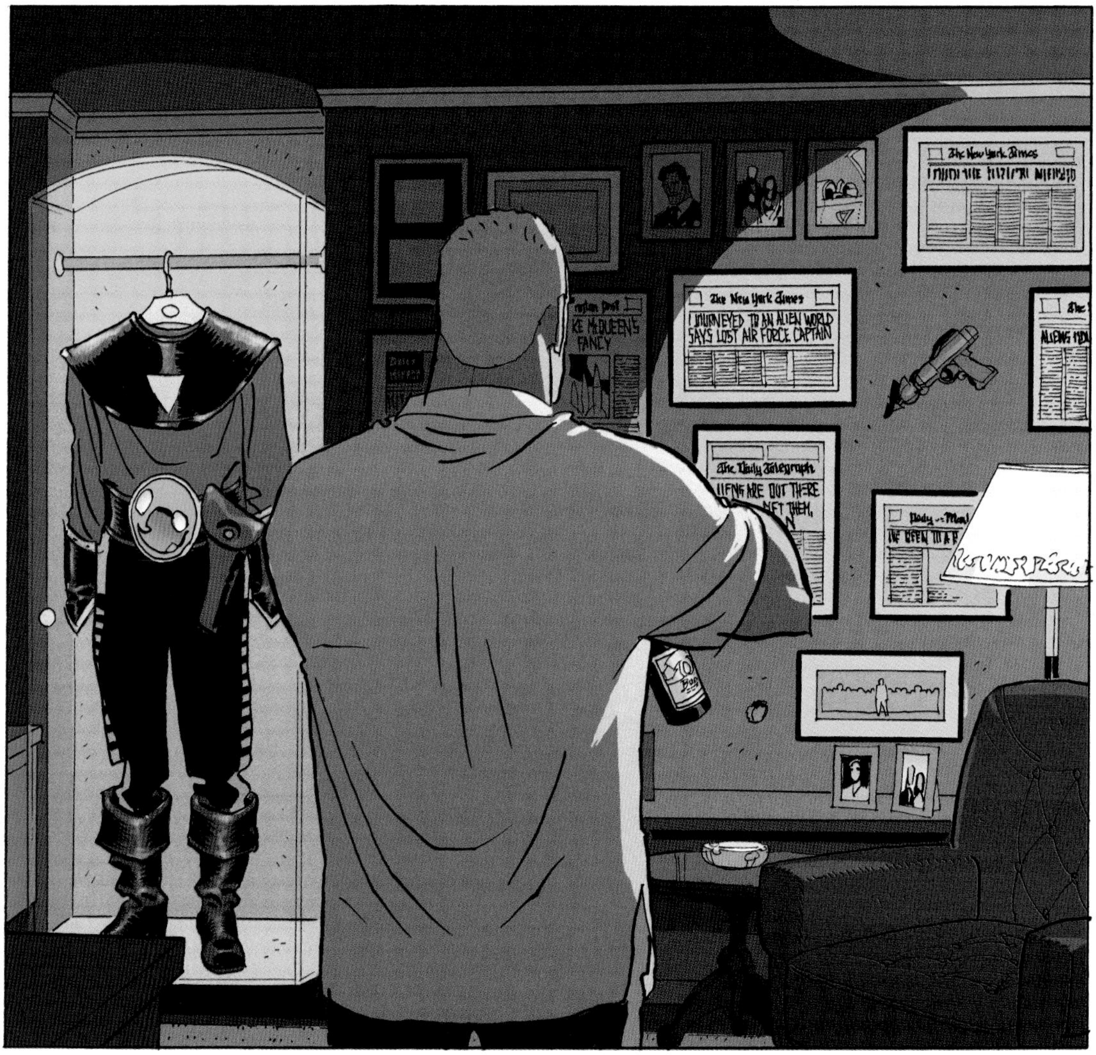
The New York Times
I JOURNEYED TO AN ALIEN WORLD SAYS LOST AIR FORCE CAPTAIN
The Daily Telegraph

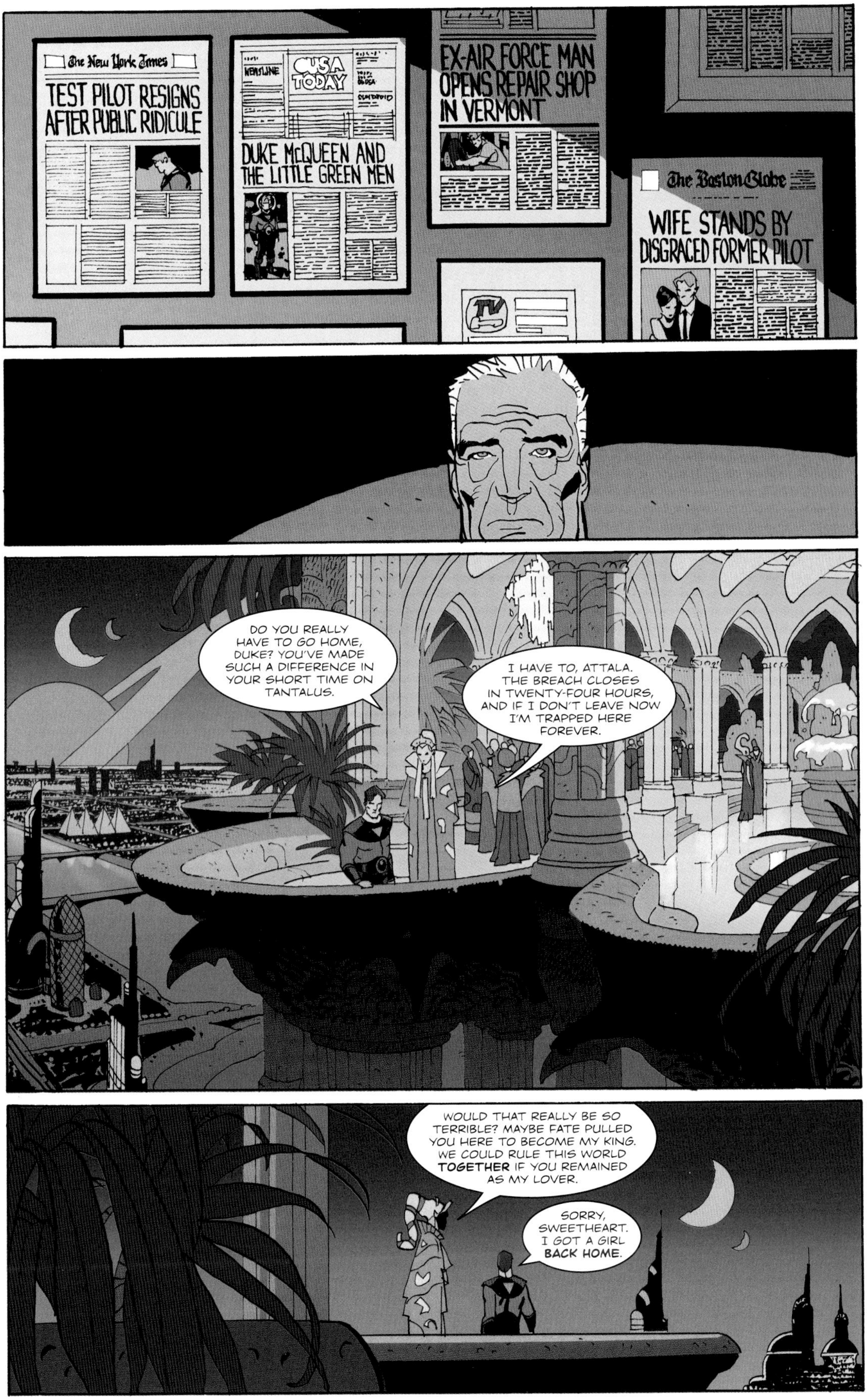
The New York Times
TEST PILOT RESIGNS AFTER PUBLIC RIDICULE
USA TODAY
DUKE McQUEEN AND THE LITTLE GREEN MEN
EX-AIR FORCE MAN OPENS REPAIR SHOP IN VERMONT
The Boston Globe
WIFE STANDS BY DISGRACED FORMER PILOT
DO YOU REALLY HAVE TO GO HOME, DUKE? YOU'VE MADE SUCH A DIFFERENCE IN YOUR SHORT TIME ON TANTALUS.
I HAVE TO, ATTALA. THE BREACH CLOSES IN TWENTY-FOUR HOURS, AND IF I DON'T LEAVE NOW I'M TRAPPED HERE FOREVER.
WOULD THAT REALLY BE SO TERRIBLE? MAYBE FATE PULLED YOU HERE TO BECOME MY KING. WE COULD RULE THIS WORLD **TOGETHER** IF YOU REMAINED AS MY LOVER.
SORRY, SWEETHEART. I GOT A GIRL **BACK HOME**.

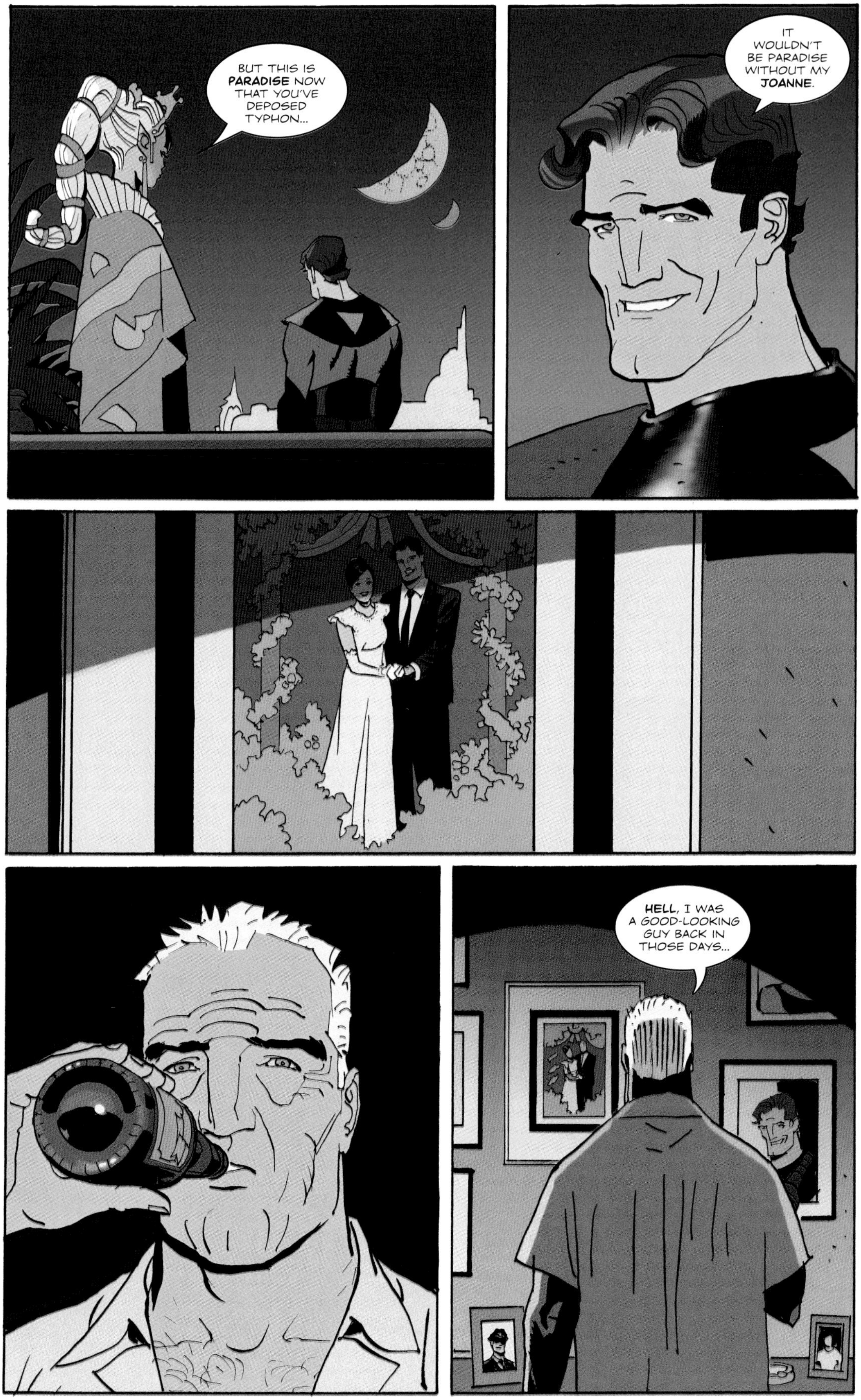
BUT THIS IS PARADISE NOW THAT YOU'VE DEPOSED TYPHON...
IT WOULDN'T BE PARADISE WITHOUT MY JOANNE.
HELL, I WAS A GOOD-LOOKING GUY BACK IN THOSE DAYS...

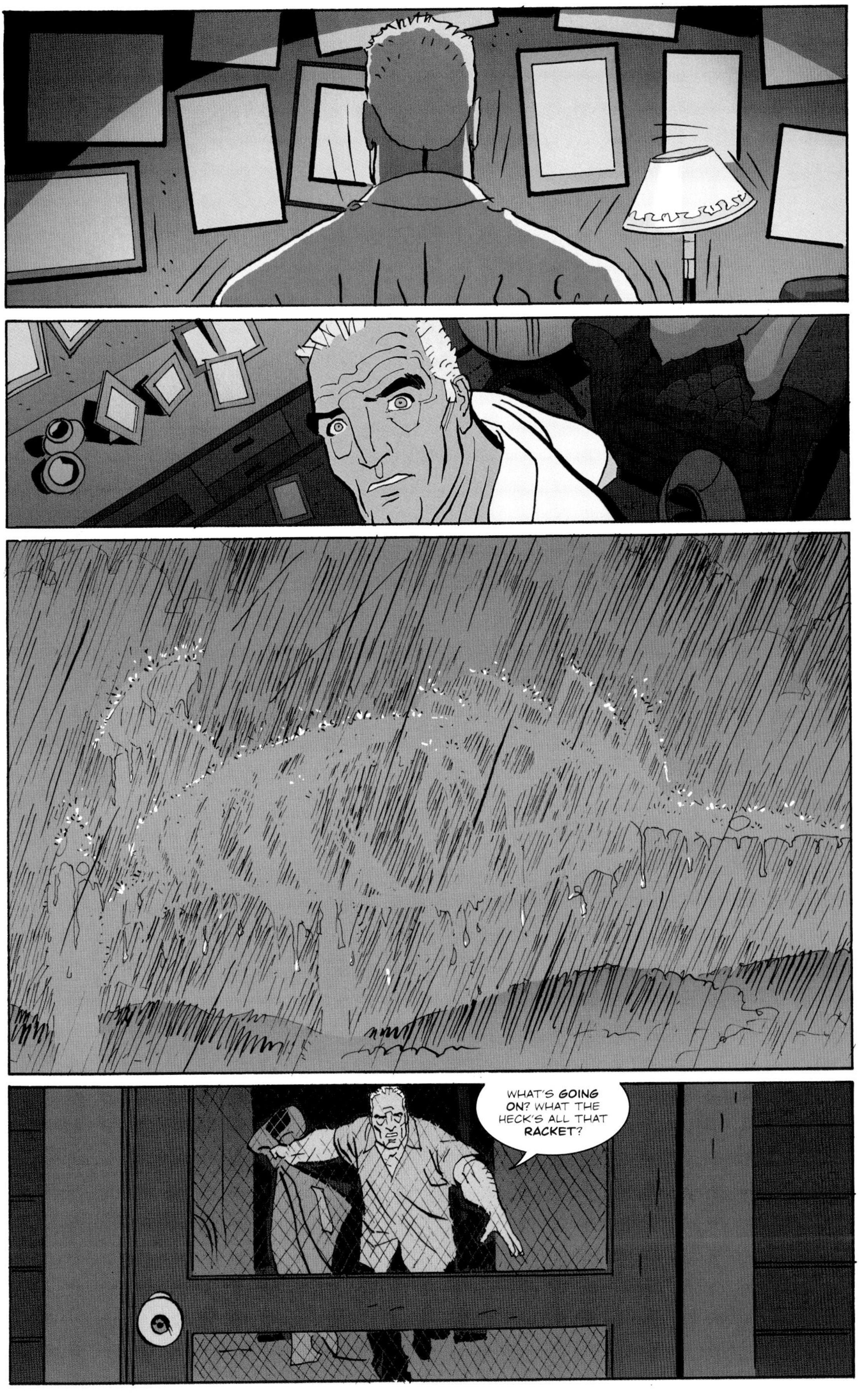
WHAT'S GOING ON? WHAT THE HECK'S ALL THAT RACKET?

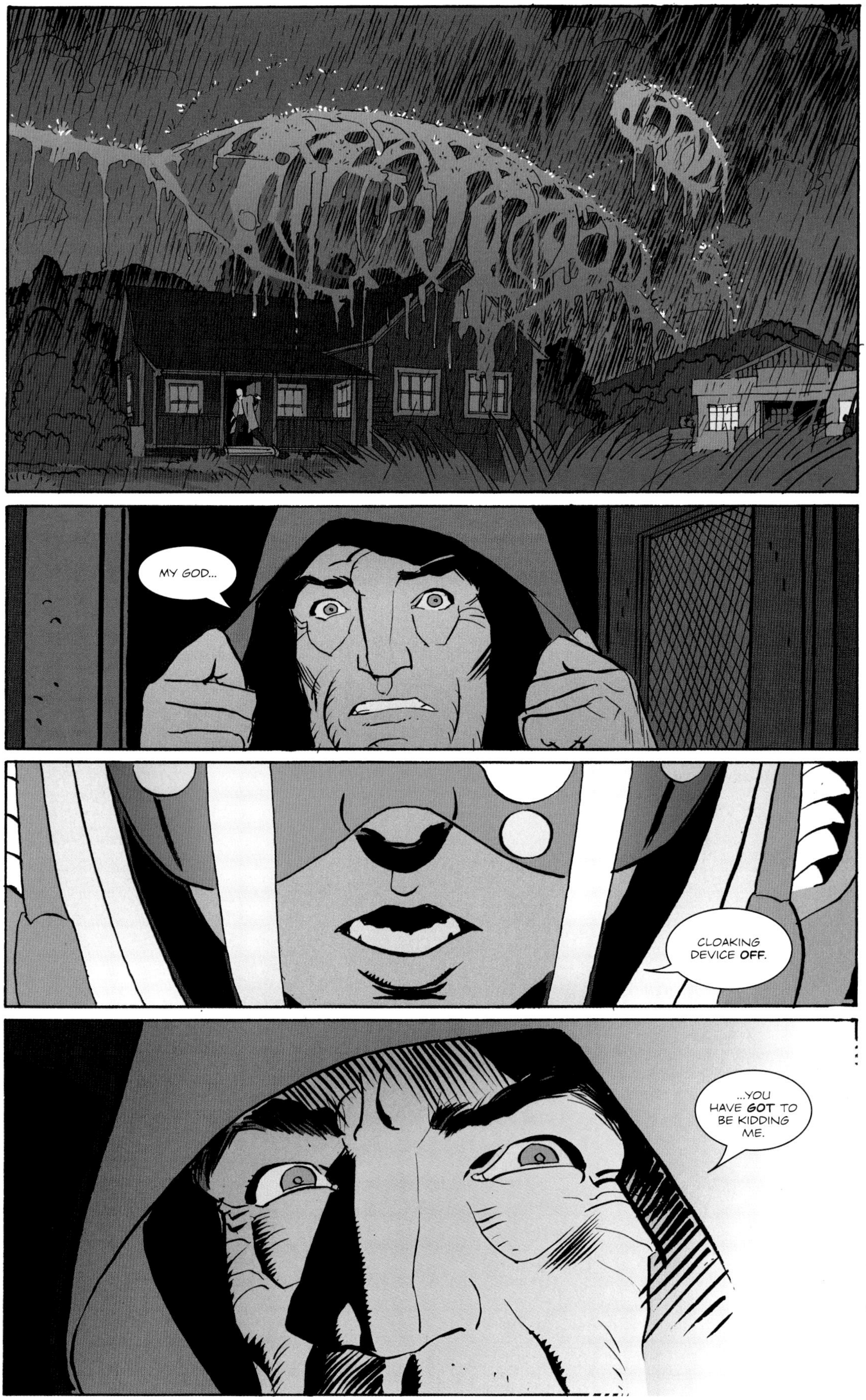
MY GOD...
CLOAKING DEVICE **OFF**.
...YOU HAVE **GOT** TO BE KIDDING ME.

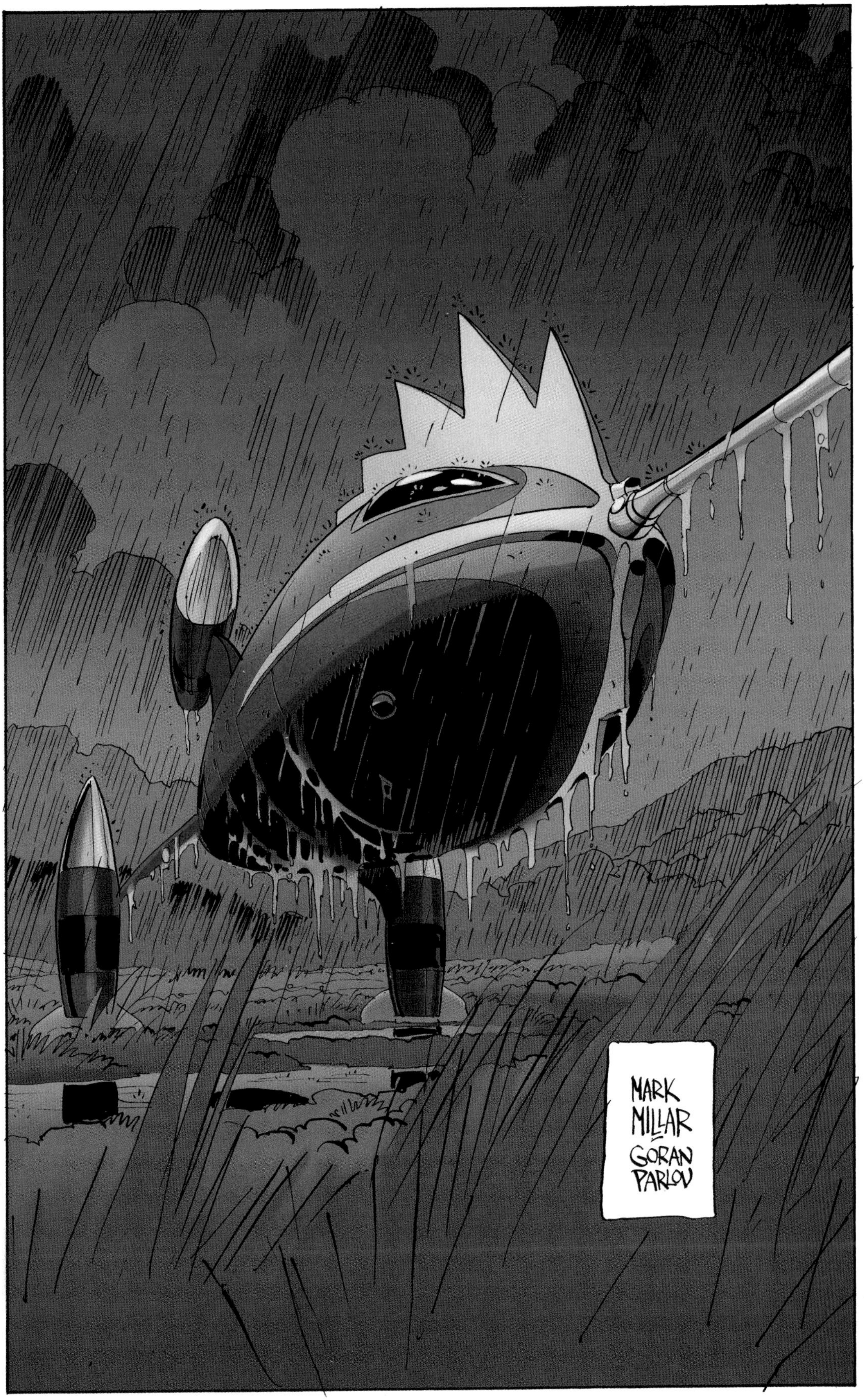
MARK
MILLAR
GORAN
PARLOV

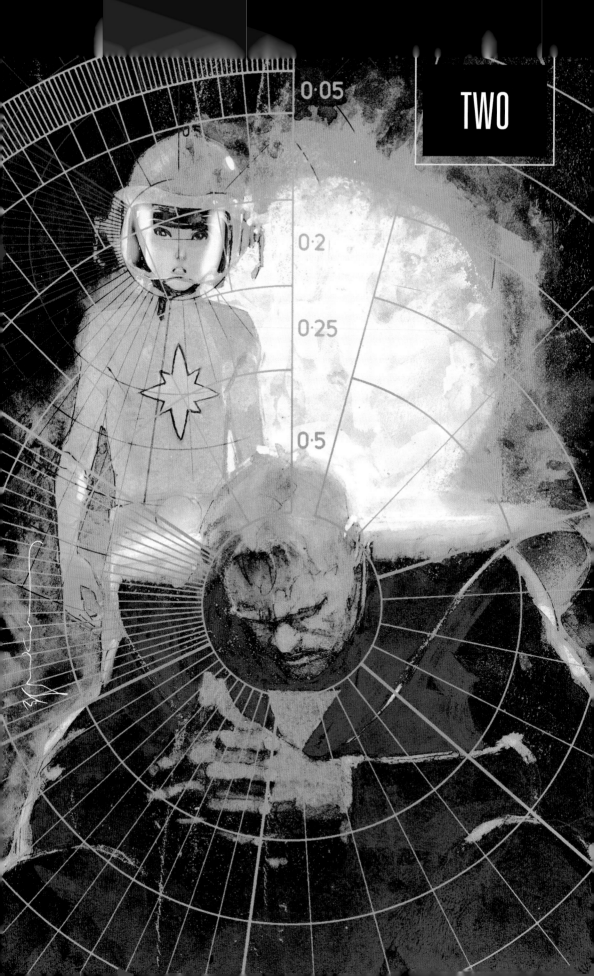

0·05

0·2

0·25

0·5

TWO

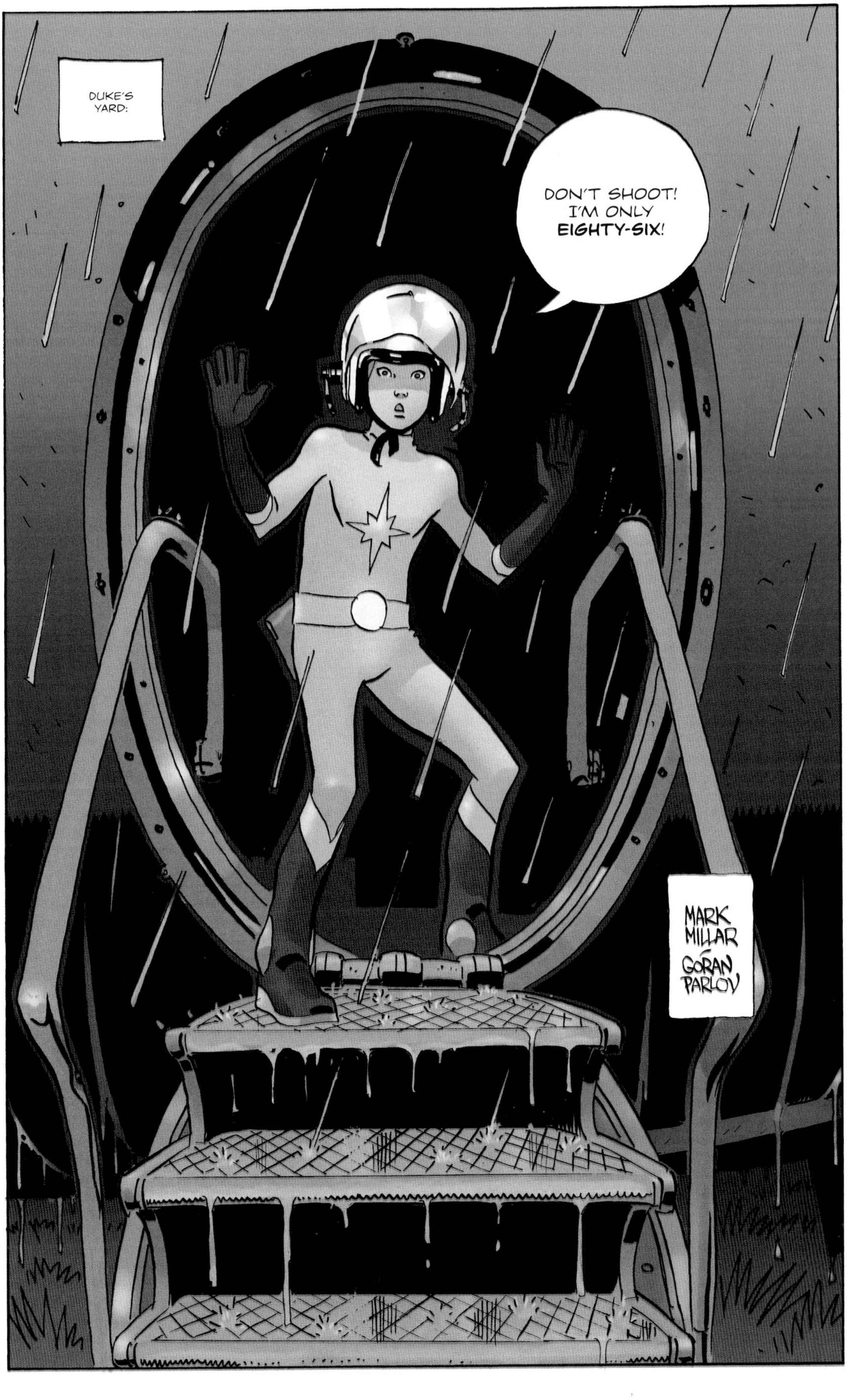
DUKE'S YARD:
DON'T SHOOT! I'M ONLY EIGHTY-SIX!
MARK MILLAR
GÓRAN PARLOV

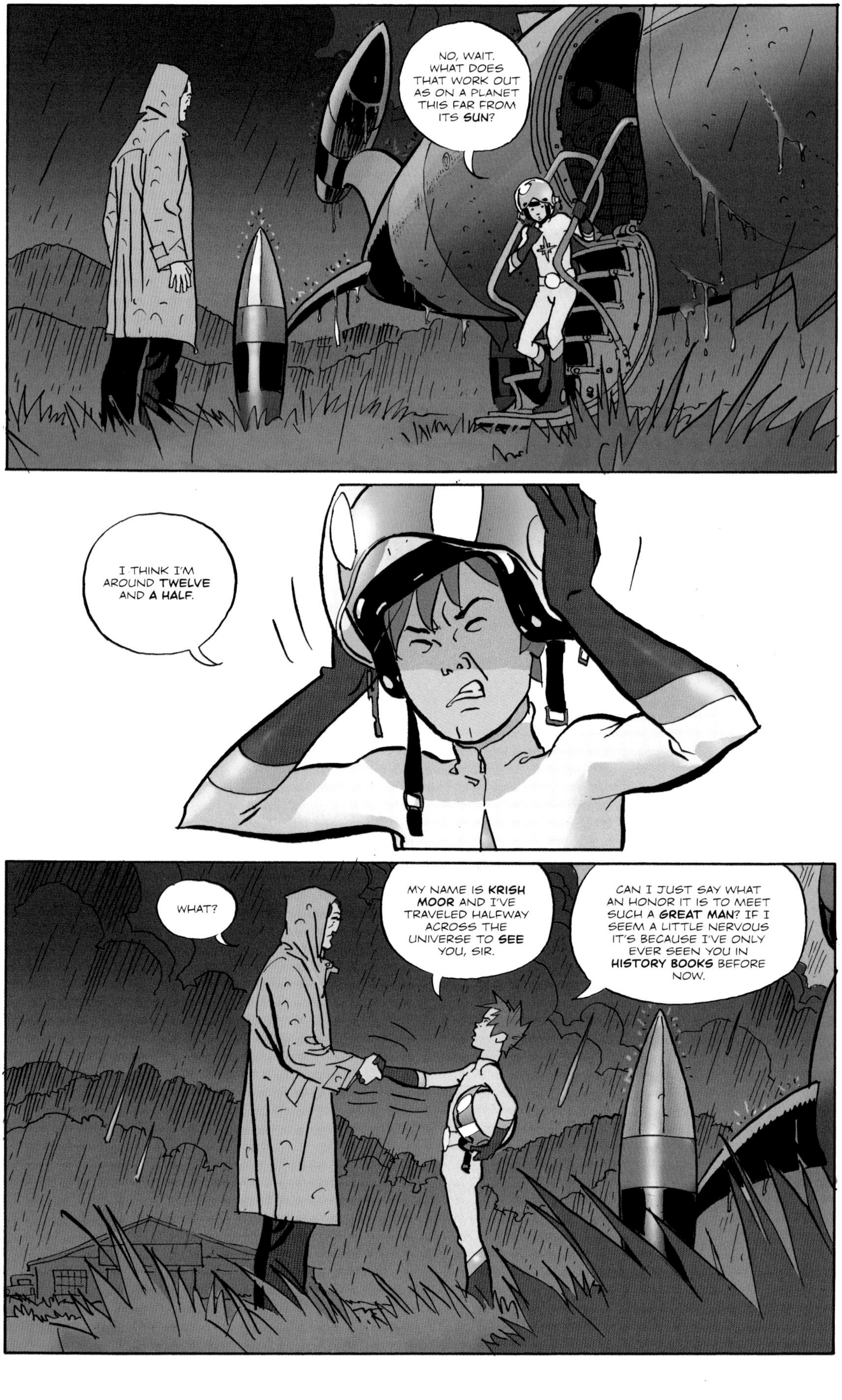
NO, WAIT. WHAT DOES THAT WORK OUT AS ON A PLANET THIS FAR FROM ITS SUN?
I THINK I'M AROUND TWELVE AND A HALF.
WHAT?
MY NAME IS KRISH MOOR AND I'VE TRAVELED HALFWAY ACROSS THE UNIVERSE TO SEE YOU, SIR.
CAN I JUST SAY WHAT AN HONOR IT IS TO MEET SUCH A GREAT MAN? IF I SEEM A LITTLE NERVOUS IT'S BECAUSE I'VE ONLY EVER SEEN YOU IN HISTORY BOOKS BEFORE NOW.

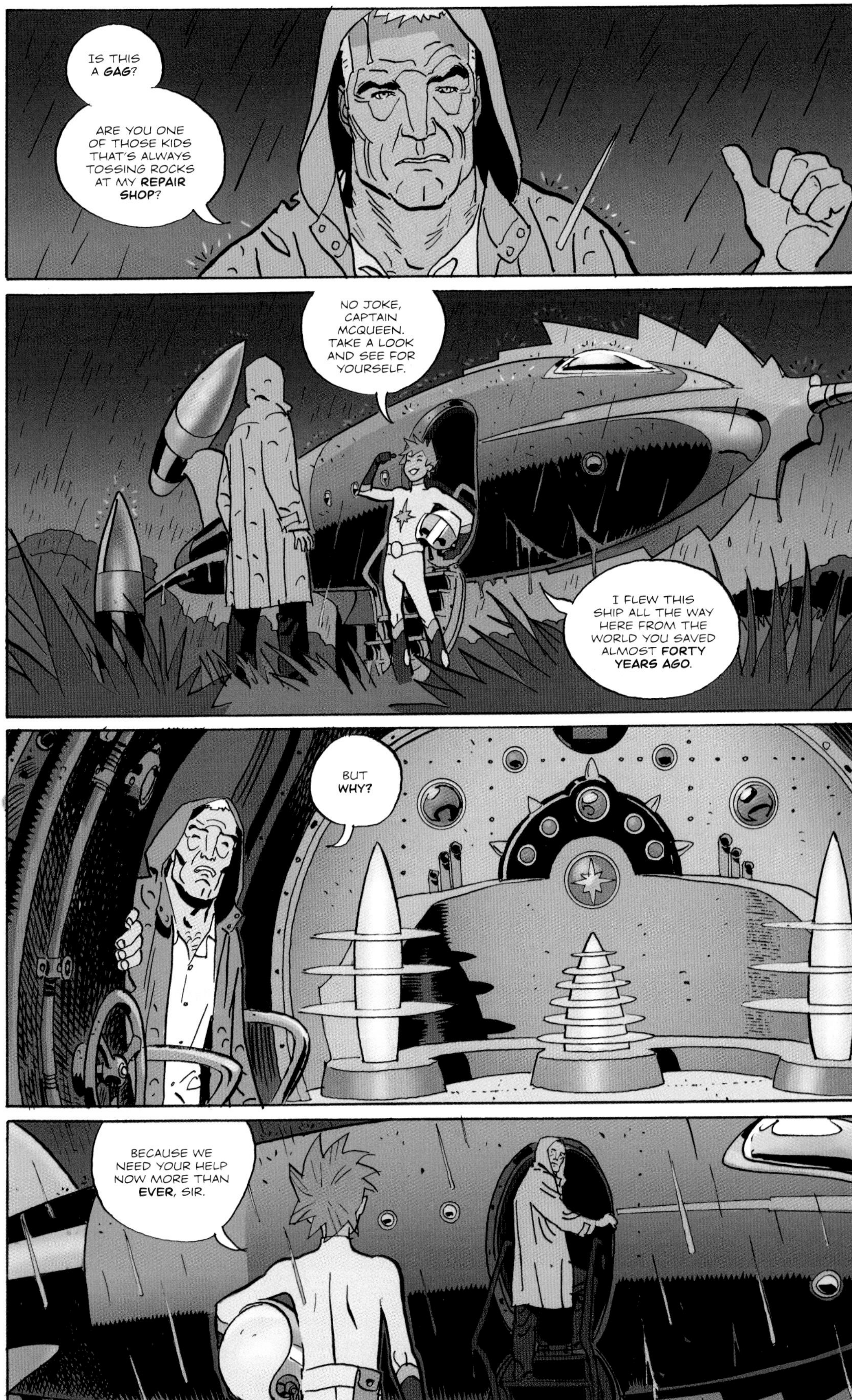
IS THIS A GAG?
ARE YOU ONE OF THOSE KIDS THAT'S ALWAYS TOSSING ROCKS AT MY REPAIR SHOP?
NO JOKE, CAPTAIN MCQUEEN. TAKE A LOOK AND SEE FOR YOURSELF.
I FLEW THIS SHIP ALL THE WAY HERE FROM THE WORLD YOU SAVED ALMOST FORTY YEARS AGO.
BUT WHY?
BECAUSE WE NEED YOUR HELP NOW MORE THAN EVER, SIR.

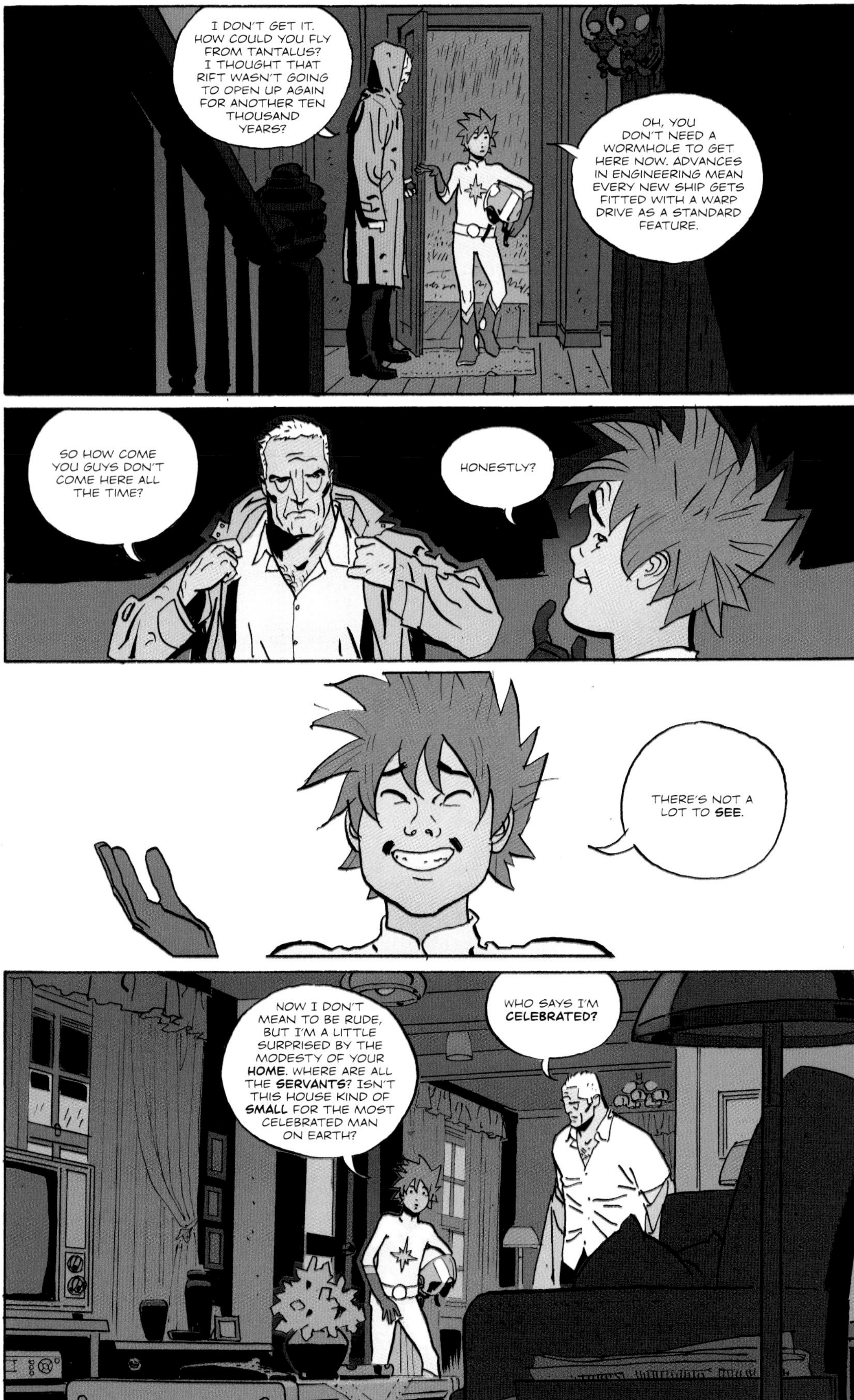
I DON'T GET IT. HOW COULD YOU FLY FROM TANTALUS? I THOUGHT THAT RIFT WASN'T GOING TO OPEN UP AGAIN FOR ANOTHER TEN THOUSAND YEARS?
OH, YOU DON'T NEED A WORMHOLE TO GET HERE NOW. ADVANCES IN ENGINEERING MEAN EVERY NEW SHIP GETS FITTED WITH A WARP DRIVE AS A STANDARD FEATURE.
SO HOW COME YOU GUYS DON'T COME HERE ALL THE TIME?
HONESTLY?
THERE'S NOT A LOT TO **SEE**.
NOW I DON'T MEAN TO BE RUDE, BUT I'M A LITTLE SURPRISED BY THE MODESTY OF YOUR **HOME**. WHERE ARE ALL THE **SERVANTS**? ISN'T THIS HOUSE KIND OF **SMALL** FOR THE MOST CELEBRATED MAN ON EARTH?
WHO SAYS I'M **CELEBRATED?**

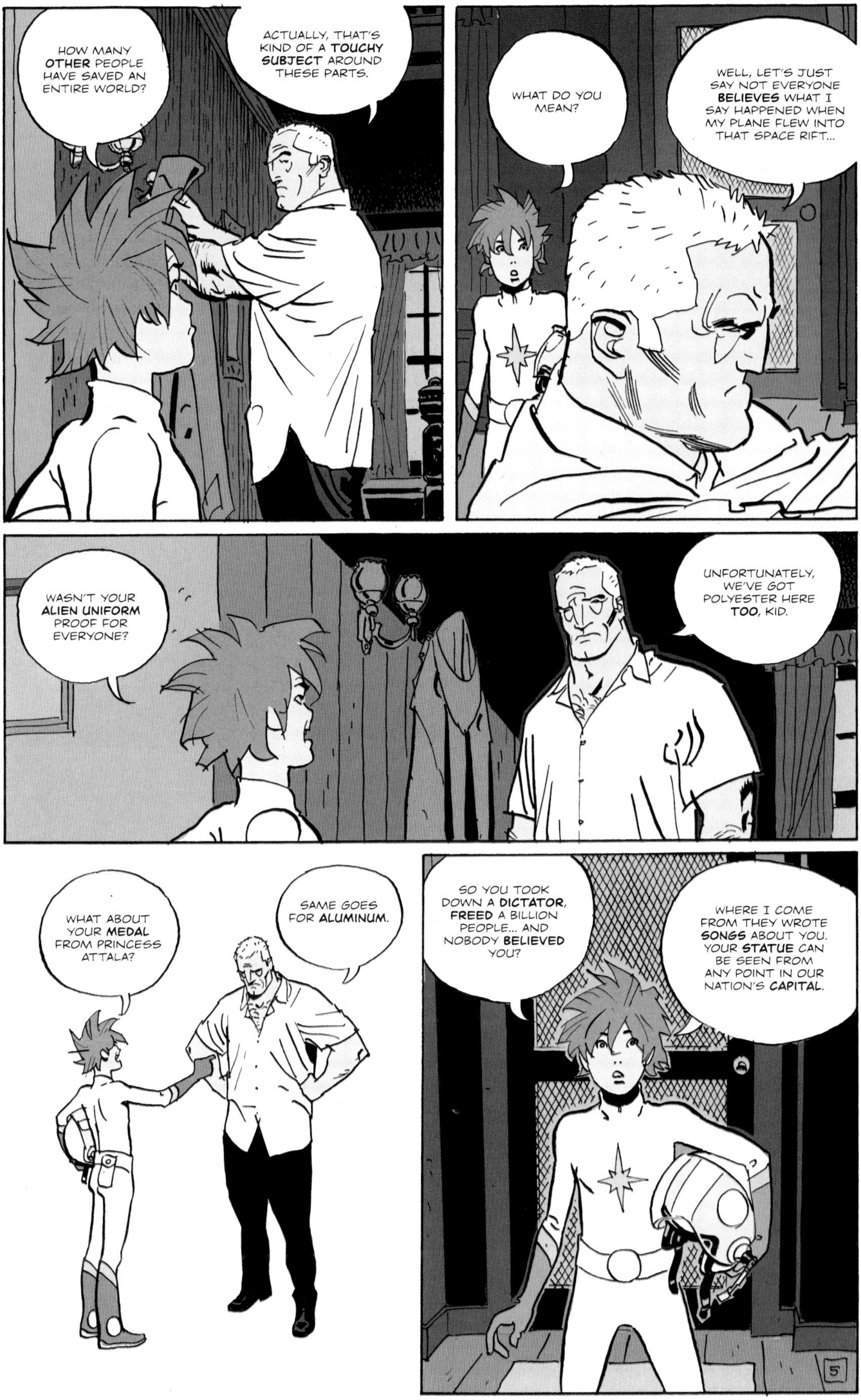
HOW MANY OTHER PEOPLE HAVE SAVED AN ENTIRE WORLD?
ACTUALLY, THAT'S KIND OF A TOUCHY SUBJECT AROUND THESE PARTS.
WHAT DO YOU MEAN?
WELL, LET'S JUST SAY NOT EVERYONE BELIEVES WHAT I SAY HAPPENED WHEN MY PLANE FLEW INTO THAT SPACE RIFT...
WASN'T YOUR ALIEN UNIFORM PROOF FOR EVERYONE?
UNFORTUNATELY, WE'VE GOT POLYESTER HERE TOO, KID.
WHAT ABOUT YOUR MEDAL FROM PRINCESS ATTALA?
SAME GOES FOR ALUMINUM.
SO YOU TOOK DOWN A DICTATOR, FREED A BILLION PEOPLE... AND NOBODY BELIEVED YOU?
WHERE I COME FROM THEY WROTE SONGS ABOUT YOU. YOUR STATUE CAN BE SEEN FROM ANY POINT IN OUR NATION'S CAPITAL.
5

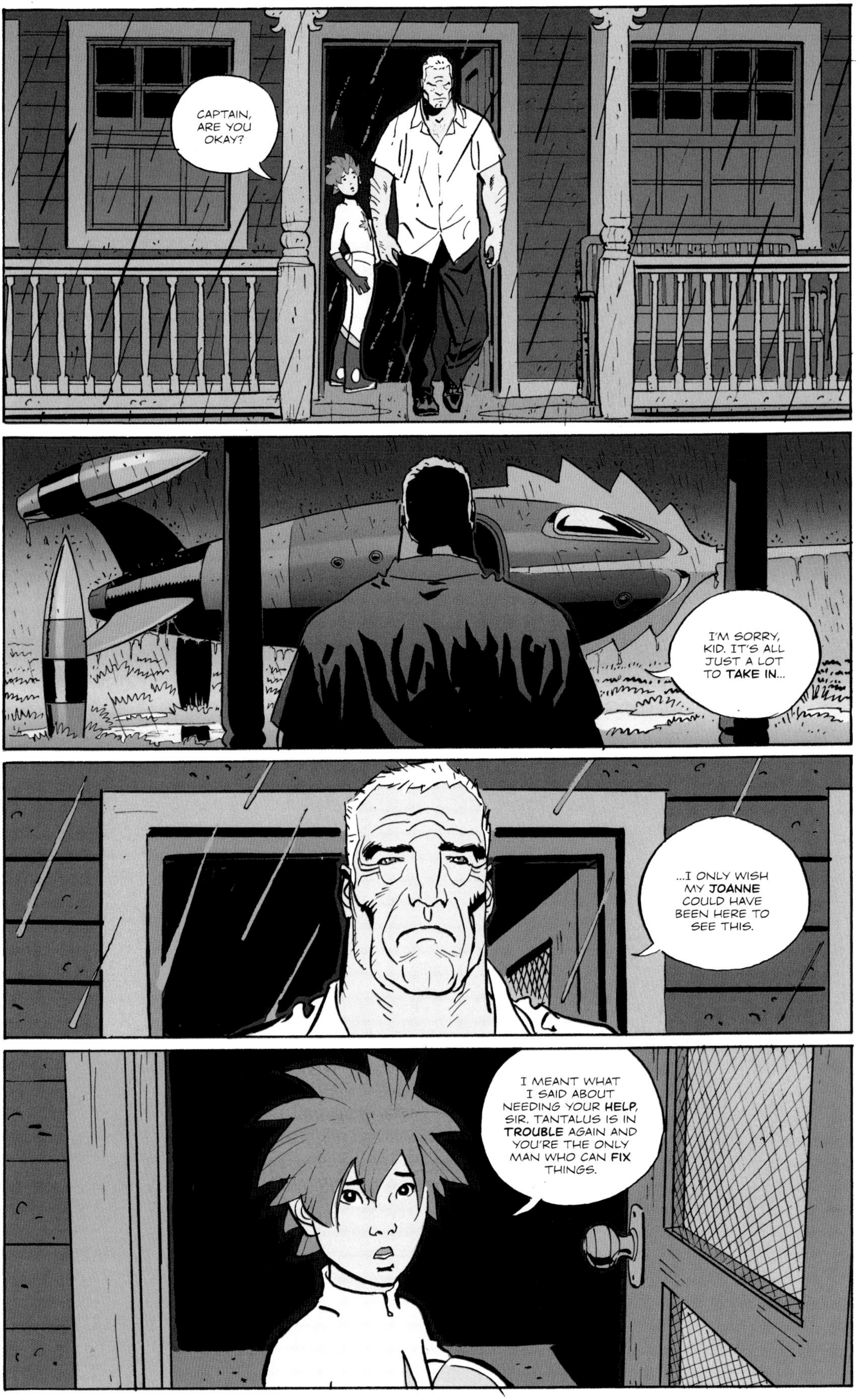
CAPTAIN, ARE YOU OKAY?
I'M SORRY, KID. IT'S ALL JUST A LOT TO **TAKE IN**...
...I ONLY WISH MY **JOANNE** COULD HAVE BEEN HERE TO SEE THIS.
I MEANT WHAT I SAID ABOUT NEEDING YOUR **HELP**, SIR. TANTALUS IS IN **TROUBLE** AGAIN AND YOU'RE THE ONLY MAN WHO CAN **FIX** THINGS.

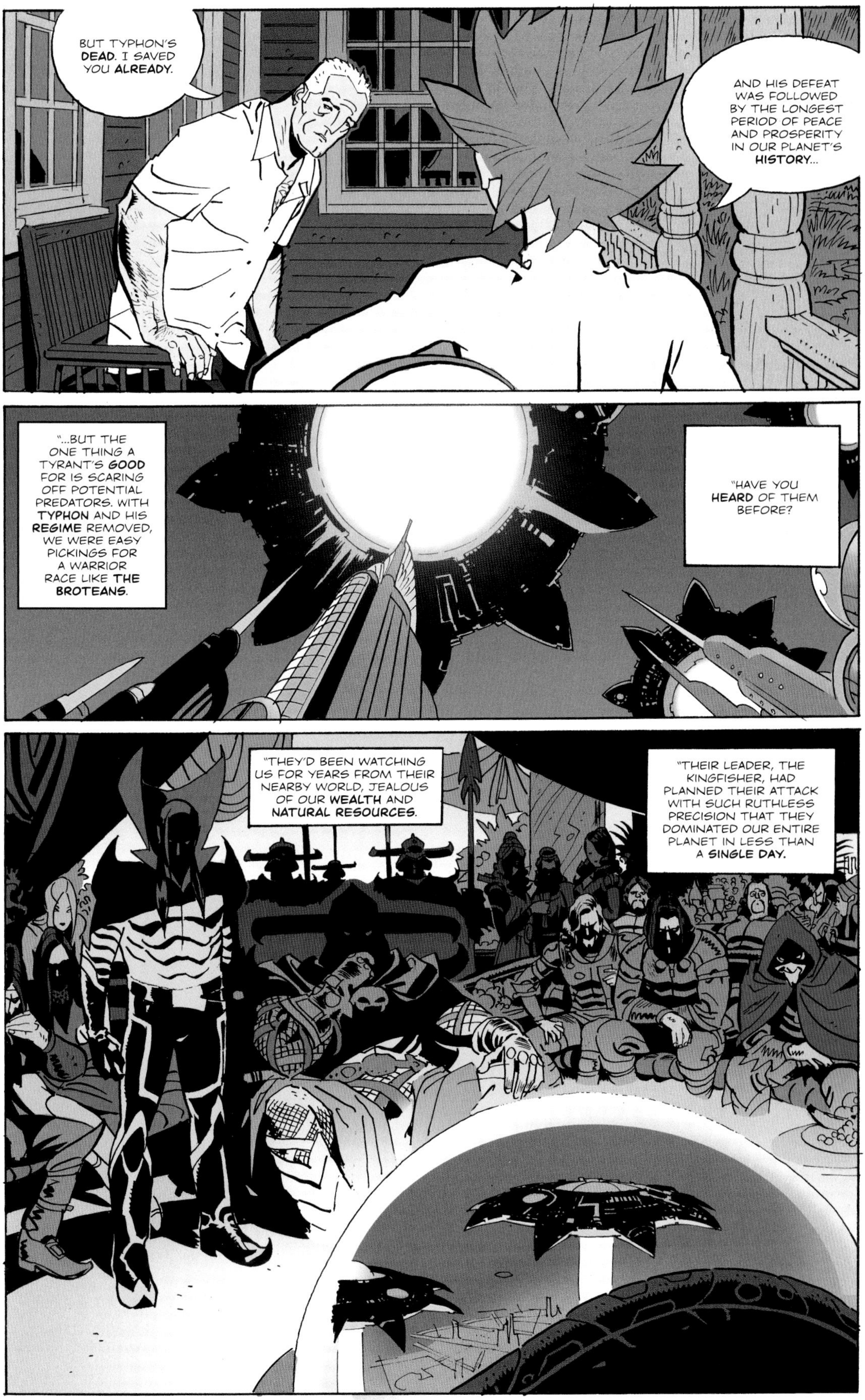
BUT TYPHON'S DEAD. I SAVED YOU ALREADY.
AND HIS DEFEAT WAS FOLLOWED BY THE LONGEST PERIOD OF PEACE AND PROSPERITY IN OUR PLANET'S HISTORY...
"...BUT THE ONE THING A TYRANT'S GOOD FOR IS SCARING OFF POTENTIAL PREDATORS. WITH TYPHON AND HIS REGIME REMOVED, WE WERE EASY PICKINGS FOR A WARRIOR RACE LIKE THE BROTEANS.
"HAVE YOU HEARD OF THEM BEFORE?
"THEY'D BEEN WATCHING US FOR YEARS FROM THEIR NEARBY WORLD, JEALOUS OF OUR WEALTH AND NATURAL RESOURCES.
"THEIR LEADER, THE KINGFISHER, HAD PLANNED THEIR ATTACK WITH SUCH RUTHLESS PRECISION THAT THEY DOMINATED OUR ENTIRE PLANET IN LESS THAN A SINGLE DAY.

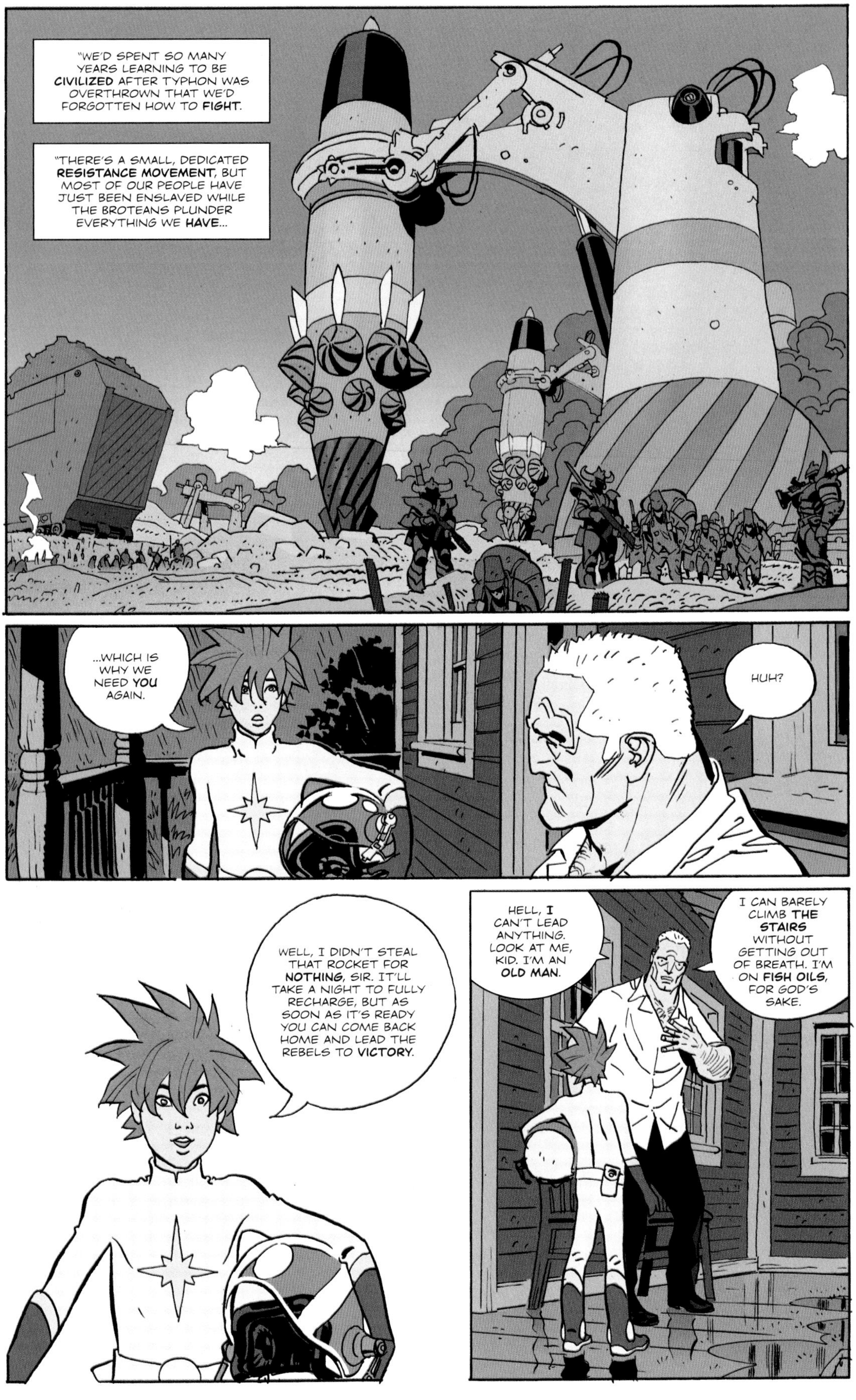
"WE'D SPENT SO MANY YEARS LEARNING TO BE CIVILIZED AFTER TYPHON WAS OVERTHROWN THAT WE'D FORGOTTEN HOW TO FIGHT.
"THERE'S A SMALL, DEDICATED RESISTANCE MOVEMENT, BUT MOST OF OUR PEOPLE HAVE JUST BEEN ENSLAVED WHILE THE BROTEANS PLUNDER EVERYTHING WE HAVE...
...WHICH IS WHY WE NEED YOU AGAIN.
HUH?
WELL, I DIDN'T STEAL THAT ROCKET FOR NOTHING, SIR. IT'LL TAKE A NIGHT TO FULLY RECHARGE, BUT AS SOON AS IT'S READY YOU CAN COME BACK HOME AND LEAD THE REBELS TO VICTORY.
HELL, I CAN'T LEAD ANYTHING. LOOK AT ME, KID. I'M AN OLD MAN.
I CAN BARELY CLIMB THE STAIRS WITHOUT GETTING OUT OF BREATH. I'M ON FISH OILS, FOR GOD'S SAKE.

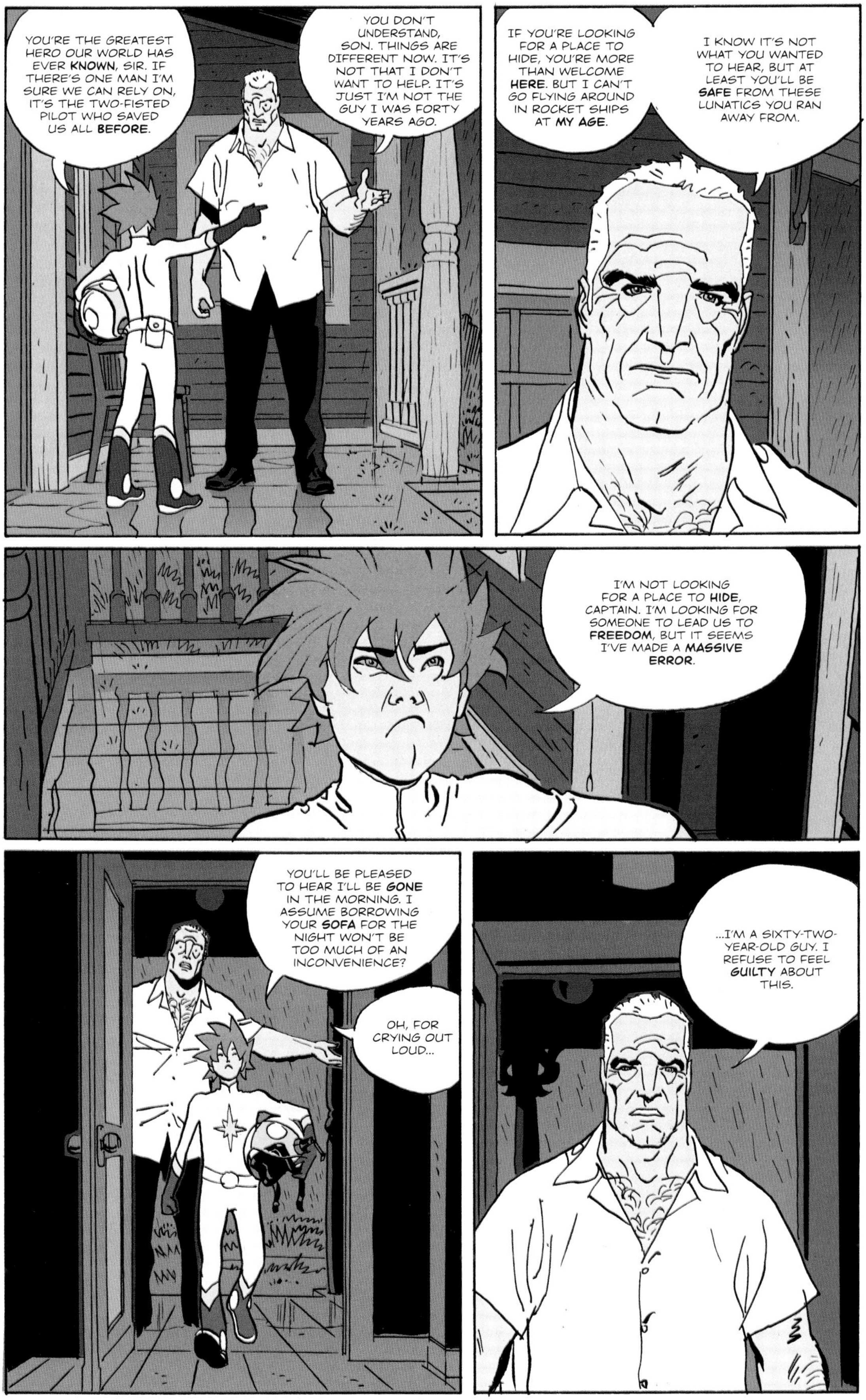

YOU'RE THE GREATEST HERO OUR WORLD HAS EVER KNOWN, SIR. IF THERE'S ONE MAN I'M SURE WE CAN RELY ON, IT'S THE TWO-FISTED PILOT WHO SAVED US ALL BEFORE.
YOU DON'T UNDERSTAND, SON. THINGS ARE DIFFERENT NOW. IT'S NOT THAT I DON'T WANT TO HELP. IT'S JUST I'M NOT THE GUY I WAS FORTY YEARS AGO.
IF YOU'RE LOOKING FOR A PLACE TO HIDE, YOU'RE MORE THAN WELCOME HERE. BUT I CAN'T GO FLYING AROUND IN ROCKET SHIPS AT MY AGE.
I KNOW IT'S NOT WHAT YOU WANTED TO HEAR, BUT AT LEAST YOU'LL BE SAFE FROM THESE LUNATICS YOU RAN AWAY FROM.
I'M NOT LOOKING FOR A PLACE TO HIDE, CAPTAIN. I'M LOOKING FOR SOMEONE TO LEAD US TO FREEDOM, BUT IT SEEMS I'VE MADE A MASSIVE ERROR.
YOU'LL BE PLEASED TO HEAR I'LL BE GONE IN THE MORNING. I ASSUME BORROWING YOUR SOFA FOR THE NIGHT WON'T BE TOO MUCH OF AN INCONVENIENCE?
OH, FOR CRYING OUT LOUD...
...I'M A SIXTY-TWO-YEAR-OLD GUY. I REFUSE TO FEEL GUILTY ABOUT THIS.

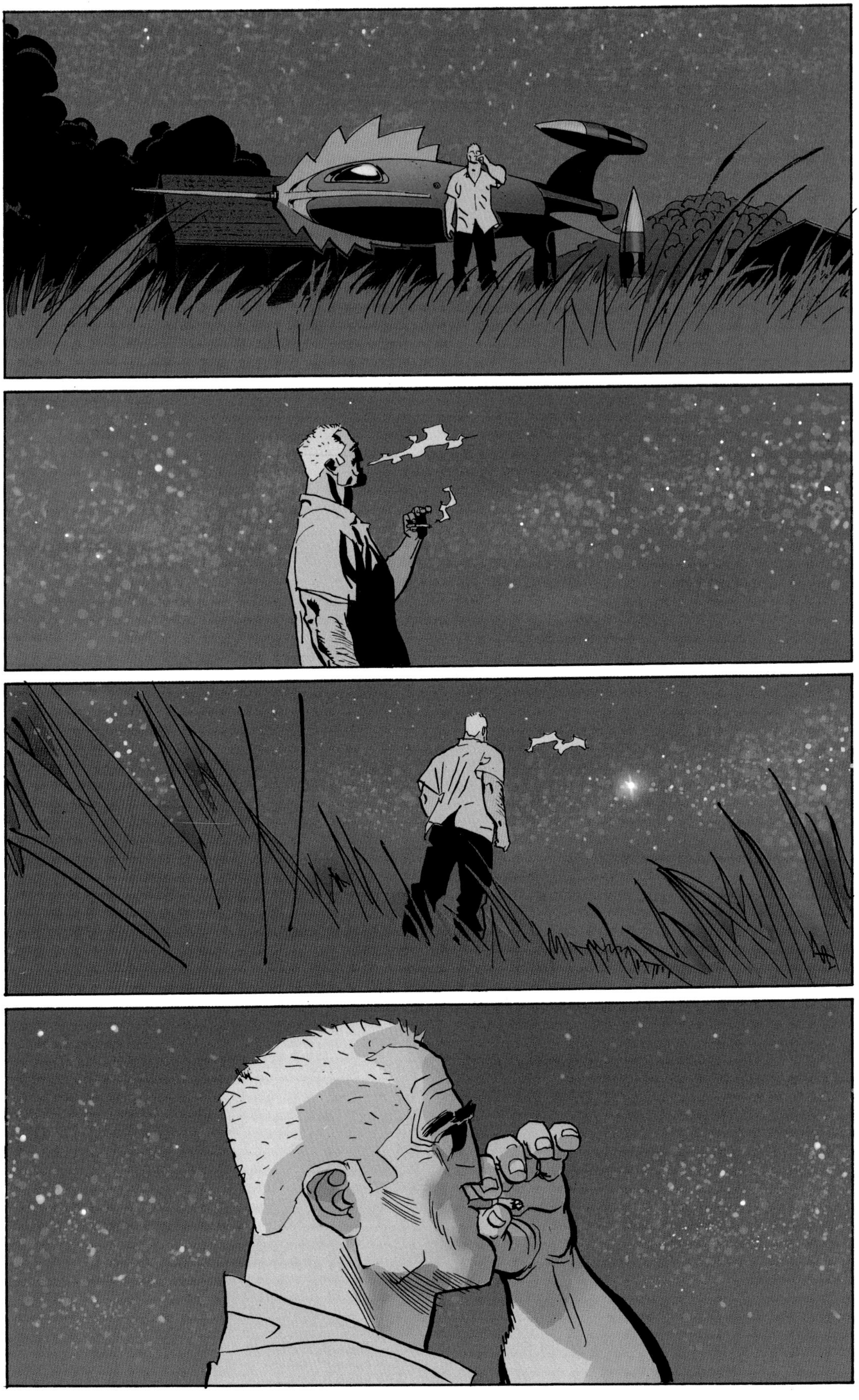

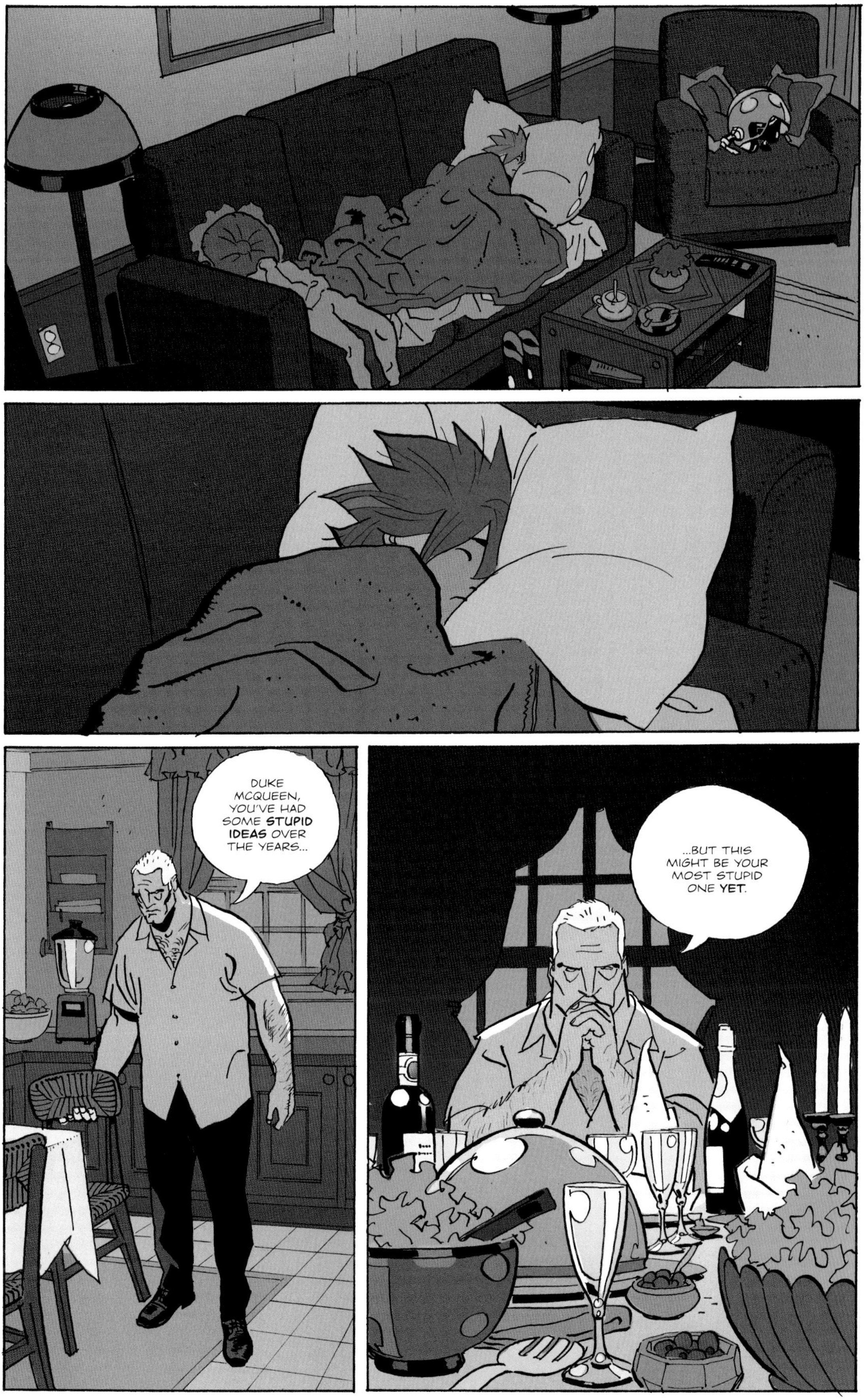
DUKE MCQUEEN, YOU'VE HAD SOME **STUPID IDEAS** OVER THE YEARS...
...BUT THIS MIGHT BE YOUR MOST STUPID ONE **YET**.

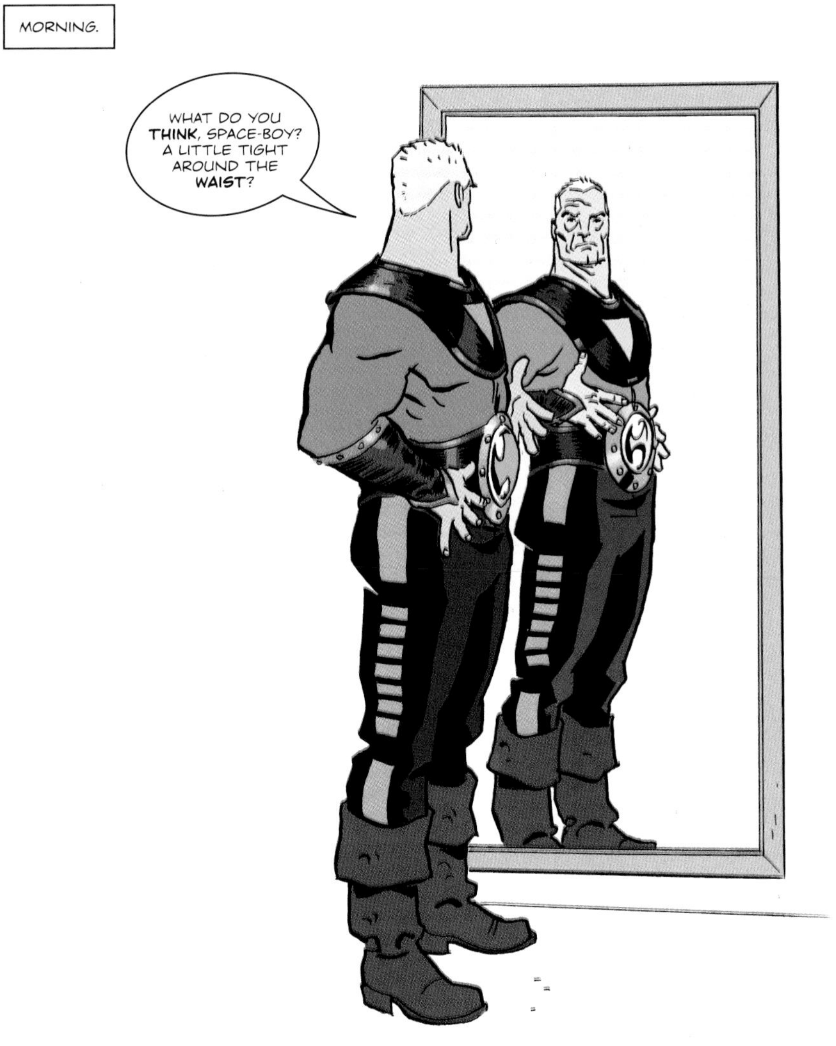
MORNING.
WHAT DO YOU THINK, SPACE-BOY? A LITTLE TIGHT AROUND THE WAIST?

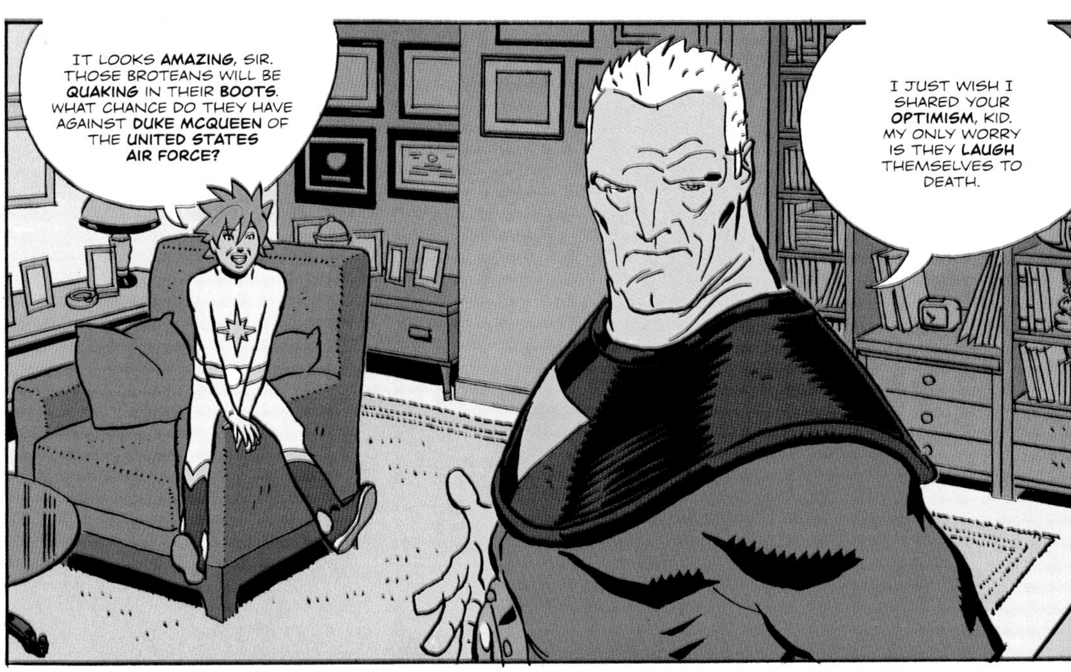
IT LOOKS AMAZING, SIR. THOSE BROTEANS WILL BE QUAKING IN THEIR BOOTS. WHAT CHANCE DO THEY HAVE AGAINST DUKE MCQUEEN OF THE UNITED STATES AIR FORCE?
I JUST WISH I SHARED YOUR OPTIMISM, KID. MY ONLY WORRY IS THEY LAUGH THEMSELVES TO DEATH.

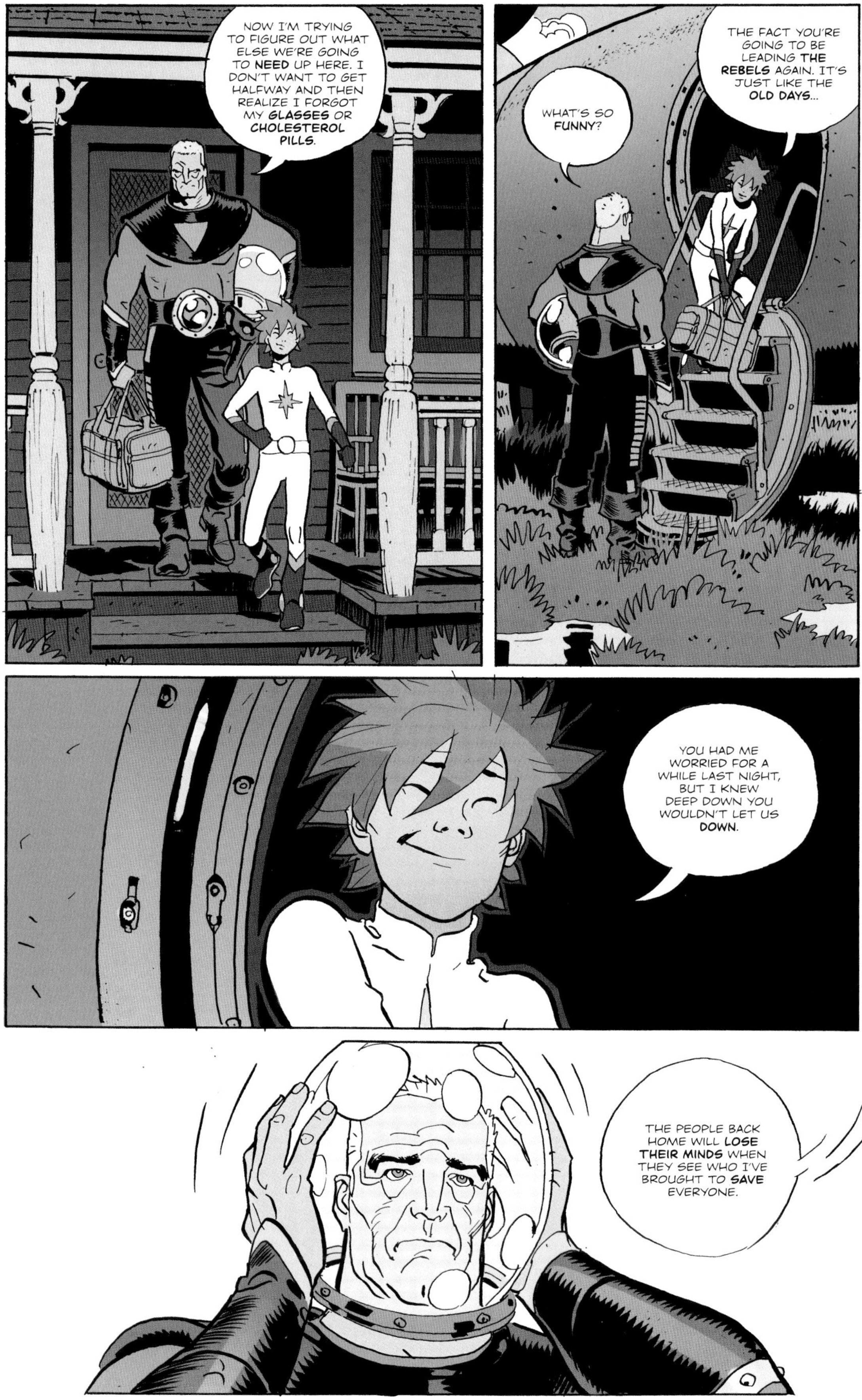
NOW I'M TRYING TO FIGURE OUT WHAT ELSE WE'RE GOING TO **NEED** UP HERE. I DON'T WANT TO GET HALFWAY AND THEN REALIZE I FORGOT MY **GLASSES** OR **CHOLESTEROL PILLS**.
WHAT'S SO **FUNNY**?
THE FACT YOU'RE GOING TO BE LEADING **THE REBELS** AGAIN. IT'S JUST LIKE THE **OLD DAYS**...
YOU HAD ME WORRIED FOR A WHILE LAST NIGHT, BUT I KNEW DEEP DOWN YOU WOULDN'T LET US **DOWN**.
THE PEOPLE BACK HOME WILL **LOSE THEIR MINDS** WHEN THEY SEE WHO I'VE BROUGHT TO **SAVE** EVERYONE.

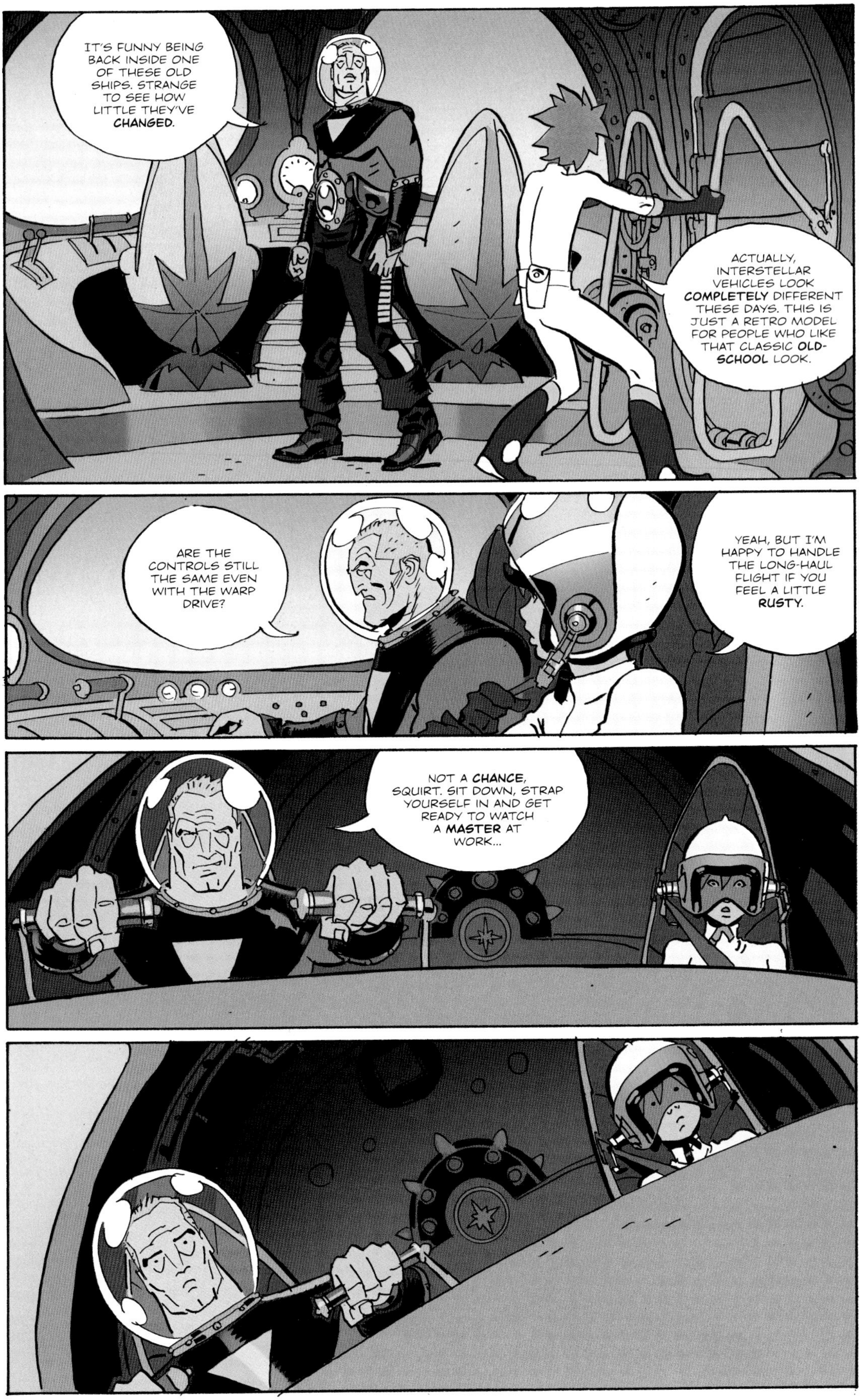
IT'S FUNNY BEING BACK INSIDE ONE OF THESE OLD SHIPS. STRANGE TO SEE HOW LITTLE THEY'VE **CHANGED**.
ACTUALLY, INTERSTELLAR VEHICLES LOOK **COMPLETELY** DIFFERENT THESE DAYS. THIS IS JUST A RETRO MODEL FOR PEOPLE WHO LIKE THAT CLASSIC **OLD-SCHOOL** LOOK.
ARE THE CONTROLS STILL THE SAME EVEN WITH THE WARP DRIVE?
YEAH, BUT I'M HAPPY TO HANDLE THE LONG-HAUL FLIGHT IF YOU FEEL A LITTLE **RUSTY**.
NOT A **CHANCE**, SQUIRT. SIT DOWN, STRAP YOURSELF IN AND GET READY TO WATCH A **MASTER** AT WORK...

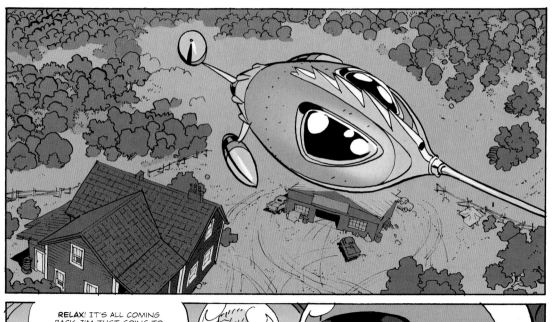

RELAX! IT'S ALL COMING BACK. I'M JUST GOING TO TAKE HER TO A NICE, SAFE HEIGHT AND THEN WE CAN PUT THIS LADY THROUGH HER **PACES.**

YOU MIGHT WANT TO SWITCH ON THE **CLOAKING DEVICE,** SIR. EXTRATERRESTRIAL VEHICLES COULD CAUSE A LITTLE **ANXIETY** IN THIS NEIGHBOR-HOOD.

ARE YOU **NUTS?** AFTER ALL THOSE YEARS OF NOBODY **BELIEVING** ME?

YOU AND I ARE GOING TO HAVE A LITTLE **FUN** FIRST...

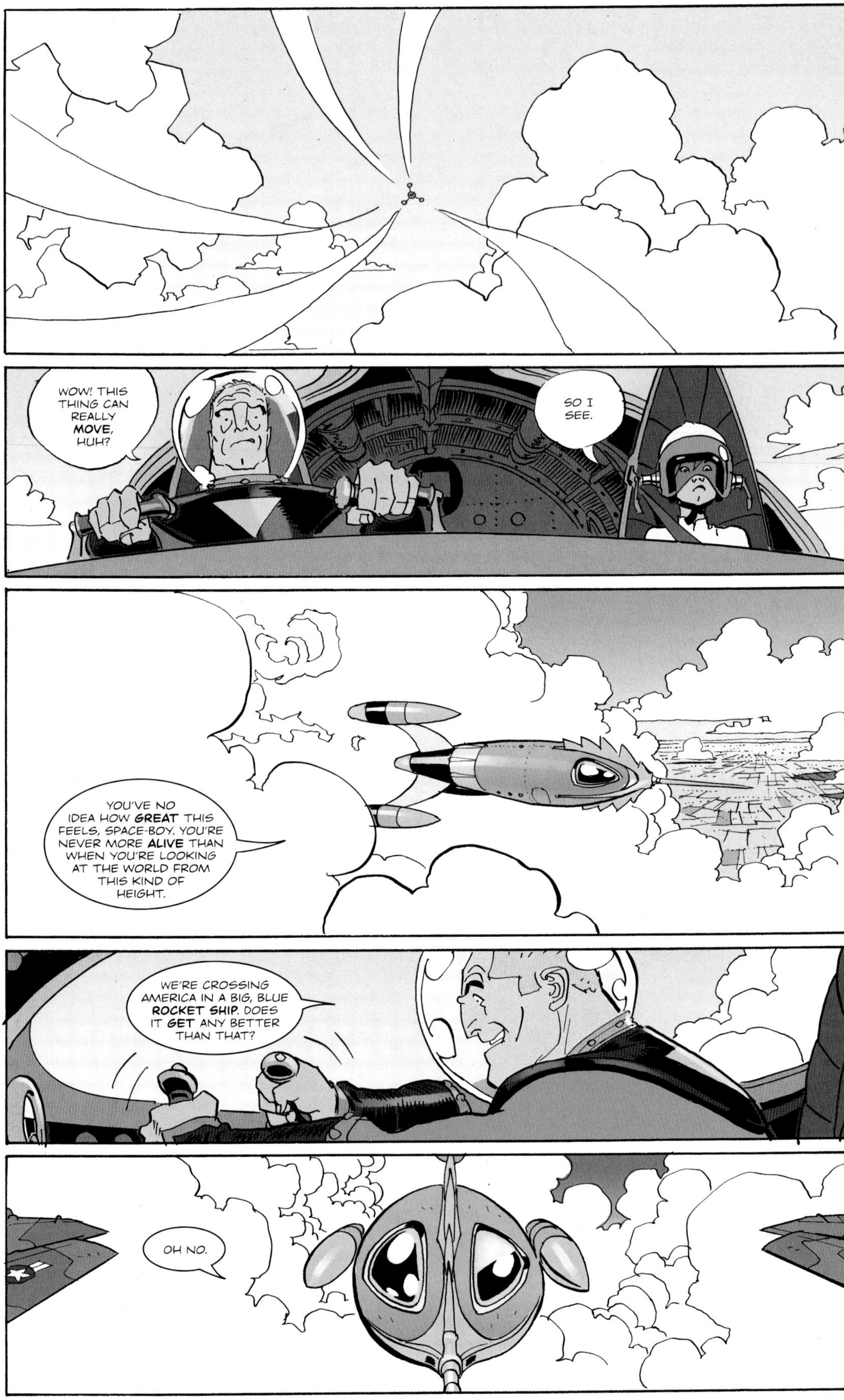
WOW! THIS THING CAN REALLY **MOVE**, HUH?
SO I SEE.
YOU'VE NO IDEA HOW **GREAT** THIS FEELS, SPACE-BOY. YOU'RE NEVER MORE **ALIVE** THAN WHEN YOU'RE LOOKING AT THE WORLD FROM THIS KIND OF HEIGHT.
WE'RE CROSSING AMERICA IN A BIG, BLUE **ROCKET SHIP**. DOES IT **GET** ANY BETTER THAN THAT?
OH NO.

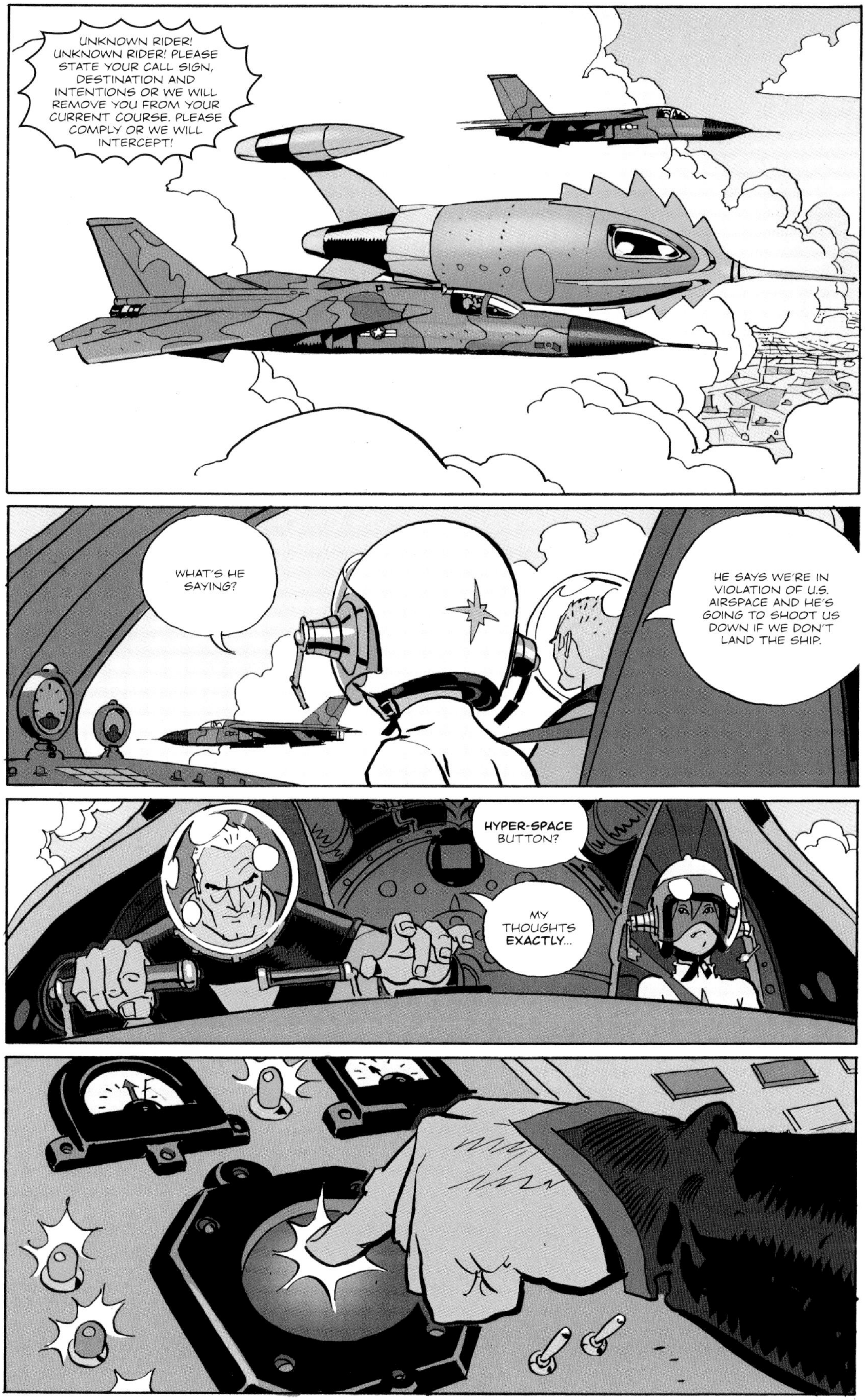
UNKNOWN RIDER! UNKNOWN RIDER! PLEASE STATE YOUR CALL SIGN, DESTINATION AND INTENTIONS OR WE WILL REMOVE YOU FROM YOUR CURRENT COURSE. PLEASE COMPLY OR WE WILL INTERCEPT!
WHAT'S HE SAYING?
HE SAYS WE'RE IN VIOLATION OF U.S. AIRSPACE AND HE'S GOING TO SHOOT US DOWN IF WE DON'T LAND THE SHIP.
HYPER-SPACE BUTTON?
MY THOUGHTS **EXACTLY**...

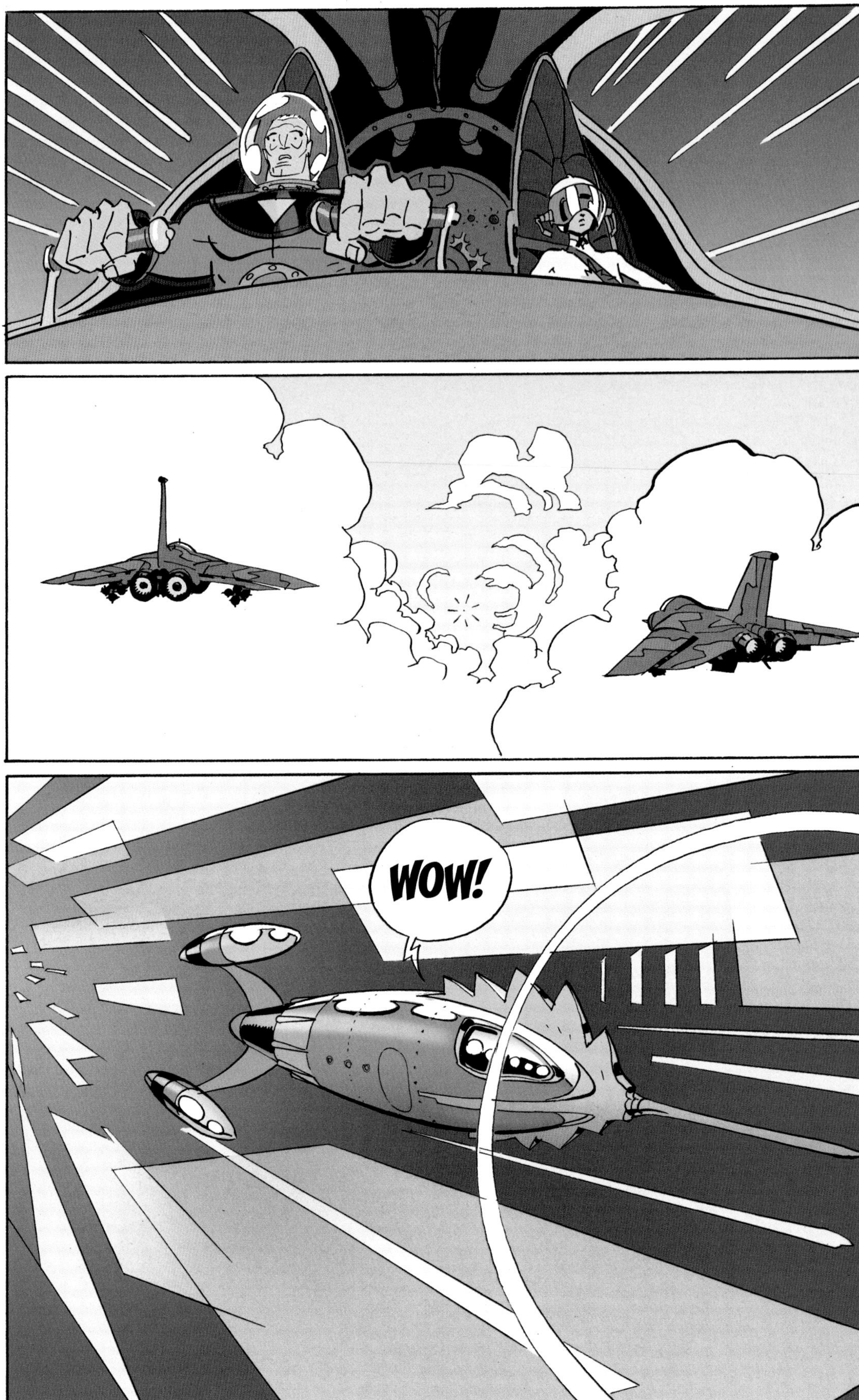
WOW!

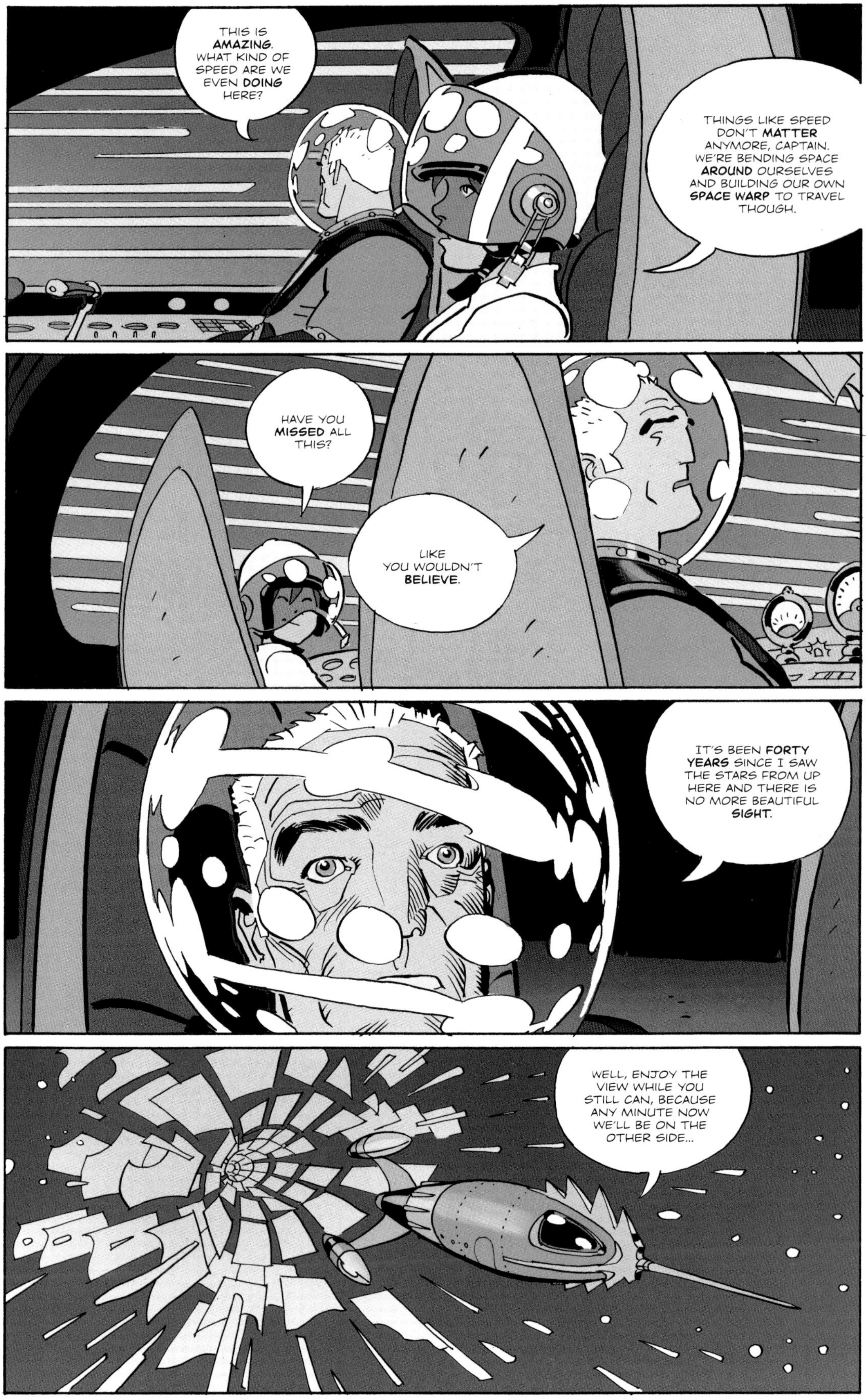
THIS IS AMAZING. WHAT KIND OF SPEED ARE WE EVEN DOING HERE?
THINGS LIKE SPEED DON'T MATTER ANYMORE, CAPTAIN. WE'RE BENDING SPACE AROUND OURSELVES AND BUILDING OUR OWN SPACE WARP TO TRAVEL THOUGH.
HAVE YOU MISSED ALL THIS?
LIKE YOU WOULDN'T BELIEVE.
IT'S BEEN FORTY YEARS SINCE I SAW THE STARS FROM UP HERE AND THERE IS NO MORE BEAUTIFUL SIGHT.
WELL, ENJOY THE VIEW WHILE YOU STILL CAN, BECAUSE ANY MINUTE NOW WE'LL BE ON THE OTHER SIDE...

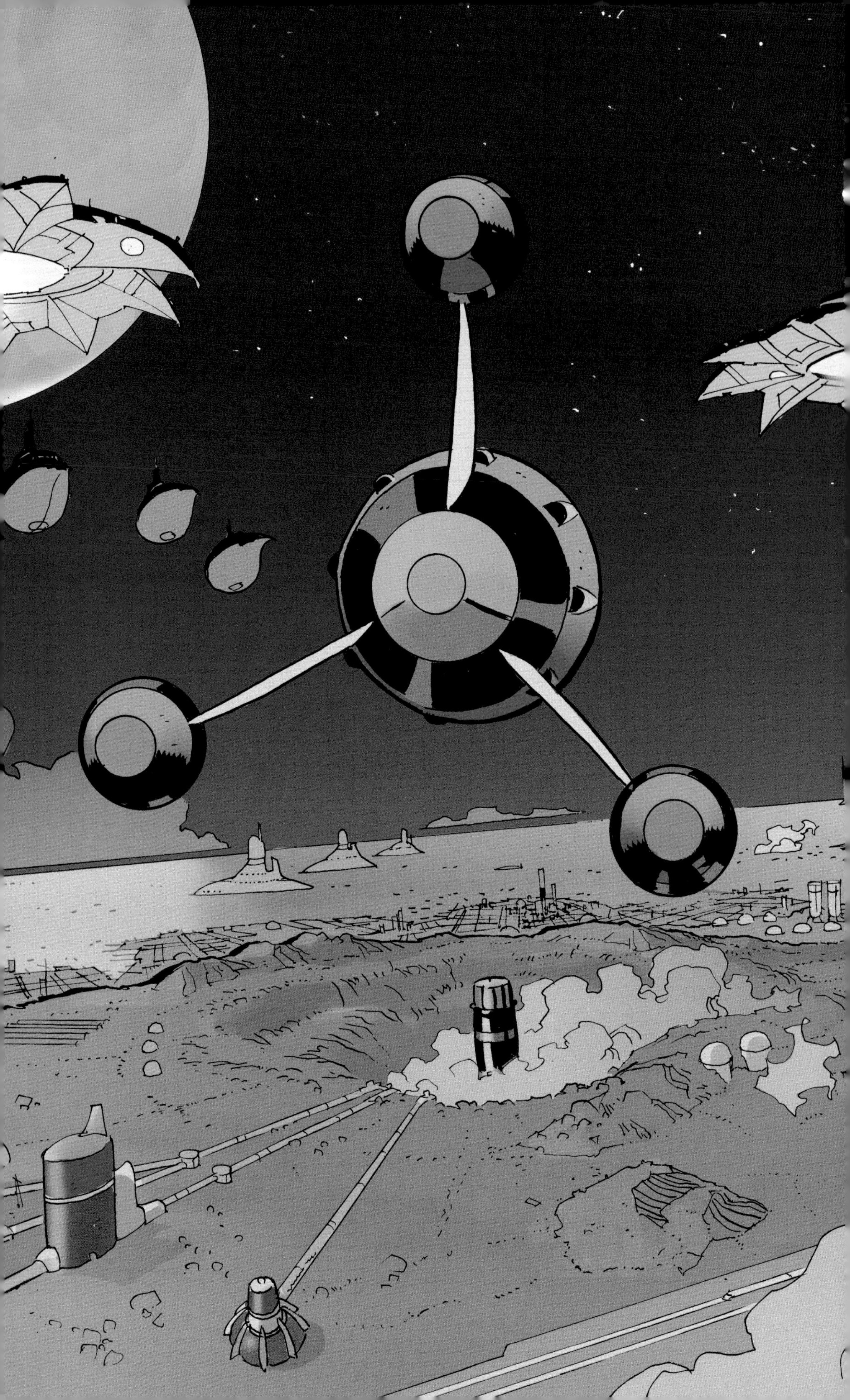

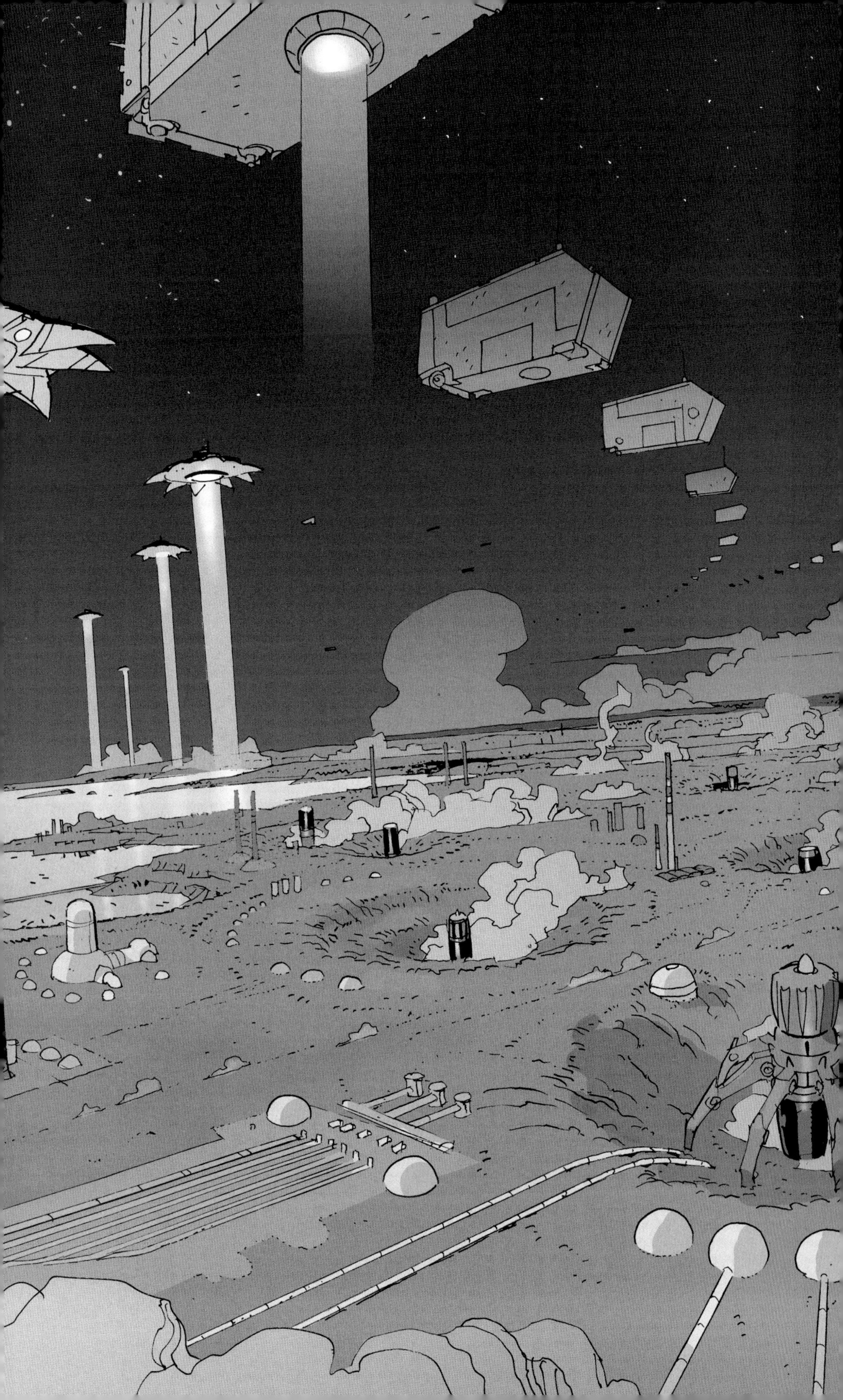

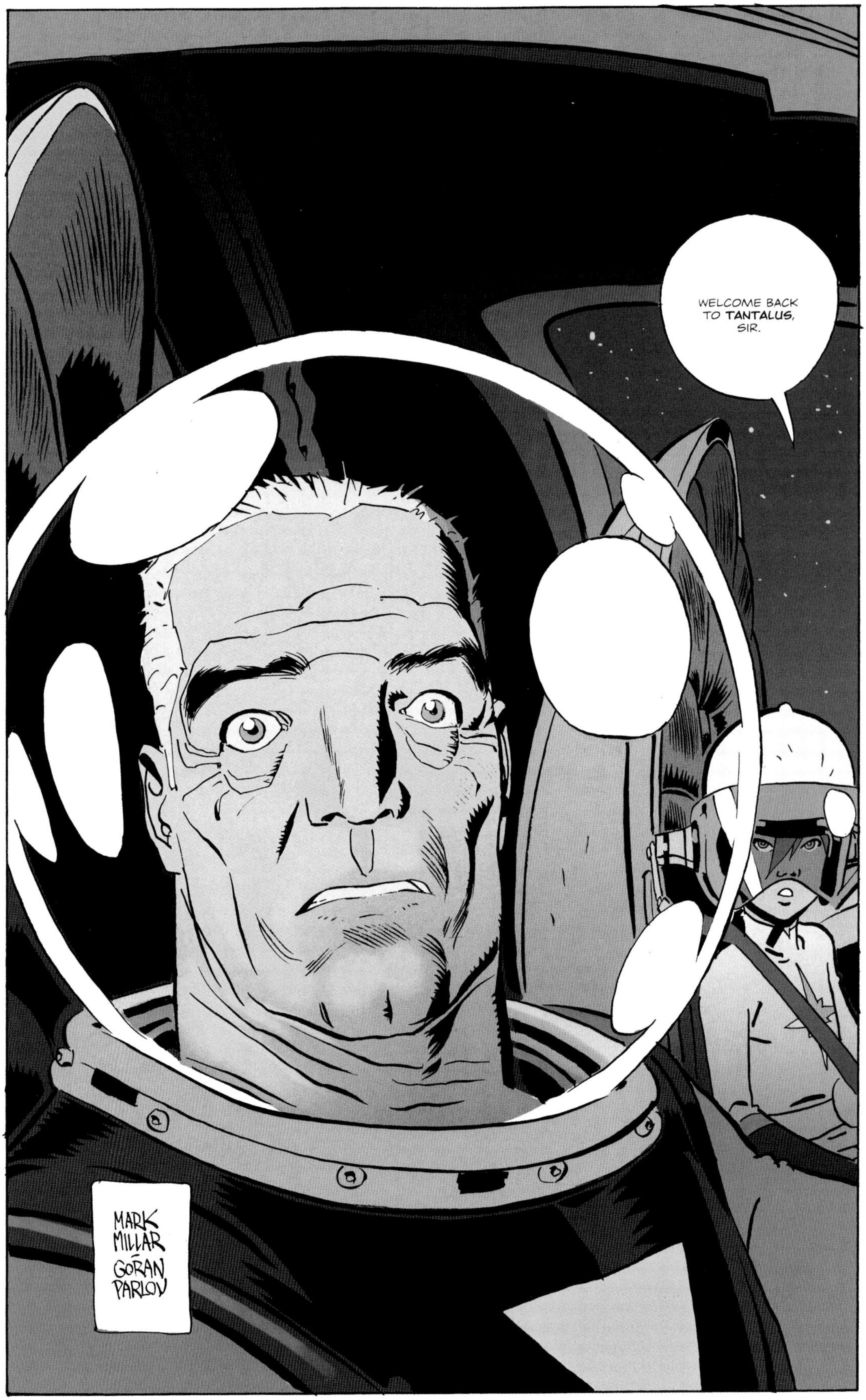
WELCOME BACK TO TANTALUS, SIR.
MARK MILLAR GORAN PARLOV

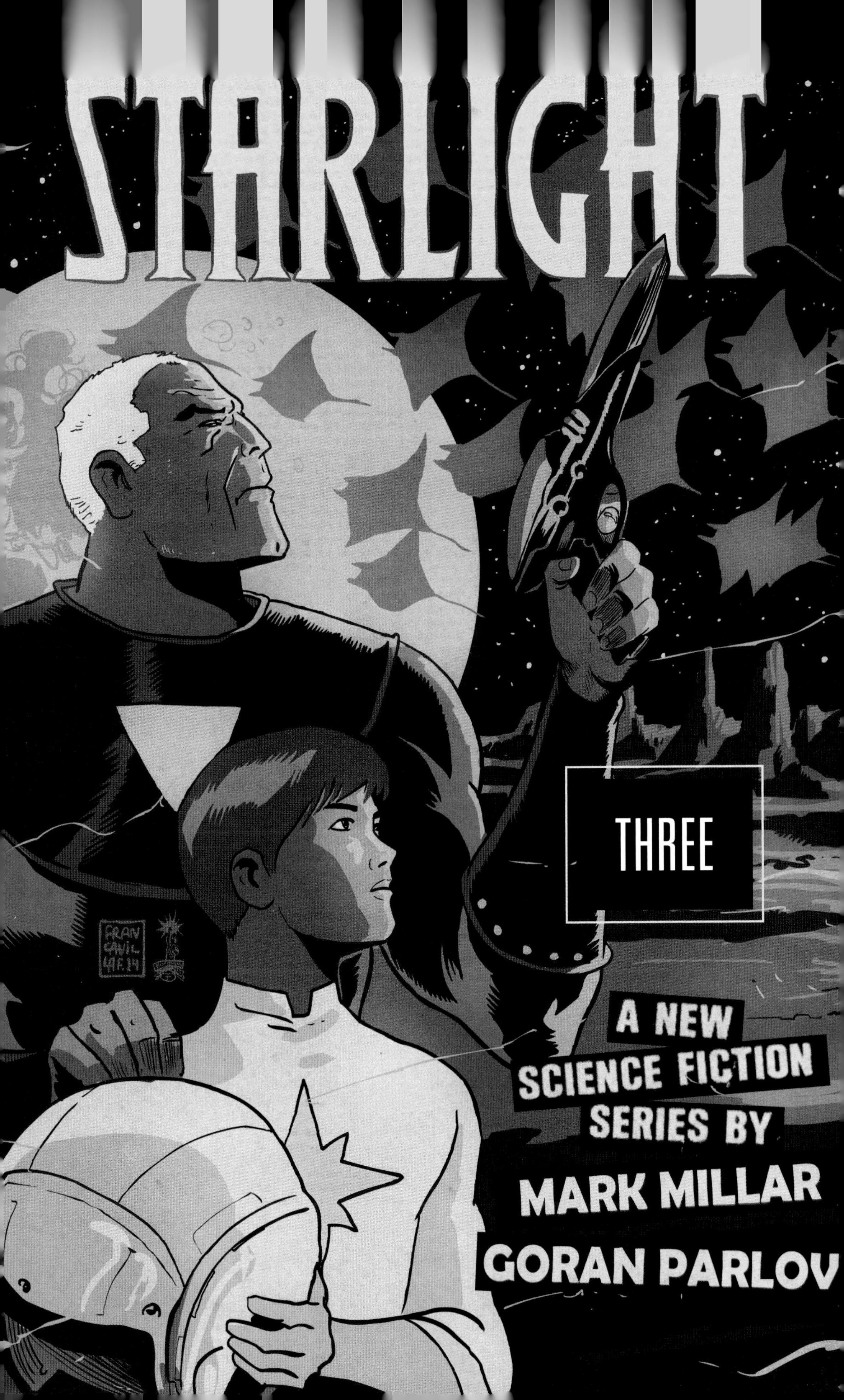
STARLIGHT
THREE
A NEW
SCIENCE FICTION
SERIES BY
MARK MILLAR
GORAN PARLOV

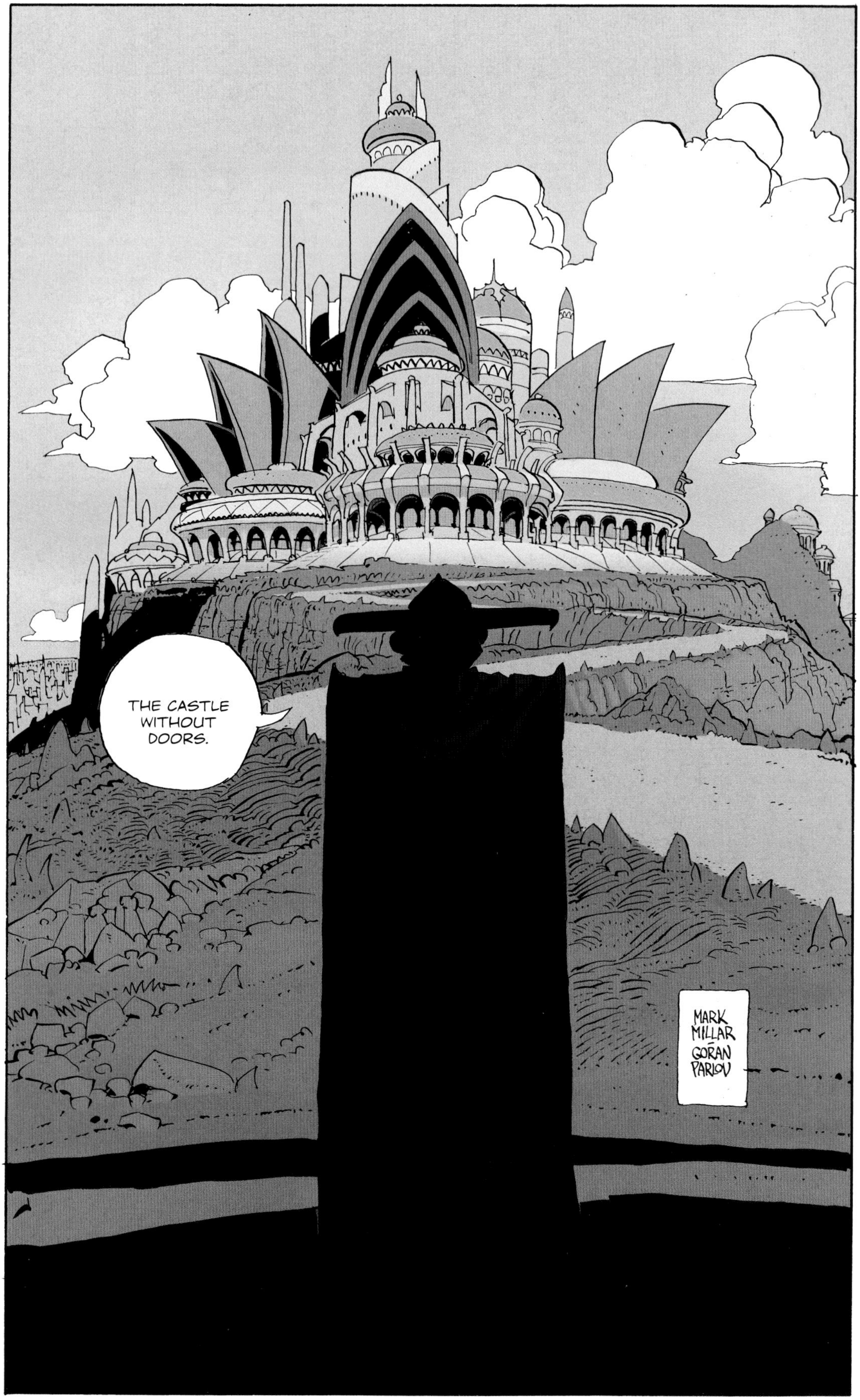

THE CASTLE WITHOUT DOORS.
MARK MILLAR GORAN PARLOV

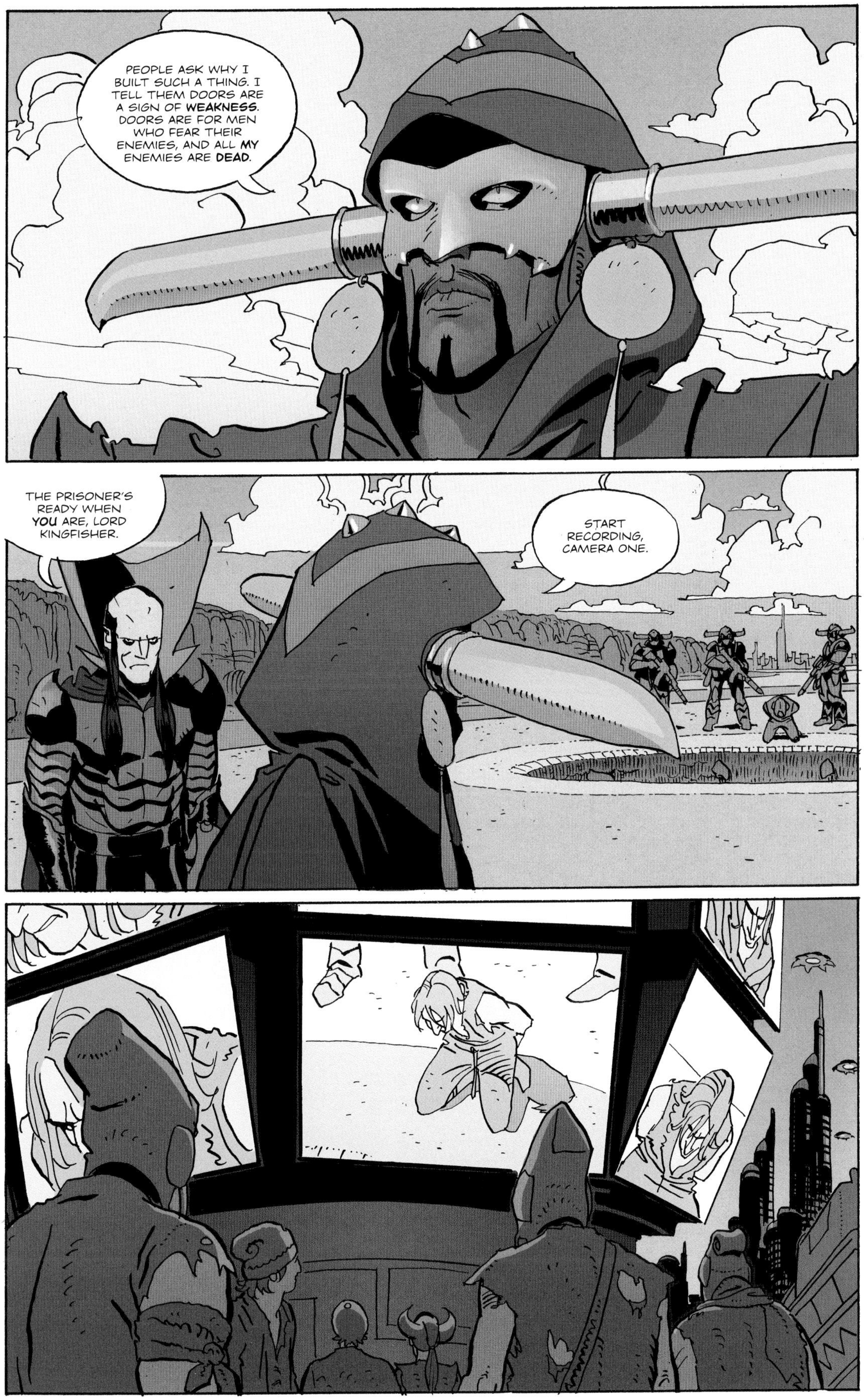
PEOPLE ASK WHY I BUILT SUCH A THING. I TELL THEM DOORS ARE A SIGN OF **WEAKNESS.** DOORS ARE FOR MEN WHO FEAR THEIR ENEMIES, AND ALL **MY** ENEMIES ARE **DEAD.**
THE PRISONER'S READY WHEN **YOU** ARE, LORD KINGFISHER.
START RECORDING, CAMERA ONE.

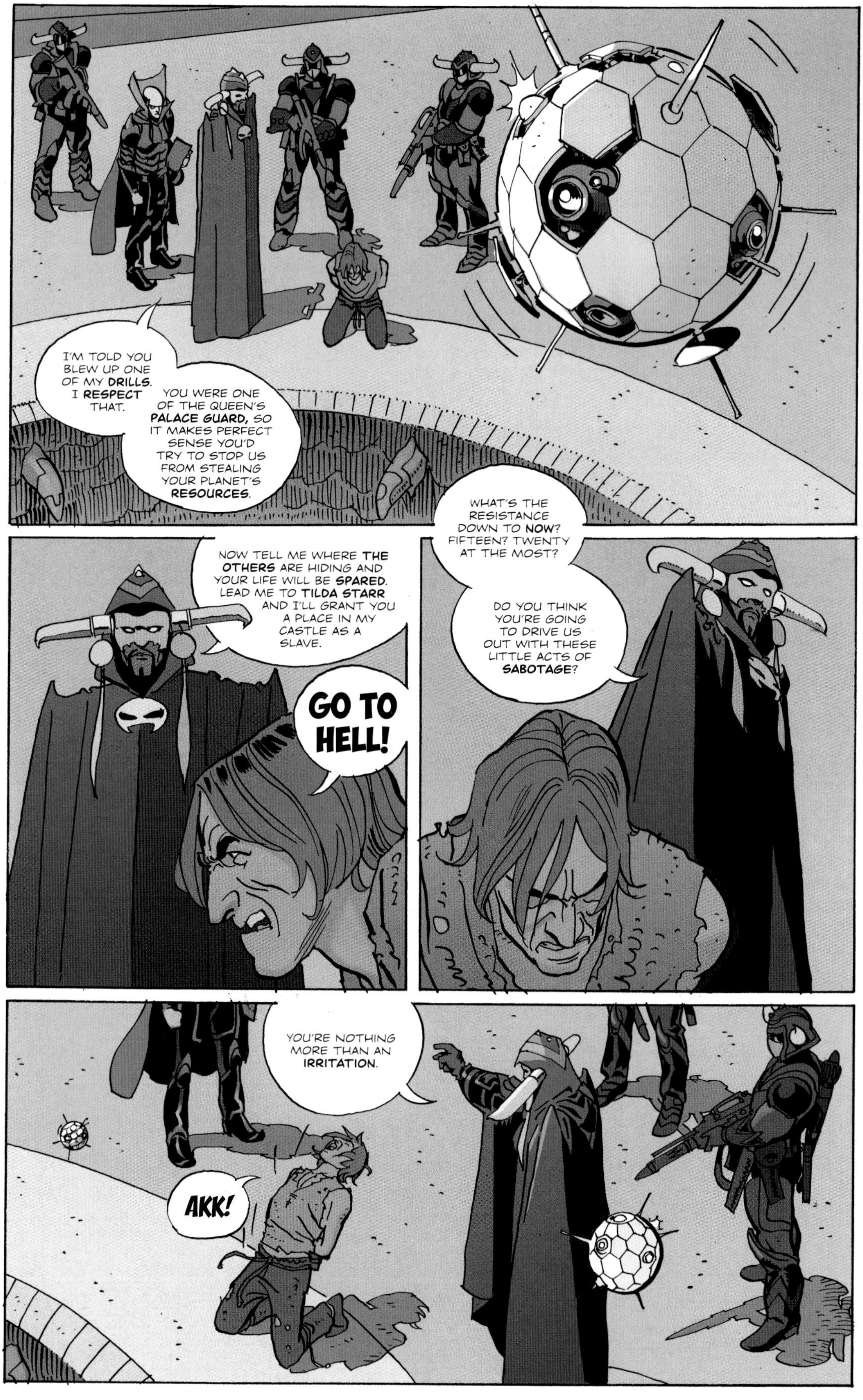
I'M TOLD YOU BLEW UP ONE OF MY DRILLS. I RESPECT THAT.
YOU WERE ONE OF THE QUEEN'S PALACE GUARD, SO IT MAKES PERFECT SENSE YOU'D TRY TO STOP US FROM STEALING YOUR PLANET'S RESOURCES.
NOW TELL ME WHERE THE OTHERS ARE HIDING AND YOUR LIFE WILL BE SPARED. LEAD ME TO TILDA STARR AND I'LL GRANT YOU A PLACE IN MY CASTLE AS A SLAVE.
GO TO HELL!
WHAT'S THE RESISTANCE DOWN TO NOW? FIFTEEN? TWENTY AT THE MOST?
DO YOU THINK YOU'RE GOING TO DRIVE US OUT WITH THESE LITTLE ACTS OF SABOTAGE?
YOU'RE NOTHING MORE THAN AN IRRITATION.
AKK!

THESE GLOVES
I BOUGHT GIVE
ME LIMITED
TELEKINESIS
AND I'VE BEEN
PRACTICING
WITH THEM FOR
MONTHS NOW.

UGH!

CAN YOU FEEL
ME MAKING YOUR
BONES SNAP? ALL
YOUR ORGANS
BURSTING AND
DEFLATING?

I PAID FOR THIS WITH
A YEAR'S SUPPLY OF
YOUR PLANET'S MOST
PRECIOUS MINERALS.
THINK ABOUT **THAT**
AS YOU DIE.

BECAUSE
THAT'S WHAT
I'M SPENDING
YOUR MONEY
ON, LOYAL
SOLDIER...

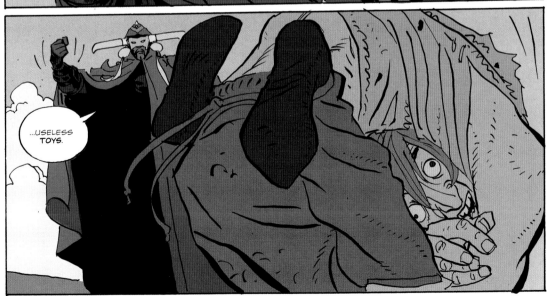

...USELESS
TOYS.

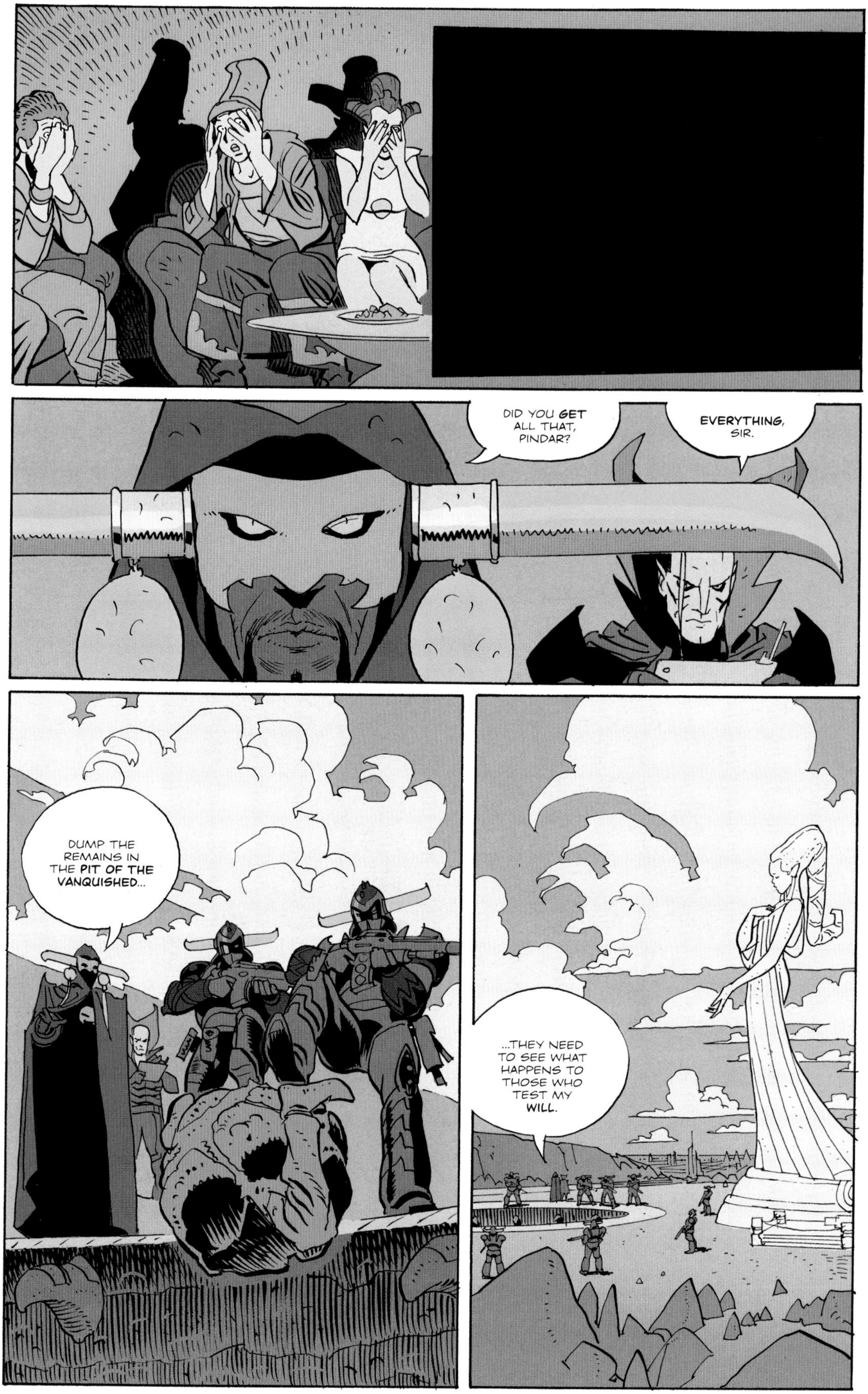
DID YOU GET ALL THAT, PINDAR?
EVERYTHING, SIR.
DUMP THE REMAINS IN THE PIT OF THE VANQUISHED...
...THEY NEED TO SEE WHAT HAPPENS TO THOSE WHO TEST MY WILL.

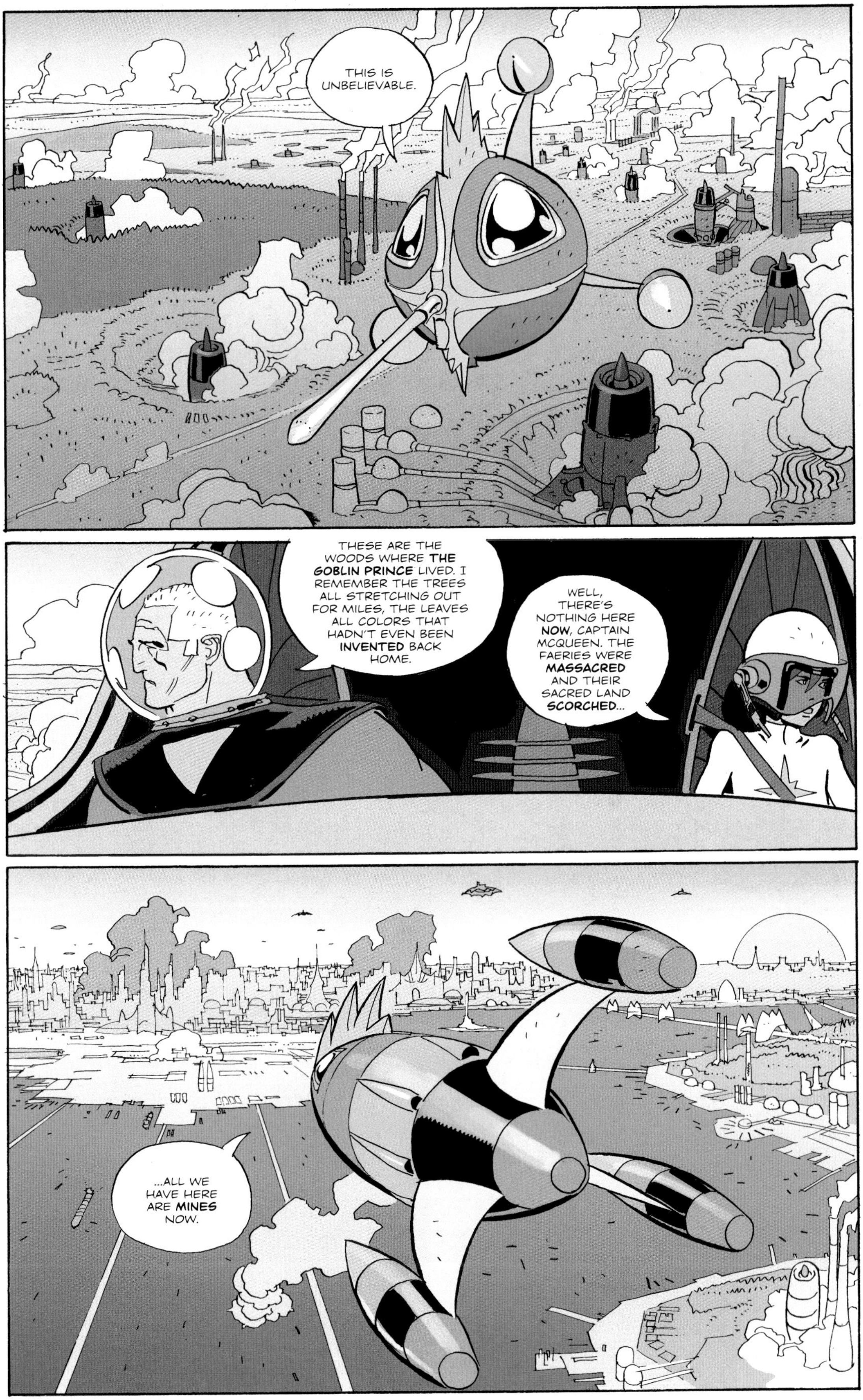
THIS IS UNBELIEVABLE.
THESE ARE THE WOODS WHERE **THE GOBLIN PRINCE** LIVED. I REMEMBER THE TREES ALL STRETCHING OUT FOR MILES, THE LEAVES ALL COLORS THAT HADN'T EVEN BEEN **INVENTED** BACK HOME.
WELL, THERE'S NOTHING HERE **NOW**, CAPTAIN MCQUEEN. THE FAERIES WERE **MASSACRED** AND THEIR SACRED LAND **SCORCHED**...
...ALL WE HAVE HERE ARE **MINES** NOW.

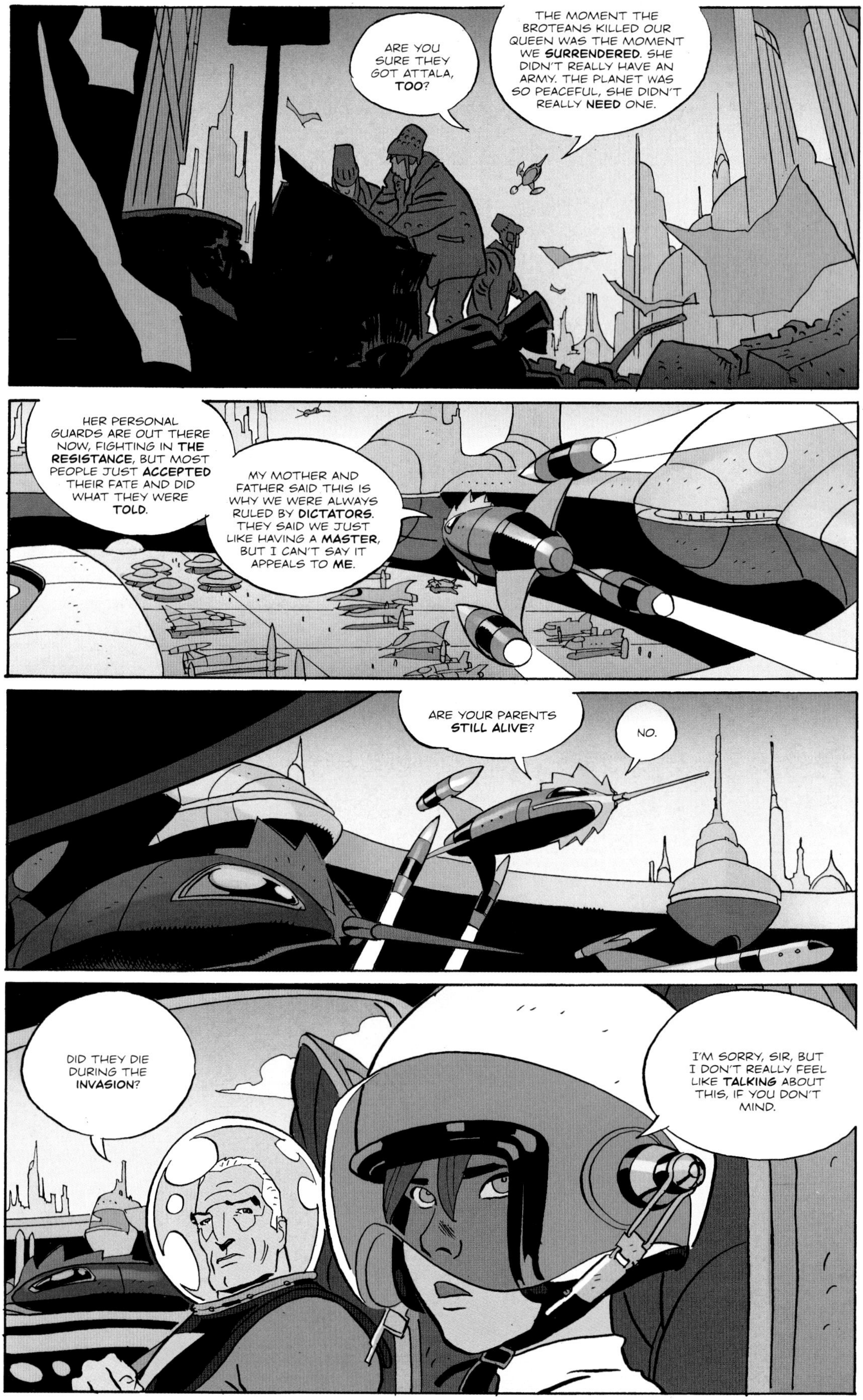
ARE YOU SURE THEY GOT ATTALA, **TOO**?
THE MOMENT THE BROTEANS KILLED OUR QUEEN WAS THE MOMENT WE **SURRENDERED**. SHE DIDN'T REALLY HAVE AN ARMY. THE PLANET WAS SO PEACEFUL, SHE DIDN'T REALLY **NEED** ONE.
HER PERSONAL GUARDS ARE OUT THERE NOW, FIGHTING IN **THE RESISTANCE**, BUT MOST PEOPLE JUST **ACCEPTED** THEIR FATE AND DID WHAT THEY WERE **TOLD**.
MY MOTHER AND FATHER SAID THIS IS WHY WE WERE ALWAYS RULED BY **DICTATORS**. THEY SAID WE JUST LIKE HAVING A **MASTER**, BUT I CAN'T SAY IT APPEALS TO **ME**.
ARE YOUR PARENTS **STILL ALIVE**?
NO.
DID THEY DIE DURING THE **INVASION**?
I'M SORRY, SIR, BUT I DON'T REALLY FEEL LIKE **TALKING** ABOUT THIS, IF YOU DON'T MIND.

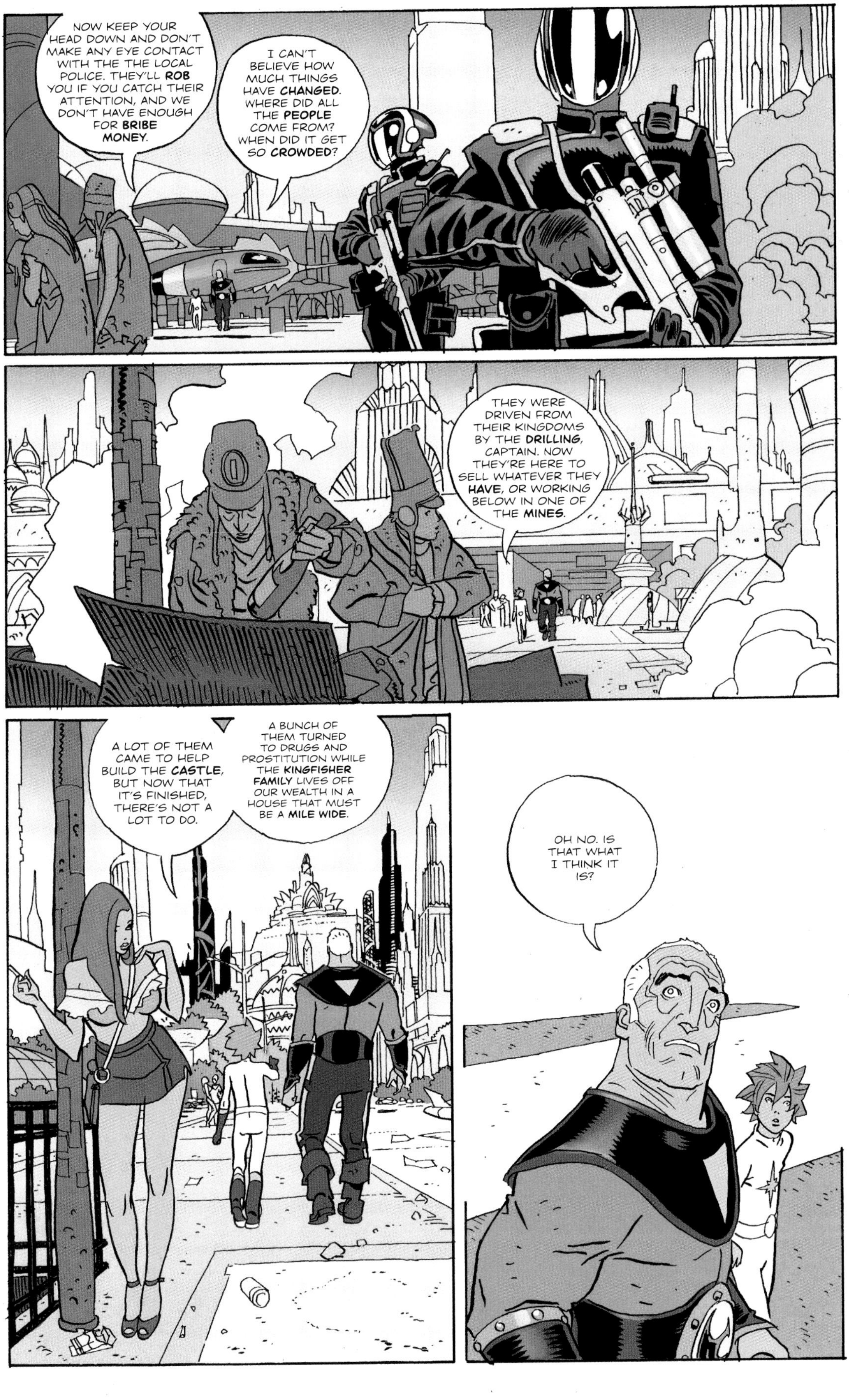
NOW KEEP YOUR HEAD DOWN AND DON'T MAKE ANY EYE CONTACT WITH THE THE LOCAL POLICE. THEY'LL ROB YOU IF YOU CATCH THEIR ATTENTION, AND WE DON'T HAVE ENOUGH FOR BRIBE MONEY.
I CAN'T BELIEVE HOW MUCH THINGS HAVE CHANGED. WHERE DID ALL THE PEOPLE COME FROM? WHEN DID IT GET SO CROWDED?
THEY WERE DRIVEN FROM THEIR KINGDOMS BY THE DRILLING, CAPTAIN. NOW THEY'RE HERE TO SELL WHATEVER THEY HAVE, OR WORKING BELOW IN ONE OF THE MINES.
A LOT OF THEM CAME TO HELP BUILD THE CASTLE, BUT NOW THAT IT'S FINISHED, THERE'S NOT A LOT TO DO.
A BUNCH OF THEM TURNED TO DRUGS AND PROSTITUTION WHILE THE KINGFISHER FAMILY LIVES OFF OUR WEALTH IN A HOUSE THAT MUST BE A MILE WIDE.
OH NO. IS THAT WHAT I THINK IT IS?

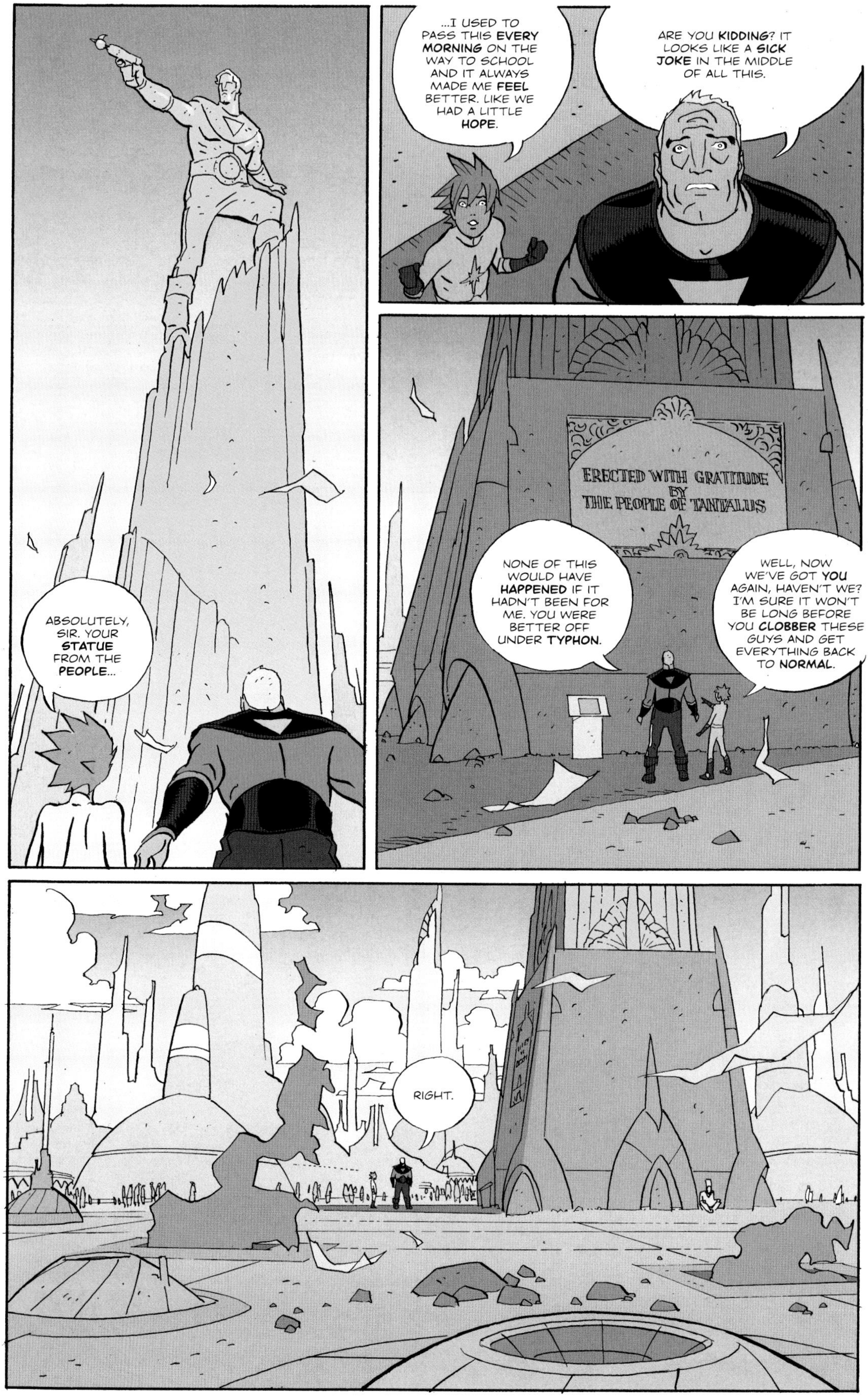
ABSOLUTELY, SIR. YOUR STATUE FROM THE PEOPLE...
...I USED TO PASS THIS EVERY MORNING ON THE WAY TO SCHOOL AND IT ALWAYS MADE ME FEEL BETTER. LIKE WE HAD A LITTLE HOPE.
ARE YOU KIDDING? IT LOOKS LIKE A SICK JOKE IN THE MIDDLE OF ALL THIS.
ERECTED WITH GRATITUDE BY THE PEOPLE OF TANTALUS
NONE OF THIS WOULD HAVE HAPPENED IF IT HADN'T BEEN FOR ME. YOU WERE BETTER OFF UNDER TYPHON.
WELL, NOW WE'VE GOT YOU AGAIN, HAVEN'T WE? I'M SURE IT WON'T BE LONG BEFORE YOU CLOBBER THESE GUYS AND GET EVERYTHING BACK TO NORMAL.
RIGHT.

WHAT'S GOING ON OVER THERE?

WE CAN'T GET INVOLVED. IT'S JUST A **POLICE MUGGING**. YOU NEED TO LIE LOW 'TIL WE FIND TILDA STARR.

TO HELL WITH **THAT**...

...LEAVE THAT GUY **ALONE**, YOU PACK OF HYENAS! YOU'RE SUPPOSED TO BE **COPS**, FOR CRYING OUT LOUD!

GET OUT OF HERE BEFORE YOU GET IT **WORSE**, OLD MAN. WHO THE HELL ARE YOU TO TELL A **BROTEAN** WHAT TO DO?

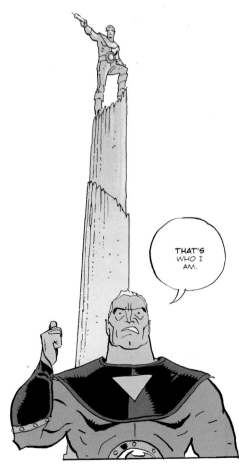

THAT'S WHO I AM.

WHO AM **I**?

NOW LEAVE HIM ALONE BEFORE I STICK MY **TOE** IN YOUR ASS!

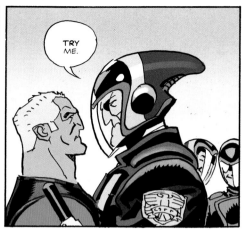

TRY ME.

KRUNCH!

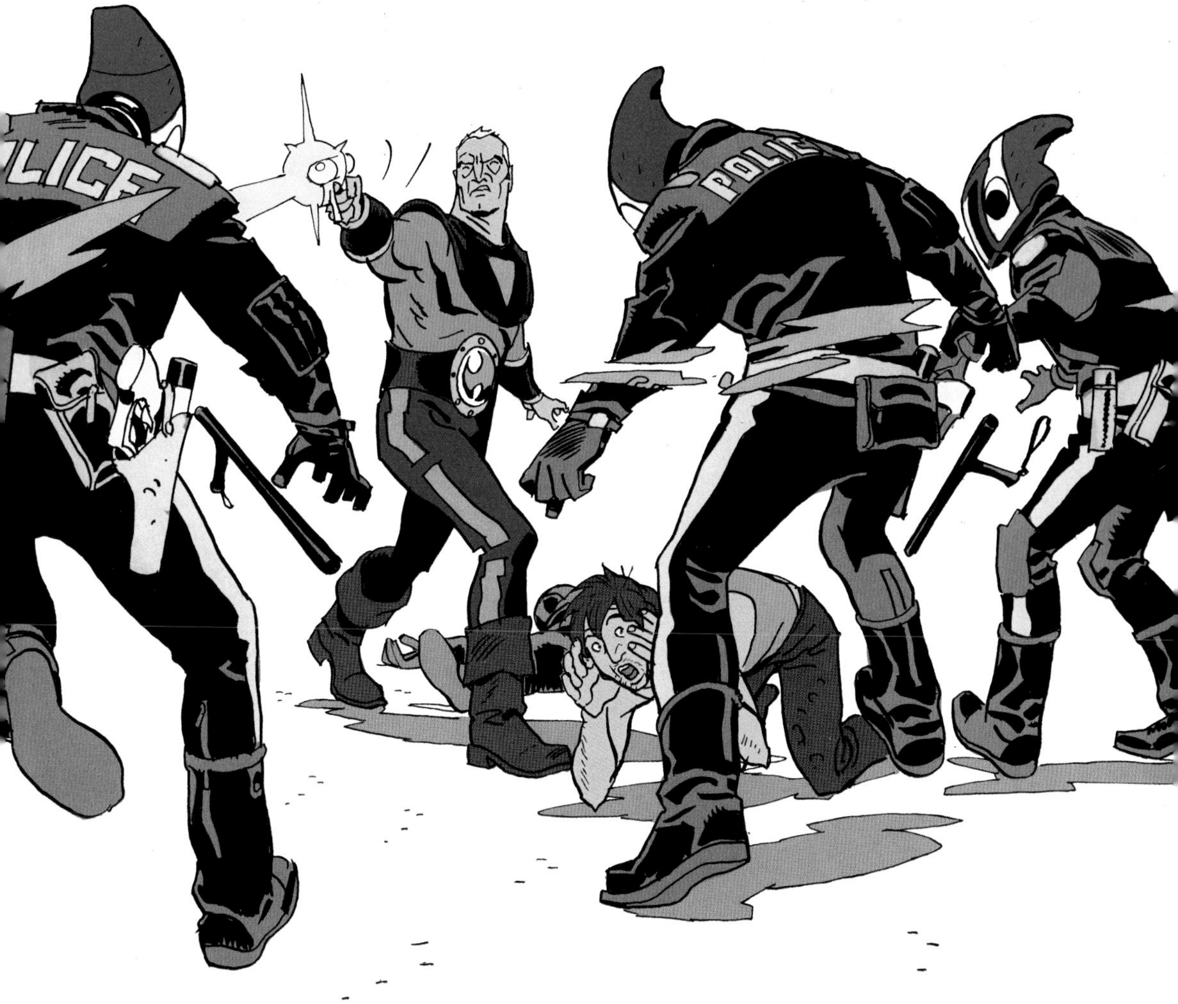

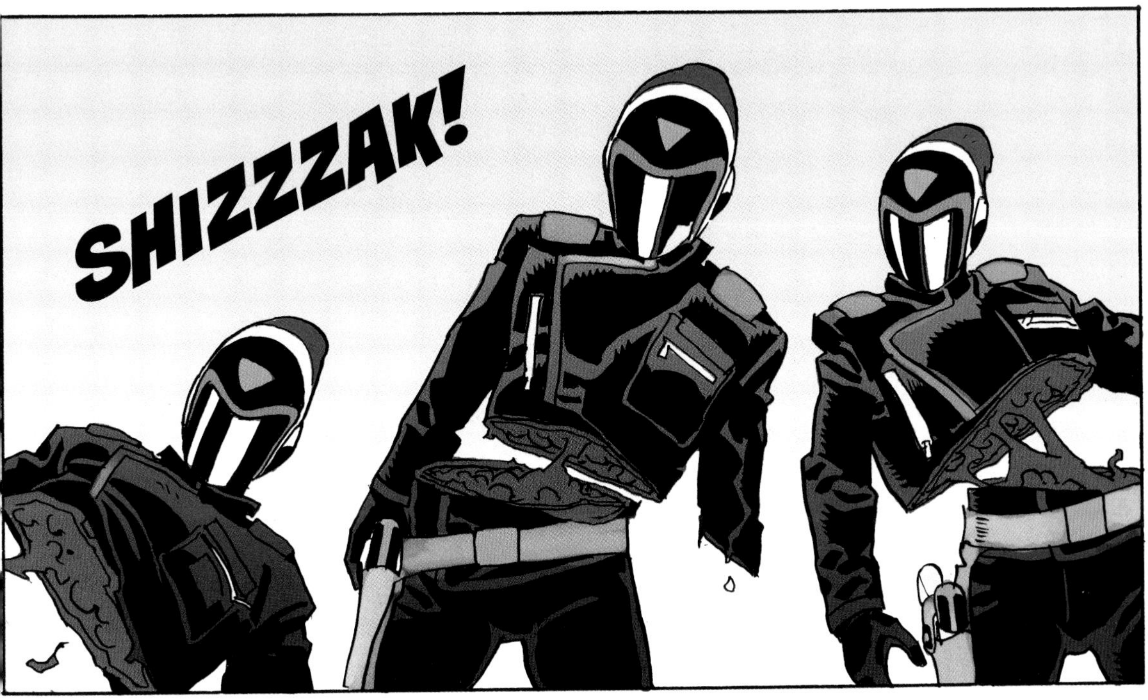
SHIZZZAK!

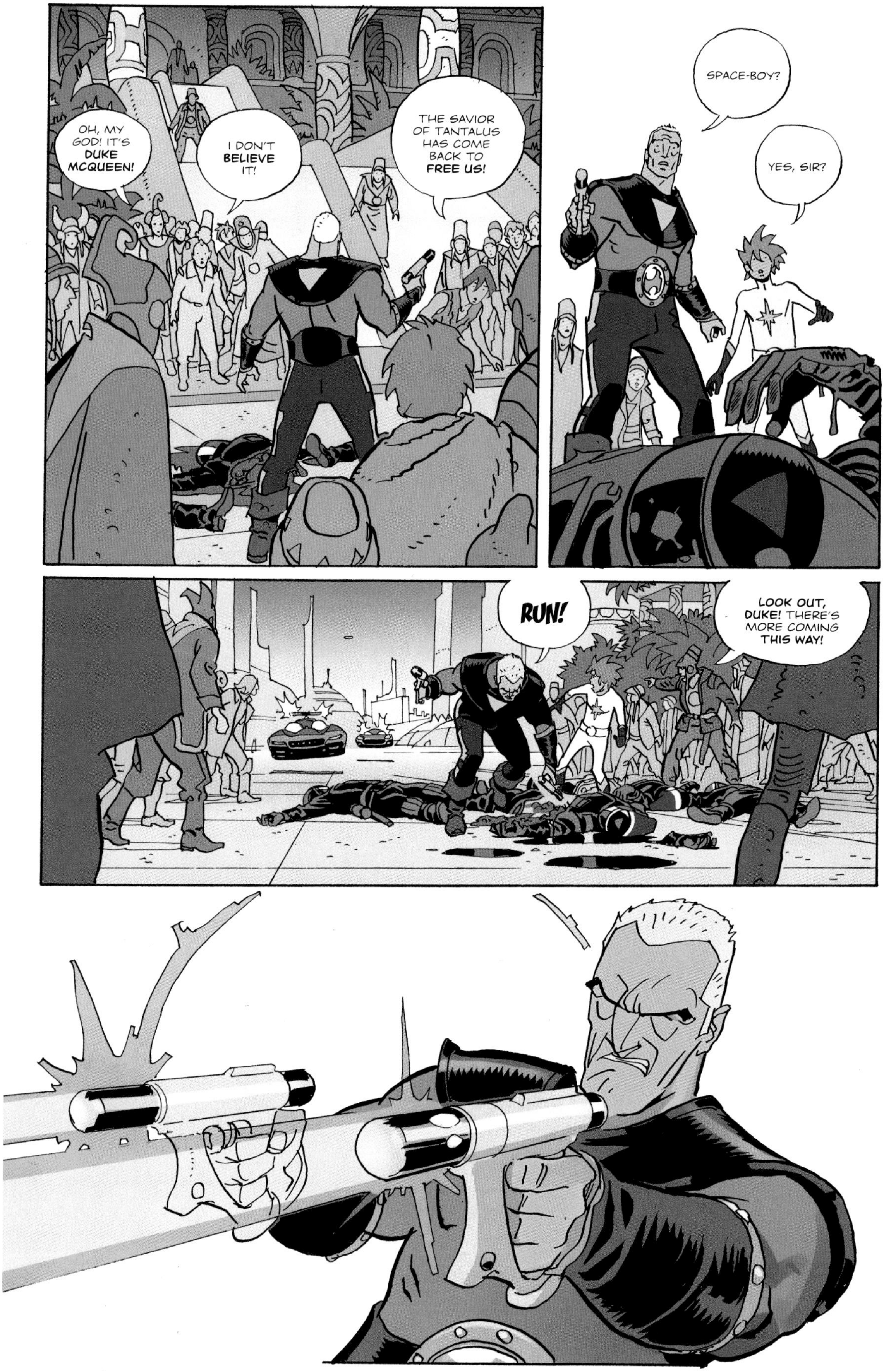
OH, MY GOD! IT'S DUKE MCQUEEN!
I DON'T BELIEVE IT!
THE SAVIOR OF TANTALUS HAS COME BACK TO FREE US!
SPACE-BOY?
YES, SIR?
RUN!
LOOK OUT, DUKE! THERE'S MORE COMING THIS WAY!

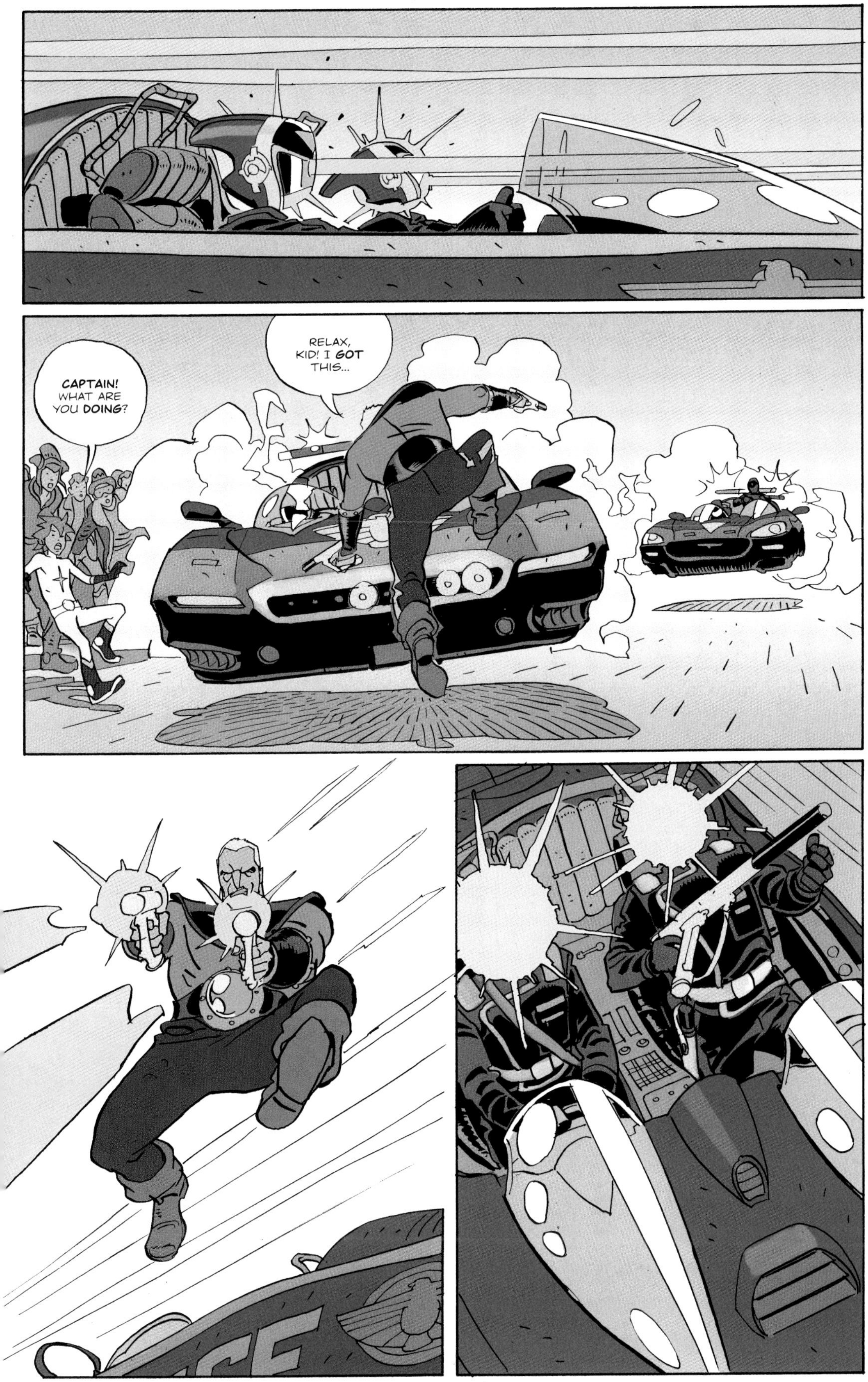
CAPTAIN! WHAT ARE YOU DOING?
RELAX, KID! I GOT THIS...

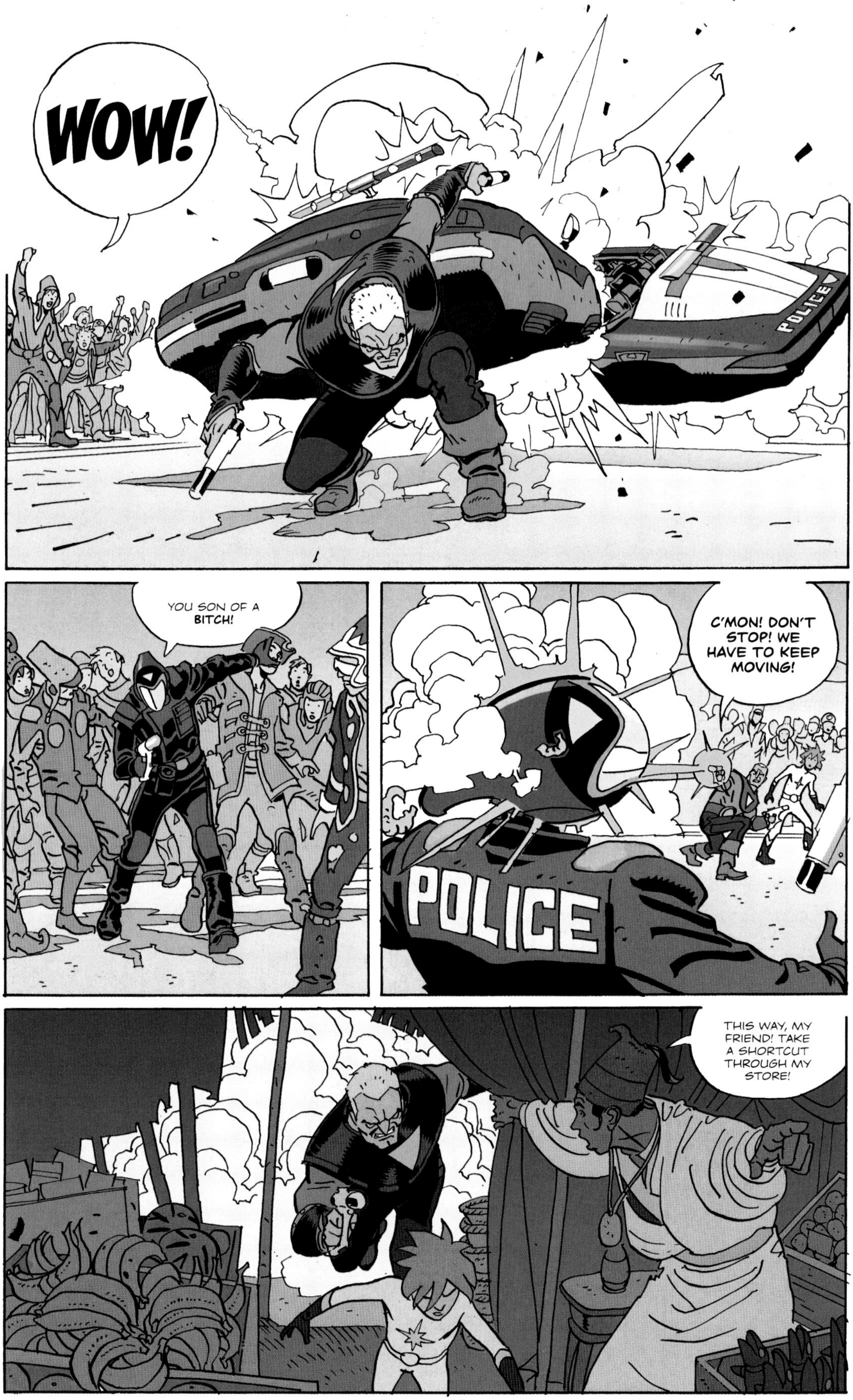
WOW!
YOU SON OF A BITCH!
C'MON! DON'T STOP! WE HAVE TO KEEP MOVING!
POLICE
THIS WAY, MY FRIEND! TAKE A SHORTCUT THROUGH MY STORE!

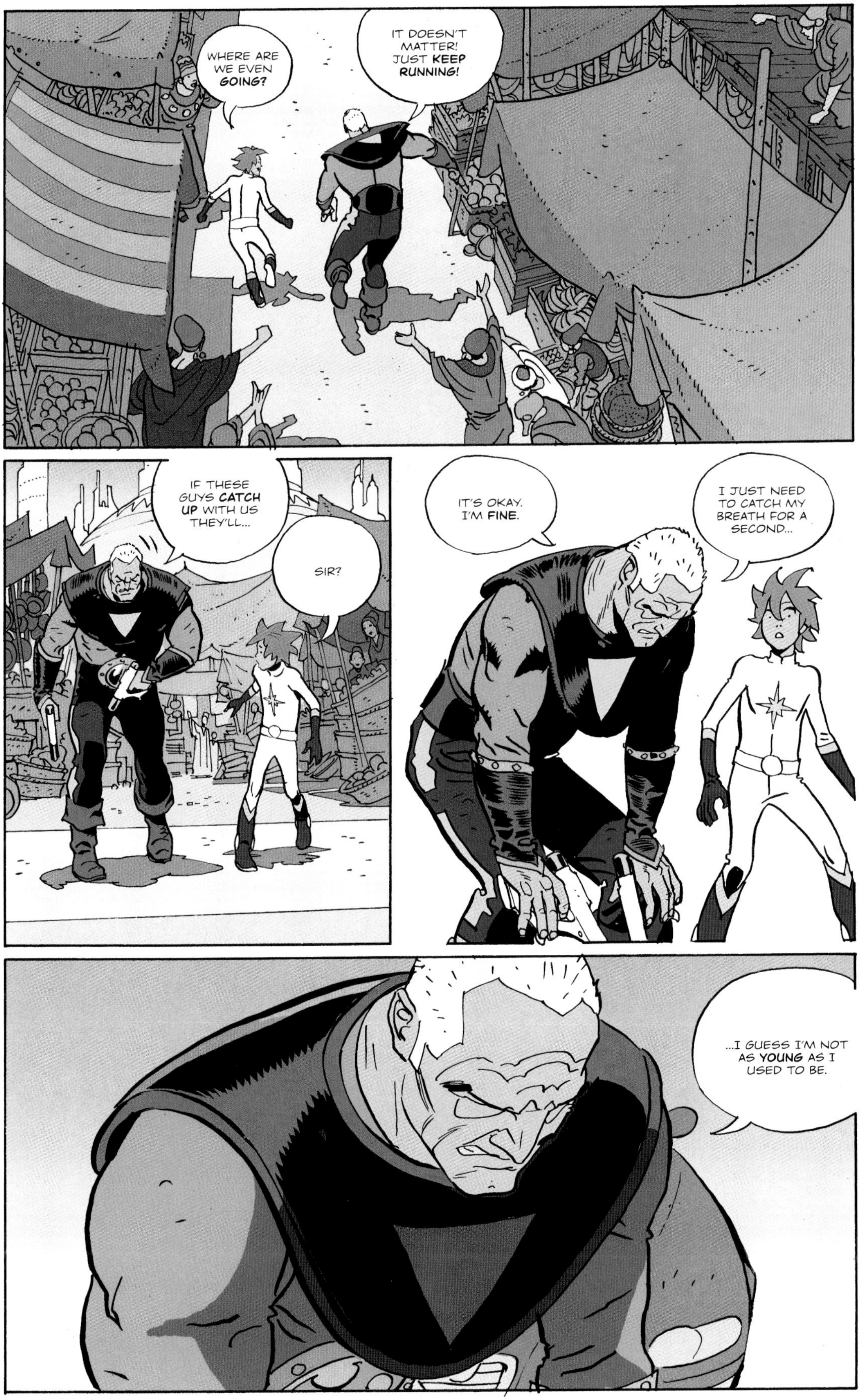
WHERE ARE WE EVEN GOING?
IT DOESN'T MATTER! JUST KEEP RUNNING!
IF THESE GUYS CATCH UP WITH US THEY'LL...
SIR?
IT'S OKAY. I'M FINE.
I JUST NEED TO CATCH MY BREATH FOR A SECOND...
...I GUESS I'M NOT AS YOUNG AS I USED TO BE.

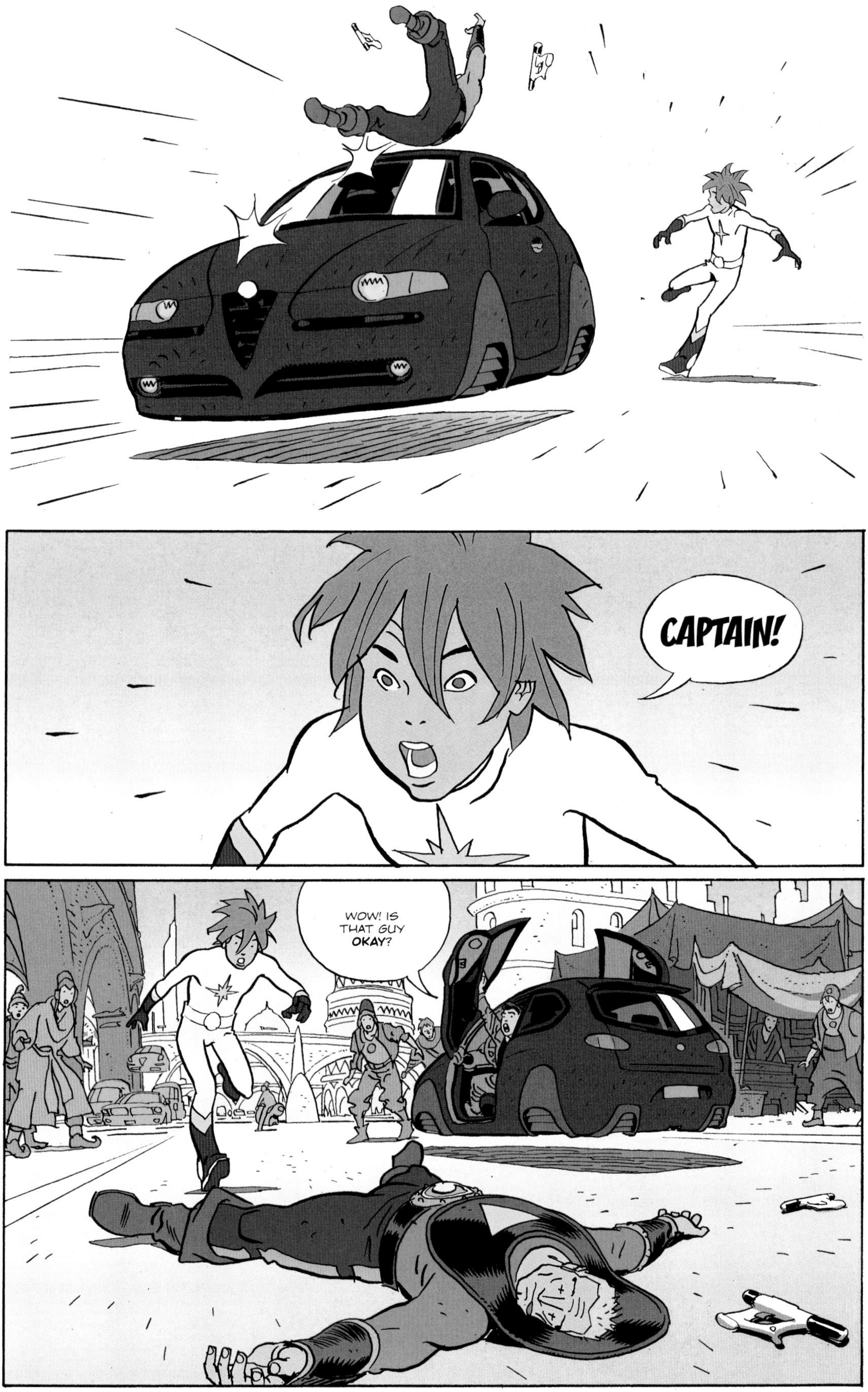
CAPTAIN!
WOW! IS THAT GUY OKAY?

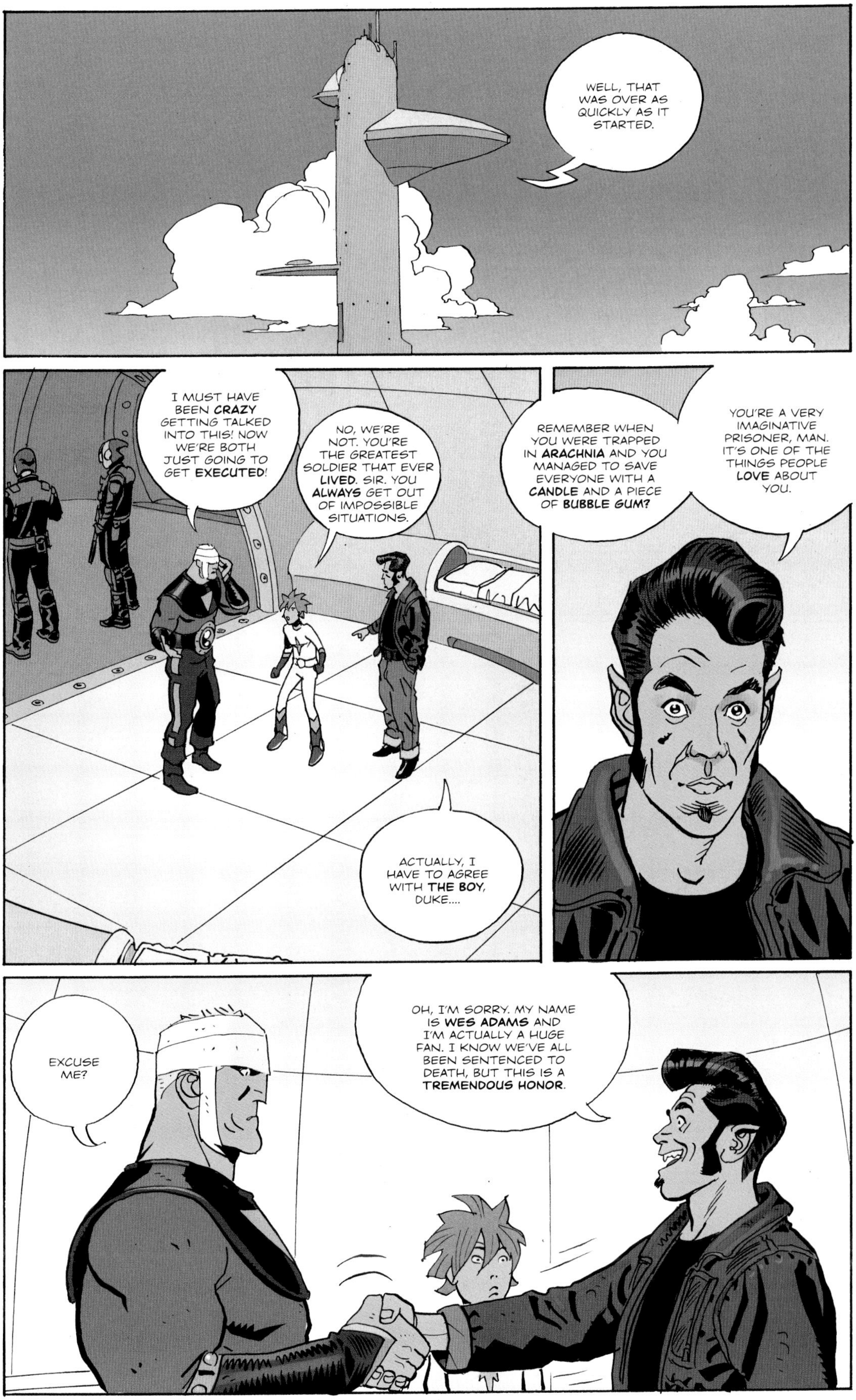
WELL, THAT WAS OVER AS QUICKLY AS IT STARTED.
I MUST HAVE BEEN CRAZY GETTING TALKED INTO THIS! NOW WE'RE BOTH JUST GOING TO GET EXECUTED!
NO, WE'RE NOT. YOU'RE THE GREATEST SOLDIER THAT EVER LIVED. SIR. YOU ALWAYS GET OUT OF IMPOSSIBLE SITUATIONS.
ACTUALLY, I HAVE TO AGREE WITH THE BOY, DUKE....
REMEMBER WHEN YOU WERE TRAPPED IN ARACHNIA AND YOU MANAGED TO SAVE EVERYONE WITH A CANDLE AND A PIECE OF BUBBLE GUM?
YOU'RE A VERY IMAGINATIVE PRISONER, MAN. IT'S ONE OF THE THINGS PEOPLE LOVE ABOUT YOU.
EXCUSE ME?
OH, I'M SORRY. MY NAME IS WES ADAMS AND I'M ACTUALLY A HUGE FAN. I KNOW WE'VE ALL BEEN SENTENCED TO DEATH, BUT THIS IS A TREMENDOUS HONOR.

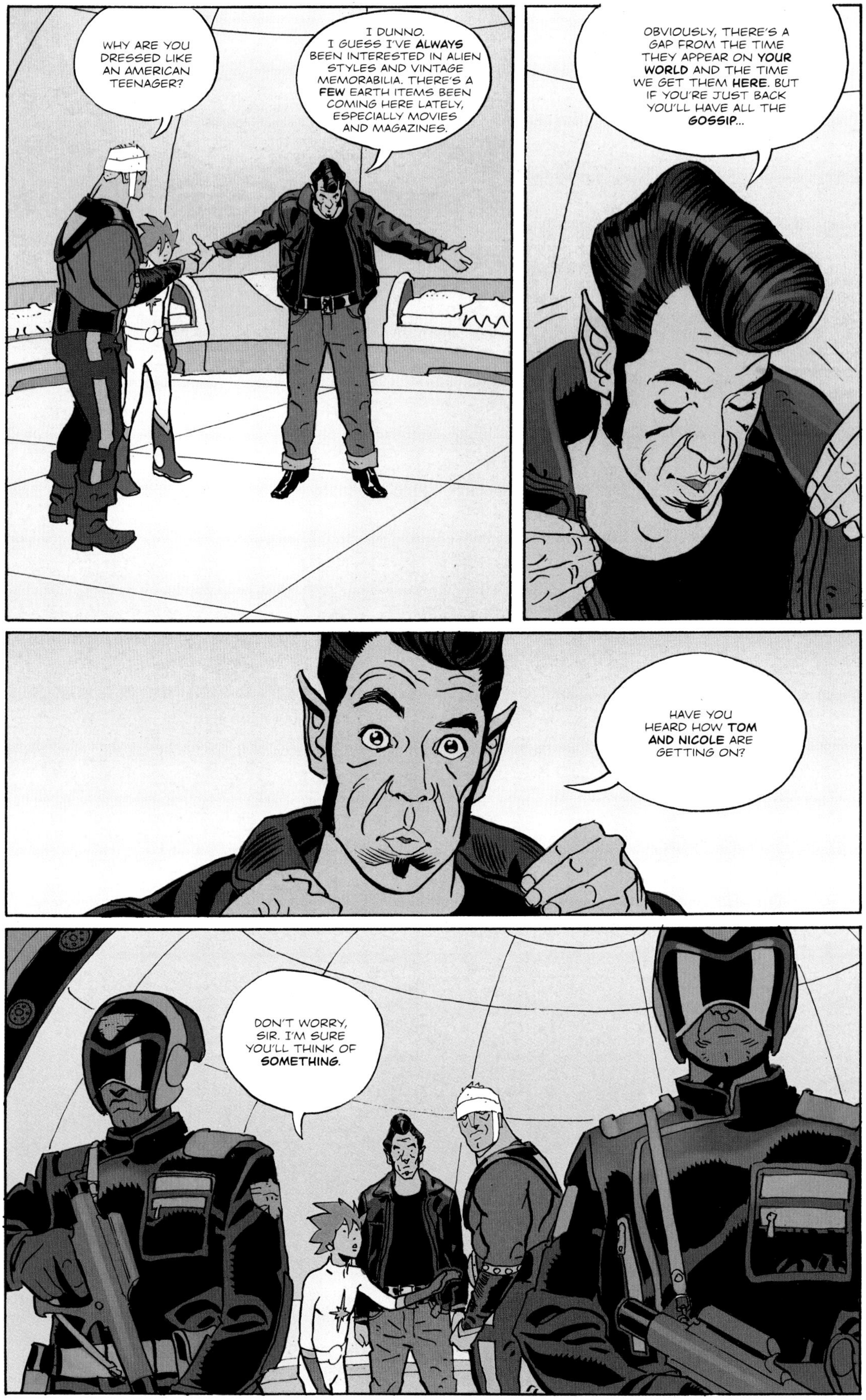
WHY ARE YOU DRESSED LIKE AN AMERICAN TEENAGER?
I DUNNO. I GUESS I'VE **ALWAYS** BEEN INTERESTED IN ALIEN STYLES AND VINTAGE MEMORABILIA. THERE'S A **FEW** EARTH ITEMS BEEN COMING HERE LATELY, ESPECIALLY MOVIES AND MAGAZINES.
OBVIOUSLY, THERE'S A GAP FROM THE TIME THEY APPEAR ON **YOUR WORLD** AND THE TIME WE GET THEM **HERE**. BUT IF YOU'RE JUST BACK YOU'LL HAVE ALL THE **GOSSIP**...
HAVE YOU HEARD HOW **TOM AND NICOLE** ARE GETTING ON?
DON'T WORRY, SIR. I'M SURE YOU'LL THINK OF **SOMETHING**.

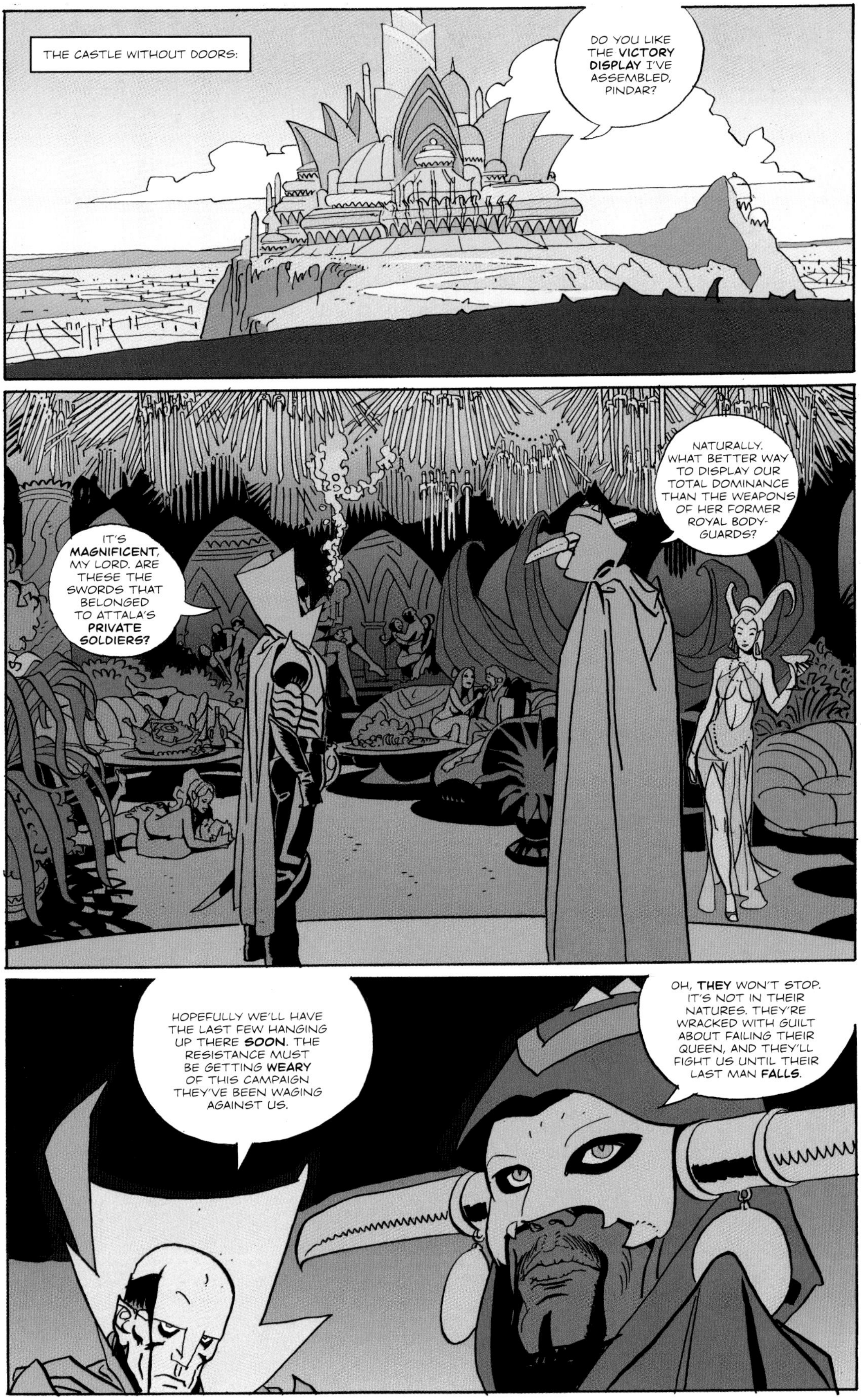
THE CASTLE WITHOUT DOORS:
DO YOU LIKE THE VICTORY DISPLAY I'VE ASSEMBLED, PINDAR?
IT'S MAGNIFICENT, MY LORD. ARE THESE THE SWORDS THAT BELONGED TO ATTALA'S PRIVATE SOLDIERS?
NATURALLY. WHAT BETTER WAY TO DISPLAY OUR TOTAL DOMINANCE THAN THE WEAPONS OF HER FORMER ROYAL BODY-GUARDS?
HOPEFULLY WE'LL HAVE THE LAST FEW HANGING UP THERE SOON. THE RESISTANCE MUST BE GETTING WEARY OF THIS CAMPAIGN THEY'VE BEEN WAGING AGAINST US.
OH, THEY WON'T STOP. IT'S NOT IN THEIR NATURES. THEY'RE WRACKED WITH GUILT ABOUT FAILING THEIR QUEEN, AND THEY'LL FIGHT US UNTIL THEIR LAST MAN FALLS.

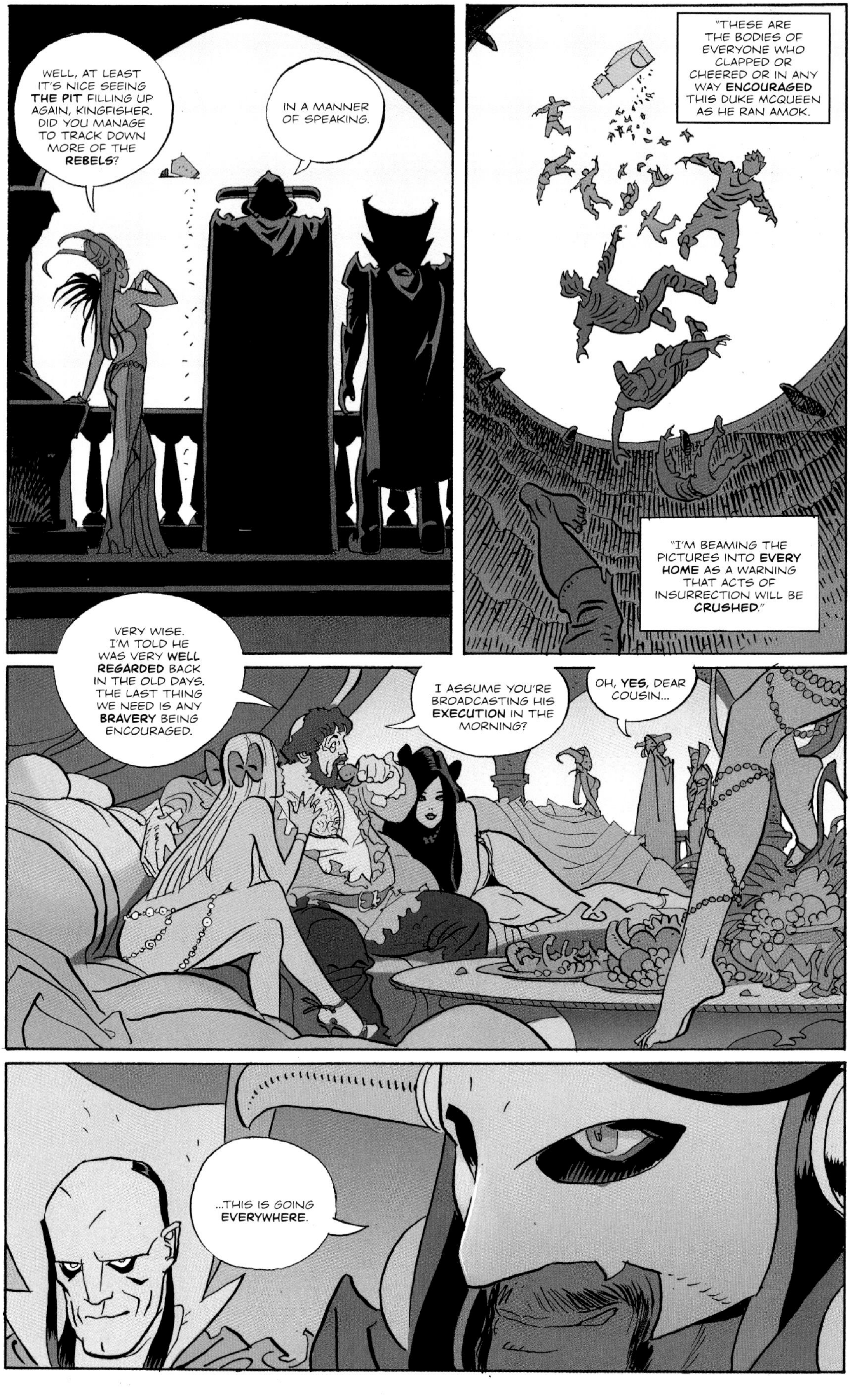
WELL, AT LEAST IT'S NICE SEEING THE PIT FILLING UP AGAIN, KINGFISHER. DID YOU MANAGE TO TRACK DOWN MORE OF THE REBELS?
IN A MANNER OF SPEAKING.
"THESE ARE THE BODIES OF EVERYONE WHO CLAPPED OR CHEERED OR IN ANY WAY ENCOURAGED THIS DUKE MCQUEEN AS HE RAN AMOK.
"I'M BEAMING THE PICTURES INTO EVERY HOME AS A WARNING THAT ACTS OF INSURRECTION WILL BE CRUSHED."
VERY WISE. I'M TOLD HE WAS VERY WELL REGARDED BACK IN THE OLD DAYS. THE LAST THING WE NEED IS ANY BRAVERY BEING ENCOURAGED.
I ASSUME YOU'RE BROADCASTING HIS EXECUTION IN THE MORNING?
OH, YES, DEAR COUSIN...
...THIS IS GOING EVERYWHERE.

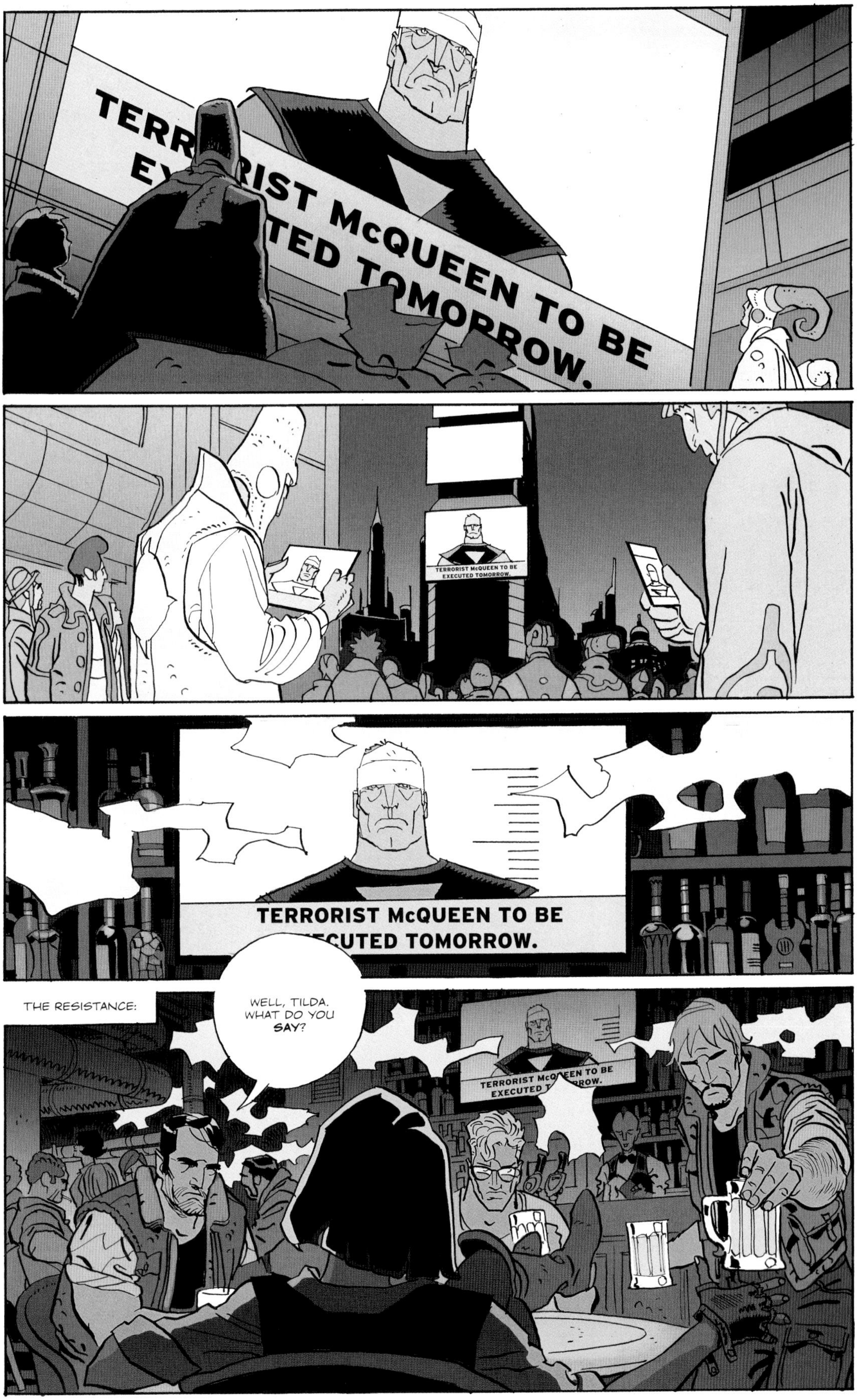
TERRORIST McQUEEN TO BE EXECUTED TOMORROW.
TERRORIST McQUEEN TO BE EXECUTED TOMORROW.
TERRORIST McQUEEN TO BE EXECUTED TOMORROW.
THE RESISTANCE:
WELL, TILDA. WHAT DO YOU SAY?
TERRORIST McQUEEN TO BE EXECUTED TOMORROW.

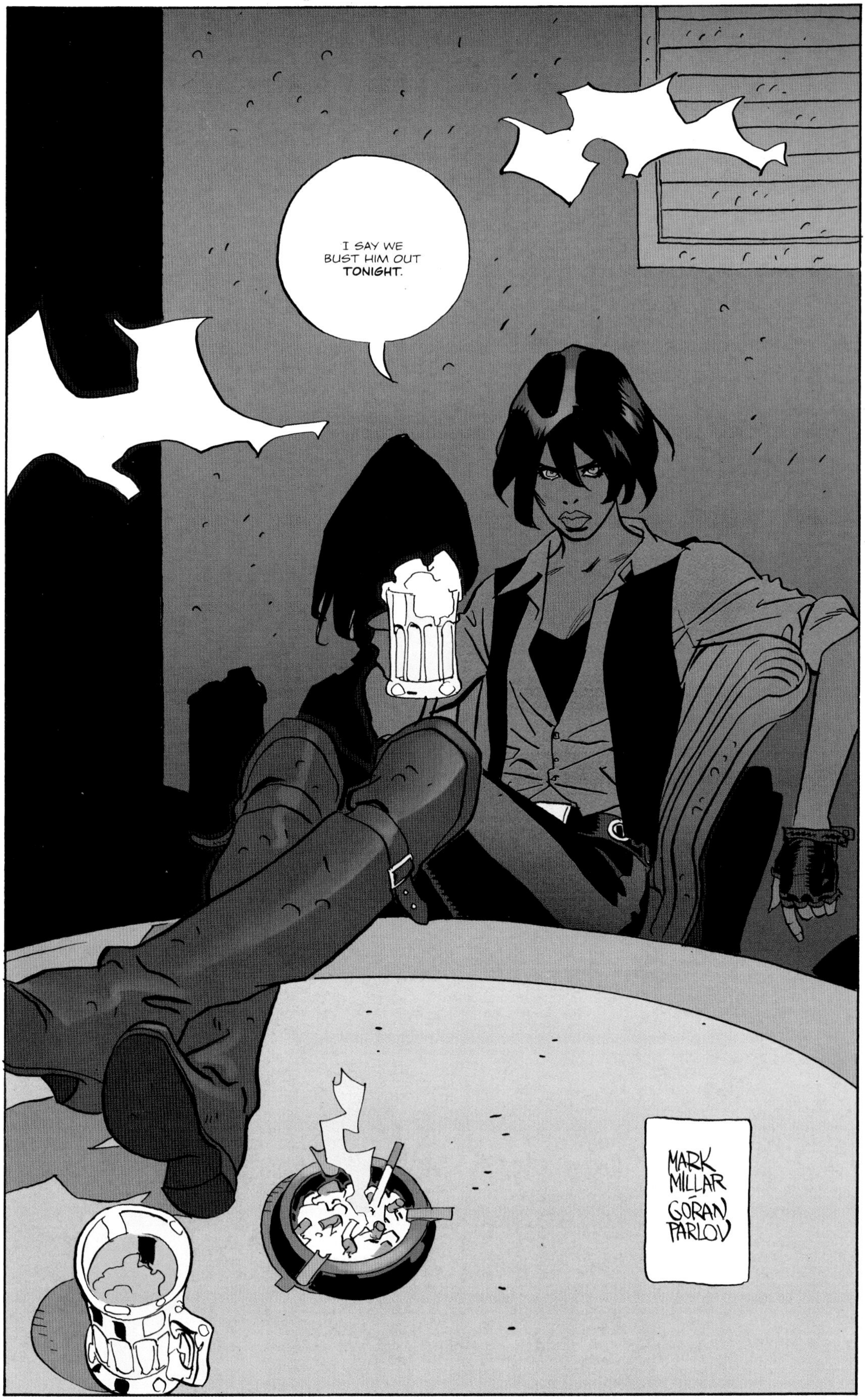
I SAY WE BUST HIM OUT TONIGHT.
MARK MILLAR GORAN PARLOV

FOUR

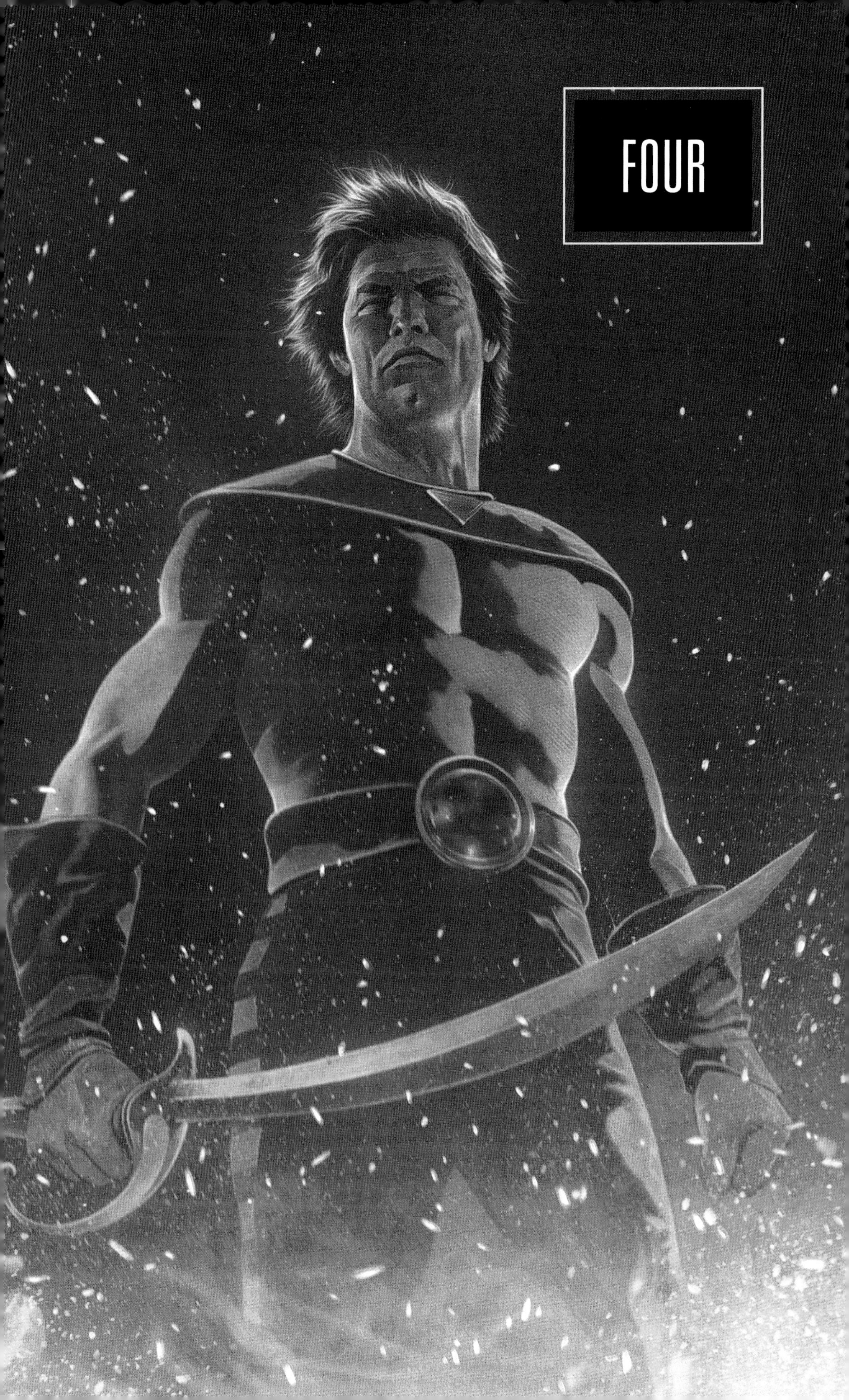

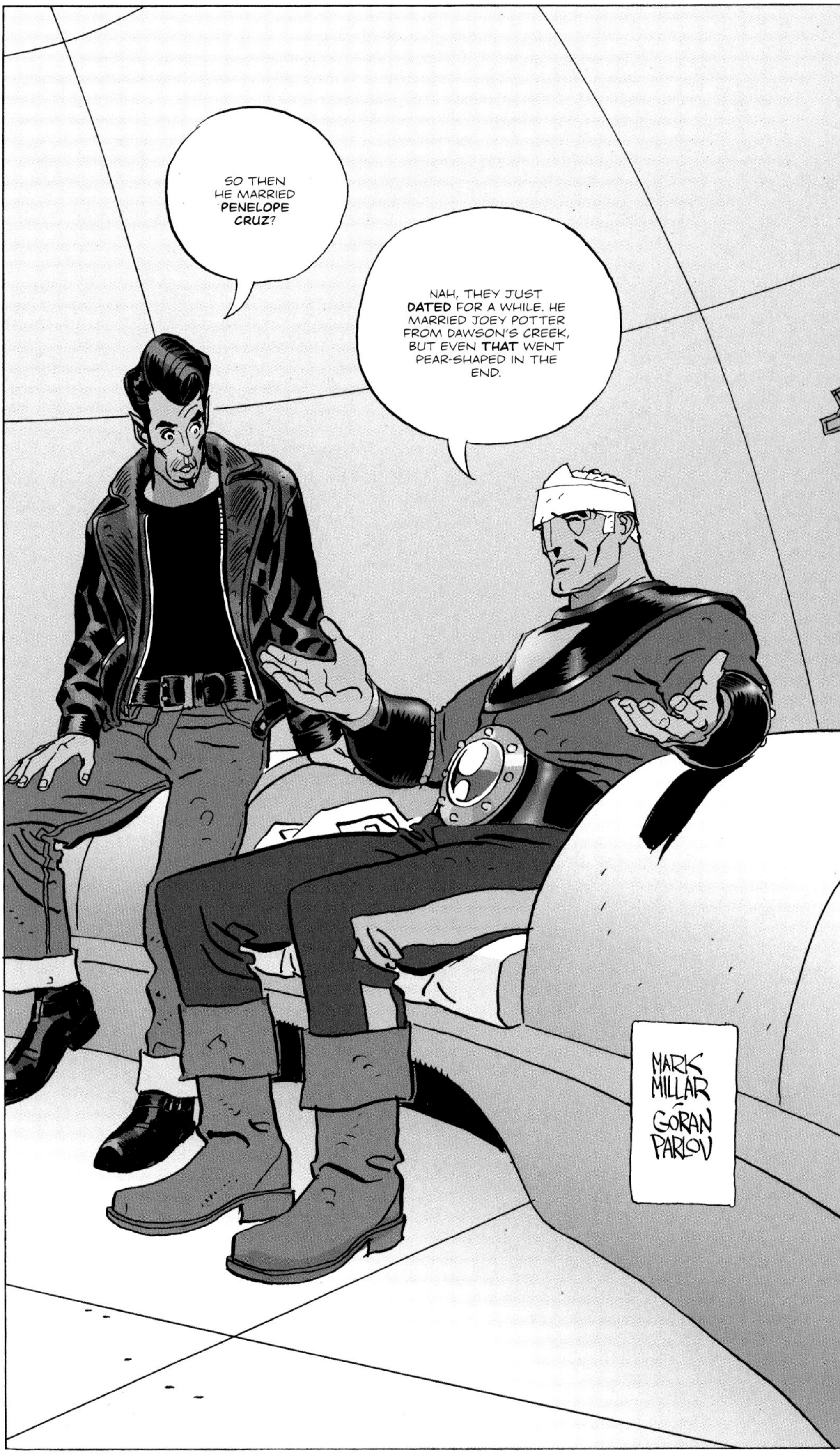

SO THEN HE MARRIED PENELOPE CRUZ?
NAH, THEY JUST DATED FOR A WHILE. HE MARRIED JOEY POTTER FROM DAWSON'S CREEK, BUT EVEN THAT WENT PEAR-SHAPED IN THE END.
MARK MILLAR GORAN PARLOV

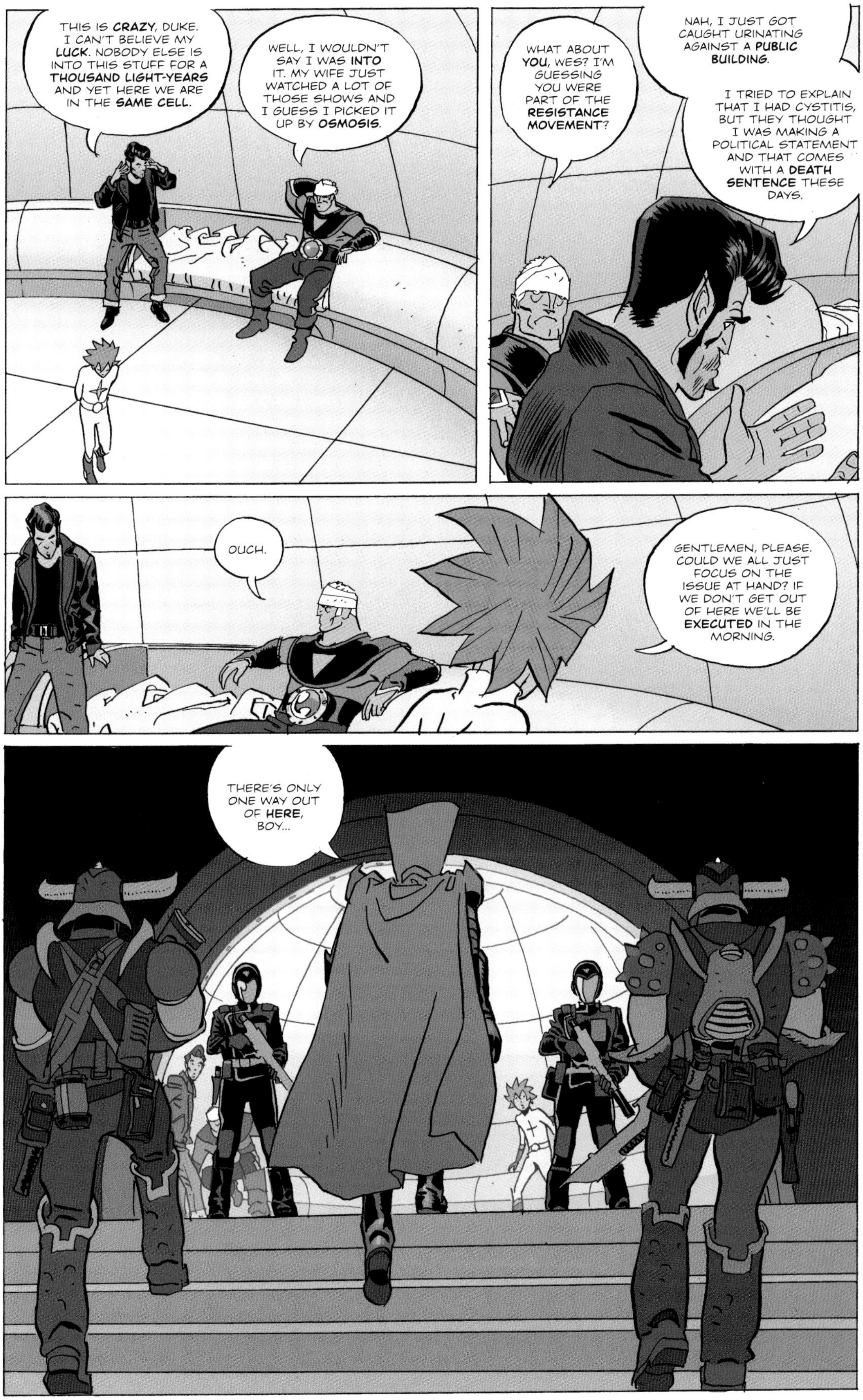
THIS IS CRAZY, DUKE. I CAN'T BELIEVE MY LUCK. NOBODY ELSE IS INTO THIS STUFF FOR A THOUSAND LIGHT-YEARS AND YET HERE WE ARE IN THE SAME CELL.
WELL, I WOULDN'T SAY I WAS INTO IT. MY WIFE JUST WATCHED A LOT OF THOSE SHOWS AND I GUESS I PICKED IT UP BY OSMOSIS.
WHAT ABOUT YOU, WES? I'M GUESSING YOU WERE PART OF THE RESISTANCE MOVEMENT?
NAH, I JUST GOT CAUGHT URINATING AGAINST A PUBLIC BUILDING.
I TRIED TO EXPLAIN THAT I HAD CYSTITIS, BUT THEY THOUGHT I WAS MAKING A POLITICAL STATEMENT AND THAT COMES WITH A DEATH SENTENCE THESE DAYS.
OUCH.
GENTLEMEN, PLEASE. COULD WE ALL JUST FOCUS ON THE ISSUE AT HAND? IF WE DON'T GET OUT OF HERE WE'LL BE EXECUTED IN THE MORNING.
THERE'S ONLY ONE WAY OUT OF HERE, BOY...

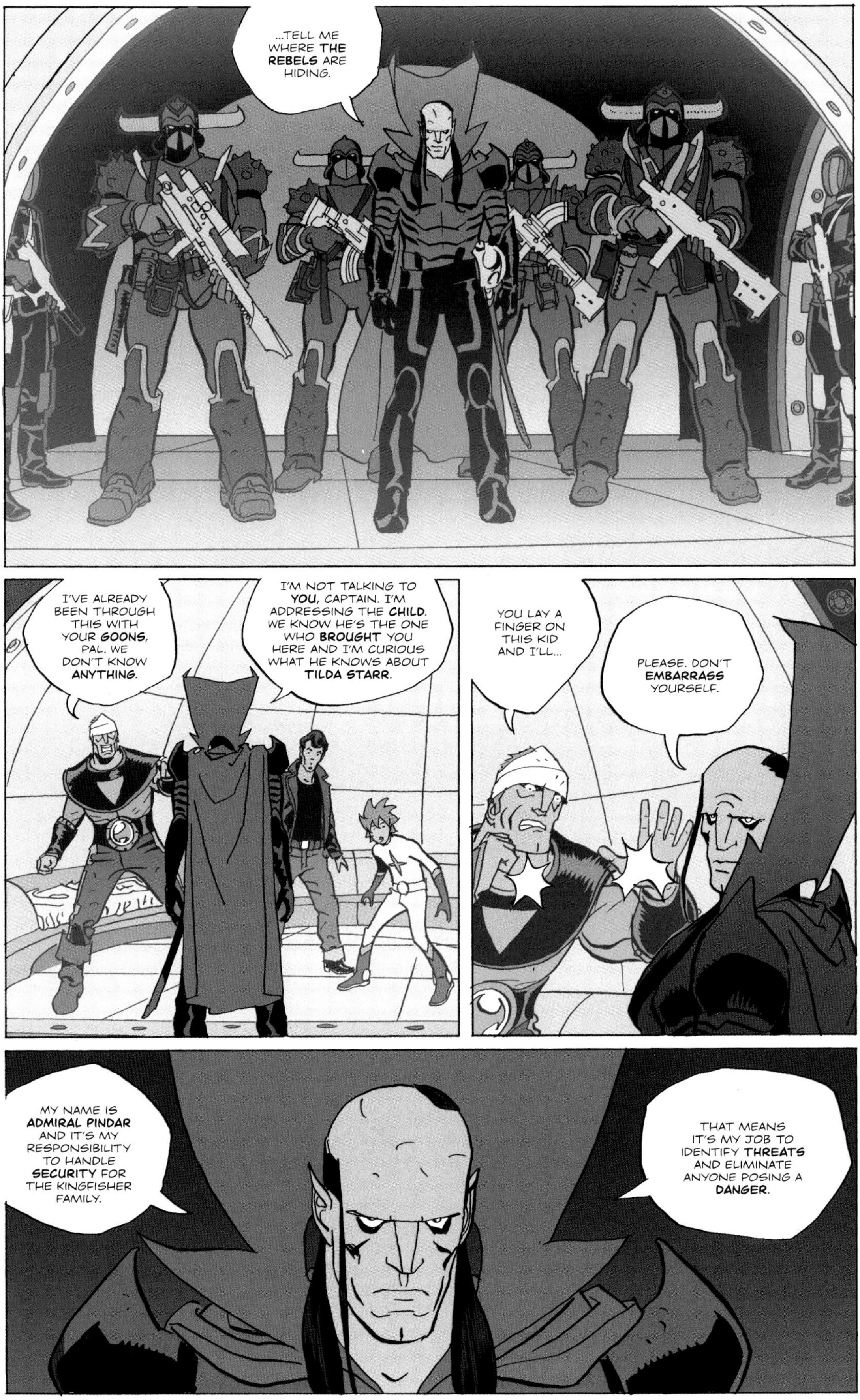
...TELL ME WHERE THE REBELS ARE HIDING.
I'VE ALREADY BEEN THROUGH THIS WITH YOUR GOONS, PAL. WE DON'T KNOW ANYTHING.
I'M NOT TALKING TO YOU, CAPTAIN. I'M ADDRESSING THE CHILD. WE KNOW HE'S THE ONE WHO BROUGHT YOU HERE AND I'M CURIOUS WHAT HE KNOWS ABOUT TILDA STARR.
YOU LAY A FINGER ON THIS KID AND I'LL...
PLEASE. DON'T EMBARRASS YOURSELF.
MY NAME IS ADMIRAL PINDAR AND IT'S MY RESPONSIBILITY TO HANDLE SECURITY FOR THE KINGFISHER FAMILY.
THAT MEANS IT'S MY JOB TO IDENTIFY THREATS AND ELIMINATE ANYONE POSING A DANGER.

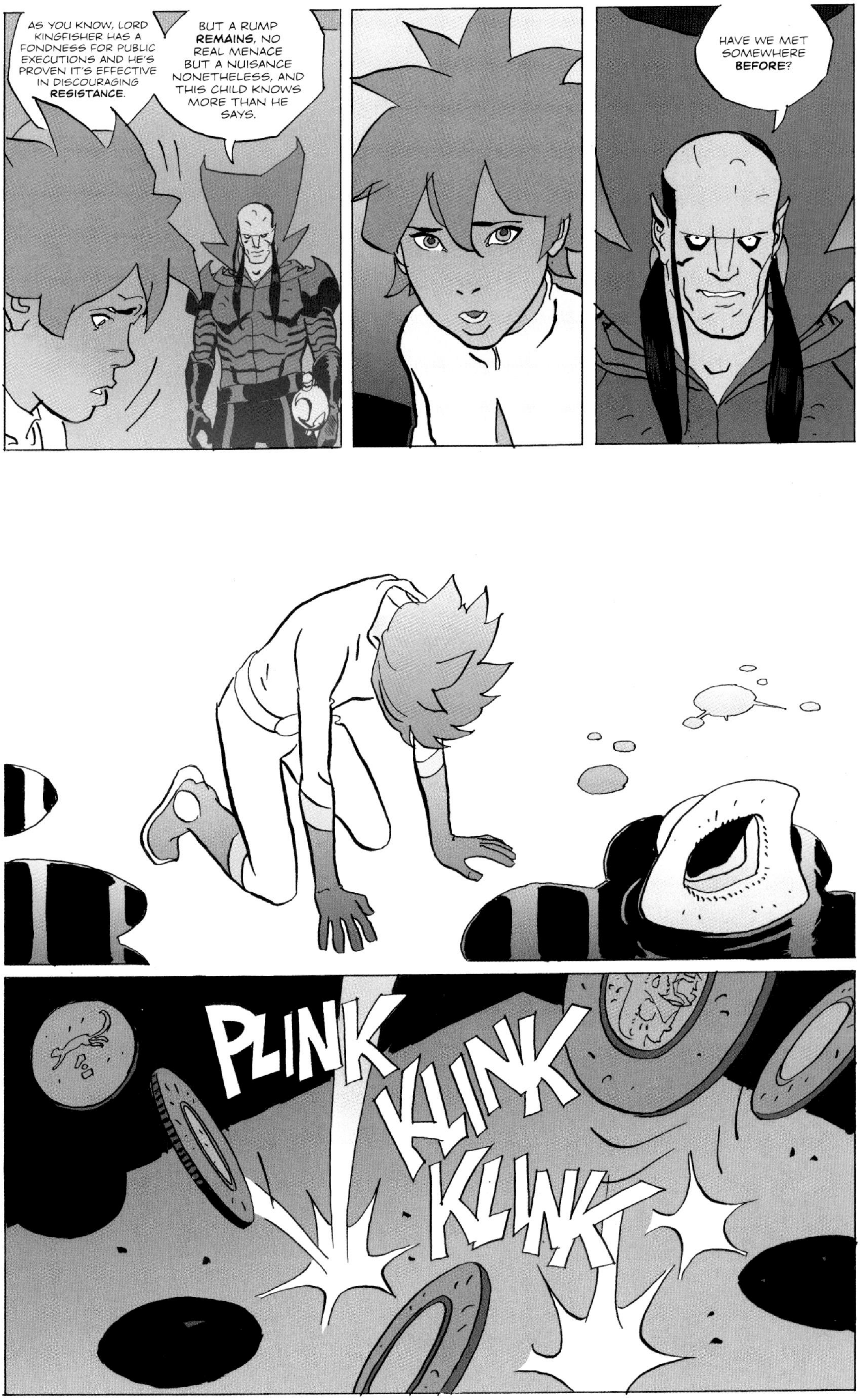
AS YOU KNOW, LORD KINGFISHER HAS A FONDNESS FOR PUBLIC EXECUTIONS AND HE'S PROVEN IT'S EFFECTIVE IN DISCOURAGING **RESISTANCE**.
BUT A RUMP **REMAINS**, NO REAL MENACE BUT A NUISANCE NONETHELESS, AND THIS CHILD KNOWS MORE THAN HE SAYS.
HAVE WE MET SOMEWHERE **BEFORE**?
PLINK
KLINK
KLINK

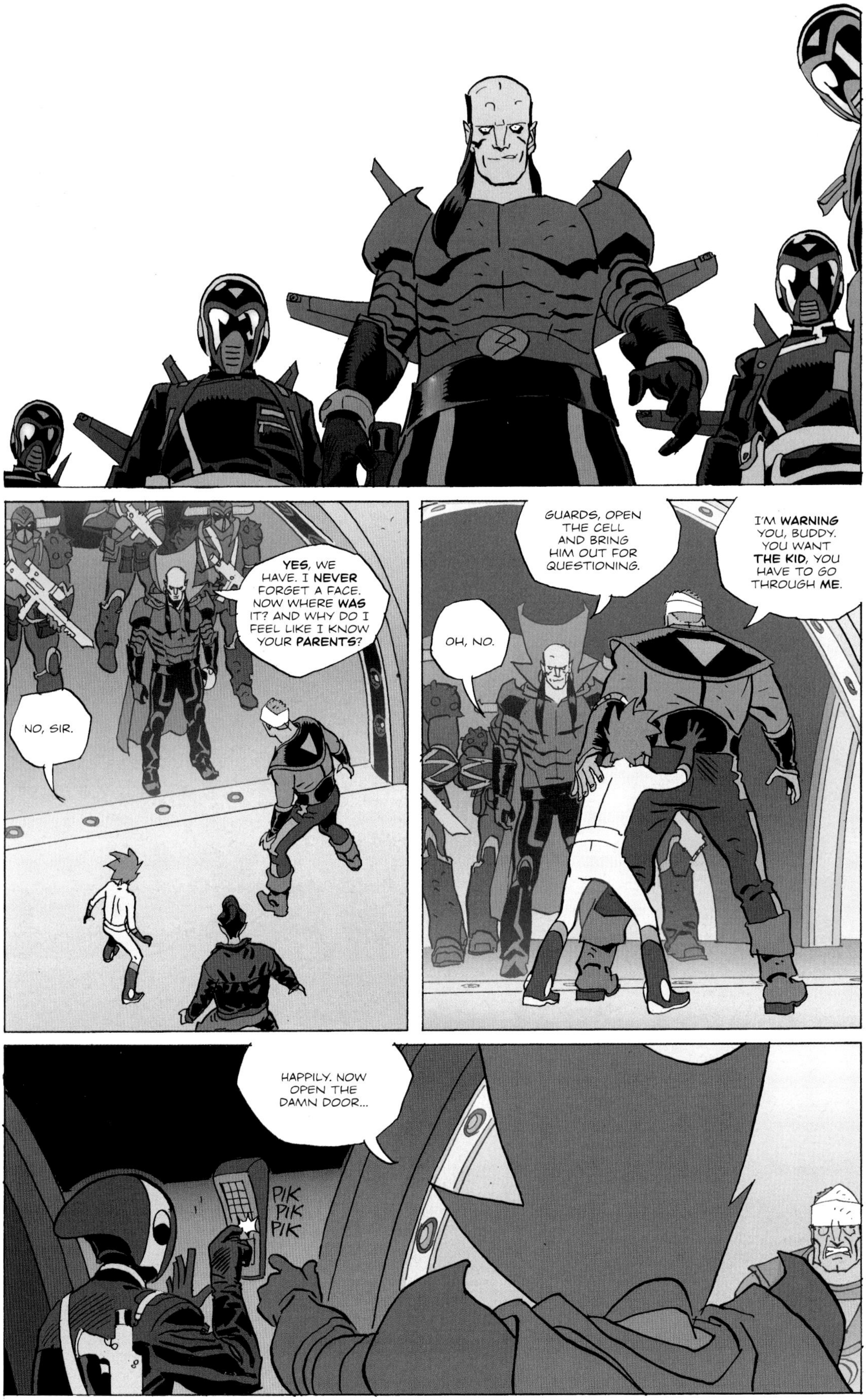
YES, WE HAVE. I NEVER FORGET A FACE. NOW WHERE WAS IT? AND WHY DO I FEEL LIKE I KNOW YOUR PARENTS?
NO, SIR.
GUARDS, OPEN THE CELL AND BRING HIM OUT FOR QUESTIONING.
I'M WARNING YOU, BUDDY. YOU WANT THE KID, YOU HAVE TO GO THROUGH ME.
OH, NO.
HAPPILY. NOW OPEN THE DAMN DOOR...
PIK PIK PIK

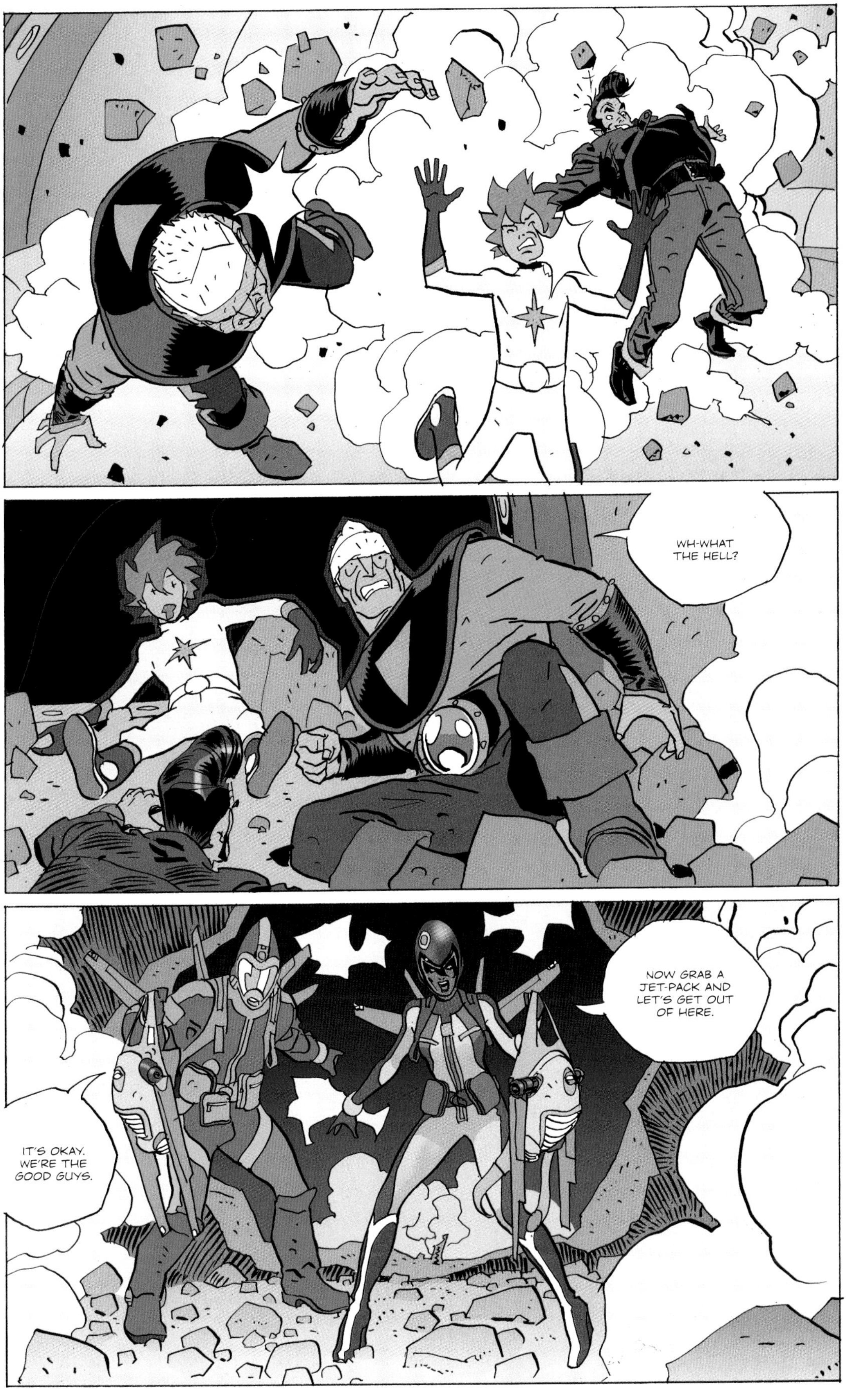
WH-WHAT THE HELL?
NOW GRAB A JET-PACK AND LET'S GET OUT OF HERE.
IT'S OKAY. WE'RE THE GOOD GUYS.

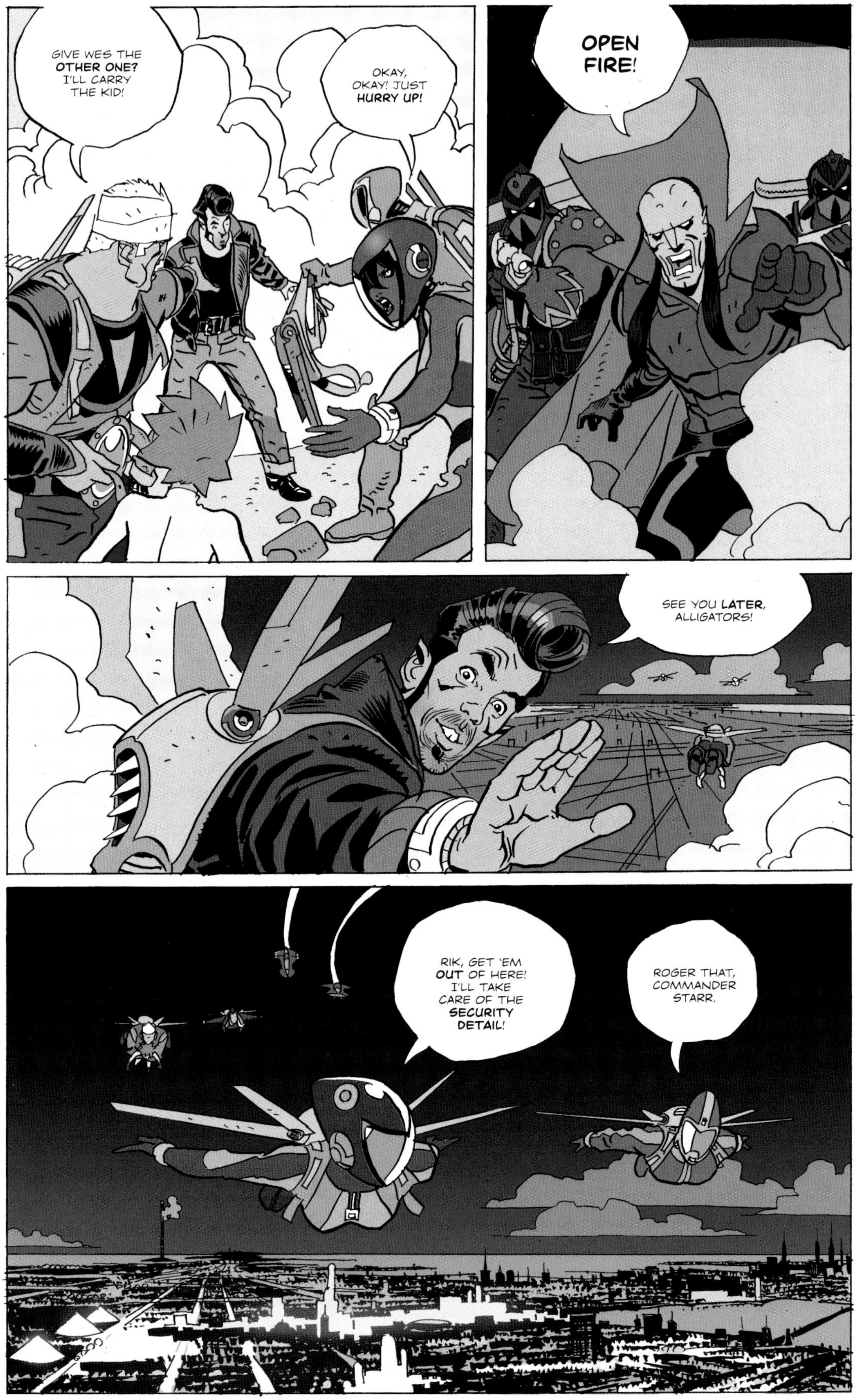
GIVE WES THE **OTHER ONE?** I'LL CARRY THE KID!
OKAY, OKAY! JUST **HURRY UP!**
OPEN FIRE!
SEE YOU **LATER,** ALLIGATORS!
RIK, GET 'EM **OUT** OF HERE! I'LL TAKE CARE OF THE **SECURITY DETAIL!**
ROGER THAT, COMMANDER STARR.

SWEET BROTEA!
JUMP! IT'S A MAGNETIC BOMB!
COULD SOMEBODY GIVE ME A HAND WITH THE BOY? HE'S TOO HEAVY FOR THIS THING TO HOLD THE TWO OF US!
UH, I DON'T THINK I'M THE ONE WHO'S TOO HEAVY, SIR.
OONF!
WHERE DO YOU THINK YOU'RE GOING, ALIEN?
TWELVE INCHES TO THE LEFT OF THAT TRUCK.
WHAT?

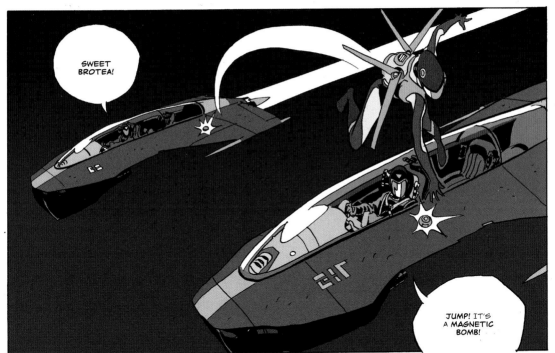

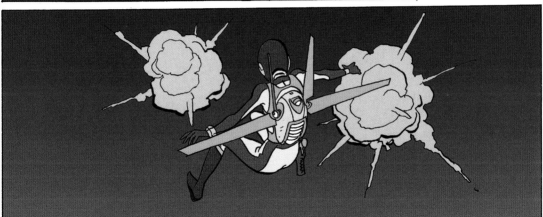

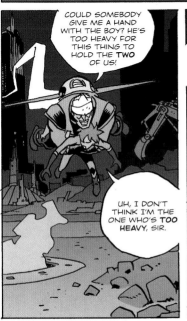

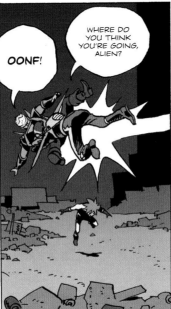

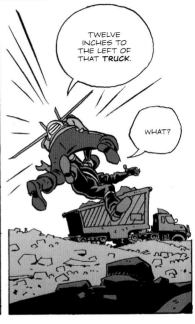

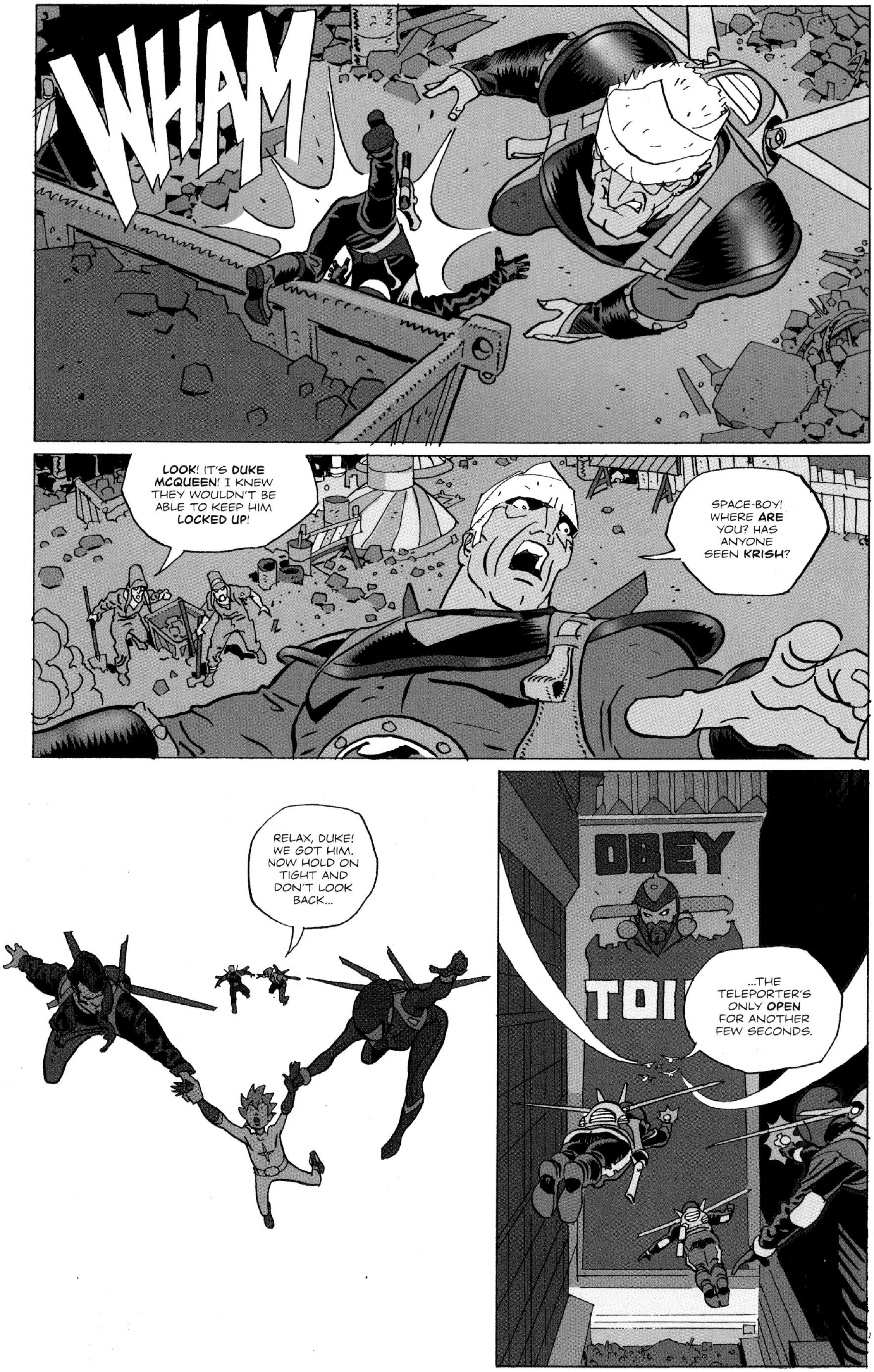
WHAM
LOOK! IT'S DUKE MCQUEEN! I KNEW THEY WOULDN'T BE ABLE TO KEEP HIM LOCKED UP!
SPACE-BOY! WHERE ARE YOU? HAS ANYONE SEEN KRISH?
RELAX, DUKE! WE GOT HIM. NOW HOLD ON TIGHT AND DON'T LOOK BACK...
OBEY
TOI
...THE TELEPORTER'S ONLY OPEN FOR ANOTHER FEW SECONDS.

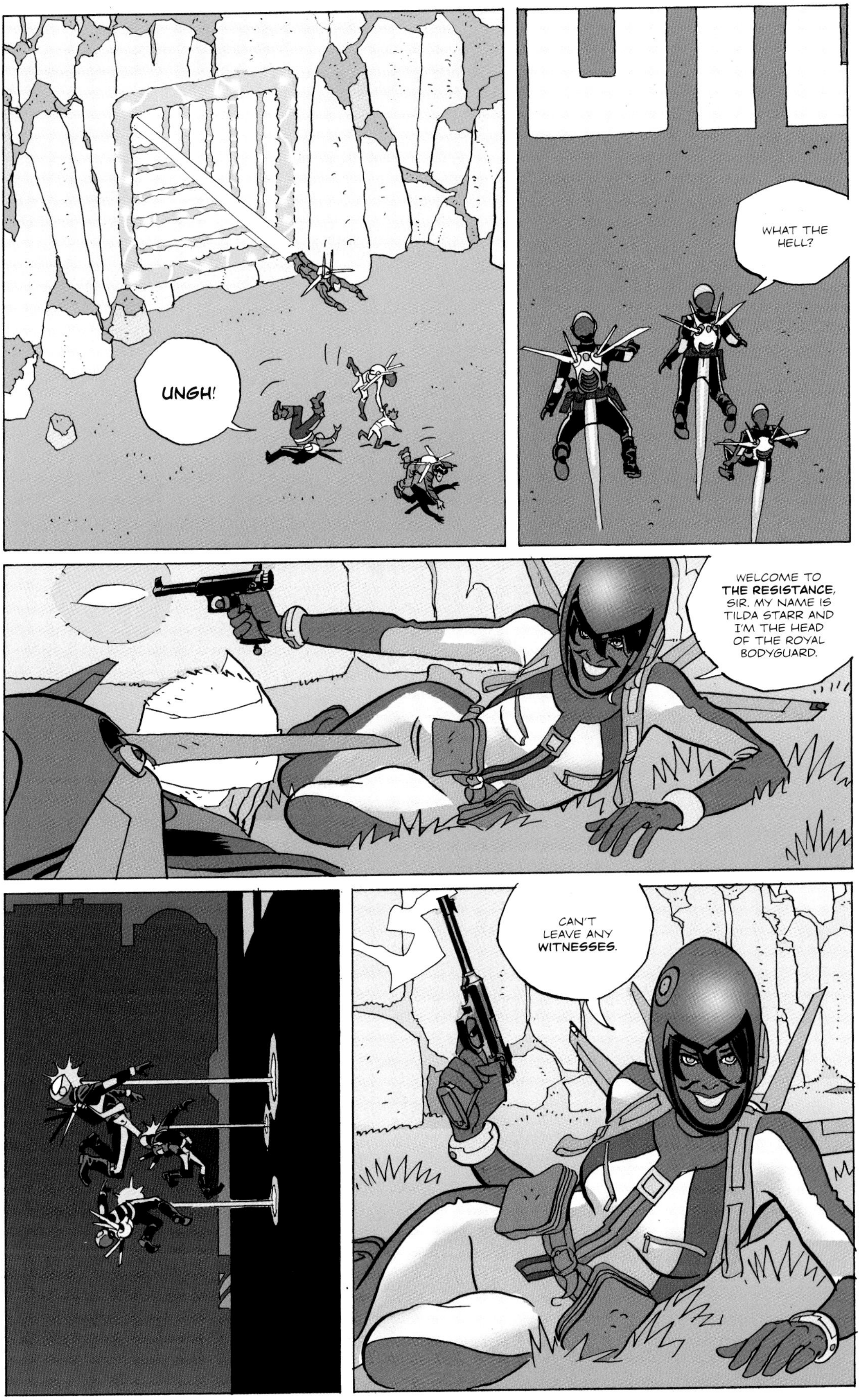
UNGH!
WHAT THE HELL?
WELCOME TO THE RESISTANCE, SIR. MY NAME IS TILDA STARR AND I'M THE HEAD OF THE ROYAL BODYGUARD.
CAN'T LEAVE ANY WITNESSES.

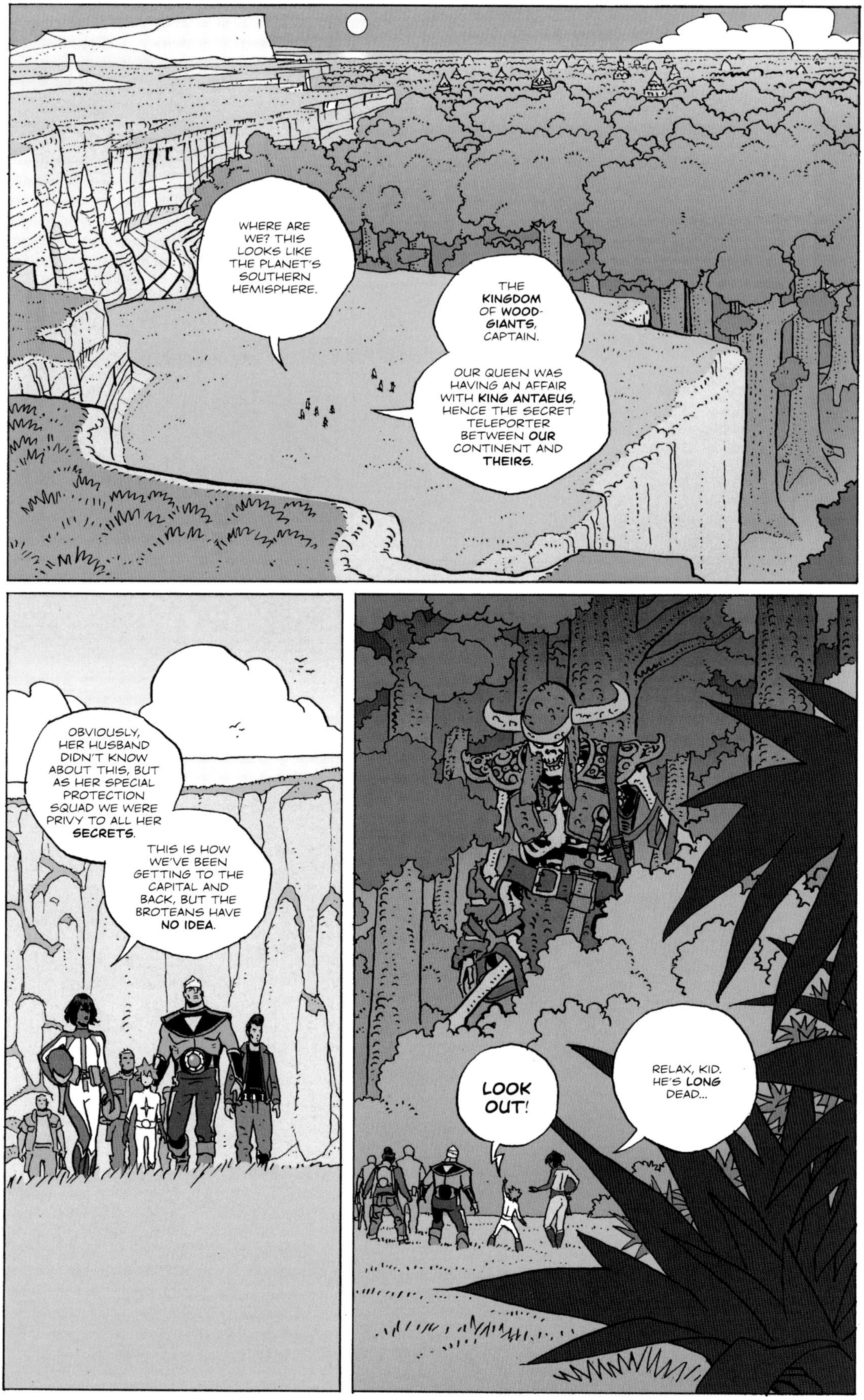

WHERE ARE WE? THIS LOOKS LIKE THE PLANET'S SOUTHERN HEMISPHERE.
THE **KINGDOM** OF **WOOD-GIANTS**, CAPTAIN.
OUR QUEEN WAS HAVING AN AFFAIR WITH **KING ANTAEUS**, HENCE THE SECRET TELEPORTER BETWEEN **OUR** CONTINENT AND **THEIRS**.
OBVIOUSLY, HER HUSBAND DIDN'T KNOW ABOUT THIS, BUT AS HER SPECIAL PROTECTION SQUAD WE WERE PRIVY TO ALL HER **SECRETS**.
THIS IS HOW WE'VE BEEN GETTING TO THE CAPITAL AND BACK, BUT THE BROTEANS HAVE **NO IDEA**.
LOOK OUT!
RELAX, KID. HE'S **LONG** DEAD...

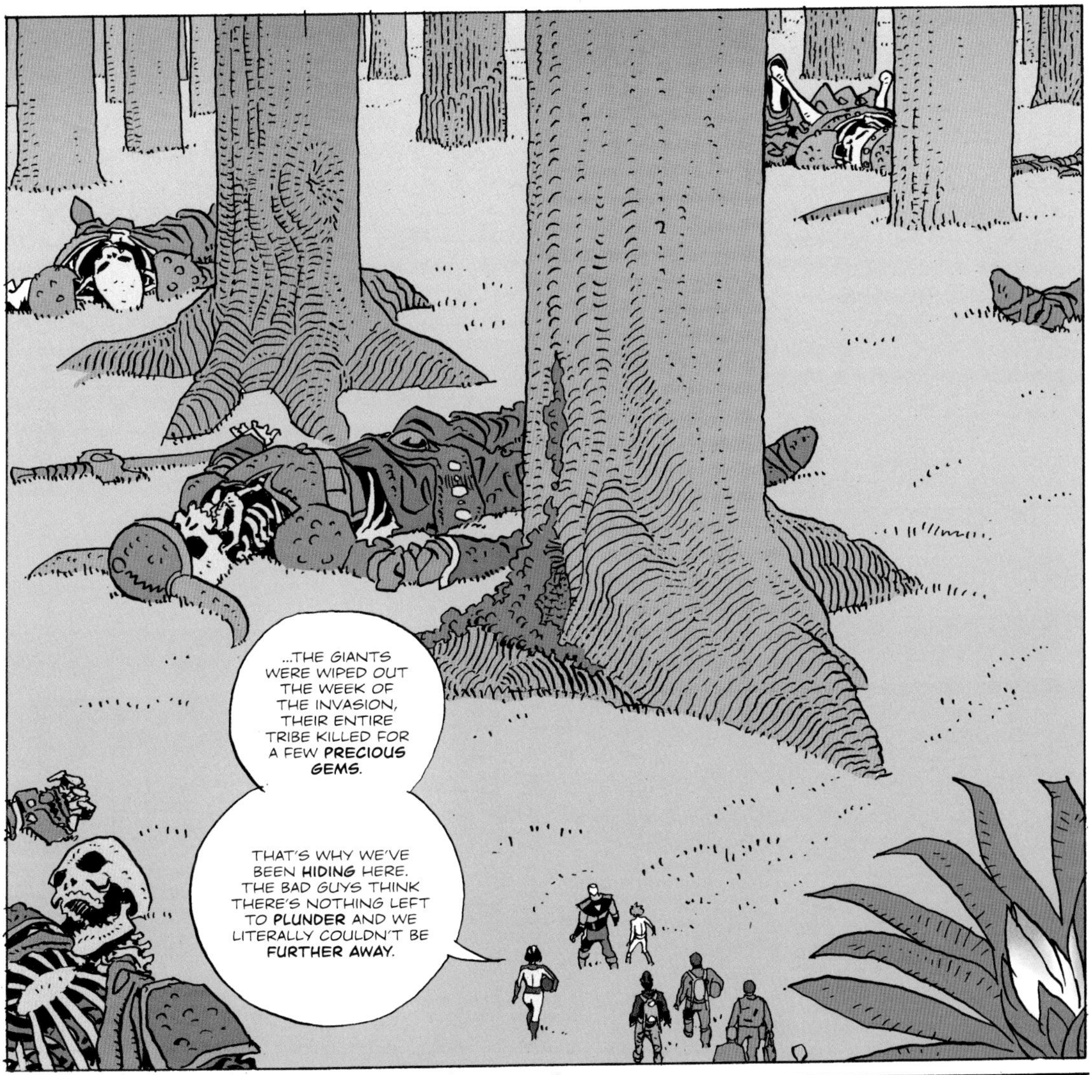
...THE GIANTS WERE WIPED OUT THE WEEK OF THE INVASION, THEIR ENTIRE TRIBE KILLED FOR A FEW **PRECIOUS GEMS**.
THAT'S WHY WE'VE BEEN **HIDING** HERE. THE BAD GUYS THINK THERE'S NOTHING LEFT TO **PLUNDER** AND WE LITERALLY COULDN'T BE **FURTHER AWAY**.

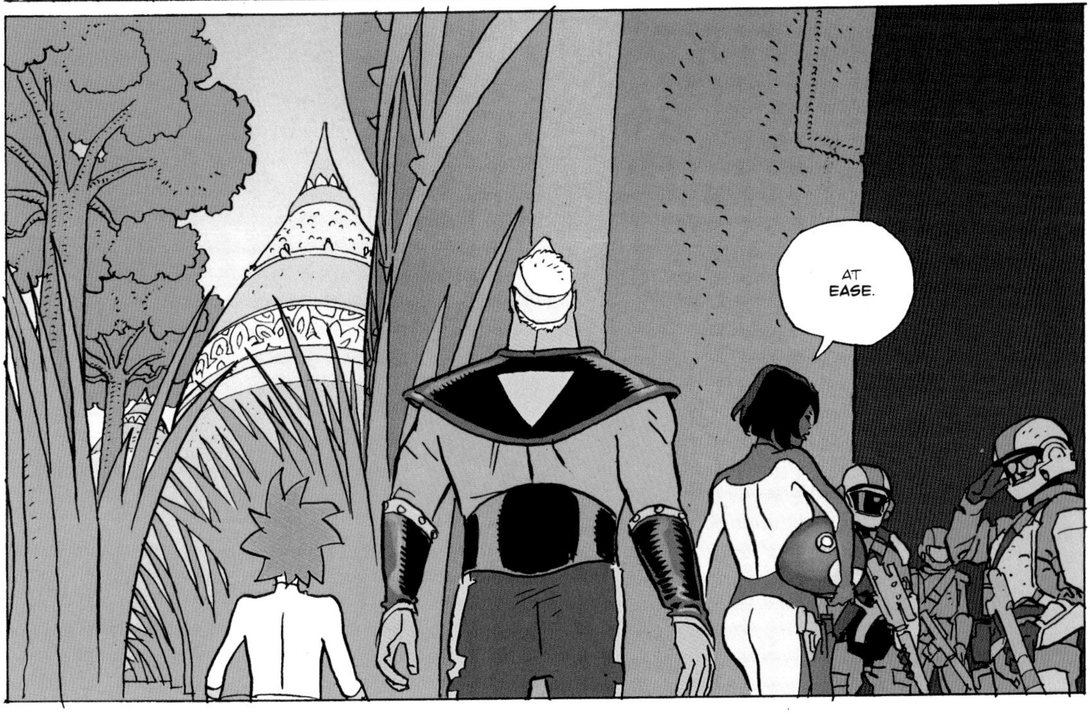
AT **EASE**.

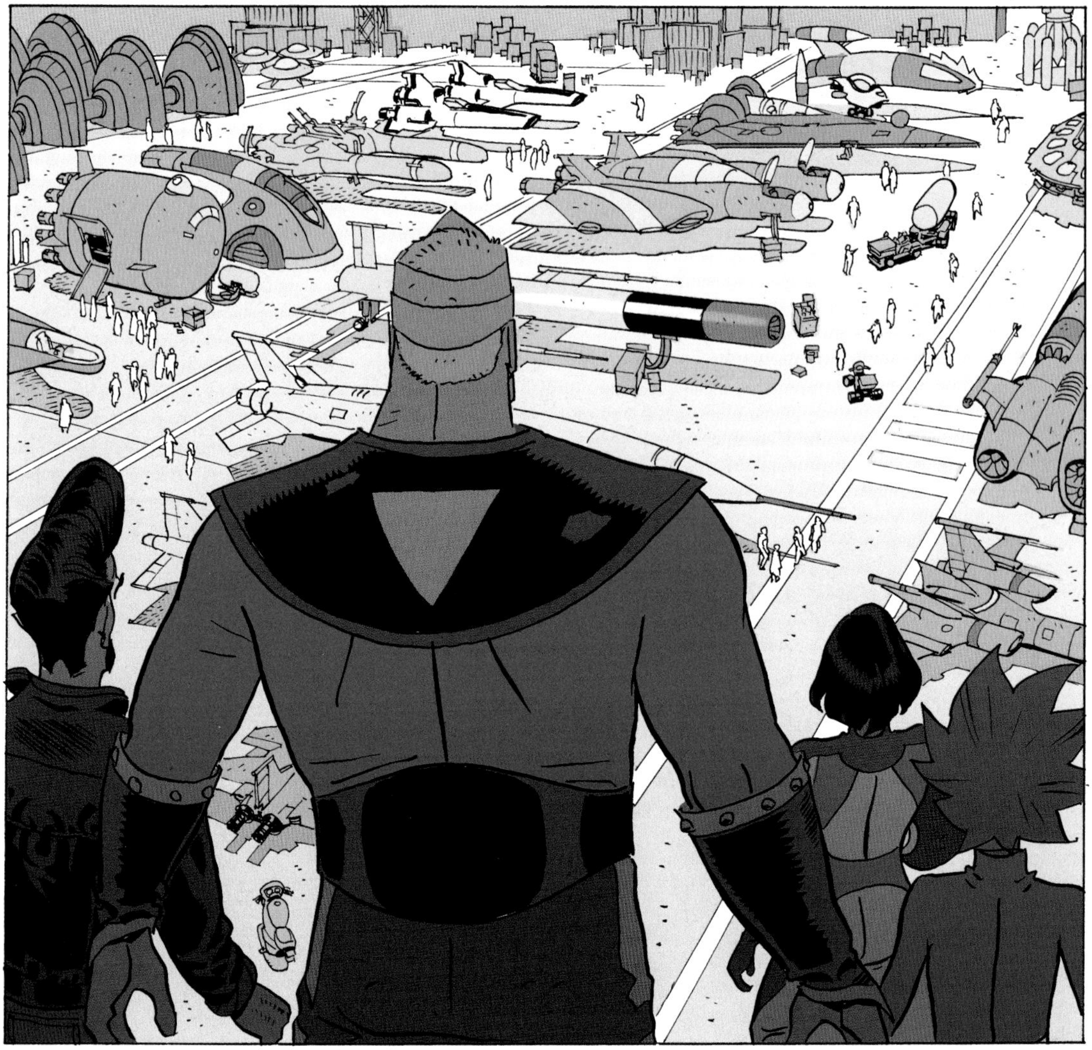

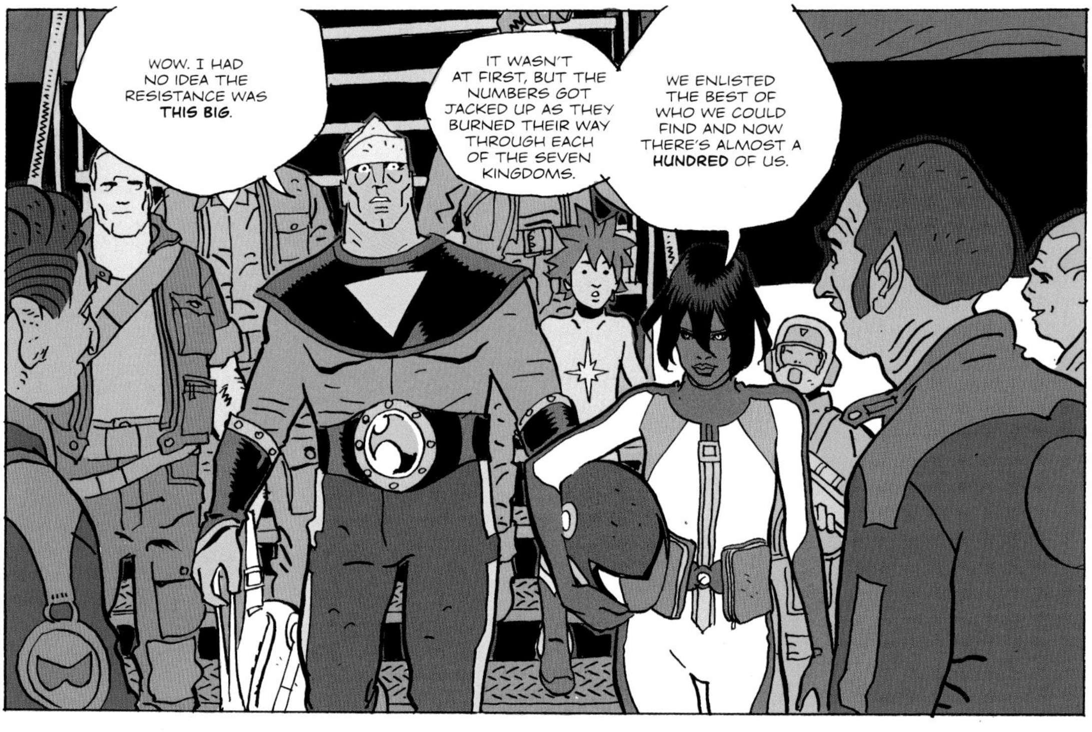
WOW. I HAD NO IDEA THE RESISTANCE WAS **THIS BIG**.
IT WASN'T AT FIRST, BUT THE NUMBERS GOT JACKED UP AS THEY BURNED THEIR WAY THROUGH EACH OF THE SEVEN KINGDOMS.
WE ENLISTED THE BEST OF WHO WE COULD FIND AND NOW THERE'S ALMOST A **HUNDRED** OF US.

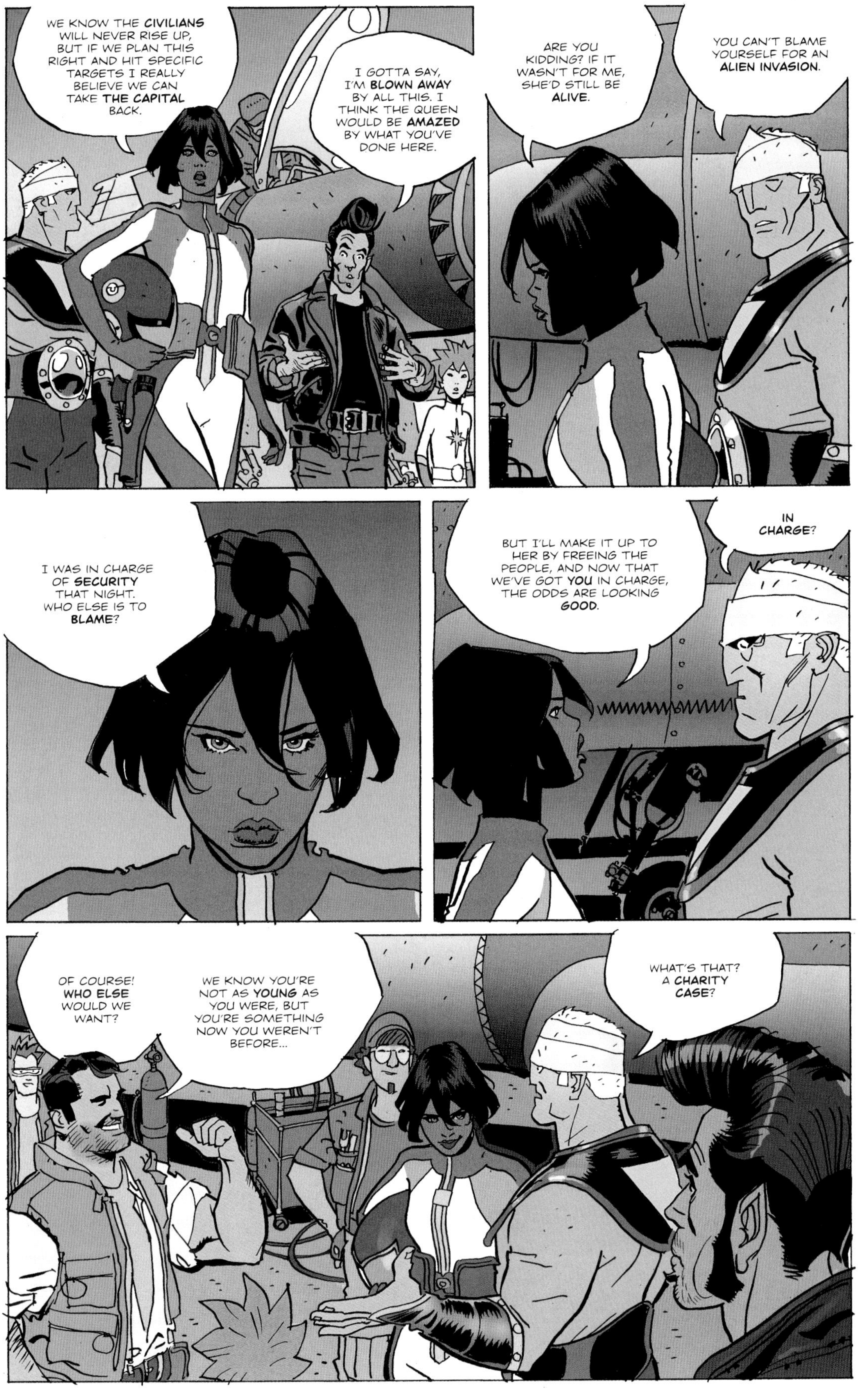
WE KNOW THE **CIVILIANS** WILL NEVER RISE UP, BUT IF WE PLAN THIS RIGHT AND HIT SPECIFIC TARGETS I REALLY BELIEVE WE CAN TAKE **THE CAPITAL** BACK.
I GOTTA SAY, I'M **BLOWN AWAY** BY ALL THIS. I THINK THE QUEEN WOULD BE **AMAZED** BY WHAT YOU'VE DONE HERE.
ARE YOU KIDDING? IF IT WASN'T FOR ME, SHE'D STILL BE **ALIVE**.
YOU CAN'T BLAME YOURSELF FOR AN **ALIEN INVASION**.
I WAS IN CHARGE OF **SECURITY** THAT NIGHT. WHO ELSE IS TO **BLAME**?
BUT I'LL MAKE IT UP TO HER BY FREEING THE PEOPLE, AND NOW THAT WE'VE GOT **YOU** IN CHARGE, THE ODDS ARE LOOKING **GOOD**.
IN **CHARGE**?
OF COURSE! **WHO ELSE** WOULD WE WANT?
WE KNOW YOU'RE NOT AS **YOUNG** AS YOU WERE, BUT YOU'RE SOMETHING NOW YOU WEREN'T BEFORE...
WHAT'S THAT? A **CHARITY CASE**?

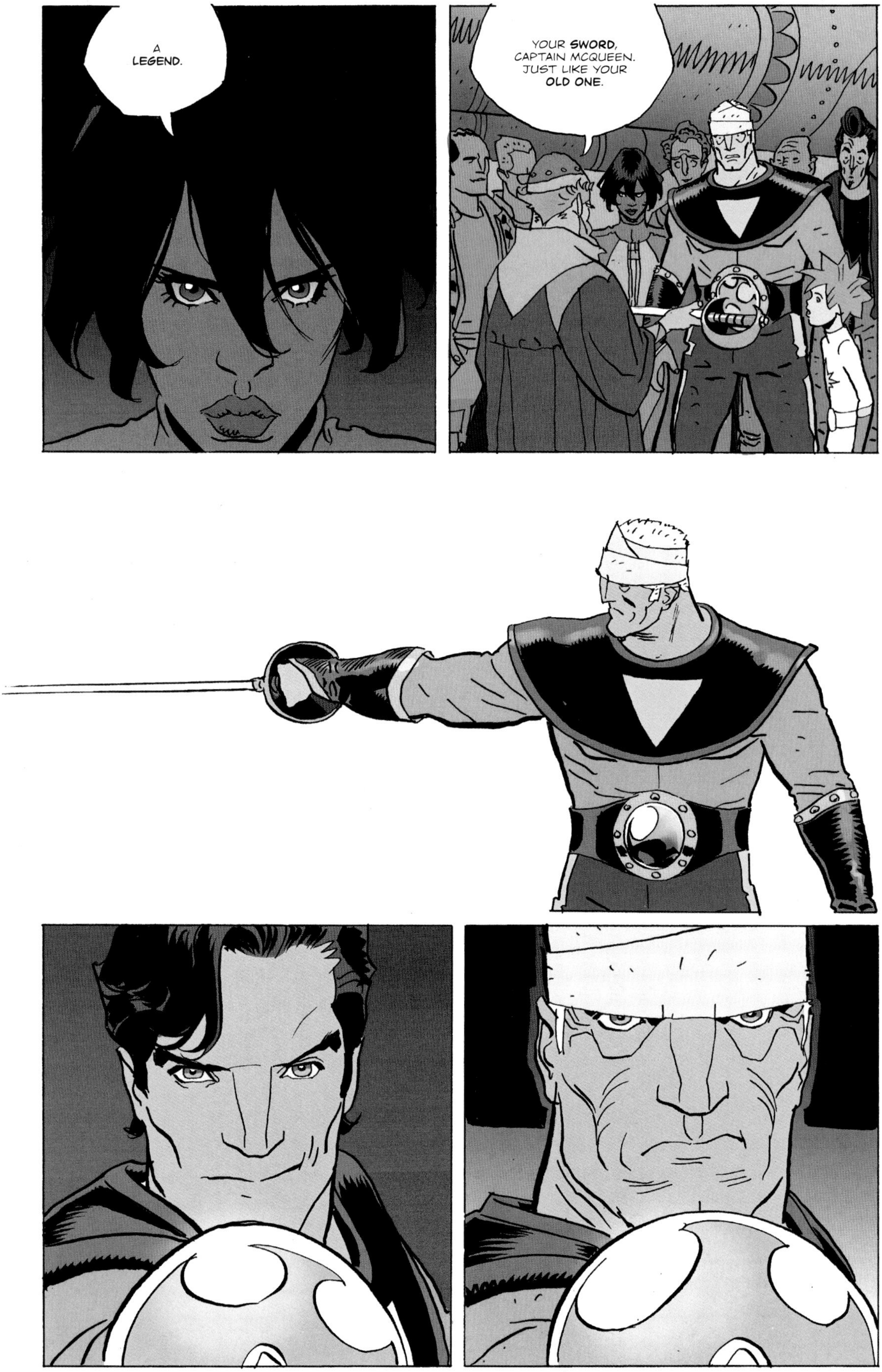
A LEGEND.
YOUR SWORD, CAPTAIN MCQUEEN. JUST LIKE YOUR OLD ONE.

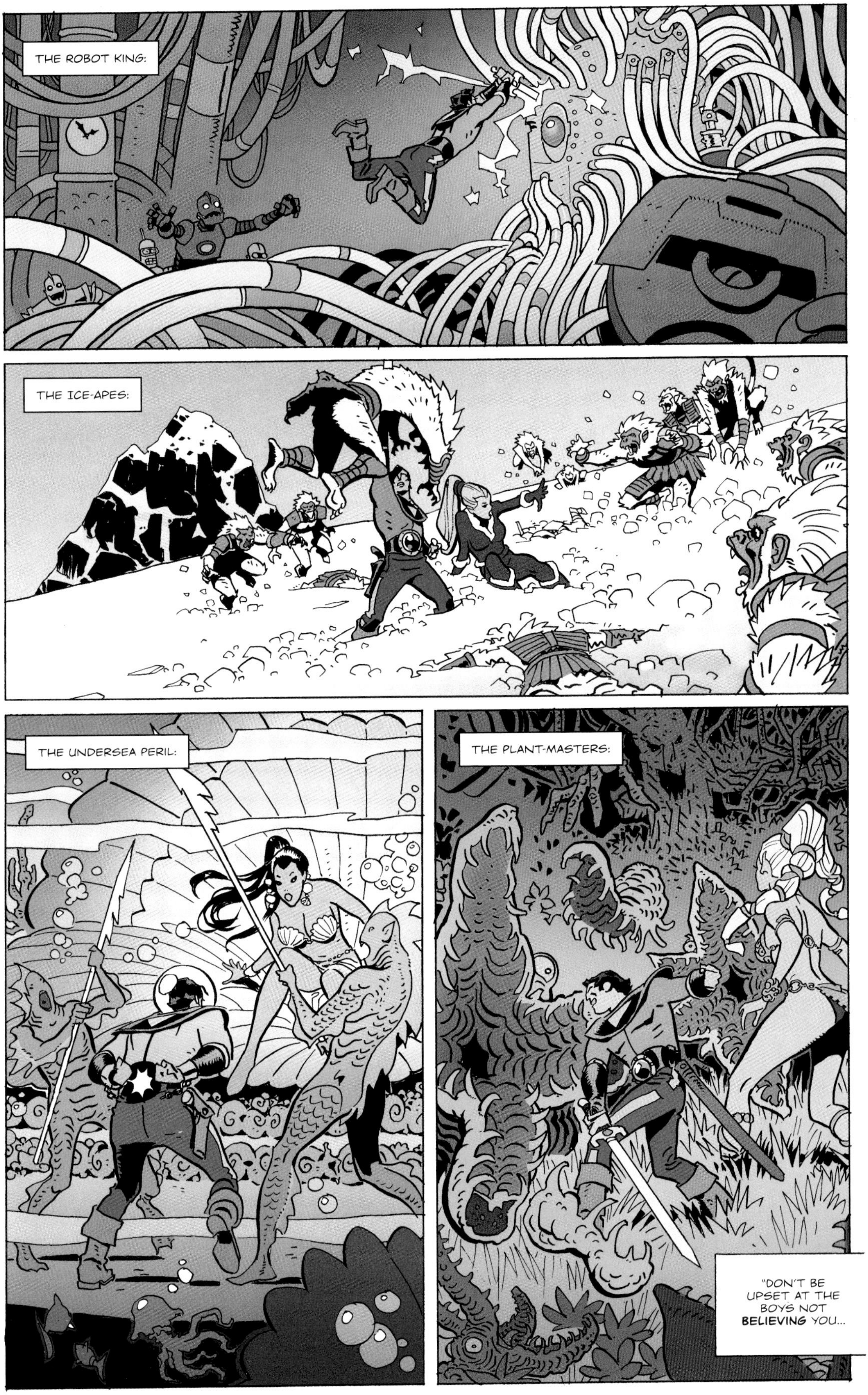
THE ROBOT KING:
THE ICE-APES:
THE UNDERSEA PERIL:
THE PLANT-MASTERS:
"DON'T BE UPSET AT THE BOYS NOT **BELIEVING** YOU...

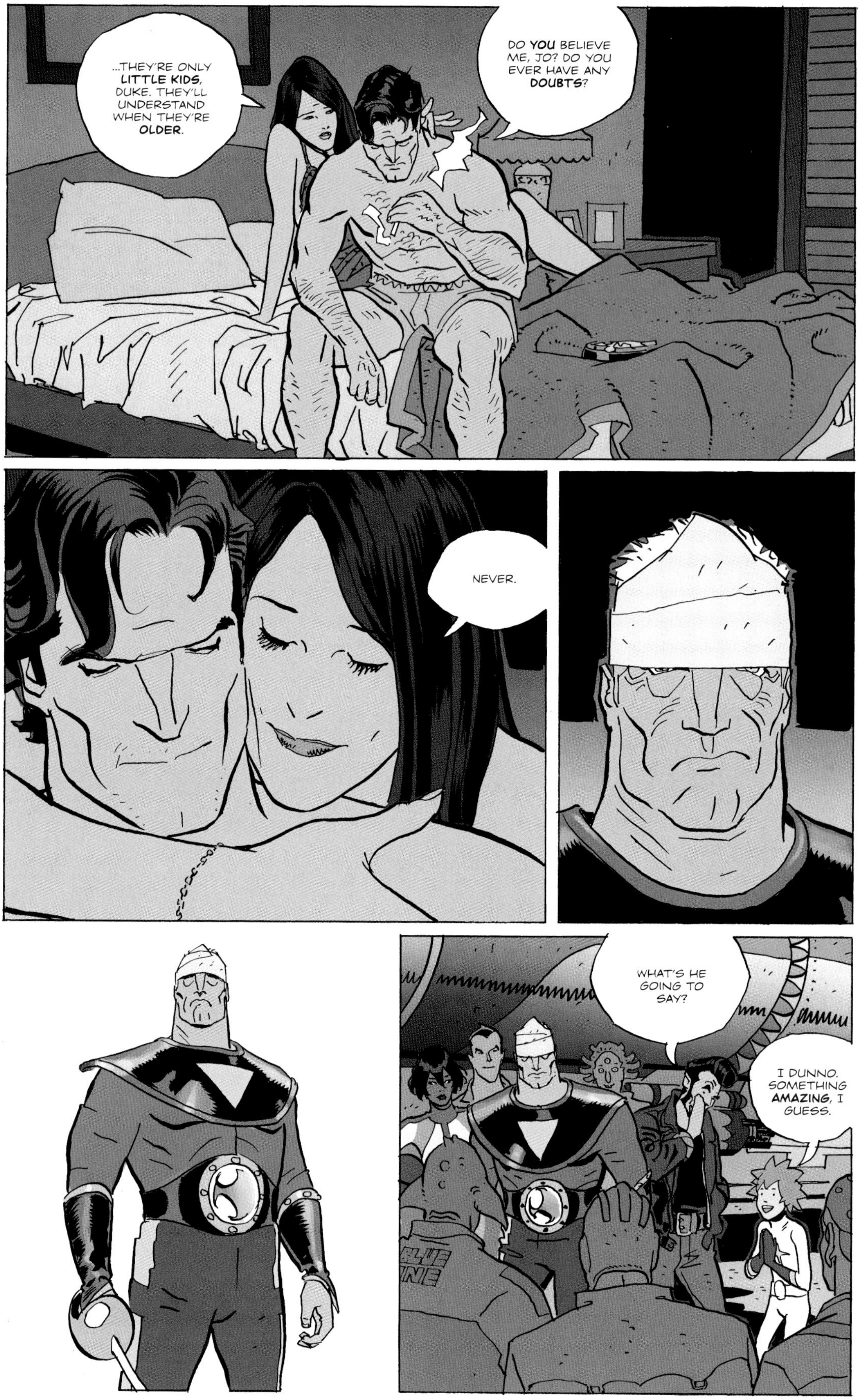
...THEY'RE ONLY LITTLE KIDS, DUKE. THEY'LL UNDERSTAND WHEN THEY'RE OLDER.
DO YOU BELIEVE ME, JO? DO YOU EVER HAVE ANY DOUBTS?
NEVER.
WHAT'S HE GOING TO SAY?
I DUNNO. SOMETHING AMAZING, I GUESS.
BLUE LINE

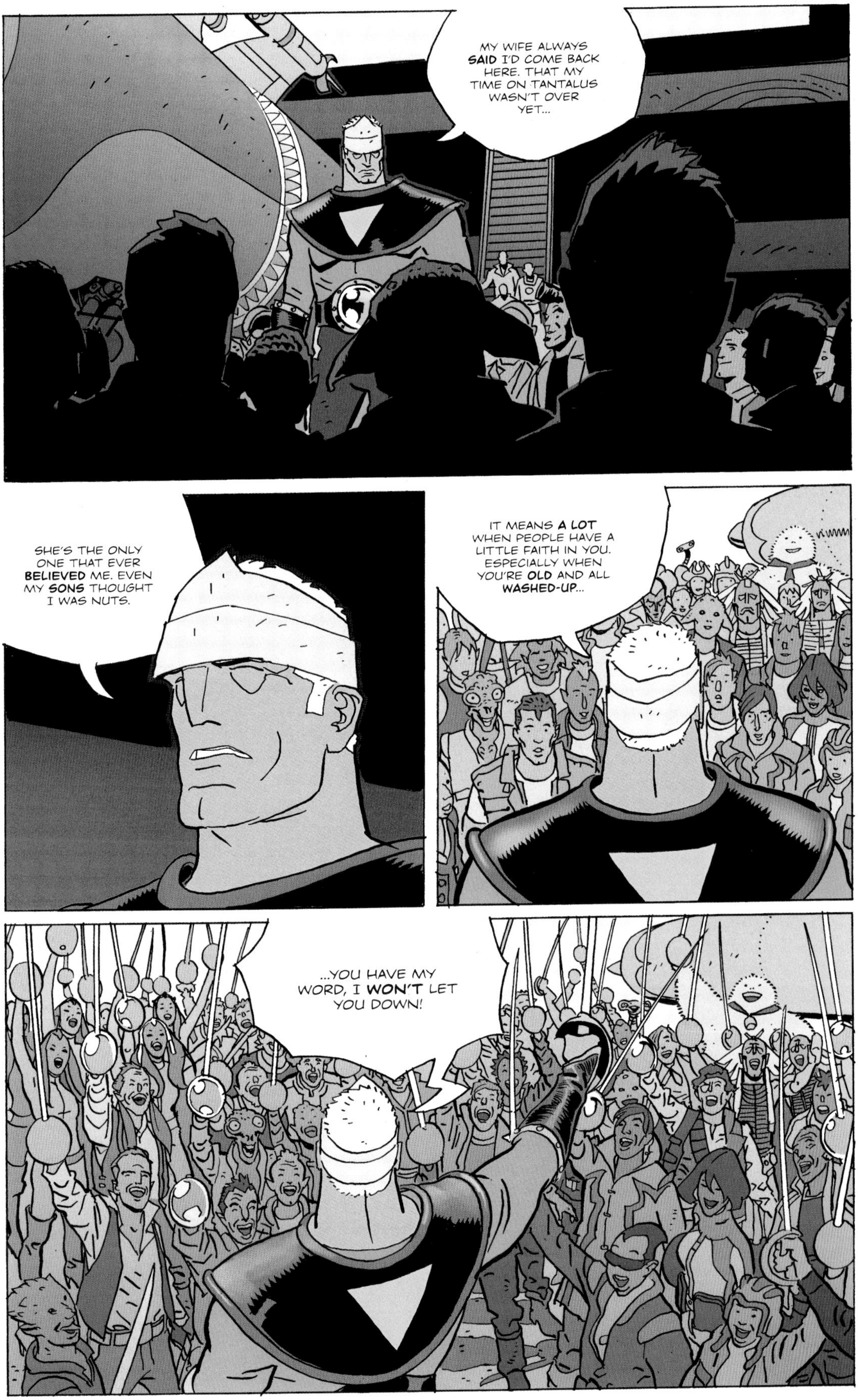
MY WIFE ALWAYS SAID I'D COME BACK HERE. THAT MY TIME ON TANTALUS WASN'T OVER YET...
SHE'S THE ONLY ONE THAT EVER BELIEVED ME. EVEN MY SONS THOUGHT I WAS NUTS.
IT MEANS A LOT WHEN PEOPLE HAVE A LITTLE FAITH IN YOU. ESPECIALLY WHEN YOU'RE OLD AND ALL WASHED-UP...
...YOU HAVE MY WORD, I WON'T LET YOU DOWN!

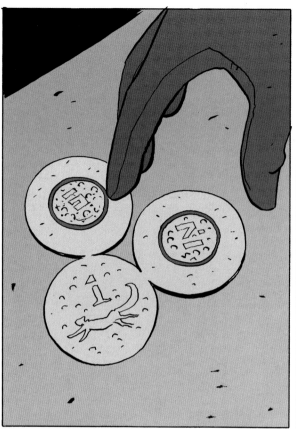

YOU OKAY?

I'M FINE.

YOU WANT TO TELL ME ABOUT THIS **PINDAR GUY**? LOOKED LIKE YOU AND HE HAVE A LITTLE **HISTORY**.

I'M SORRY, SIR. IT'S STILL TOO SOON TO **TALK** ABOUT.

THAT'S OKAY. I UNDERSTAND. I JUST WANTED TO COME OVER AND SAY THANKS FOR GETTING ME **BACK HERE**, KIDDO. I KNOW I DIDN'T SEEM **INTO** IT AT FIRST, BUT THAT WAS JUST THE **FEAR** TALKING.

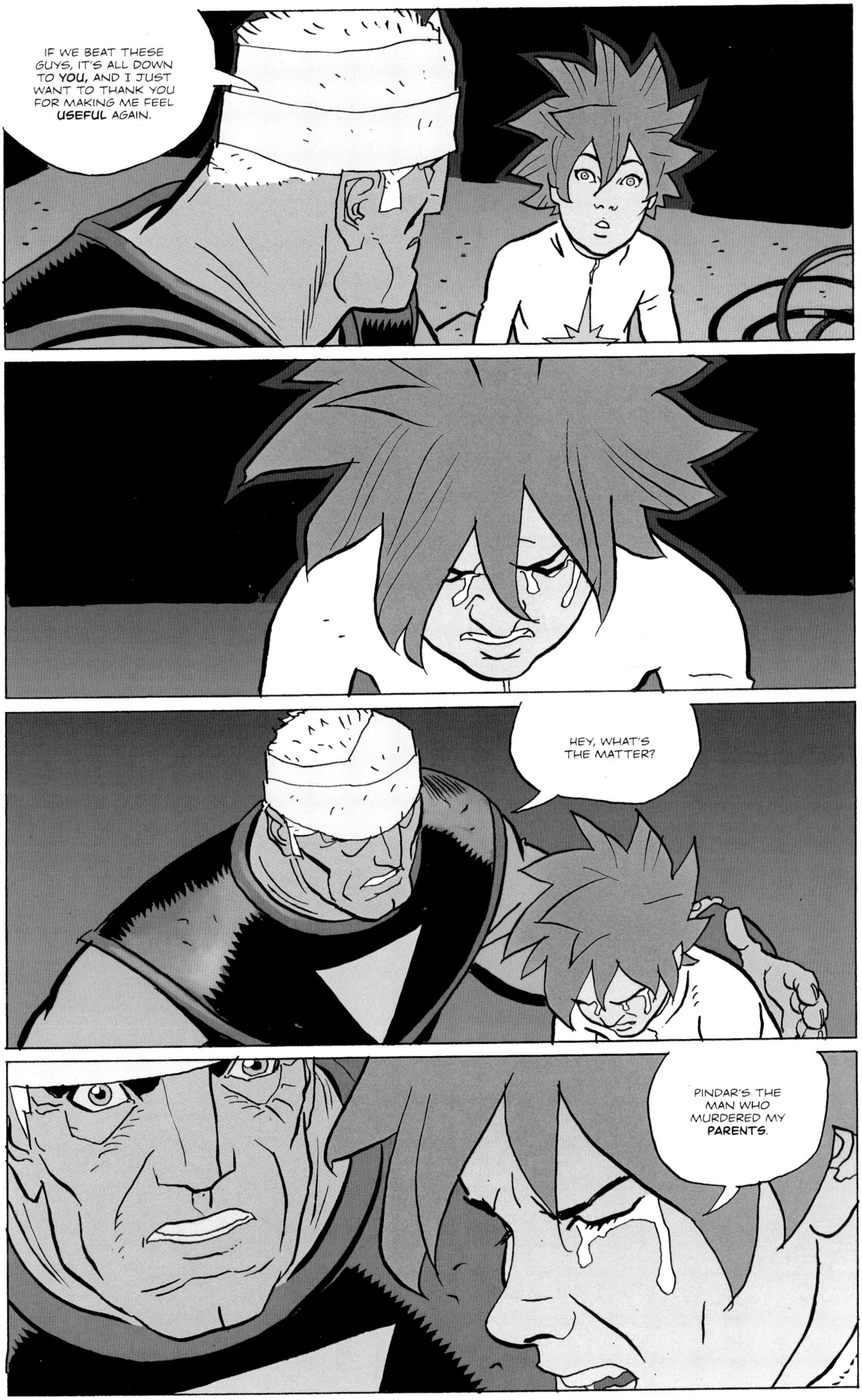
IF WE BEAT THESE GUYS, IT'S ALL DOWN TO **YOU,** AND I JUST WANT TO THANK YOU FOR MAKING ME FEEL **USEFUL** AGAIN.
HEY, WHAT'S THE MATTER?
PINDAR'S THE MAN WHO MURDERED MY **PARENTS**.

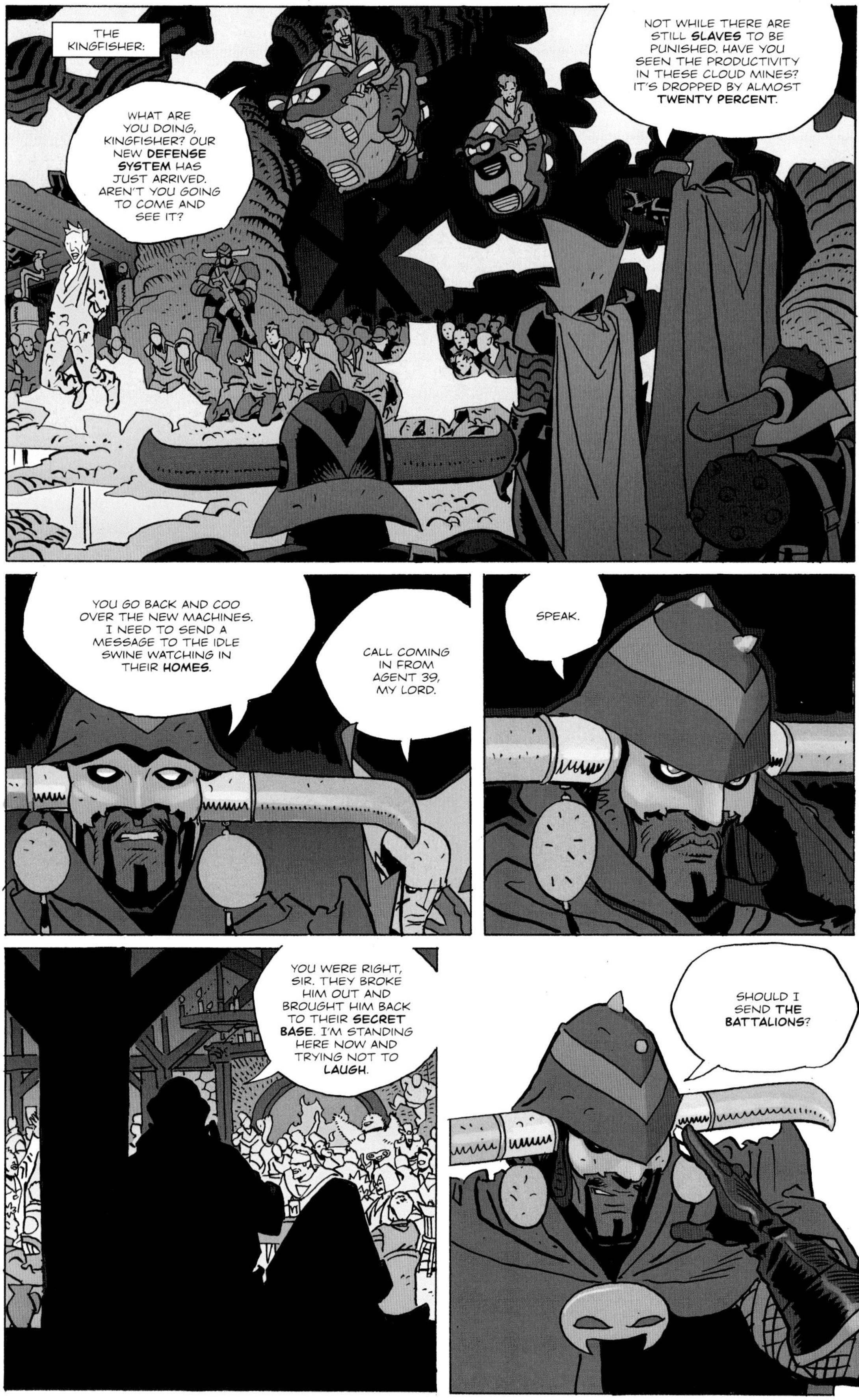
THE KINGFISHER:
WHAT ARE YOU DOING, KINGFISHER? OUR NEW **DEFENSE SYSTEM** HAS JUST ARRIVED. AREN'T YOU GOING TO COME AND SEE IT?
NOT WHILE THERE ARE STILL **SLAVES** TO BE PUNISHED. HAVE YOU SEEN THE PRODUCTIVITY IN THESE CLOUD MINES? IT'S DROPPED BY ALMOST **TWENTY PERCENT**.
YOU GO BACK AND COO OVER THE NEW MACHINES. I NEED TO SEND A MESSAGE TO THE IDLE SWINE WATCHING IN THEIR **HOMES**.
CALL COMING IN FROM AGENT 39, MY LORD.
SPEAK.
YOU WERE RIGHT, SIR. THEY BROKE HIM OUT AND BROUGHT HIM BACK TO THEIR **SECRET BASE**. I'M STANDING HERE NOW AND TRYING NOT TO **LAUGH**.
SHOULD I SEND **THE BATTALIONS**?

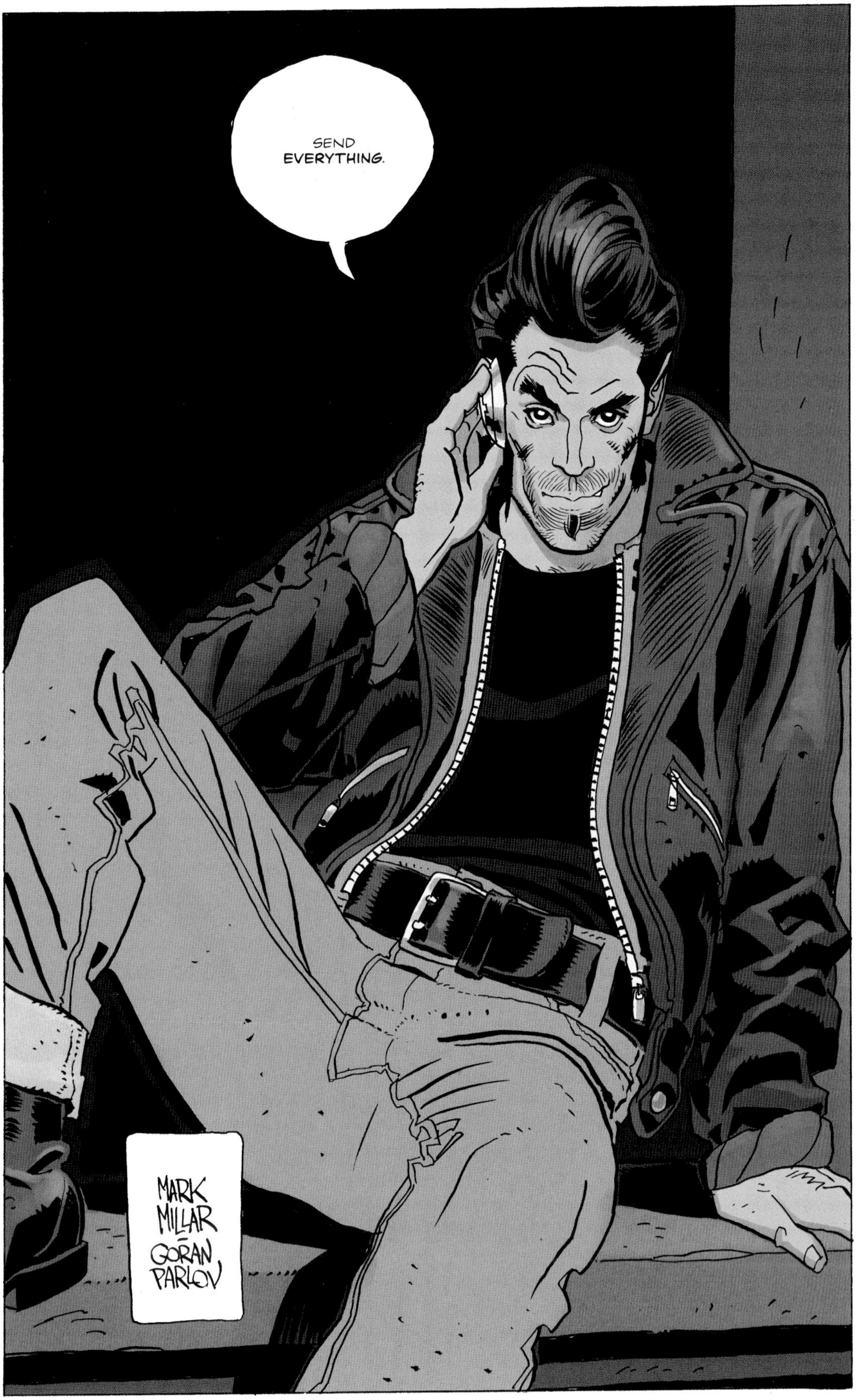
SEND EVERYTHING.
MARK MILLAR - GORAN PARLOV

FIVE

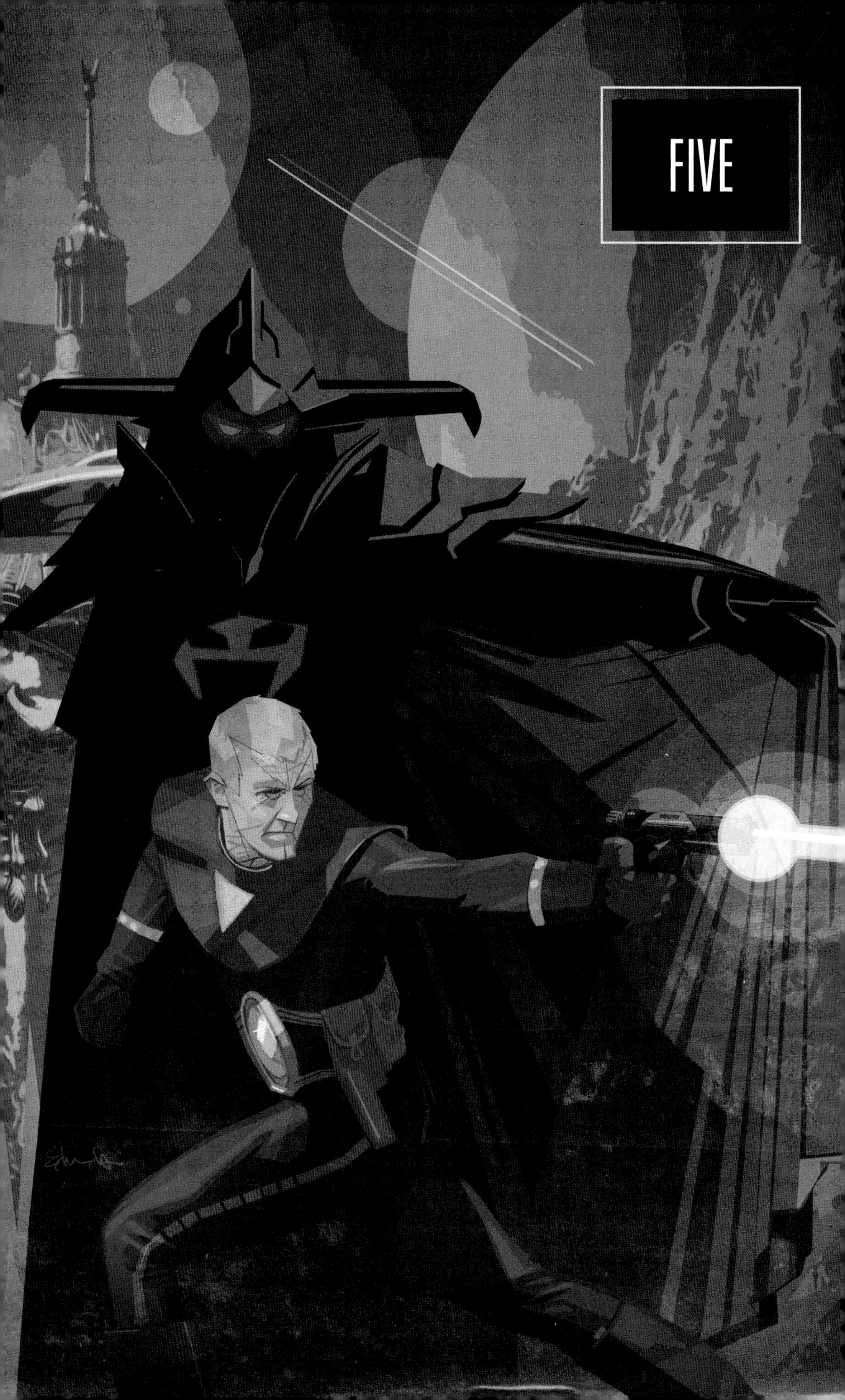

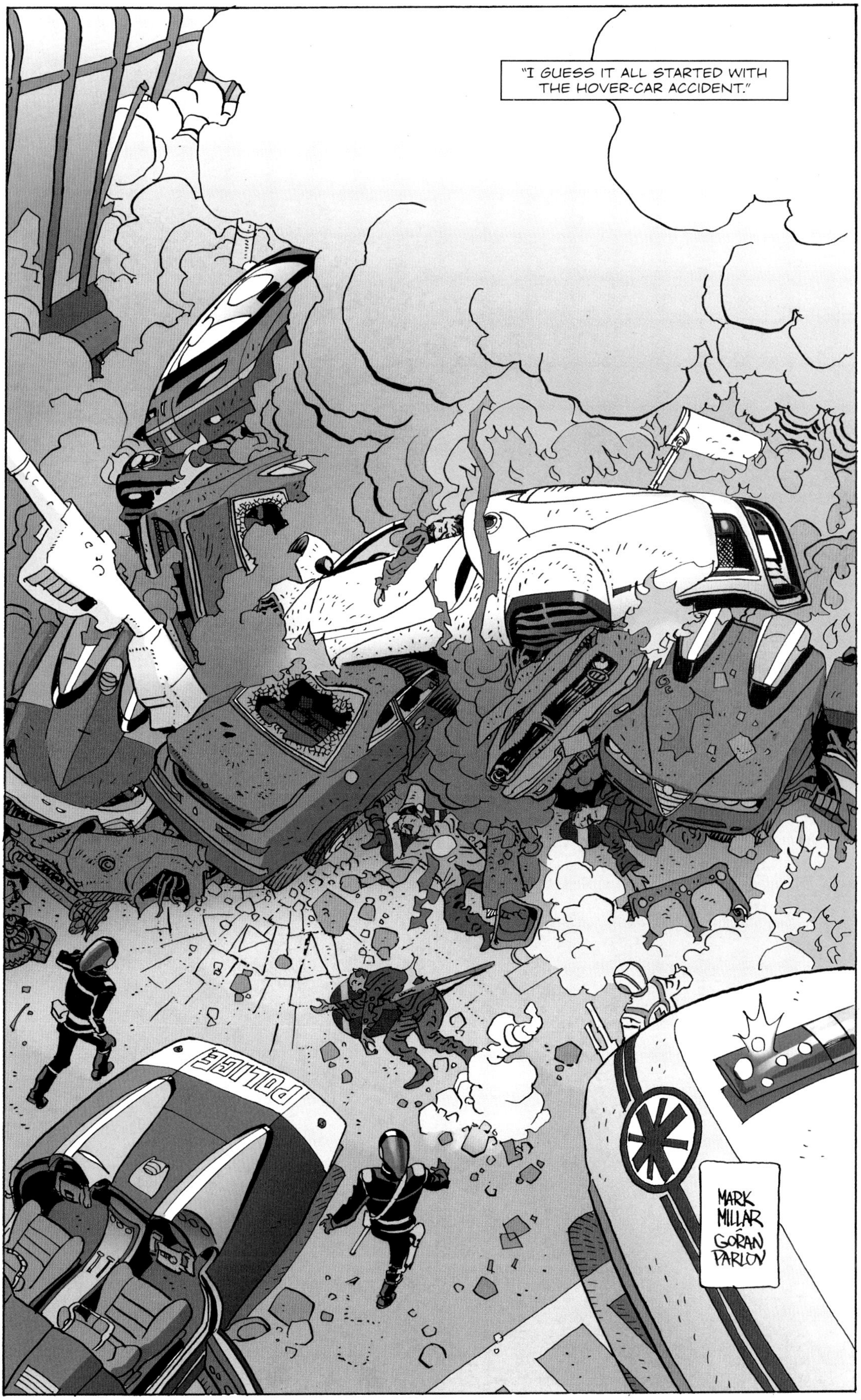
"I GUESS IT ALL STARTED WITH THE HOVER-CAR ACCIDENT."
POLICE
MARK MILLAR GORAN PARLOV

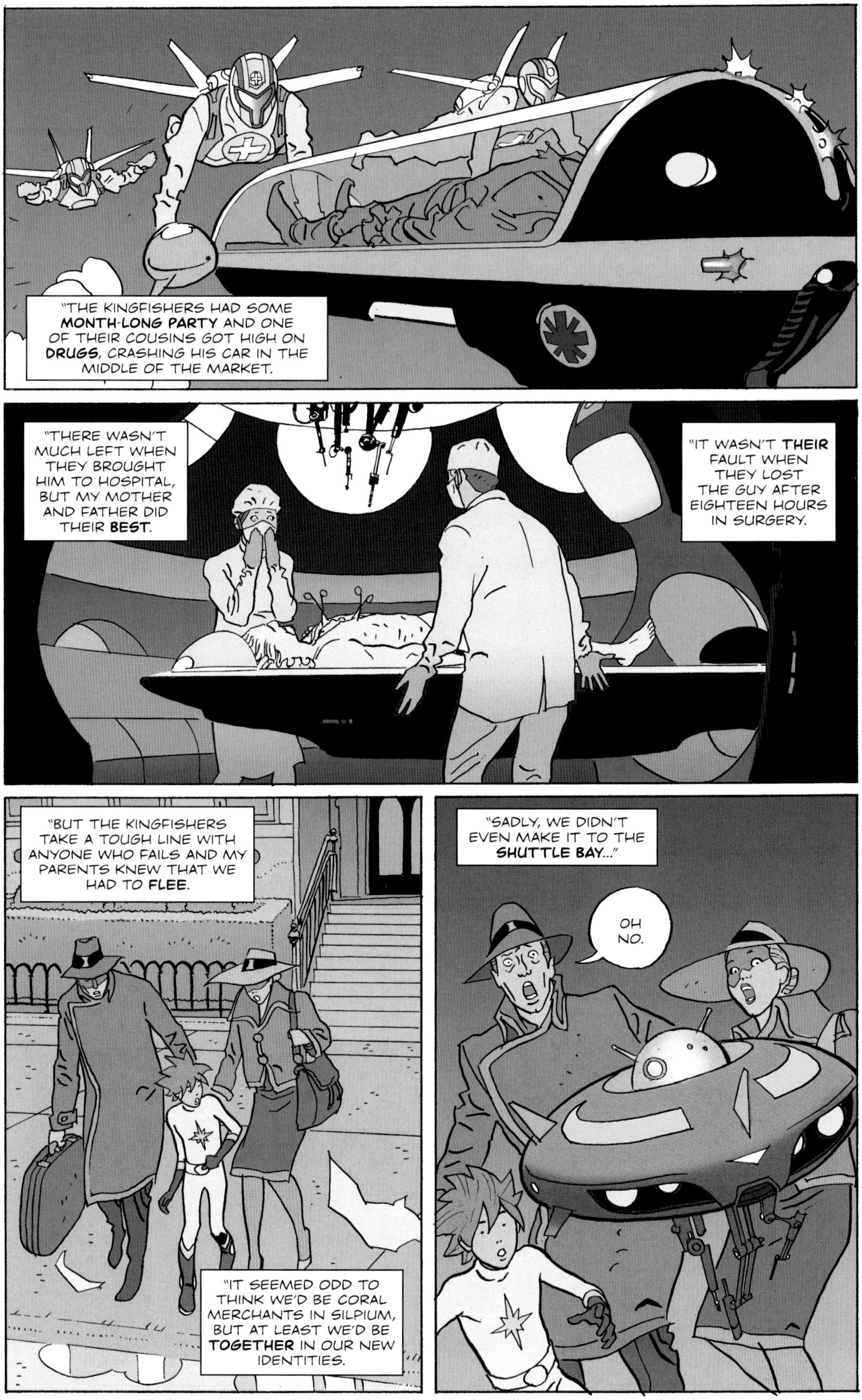
"THE KINGFISHERS HAD SOME **MONTH-LONG PARTY** AND ONE OF THEIR COUSINS GOT HIGH ON **DRUGS**, CRASHING HIS CAR IN THE MIDDLE OF THE MARKET.
"THERE WASN'T MUCH LEFT WHEN THEY BROUGHT HIM TO HOSPITAL, BUT MY MOTHER AND FATHER DID THEIR **BEST**.
"IT WASN'T **THEIR** FAULT WHEN THEY LOST THE GUY AFTER EIGHTEEN HOURS IN SURGERY.
"BUT THE KINGFISHERS TAKE A TOUGH LINE WITH ANYONE WHO FAILS AND MY PARENTS KNEW THAT WE HAD TO **FLEE**.
"IT SEEMED ODD TO THINK WE'D BE CORAL MERCHANTS IN SILPIUM, BUT AT LEAST WE'D BE **TOGETHER** IN OUR NEW IDENTITIES.
"SADLY, WE DIDN'T EVEN MAKE IT TO THE **SHUTTLE BAY**..."
OH NO.

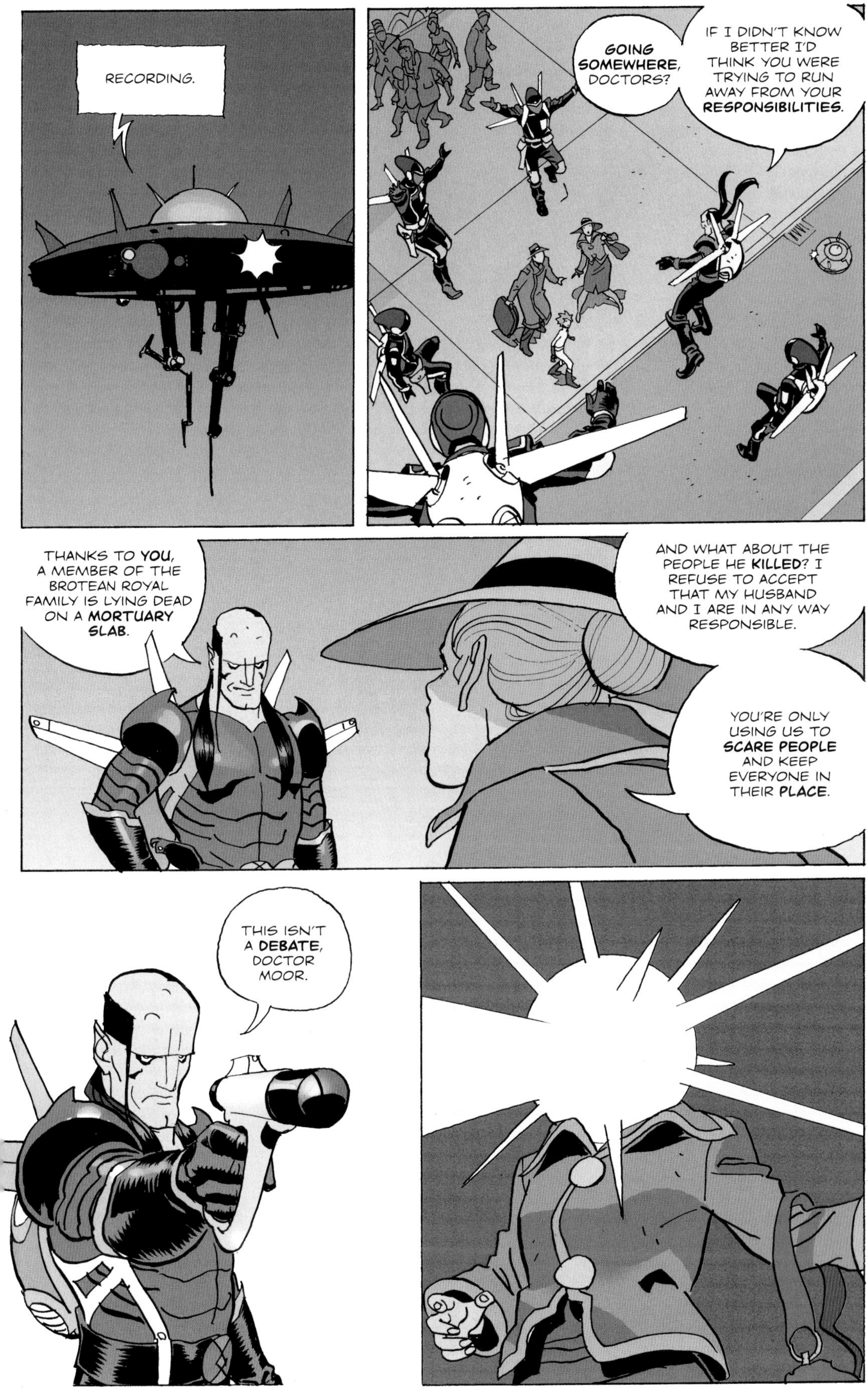
RECORDING.
GOING SOMEWHERE, DOCTORS?
IF I DIDN'T KNOW BETTER I'D THINK YOU WERE TRYING TO RUN AWAY FROM YOUR RESPONSIBILITIES.
THANKS TO YOU, A MEMBER OF THE BROTEAN ROYAL FAMILY IS LYING DEAD ON A MORTUARY SLAB.
AND WHAT ABOUT THE PEOPLE HE KILLED? I REFUSE TO ACCEPT THAT MY HUSBAND AND I ARE IN ANY WAY RESPONSIBLE.
YOU'RE ONLY USING US TO SCARE PEOPLE AND KEEP EVERYONE IN THEIR PLACE.
THIS ISN'T A DEBATE, DOCTOR MOOR.

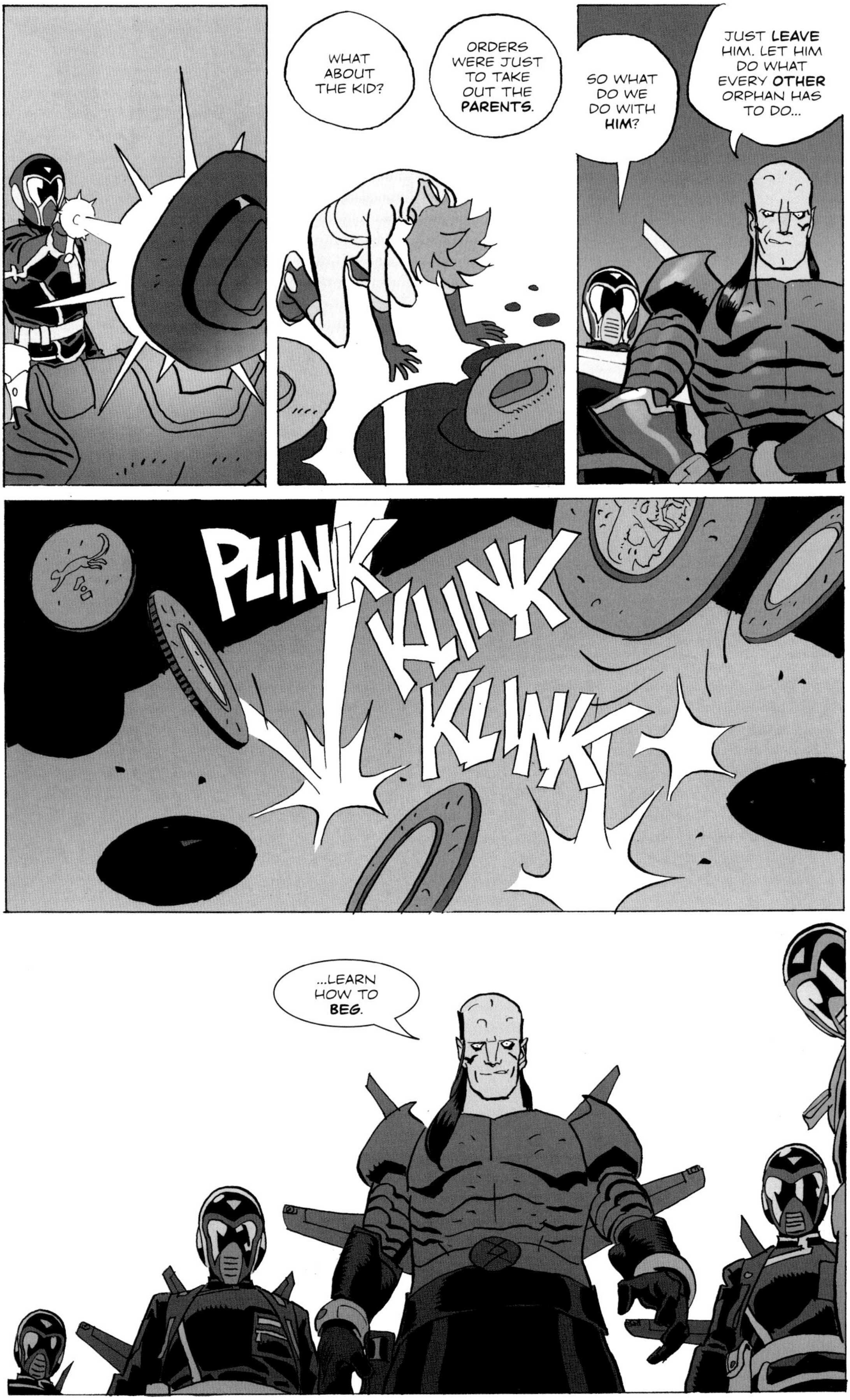
WHAT ABOUT THE KID?
ORDERS WERE JUST TO TAKE OUT THE **PARENTS**.
SO WHAT DO WE DO WITH **HIM**?
JUST **LEAVE** HIM. LET HIM DO WHAT EVERY **OTHER** ORPHAN HAS TO DO...
PLINK
KLINK
KLINK
...LEARN HOW TO **BEG**.

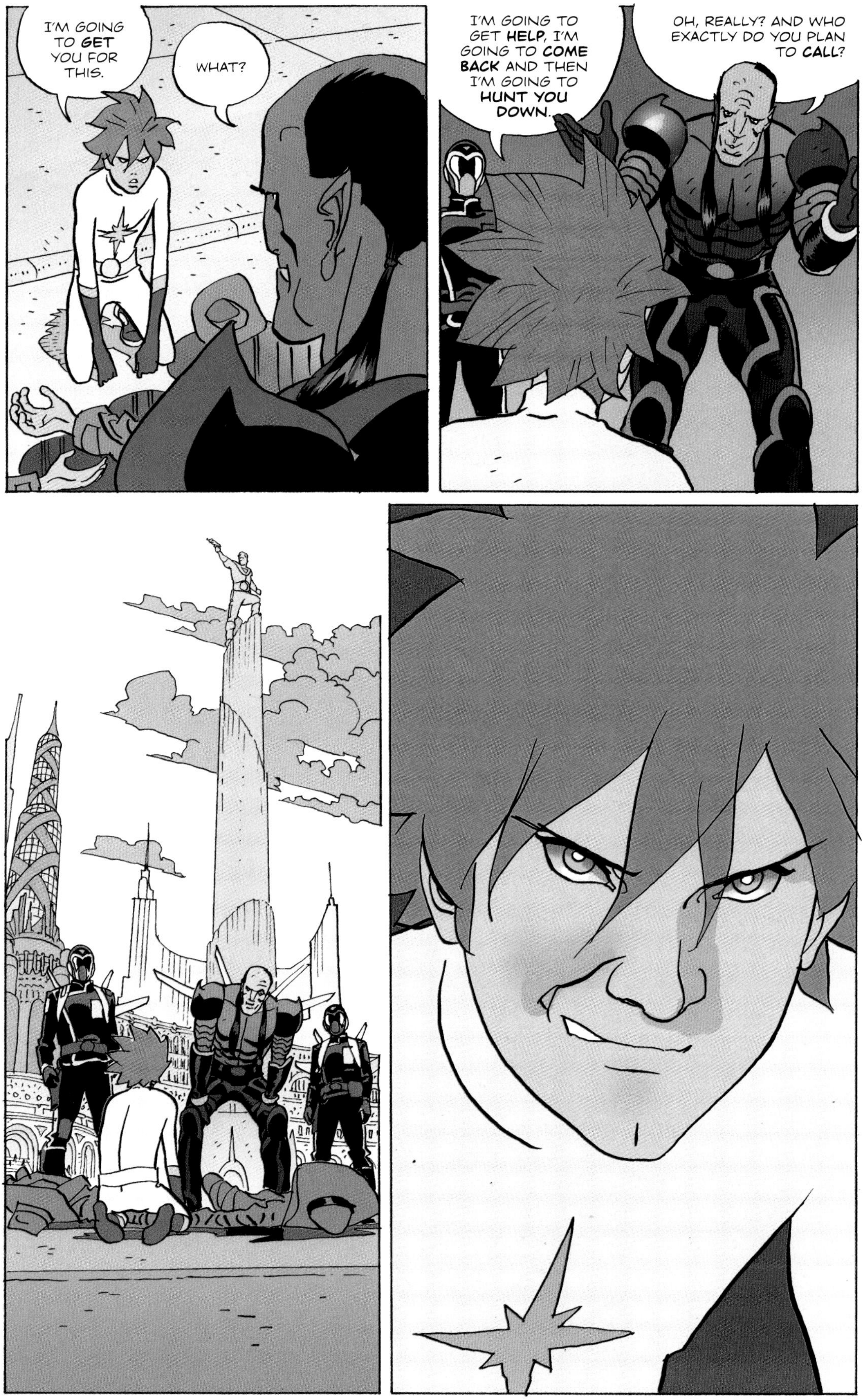
I'M GOING TO **GET** YOU FOR THIS.
WHAT?
I'M GOING TO GET **HELP**, I'M GOING TO **COME BACK** AND THEN I'M GOING TO **HUNT YOU DOWN**.
OH, REALLY? AND WHO EXACTLY DO YOU PLAN TO **CALL**?

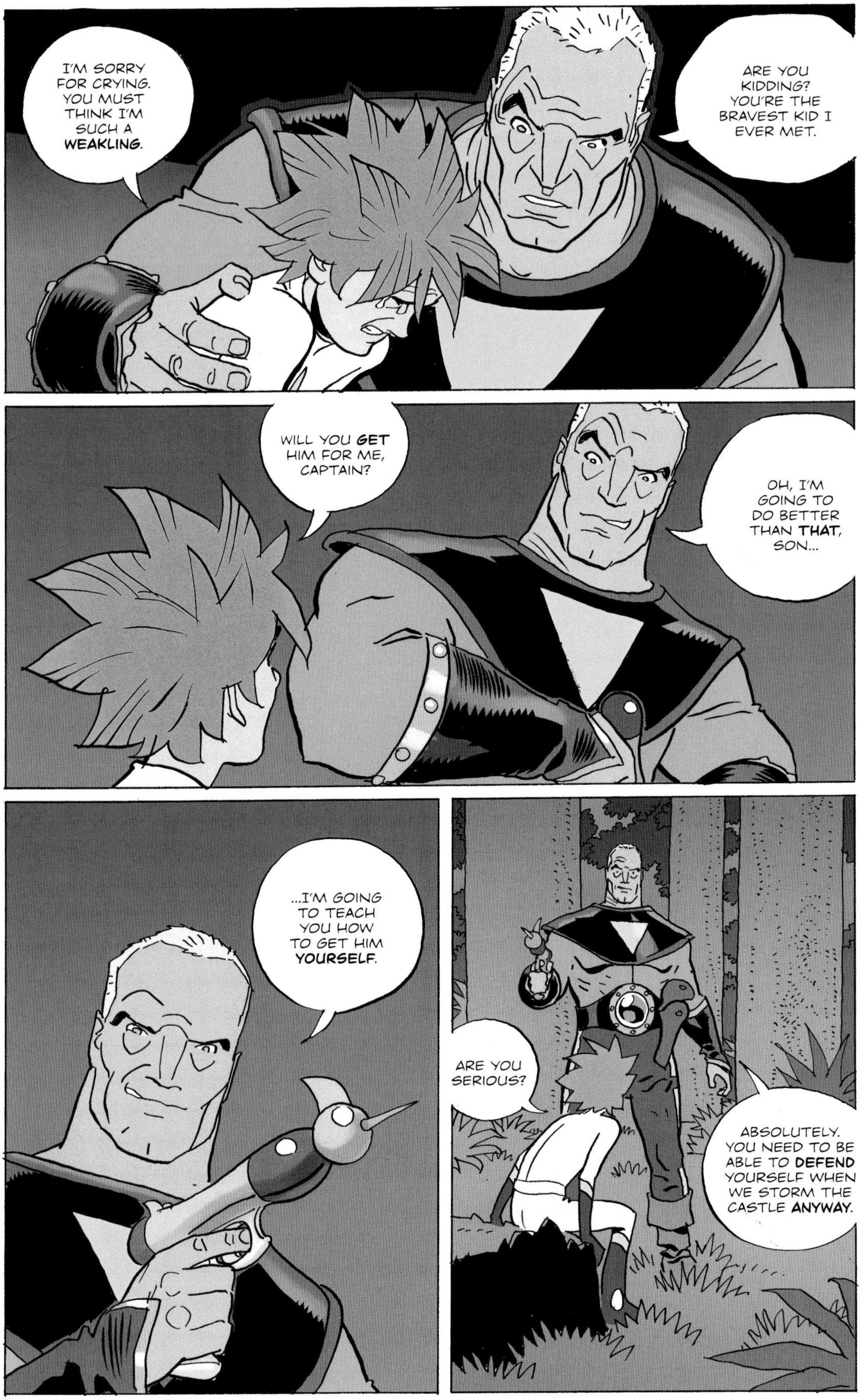
I'M SORRY FOR CRYING. YOU MUST THINK I'M SUCH A WEAKLING.
ARE YOU KIDDING? YOU'RE THE BRAVEST KID I EVER MET.
WILL YOU GET HIM FOR ME, CAPTAIN?
OH, I'M GOING TO DO BETTER THAN THAT, SON...
...I'M GOING TO TEACH YOU HOW TO GET HIM YOURSELF.
ARE YOU SERIOUS?
ABSOLUTELY. YOU NEED TO BE ABLE TO DEFEND YOURSELF WHEN WE STORM THE CASTLE ANYWAY.

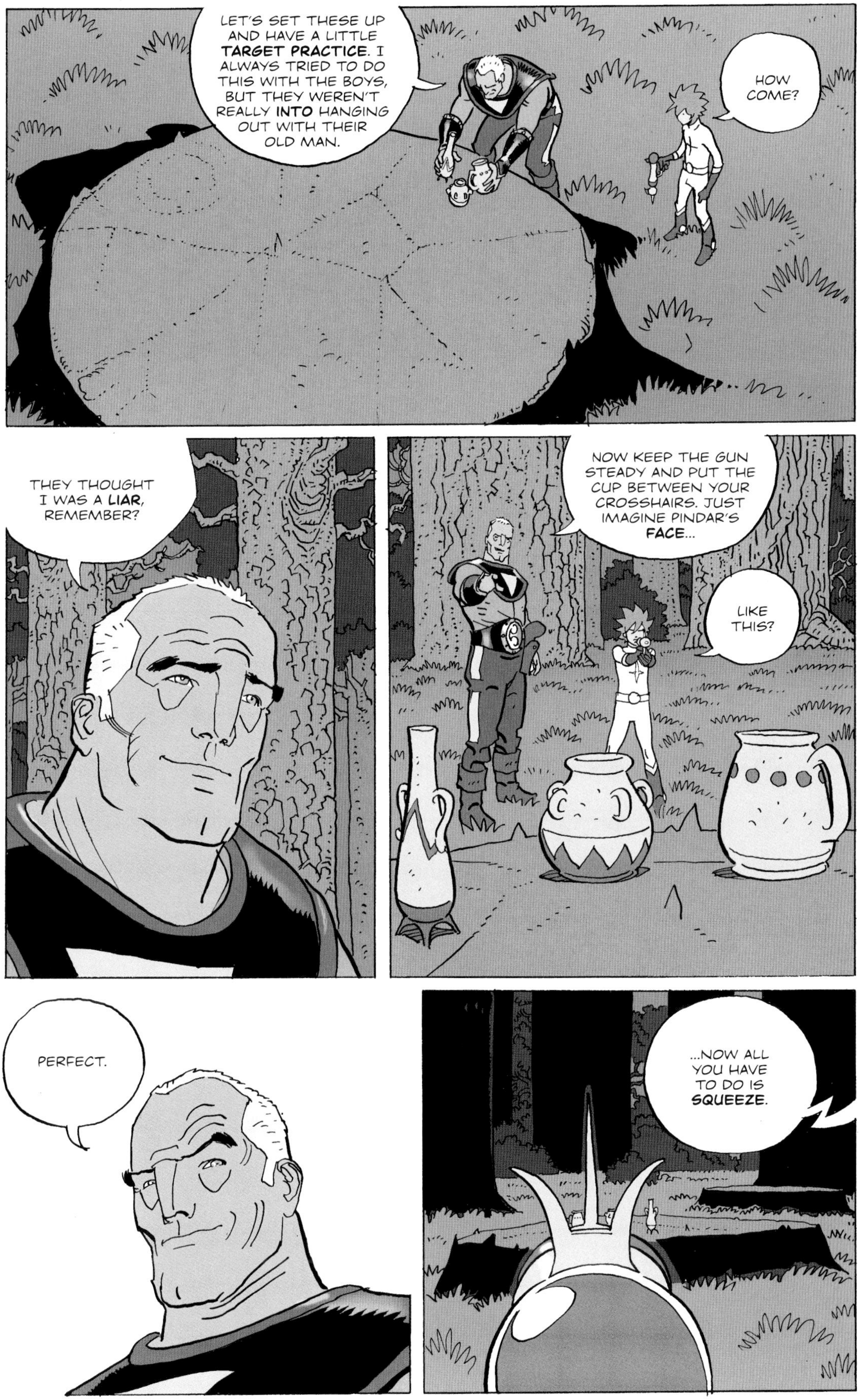
LET'S SET THESE UP AND HAVE A LITTLE **TARGET PRACTICE**. I ALWAYS TRIED TO DO THIS WITH THE BOYS, BUT THEY WEREN'T REALLY **INTO** HANGING OUT WITH THEIR OLD MAN.
HOW COME?
THEY THOUGHT I WAS A **LIAR**, REMEMBER?
NOW KEEP THE GUN STEADY AND PUT THE CUP BETWEEN YOUR CROSSHAIRS. JUST IMAGINE PINDAR'S **FACE**...
LIKE THIS?
PERFECT.
...NOW ALL YOU HAVE TO DO IS **SQUEEZE**.

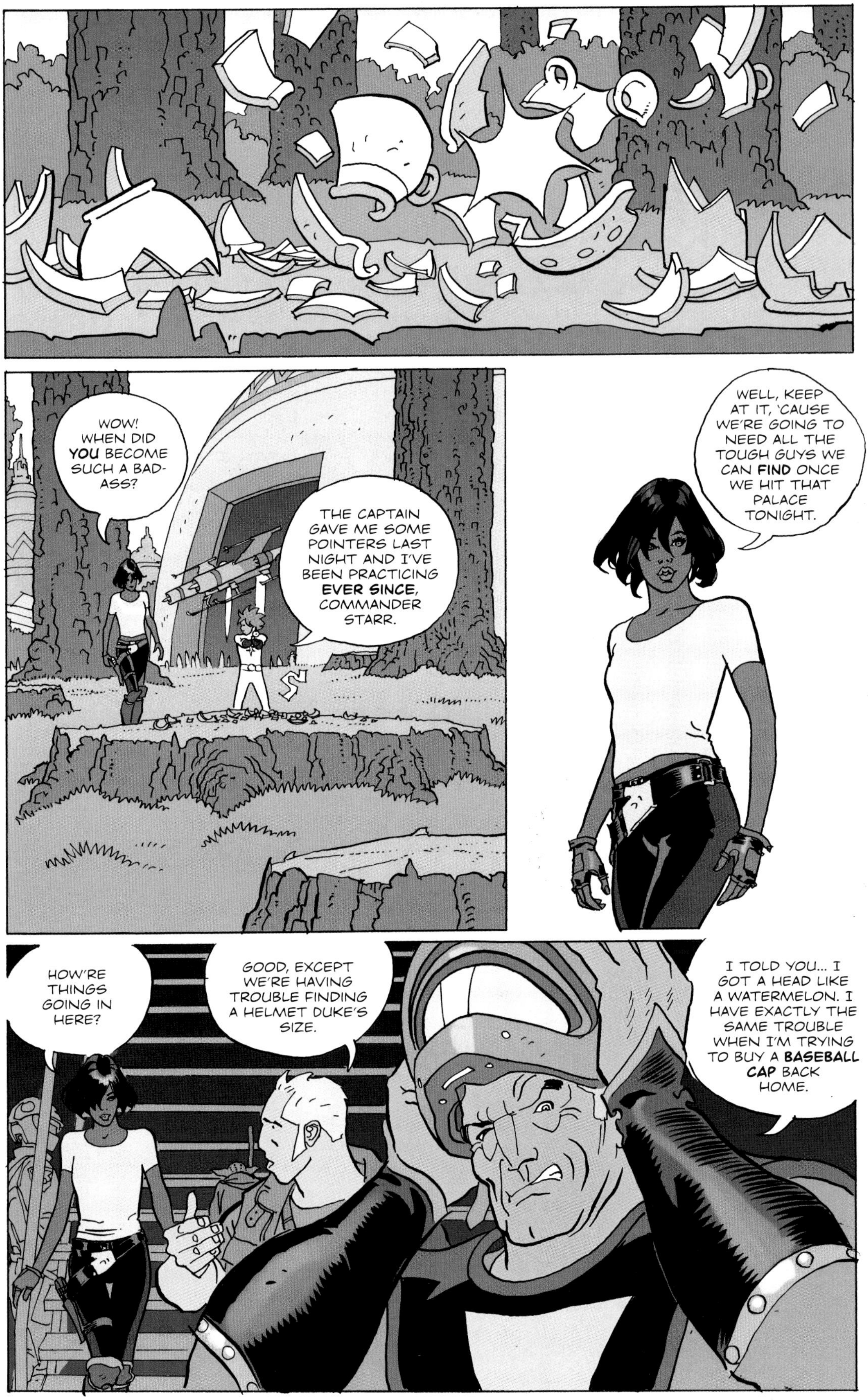
WOW! WHEN DID **YOU** BECOME SUCH A BAD-ASS?
THE CAPTAIN GAVE ME SOME POINTERS LAST NIGHT AND I'VE BEEN PRACTICING **EVER SINCE**, COMMANDER STARR.
WELL, KEEP AT IT, 'CAUSE WE'RE GOING TO NEED ALL THE TOUGH GUYS WE CAN **FIND** ONCE WE HIT THAT PALACE TONIGHT.
HOW'RE THINGS GOING IN HERE?
GOOD, EXCEPT WE'RE HAVING TROUBLE FINDING A HELMET DUKE'S SIZE.
I TOLD YOU... I GOT A HEAD LIKE A WATERMELON. I HAVE EXACTLY THE SAME TROUBLE WHEN I'M TRYING TO BUY A **BASEBALL CAP** BACK HOME.

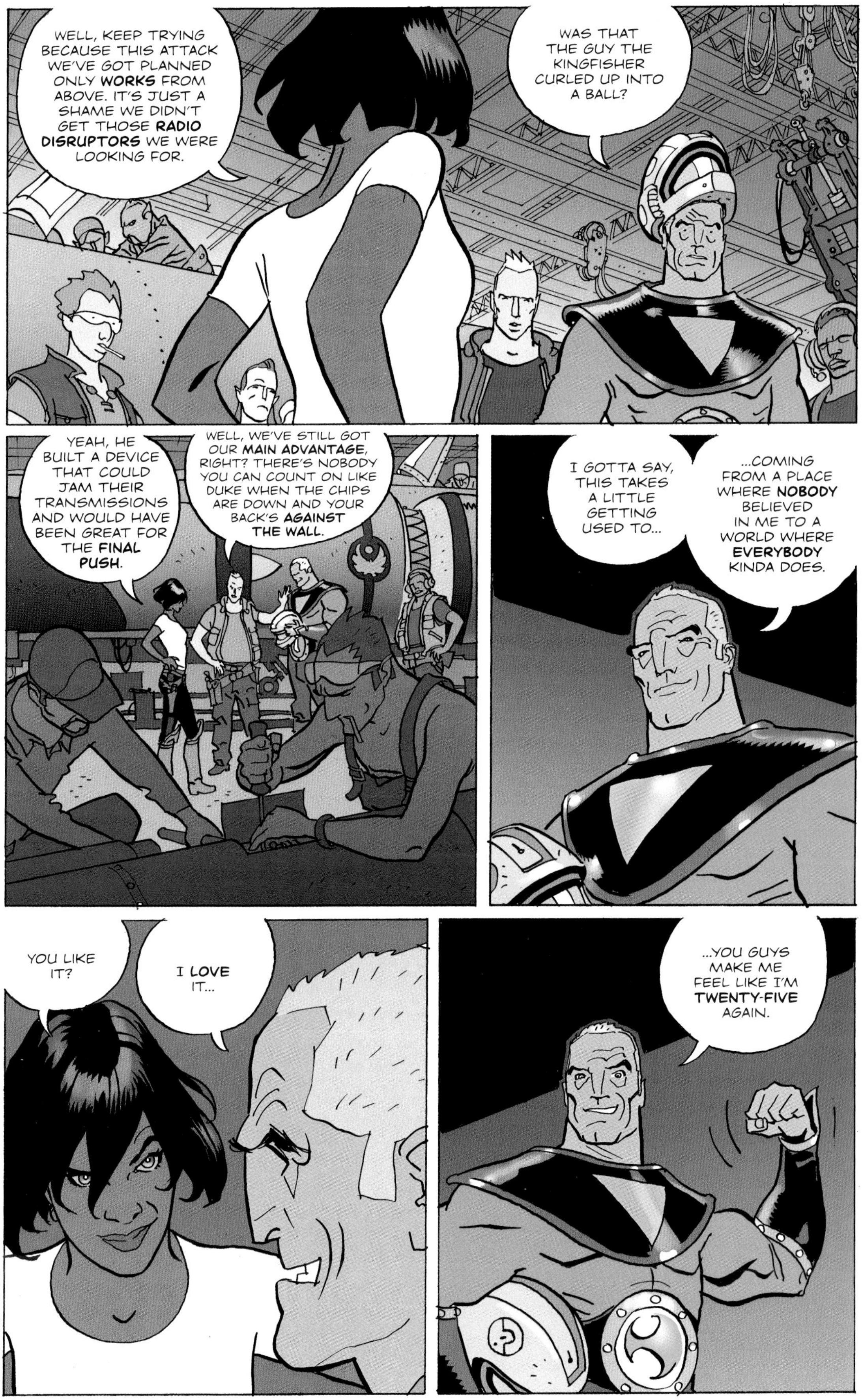
WELL, KEEP TRYING BECAUSE THIS ATTACK WE'VE GOT PLANNED ONLY **WORKS** FROM ABOVE. IT'S JUST A SHAME WE DIDN'T GET THOSE **RADIO DISRUPTORS** WE WERE LOOKING FOR.
WAS THAT THE GUY THE KINGFISHER CURLED UP INTO A BALL?
YEAH, HE BUILT A DEVICE THAT COULD JAM THEIR TRANSMISSIONS AND WOULD HAVE BEEN GREAT FOR THE **FINAL PUSH**.
WELL, WE'VE STILL GOT OUR **MAIN ADVANTAGE**, RIGHT? THERE'S NOBODY YOU CAN COUNT ON LIKE DUKE WHEN THE CHIPS ARE DOWN AND YOUR BACK'S **AGAINST THE WALL**.
I GOTTA SAY, THIS TAKES A LITTLE GETTING USED TO...
...COMING FROM A PLACE WHERE **NOBODY** BELIEVED IN ME TO A WORLD WHERE **EVERYBODY** KINDA DOES.
YOU LIKE IT?
I **LOVE** IT...
...YOU GUYS MAKE ME FEEL LIKE I'M **TWENTY-FIVE** AGAIN.

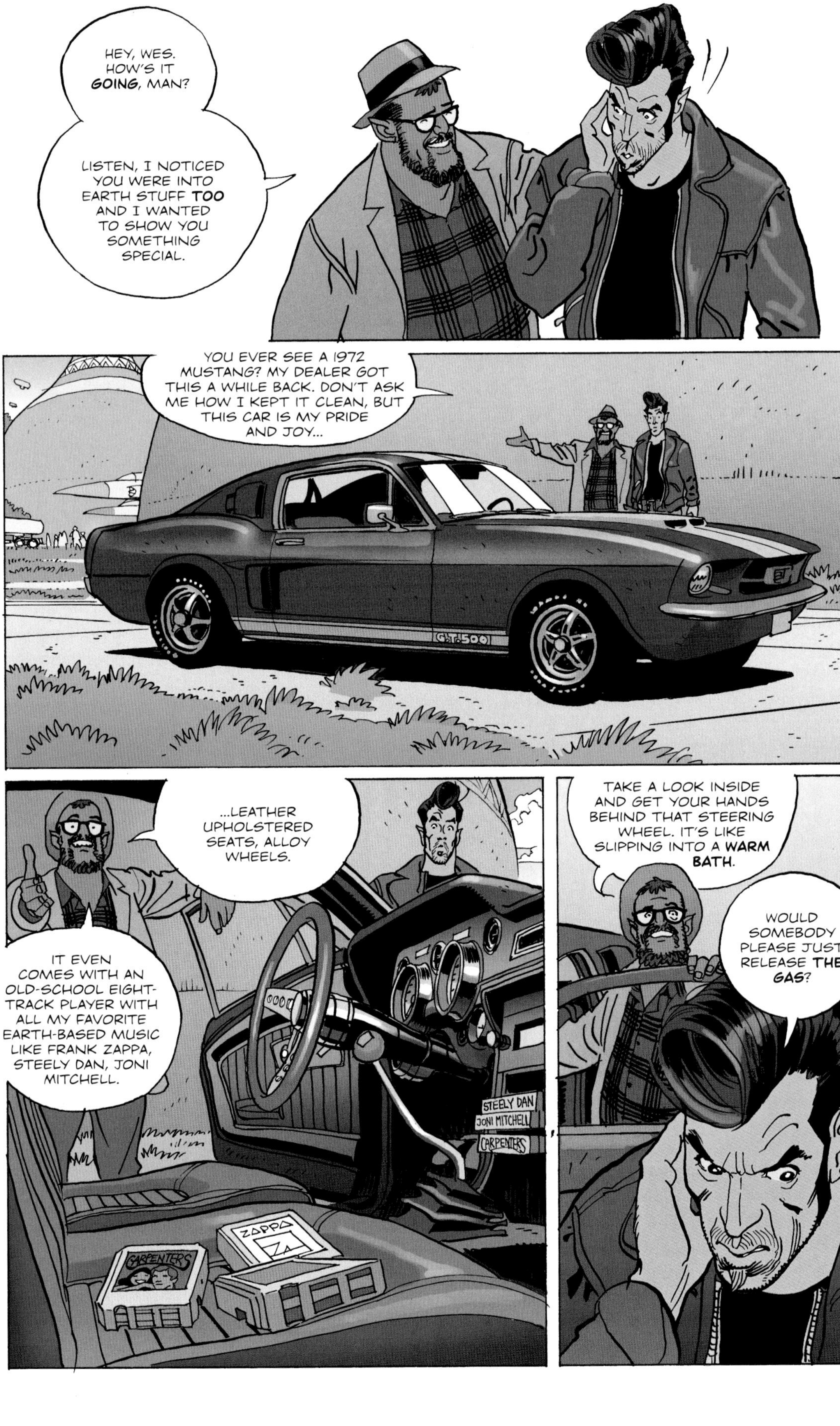
HEY, WES. HOW'S IT **GOING**, MAN?
LISTEN, I NOTICED YOU WERE INTO EARTH STUFF **TOO** AND I WANTED TO SHOW YOU SOMETHING SPECIAL.
YOU EVER SEE A 1972 MUSTANG? MY DEALER GOT THIS A WHILE BACK. DON'T ASK ME HOW I KEPT IT CLEAN, BUT THIS CAR IS MY PRIDE AND JOY...
G.T. 500
...LEATHER UPHOLSTERED SEATS, ALLOY WHEELS.
IT EVEN COMES WITH AN OLD-SCHOOL EIGHT-TRACK PLAYER WITH ALL MY FAVORITE EARTH-BASED MUSIC LIKE FRANK ZAPPA, STEELY DAN, JONI MITCHELL.
STEELY DAN
JONI MITCHELL
CARPENTERS
ZAPPA
CARPENTERS
TAKE A LOOK INSIDE AND GET YOUR HANDS BEHIND THAT STEERING WHEEL. IT'S LIKE SLIPPING INTO A **WARM BATH**.
WOULD SOMEBODY PLEASE JUST RELEASE **THE GAS**?

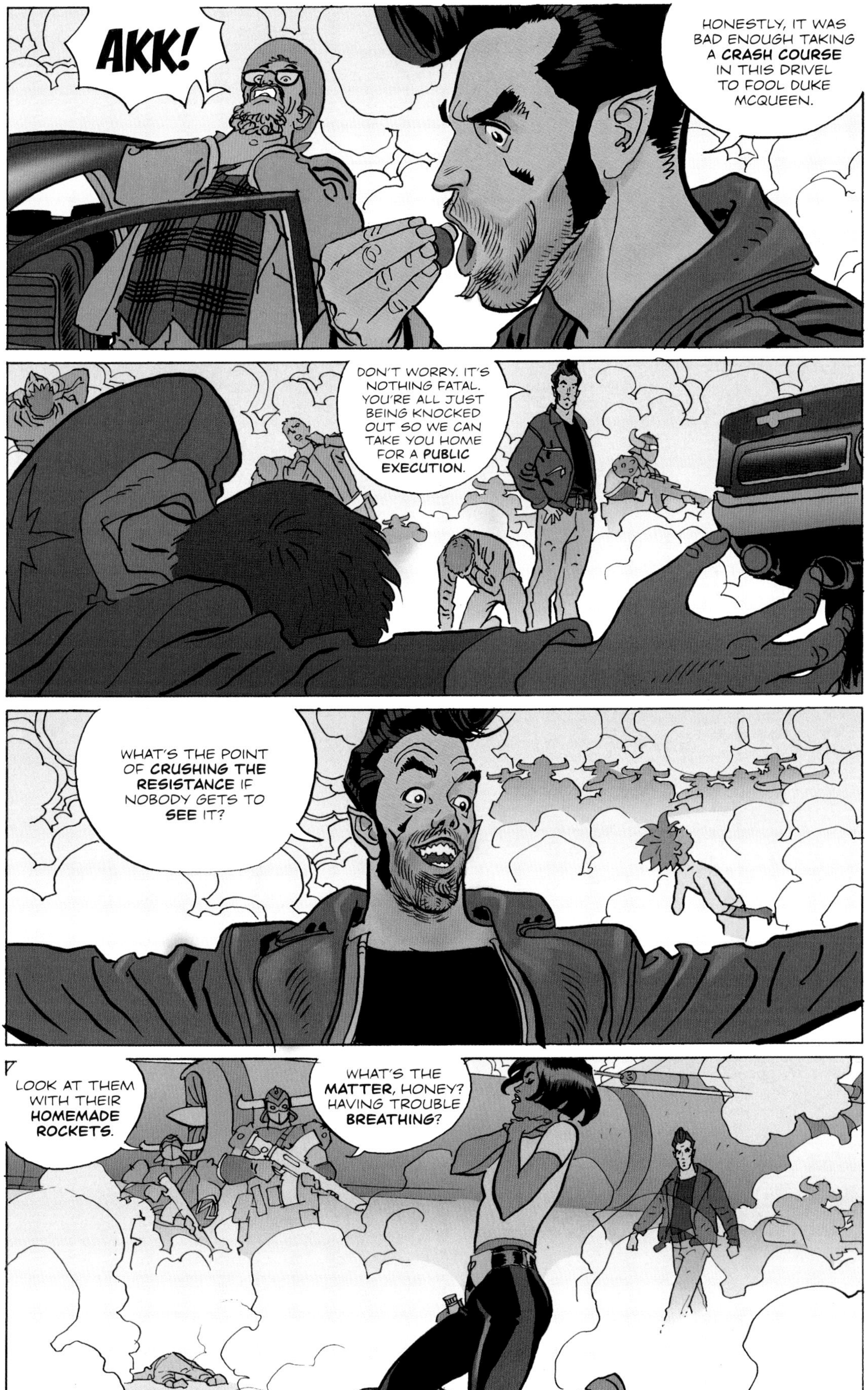
AKK!
HONESTLY, IT WAS BAD ENOUGH TAKING A CRASH COURSE IN THIS DRIVEL TO FOOL DUKE McQUEEN.
DON'T WORRY. IT'S NOTHING FATAL. YOU'RE ALL JUST BEING KNOCKED OUT SO WE CAN TAKE YOU HOME FOR A PUBLIC EXECUTION.
WHAT'S THE POINT OF CRUSHING THE RESISTANCE IF NOBODY GETS TO SEE IT?
LOOK AT THEM WITH THEIR HOMEMADE ROCKETS.
WHAT'S THE MATTER, HONEY? HAVING TROUBLE BREATHING?

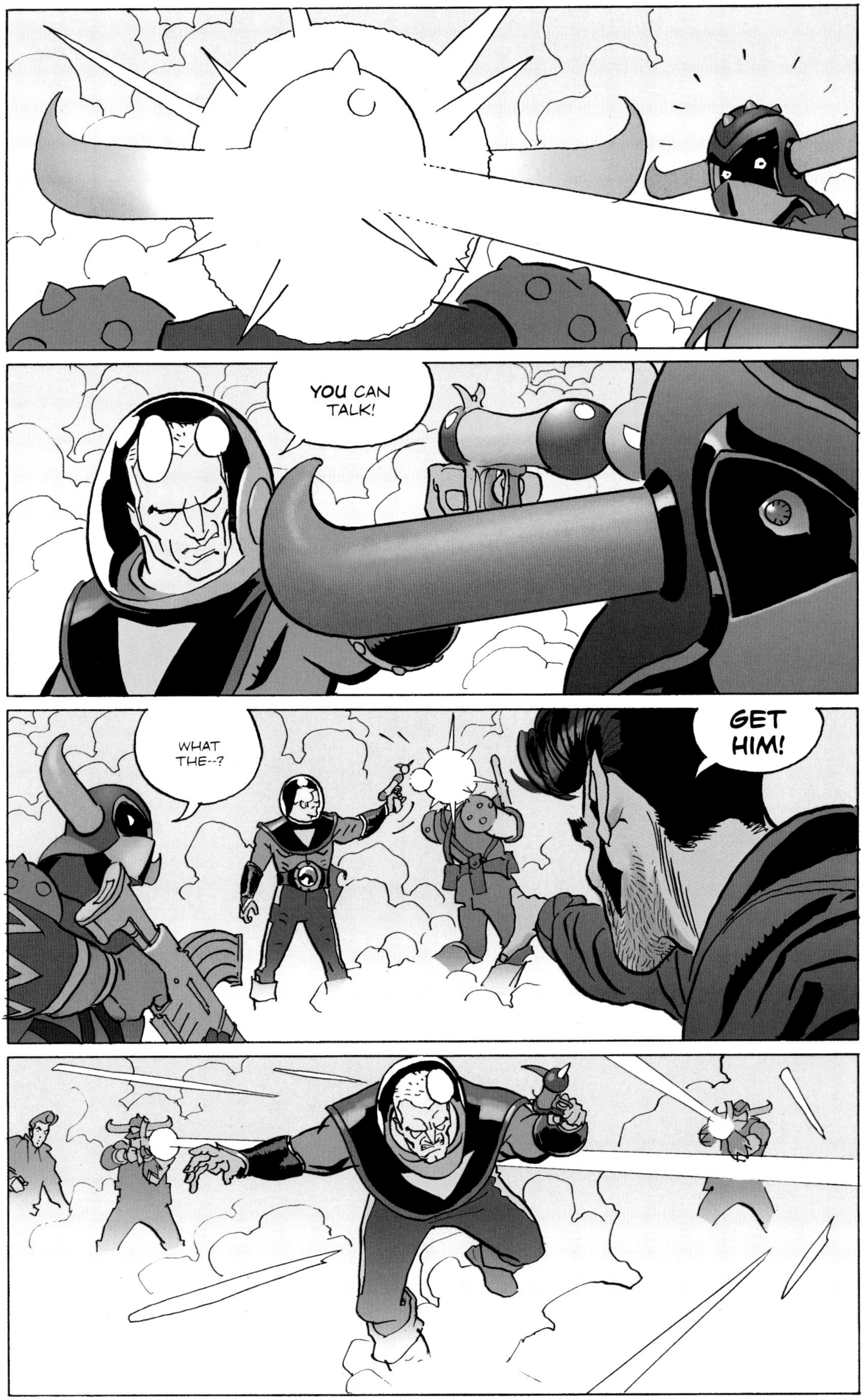
YOU CAN TALK!
WHAT THE--?
GET HIM!

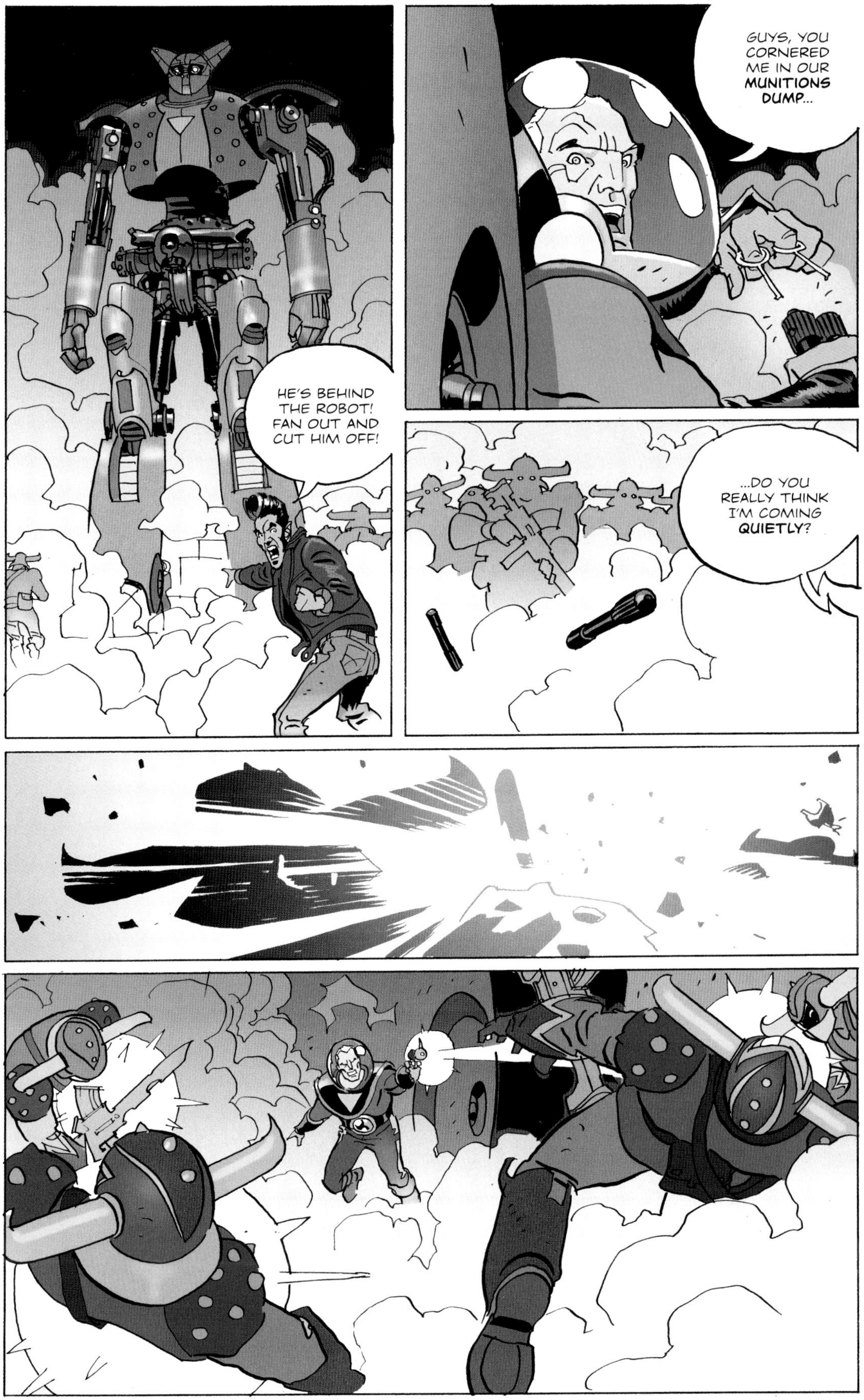
HE'S BEHIND THE ROBOT! FAN OUT AND CUT HIM OFF!
GUYS, YOU CORNERED ME IN OUR **MUNITIONS DUMP**...
...DO YOU REALLY THINK I'M COMING **QUIETLY**?

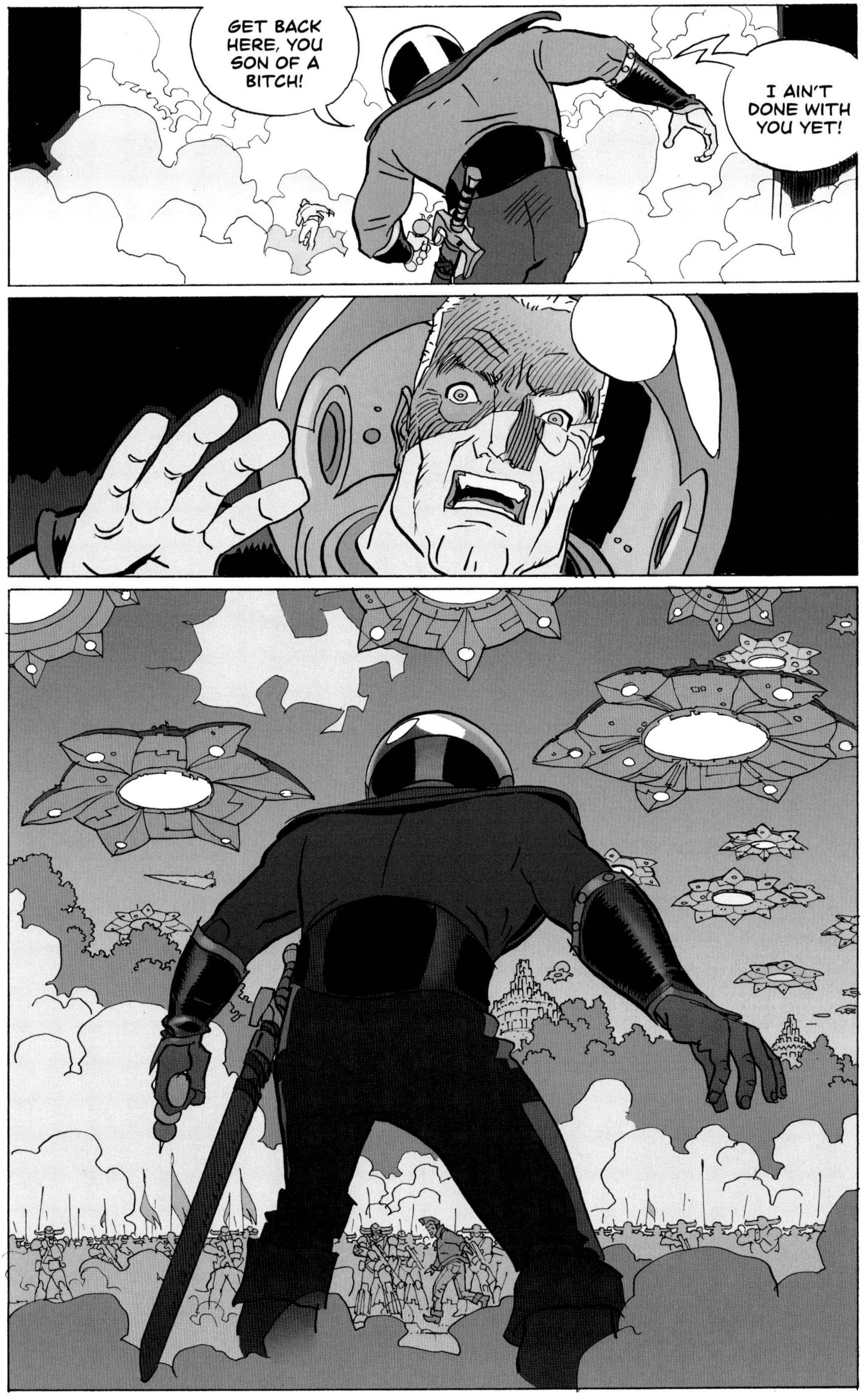
GET BACK HERE, YOU SON OF A BITCH!
I AIN'T DONE WITH YOU YET!

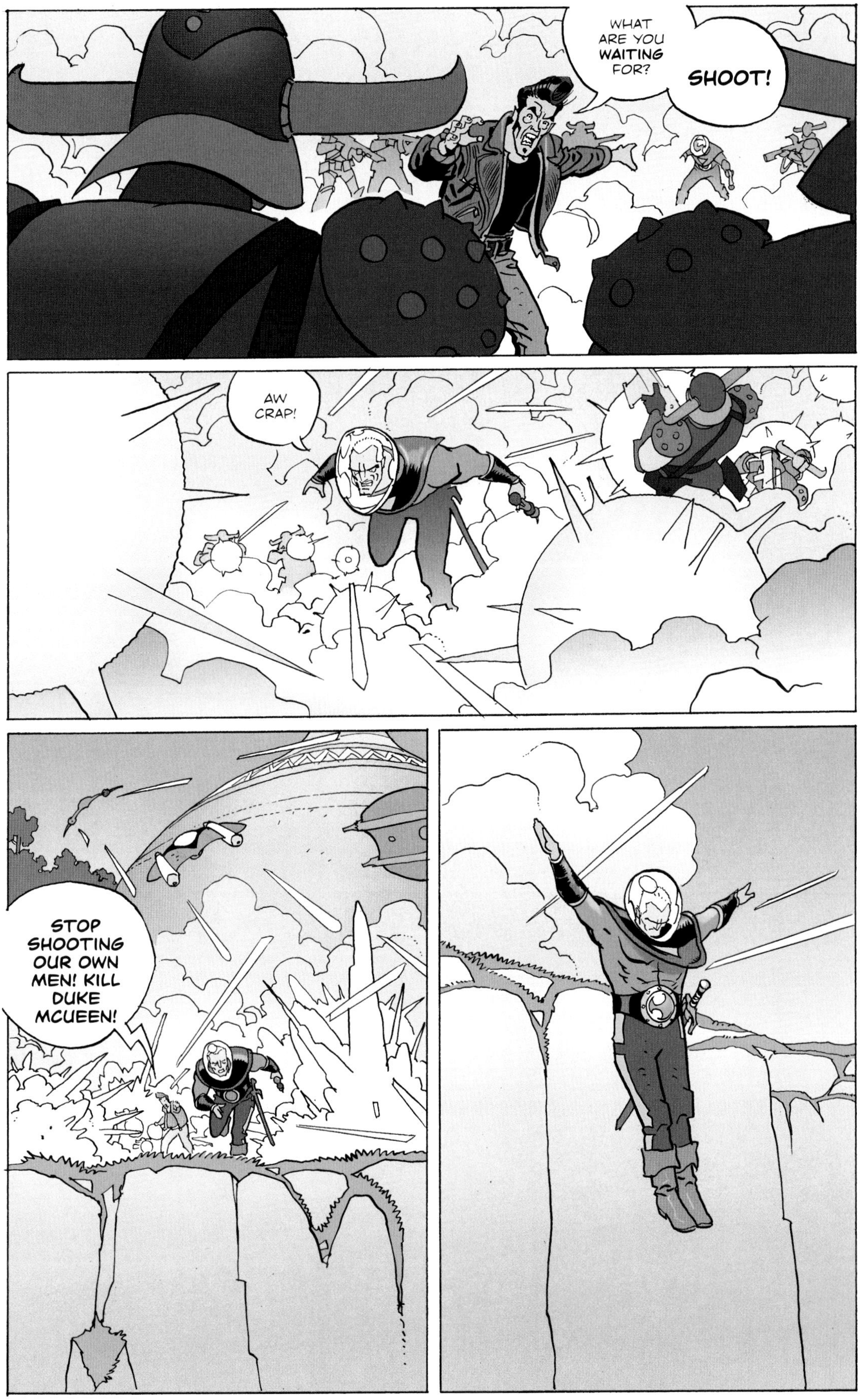
WHAT ARE YOU WAITING FOR?
SHOOT!
AW CRAP!
STOP SHOOTING OUR OWN MEN! KILL DUKE MCUEEN!

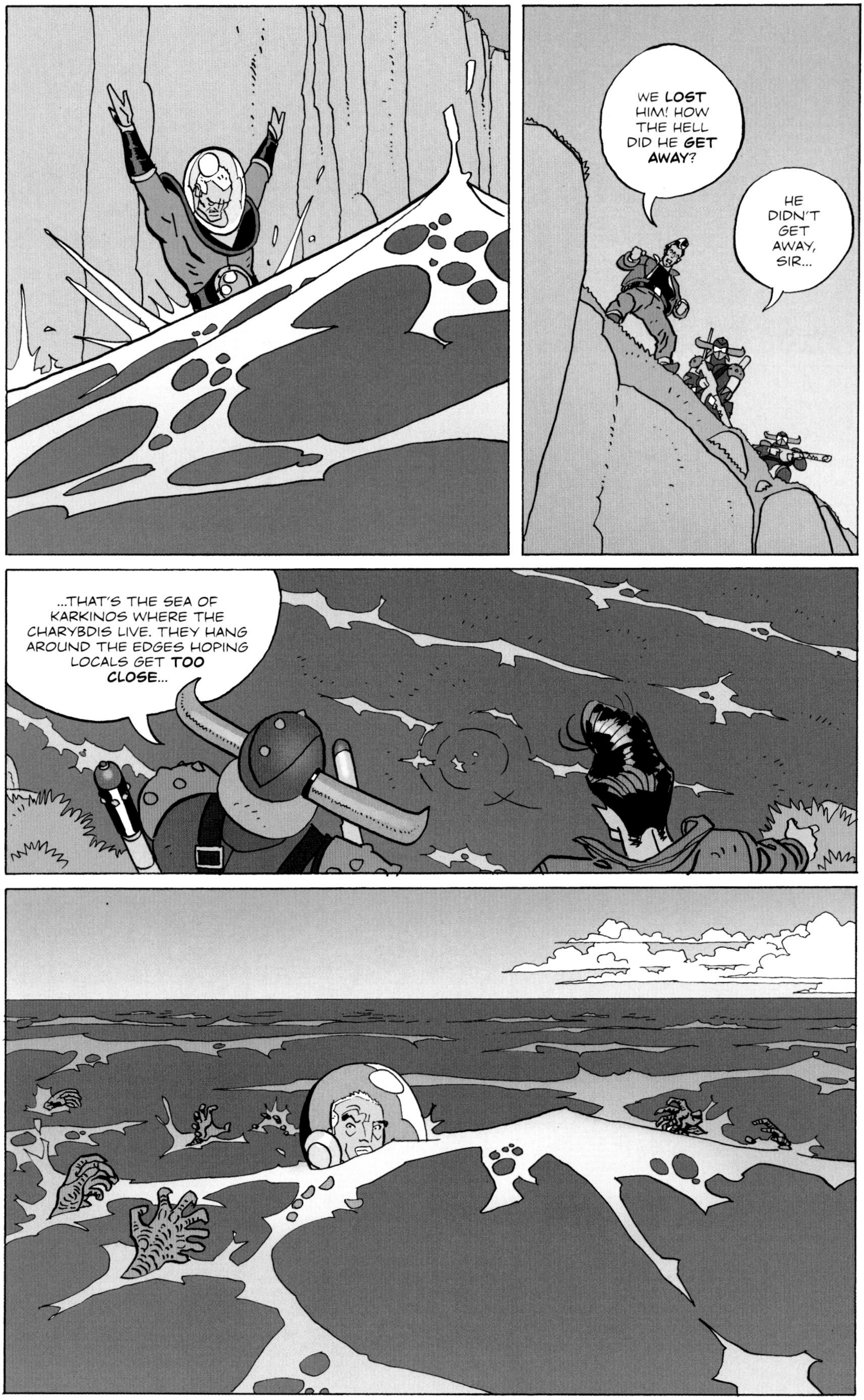
WE LOST HIM! HOW THE HELL DID HE GET AWAY?
HE DIDN'T GET AWAY, SIR...
...THAT'S THE SEA OF KARKINOS WHERE THE CHARYBDIS LIVE. THEY HANG AROUND THE EDGES HOPING LOCALS GET TOO CLOSE...

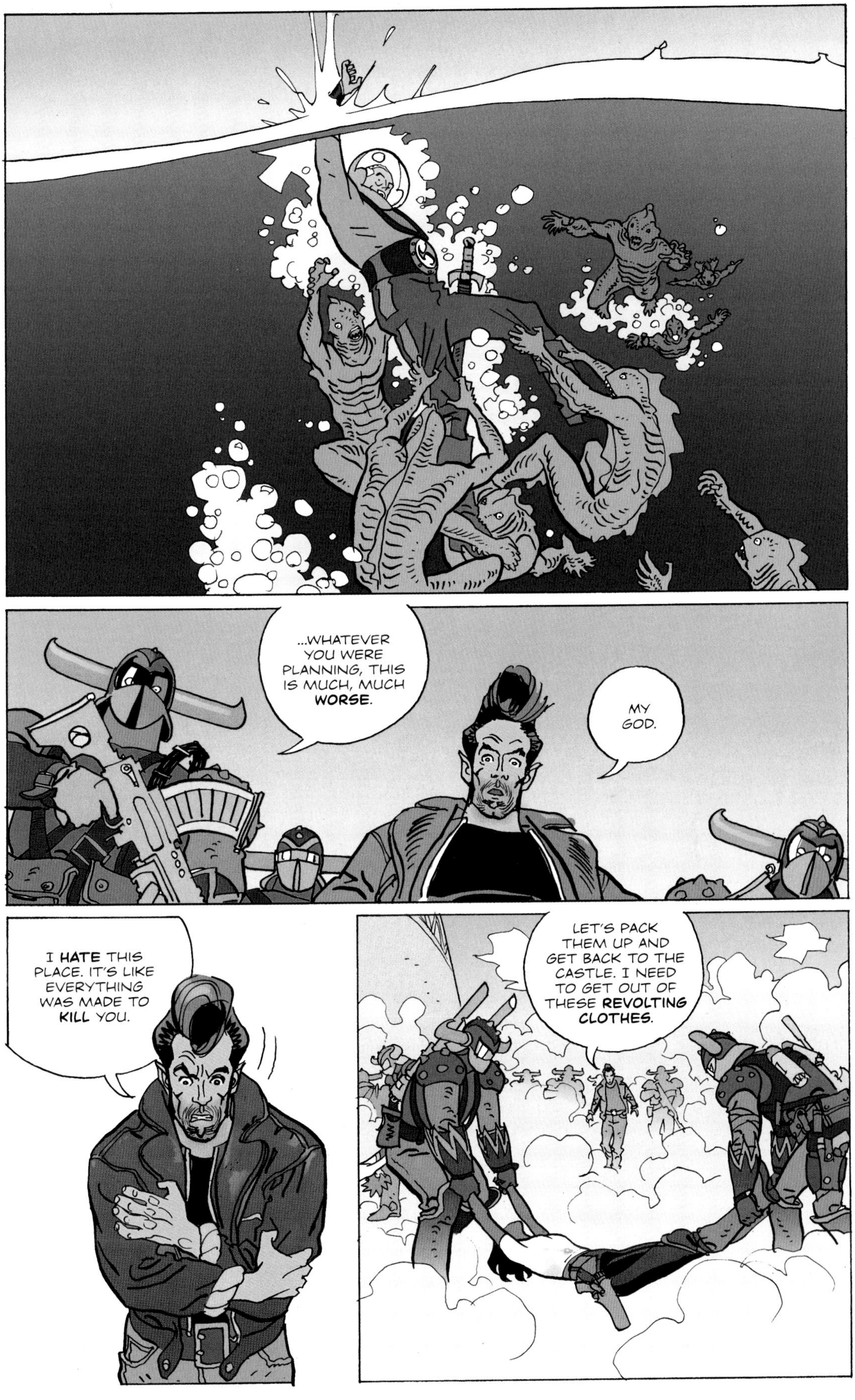
...WHATEVER YOU WERE PLANNING, THIS IS MUCH, MUCH **WORSE**.
MY GOD.
I **HATE** THIS PLACE. IT'S LIKE EVERYTHING WAS MADE TO **KILL** YOU.
LET'S PACK THEM UP AND GET BACK TO THE CASTLE. I NEED TO GET OUT OF THESE **REVOLTING CLOTHES**.

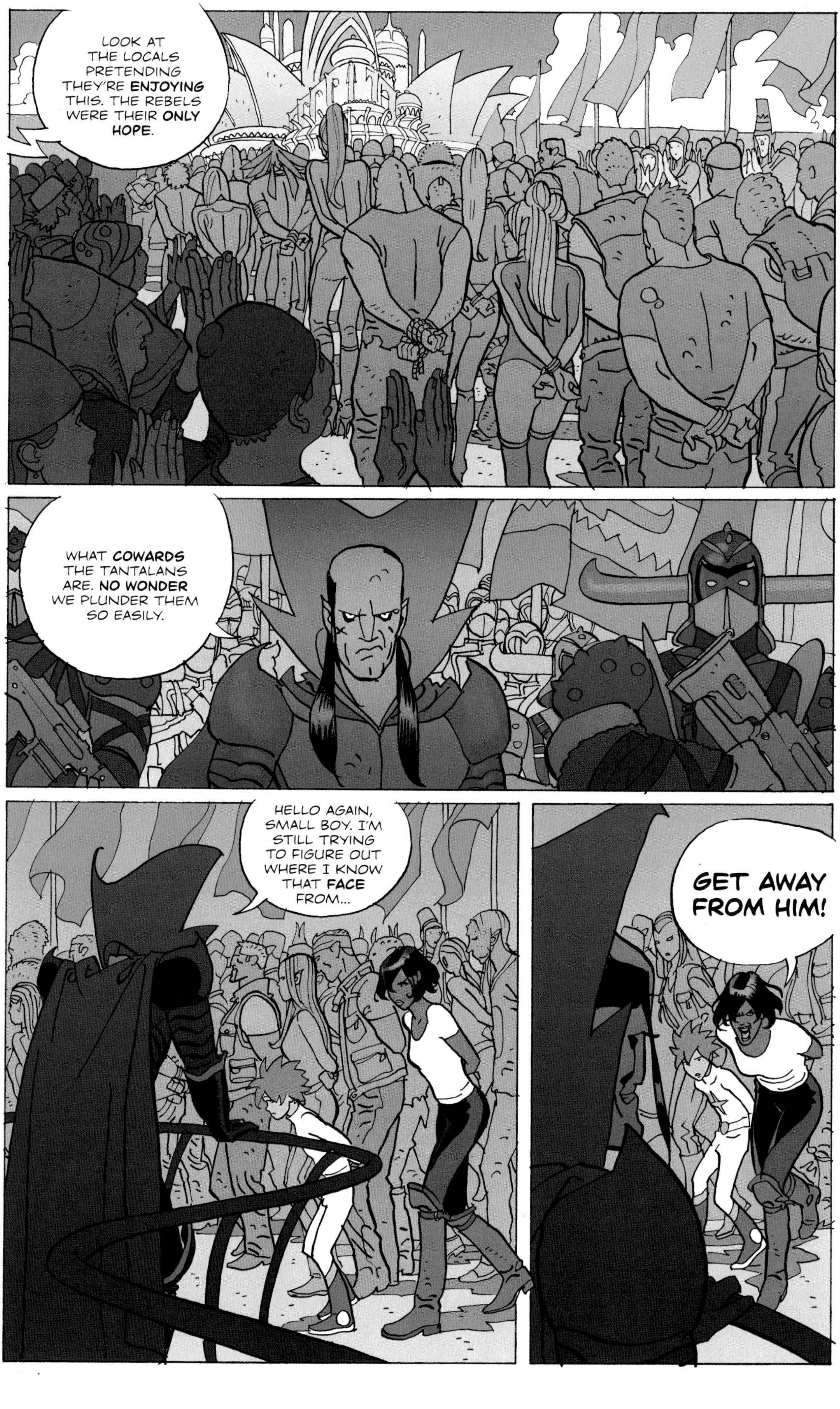
LOOK AT THE LOCALS PRETENDING THEY'RE ENJOYING THIS. THE REBELS WERE THEIR ONLY HOPE.
WHAT COWARDS THE TANTALANS ARE. NO WONDER WE PLUNDER THEM SO EASILY.
HELLO AGAIN, SMALL BOY. I'M STILL TRYING TO FIGURE OUT WHERE I KNOW THAT FACE FROM...
GET AWAY FROM HIM!

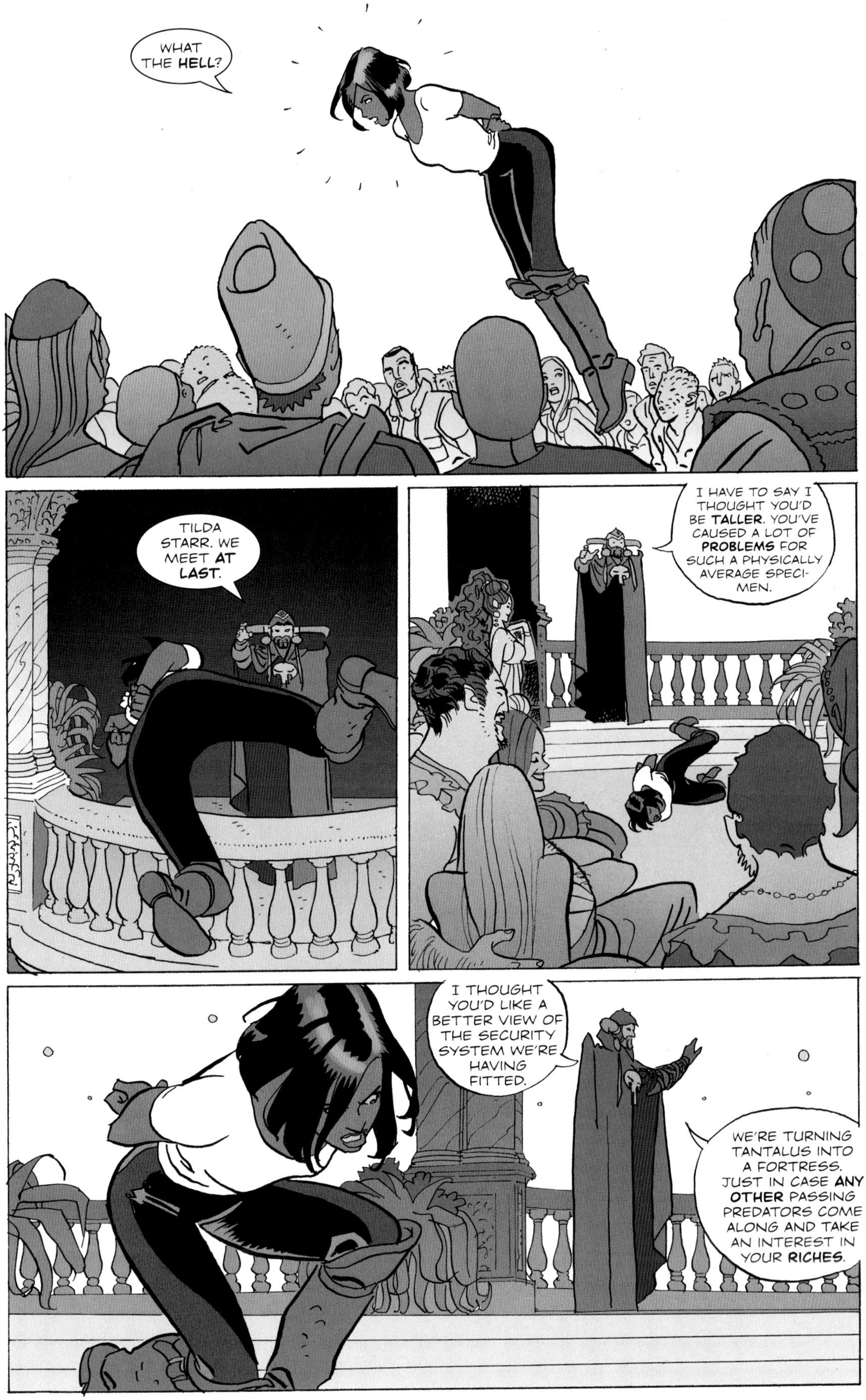
WHAT THE HELL?
TILDA STARR. WE MEET AT LAST.
I HAVE TO SAY I THOUGHT YOU'D BE TALLER. YOU'VE CAUSED A LOT OF PROBLEMS FOR SUCH A PHYSICALLY AVERAGE SPECI- MEN.
I THOUGHT YOU'D LIKE A BETTER VIEW OF THE SECURITY SYSTEM WE'RE HAVING FITTED.
WE'RE TURNING TANTALUS INTO A FORTRESS. JUST IN CASE ANY OTHER PASSING PREDATORS COME ALONG AND TAKE AN INTEREST IN YOUR RICHES.

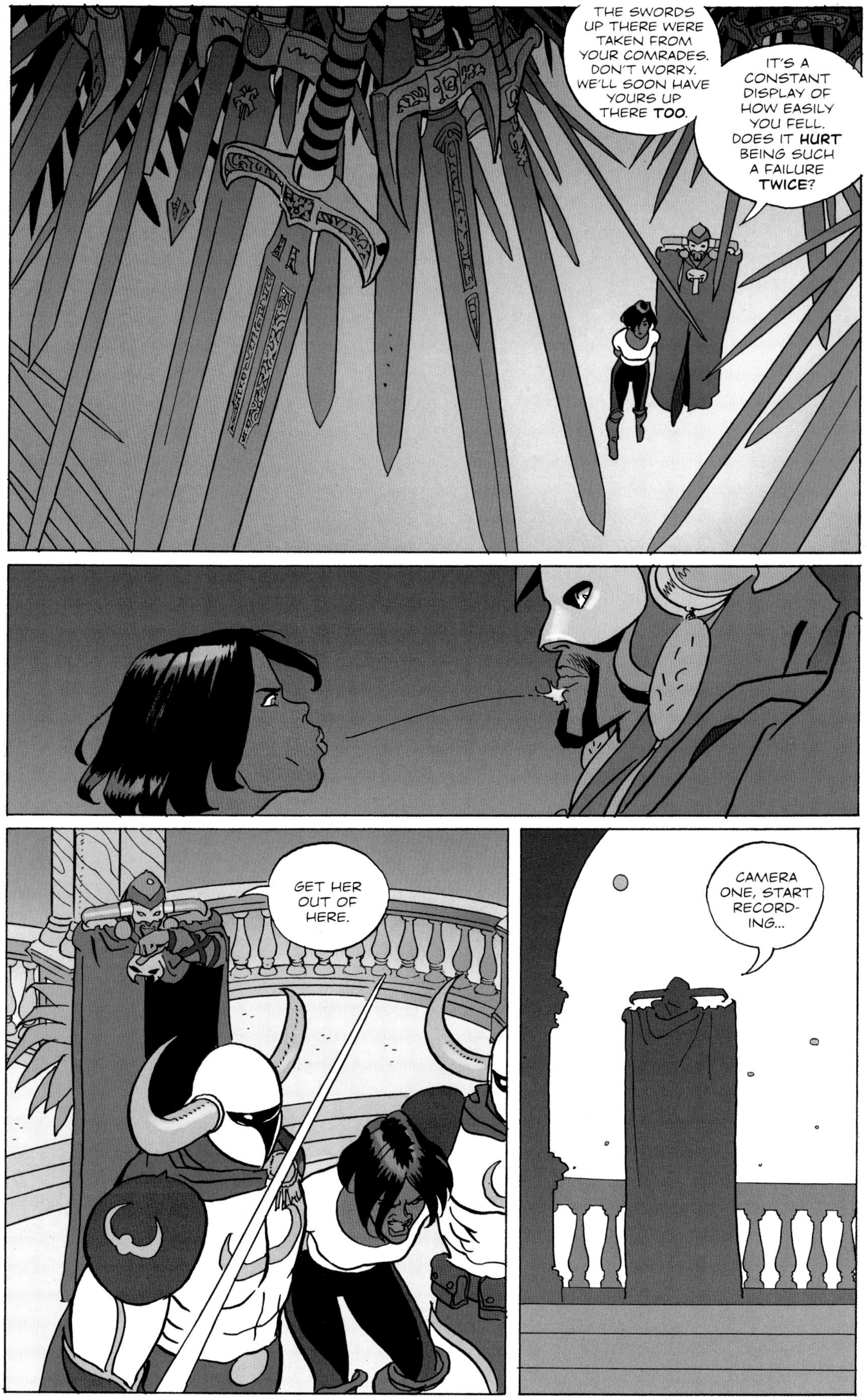
THE SWORDS UP THERE WERE TAKEN FROM YOUR COMRADES. DON'T WORRY. WE'LL SOON HAVE YOURS UP THERE **TOO**.
IT'S A CONSTANT DISPLAY OF HOW EASILY YOU FELL. DOES IT **HURT** BEING SUCH A FAILURE **TWICE**?
GET HER OUT OF HERE.
CAMERA ONE, START RECORD-ING...

"TILDA STARR HAS BEEN **DEFEATED** AND HER REBEL ARMY **CAPTURED.**

"THE RESISTANCE IS OVER, ALONG WITH ANY NOTION THAT OUR ABSOLUTE RULE IS ANYTHING BUT **INEVITABLE** NOW.

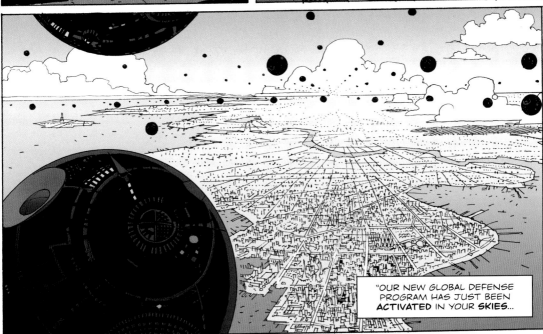

"OUR NEW GLOBAL DEFENSE PROGRAM HAS JUST BEEN **ACTIVATED** IN YOUR **SKIES**...

"...YOUR NEW WORKING DAY WILL NOW BE **THREE HOURS** LONGER.

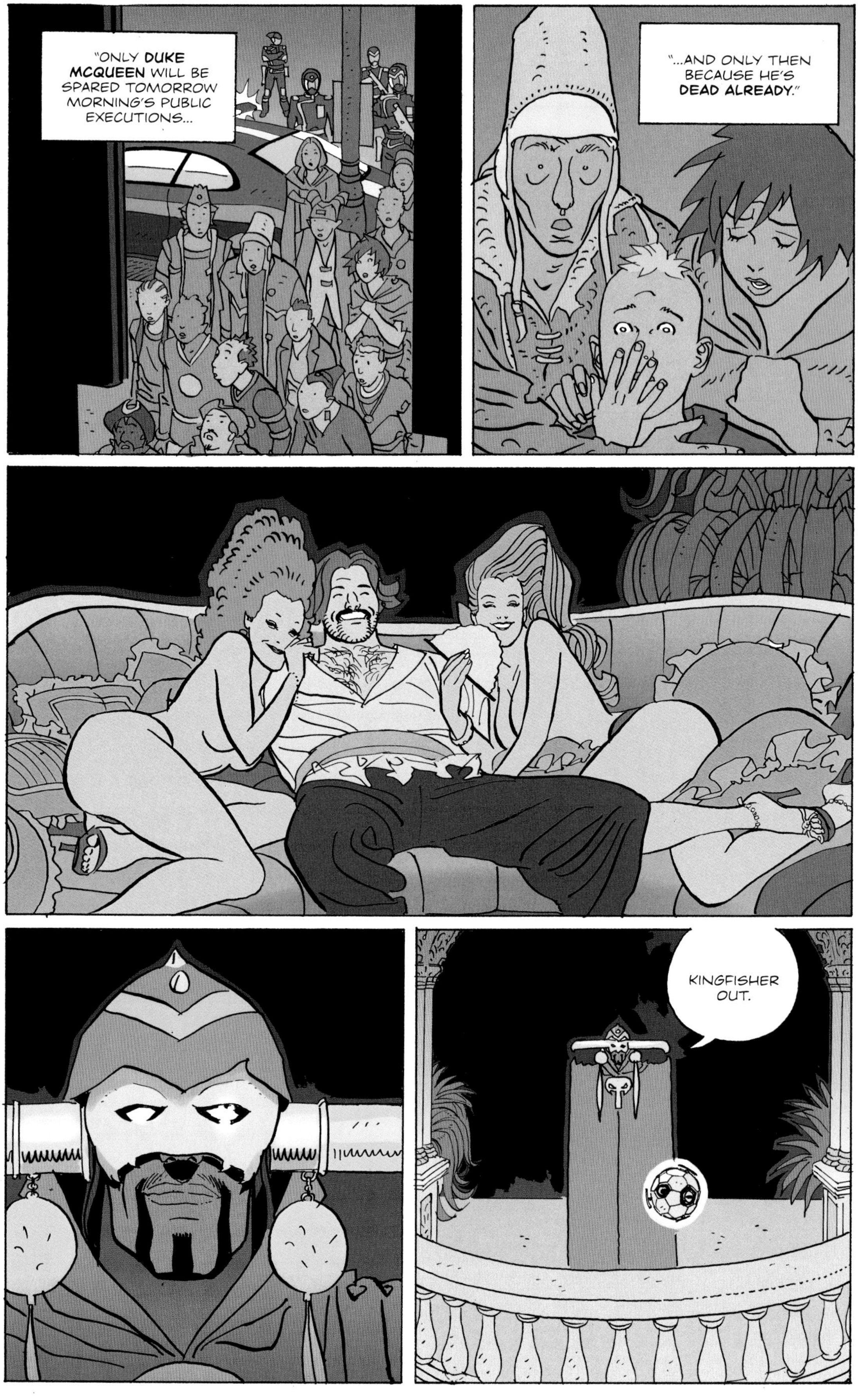
"ONLY **DUKE MCQUEEN** WILL BE SPARED TOMORROW MORNING'S PUBLIC EXECUTIONS...
"...AND ONLY THEN BECAUSE HE'S **DEAD ALREADY**."
KINGFISHER OUT.

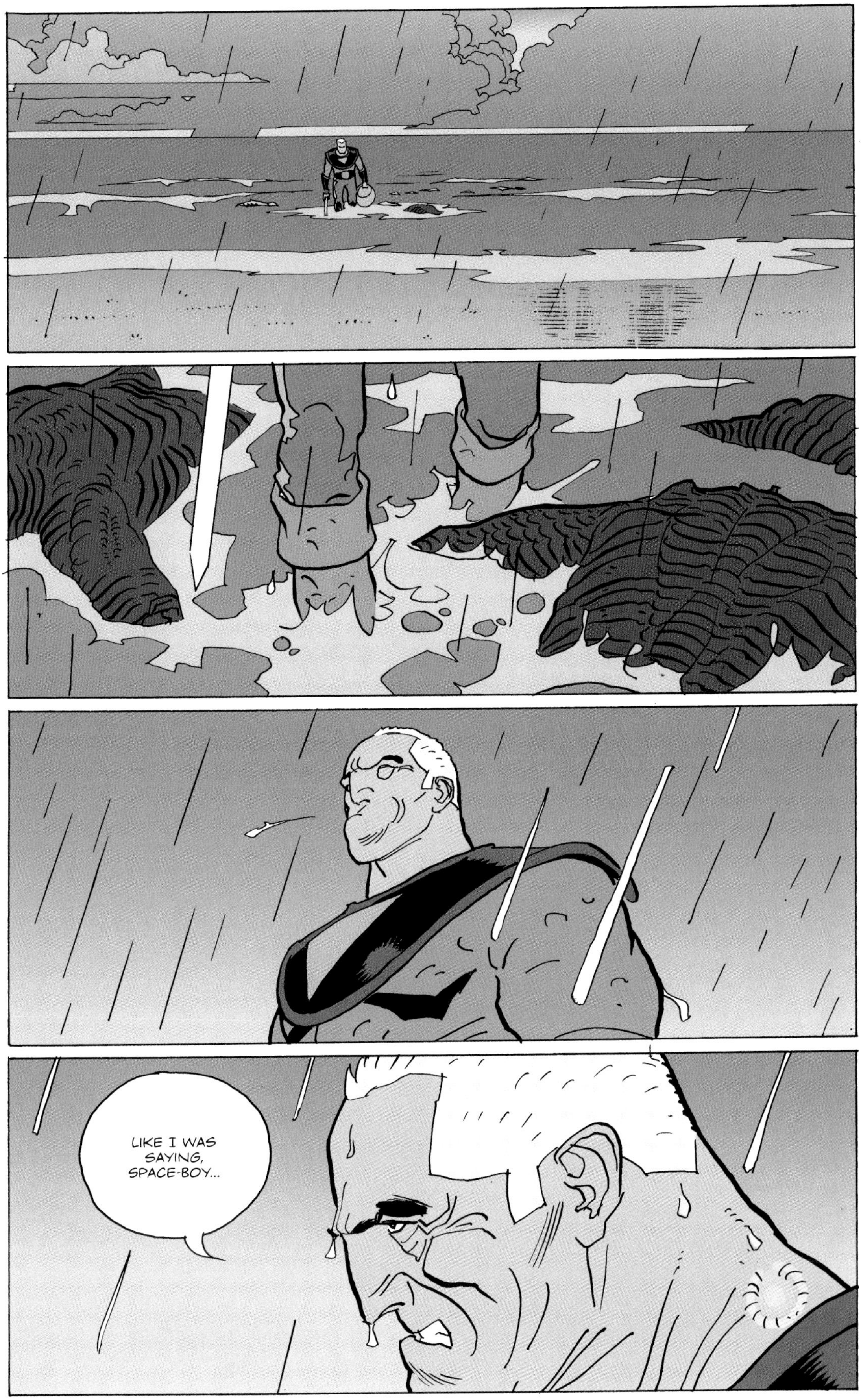
LIKE I WAS SAYING, SPACE-BOY...

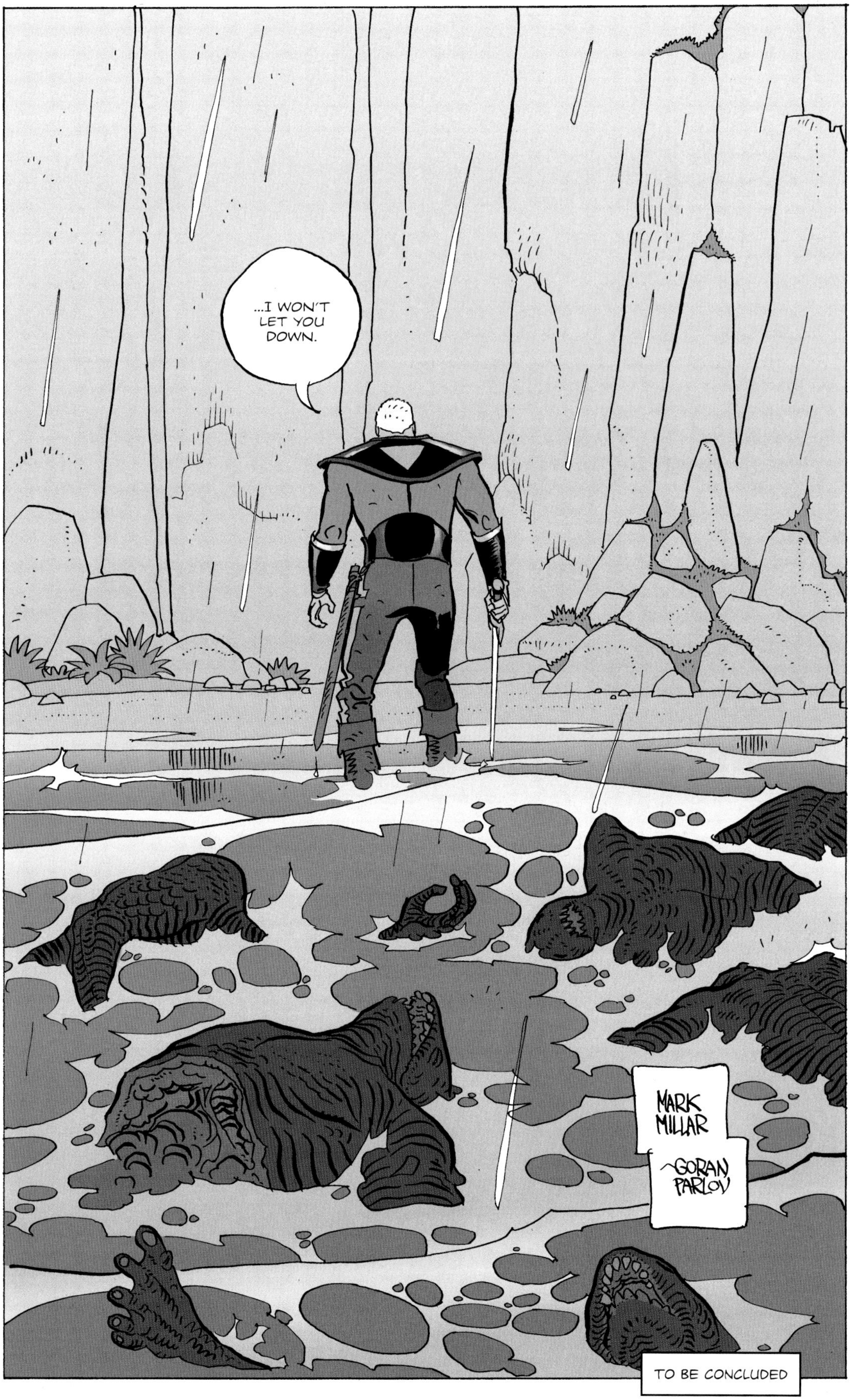
...I WON'T LET YOU DOWN.
MARK MILLAR
GORAN PARLOV
TO BE CONCLUDED

SIX

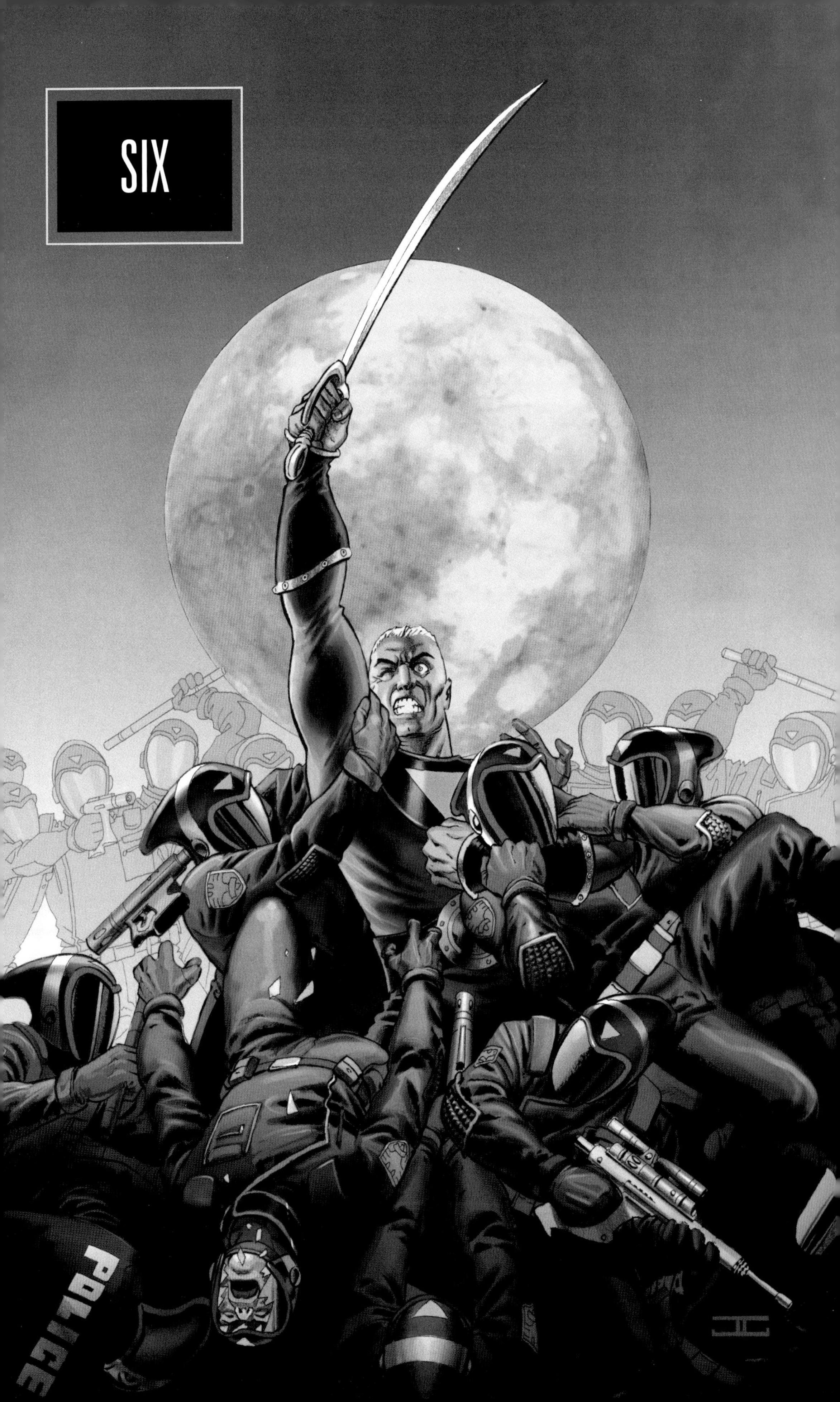
POLICE

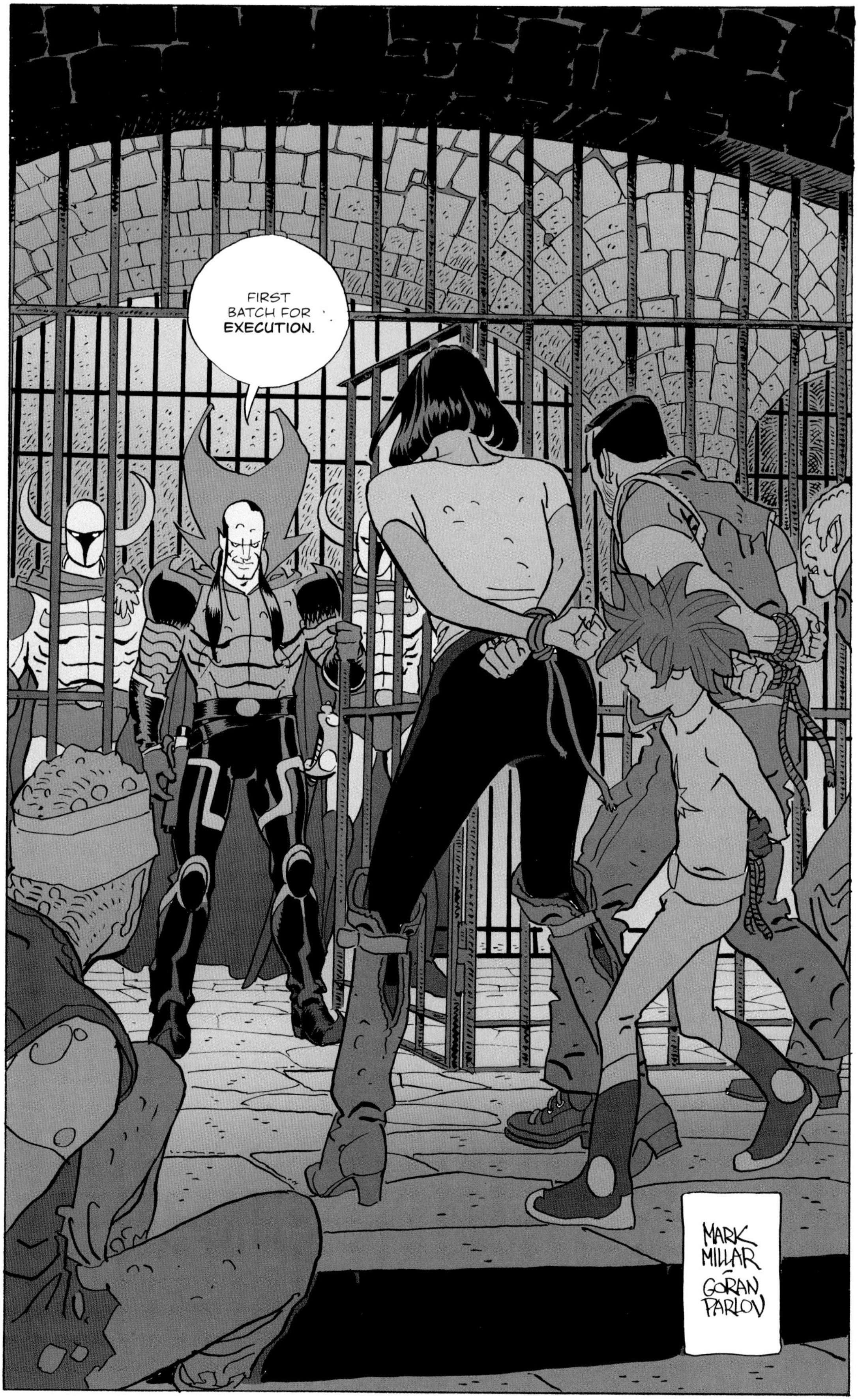
FIRST BATCH FOR EXECUTION.
MARK MILLAR
GORAN PARLOV

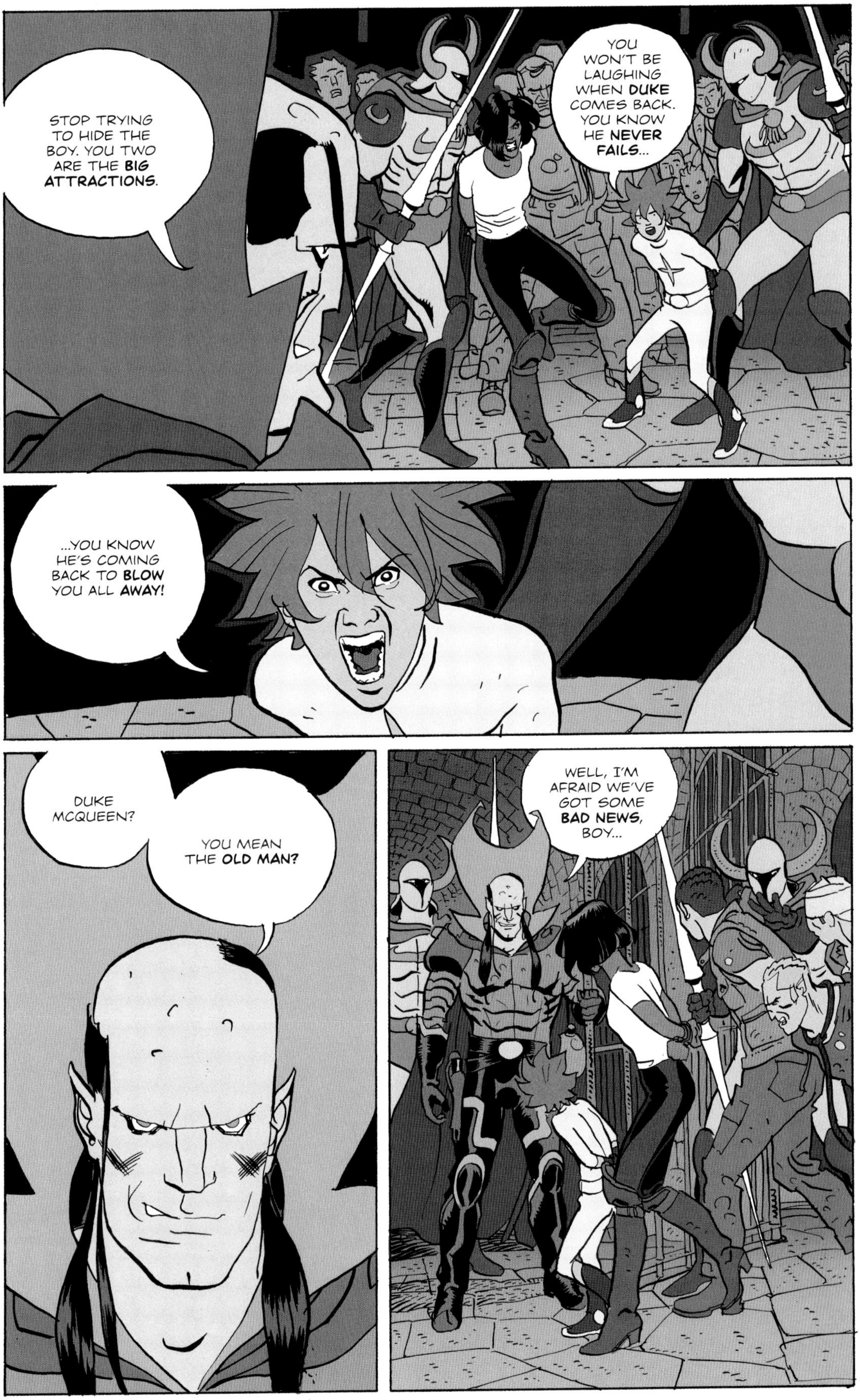
STOP TRYING TO HIDE THE BOY. YOU TWO ARE THE **BIG ATTRACTIONS**.
YOU WON'T BE LAUGHING WHEN **DUKE** COMES BACK. YOU KNOW HE **NEVER FAILS**...
...YOU KNOW HE'S COMING BACK TO **BLOW** YOU ALL **AWAY!**
DUKE MCQUEEN?
YOU MEAN THE **OLD MAN?**
WELL, I'M AFRAID WE'VE GOT SOME **BAD NEWS**, BOY...

THE PIT OF THE VANQUISHED.

THIS IS THE HOLE WHERE THEY DUMP **THE OPPOSITION**.

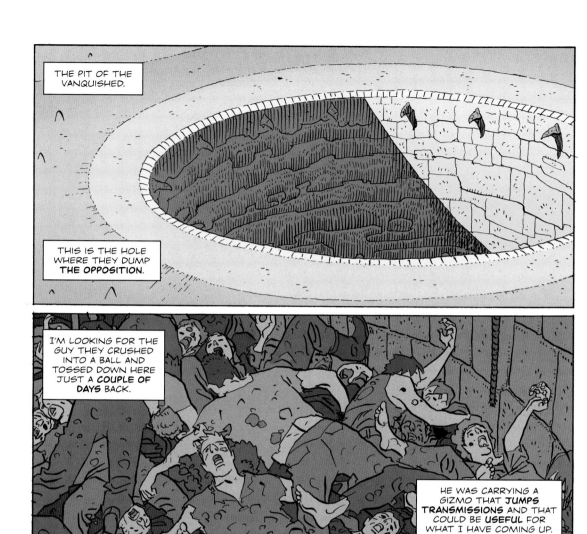

I'M LOOKING FOR THE GUY THEY CRUSHED INTO A BALL AND TOSSED DOWN HERE JUST A **COUPLE OF DAYS** BACK.

HE WAS CARRYING A GIZMO THAT **JUMPS TRANSMISSIONS** AND THAT COULD BE **USEFUL** FOR WHAT I HAVE COMING UP.

GOT IT!

HEY! WHAT THE HELL'S **GOING** ON DOWN THERE?

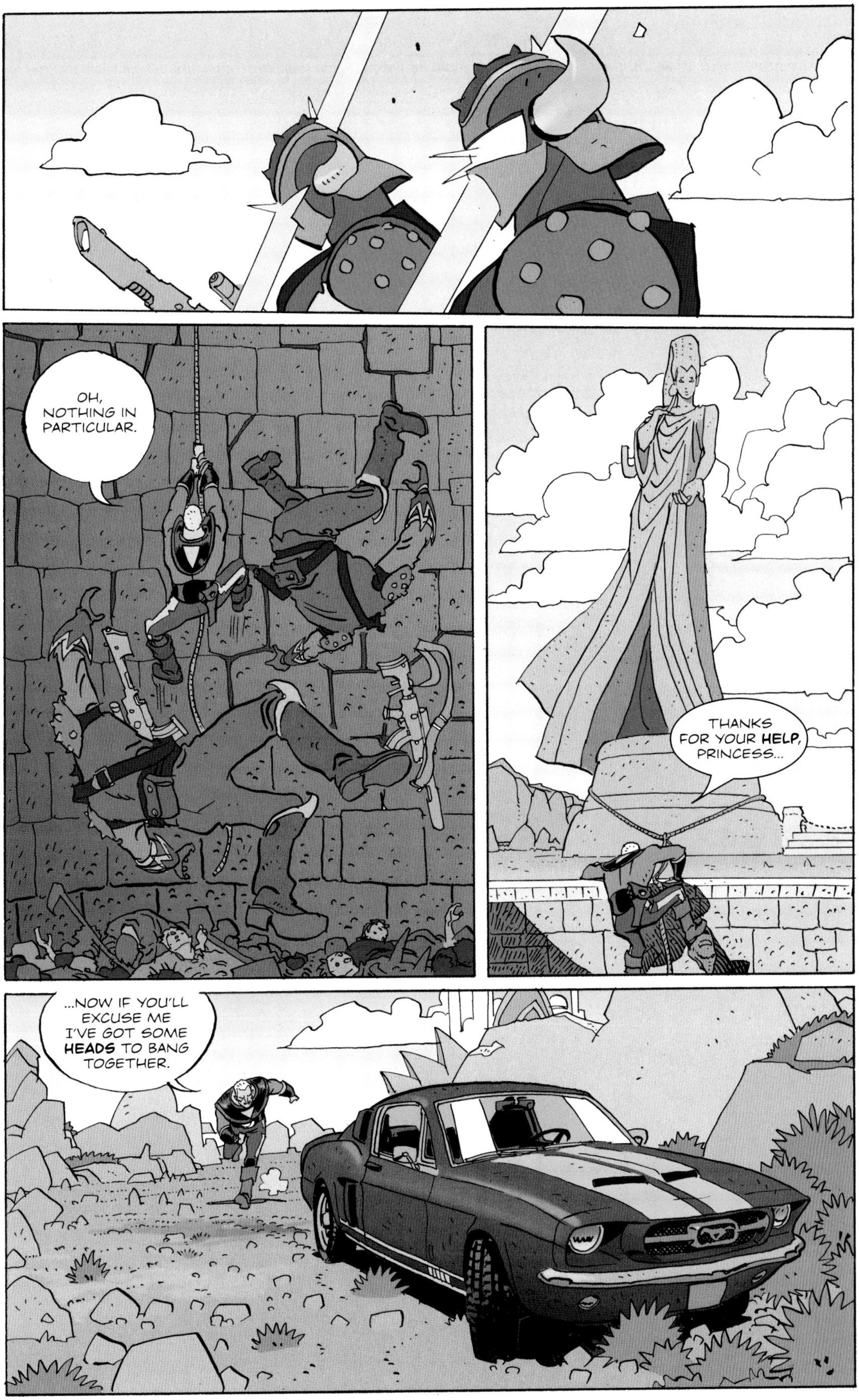
OH, NOTHING IN PARTICULAR.
THANKS FOR YOUR **HELP**, PRINCESS...
...NOW IF YOU'LL EXCUSE ME I'VE GOT SOME **HEADS** TO BANG TOGETHER.

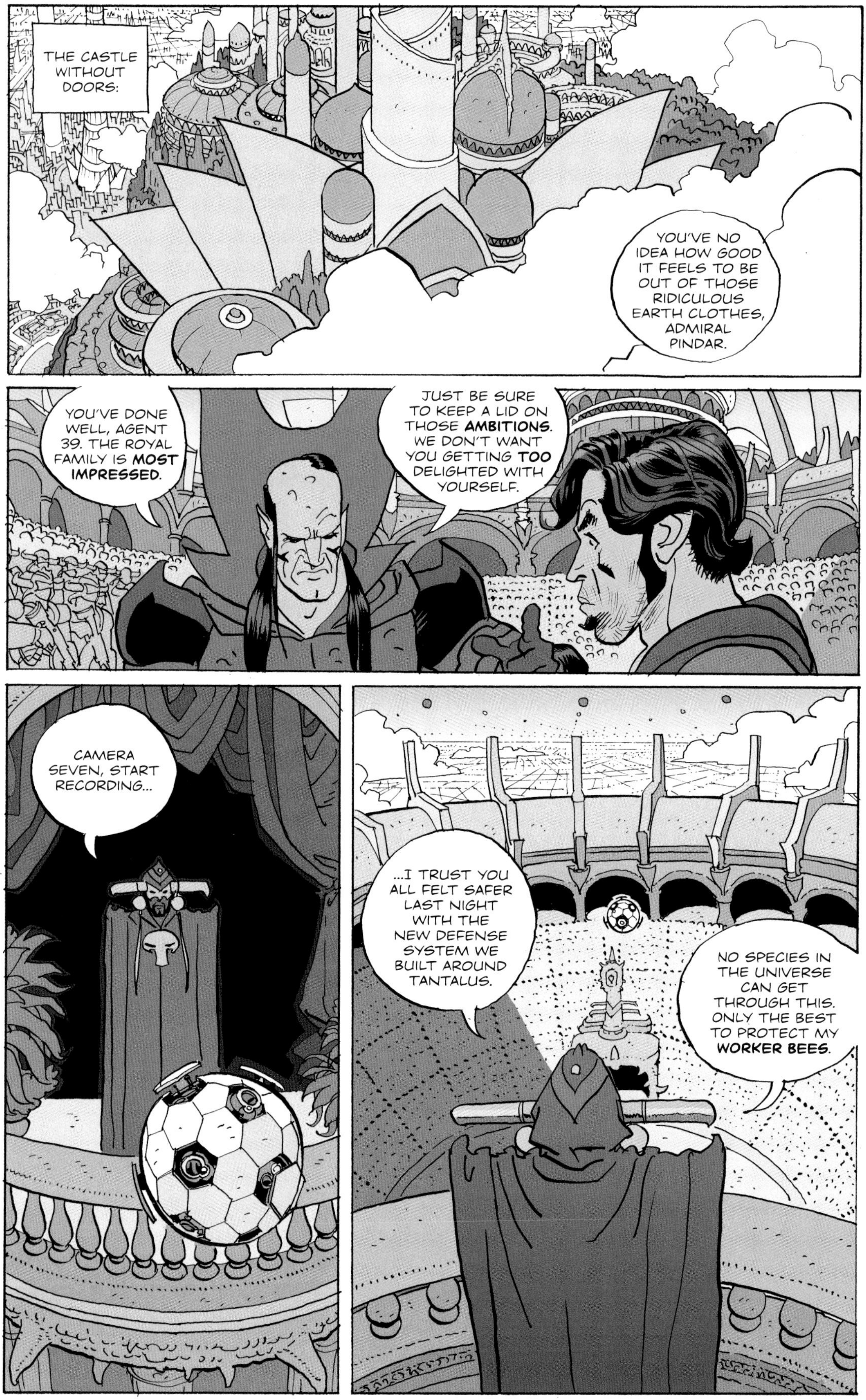
THE CASTLE WITHOUT DOORS:
YOU'VE NO IDEA HOW GOOD IT FEELS TO BE OUT OF THOSE RIDICULOUS EARTH CLOTHES, ADMIRAL PINDAR.
YOU'VE DONE WELL, AGENT 39. THE ROYAL FAMILY IS **MOST IMPRESSED**.
JUST BE SURE TO KEEP A LID ON THOSE **AMBITIONS**. WE DON'T WANT YOU GETTING **TOO** DELIGHTED WITH YOURSELF.
CAMERA SEVEN, START RECORDING...
...I TRUST YOU ALL FELT SAFER LAST NIGHT WITH THE NEW DEFENSE SYSTEM WE BUILT AROUND TANTALUS.
NO SPECIES IN THE UNIVERSE CAN GET THROUGH THIS. ONLY THE BEST TO PROTECT MY **WORKER BEES**.

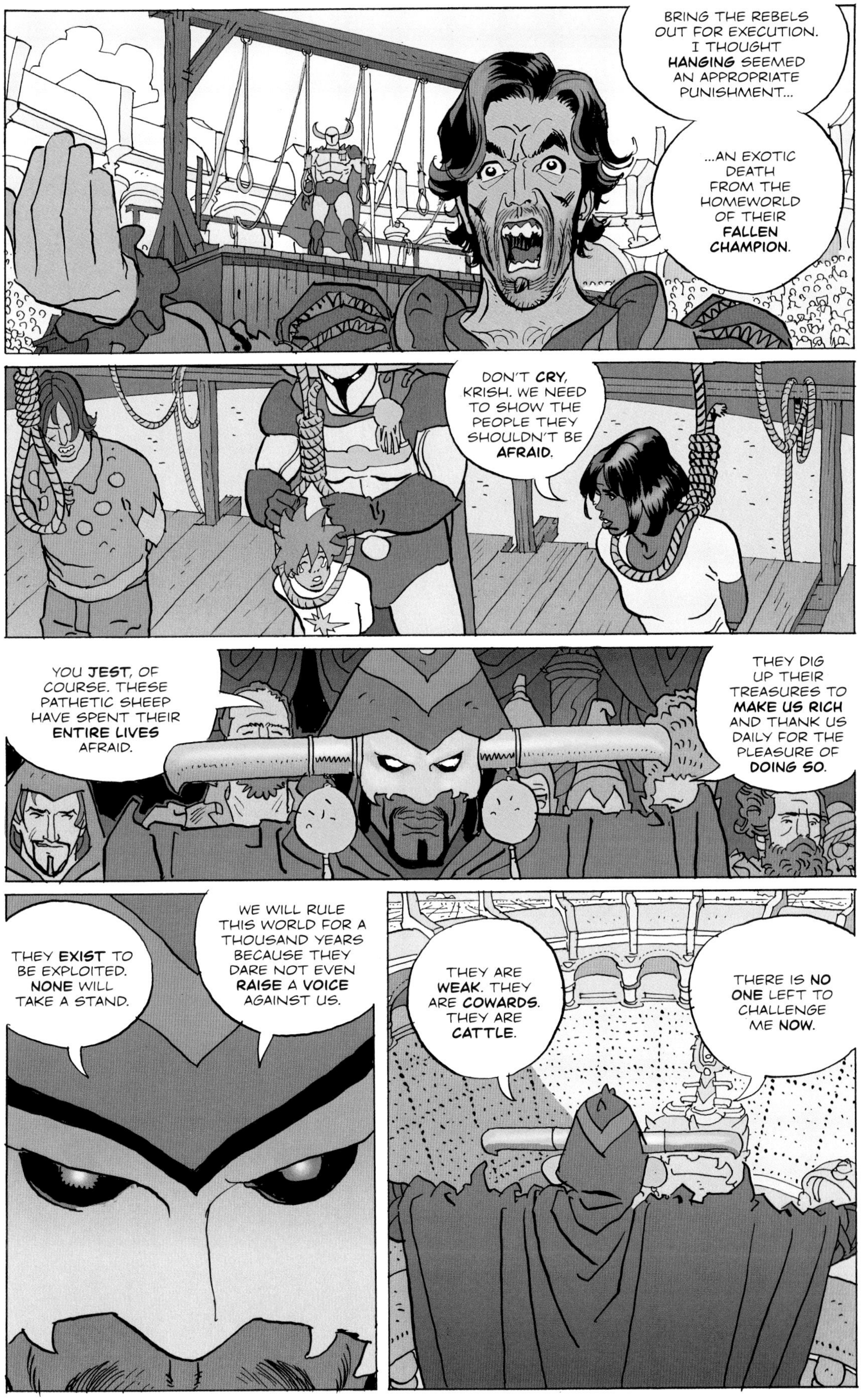
BRING THE REBELS OUT FOR EXECUTION. I THOUGHT HANGING SEEMED AN APPROPRIATE PUNISHMENT...
...AN EXOTIC DEATH FROM THE HOMEWORLD OF THEIR FALLEN CHAMPION.
DON'T CRY, KRISH. WE NEED TO SHOW THE PEOPLE THEY SHOULDN'T BE AFRAID.
YOU JEST, OF COURSE. THESE PATHETIC SHEEP HAVE SPENT THEIR ENTIRE LIVES AFRAID.
THEY DIG UP THEIR TREASURES TO MAKE US RICH AND THANK US DAILY FOR THE PLEASURE OF DOING SO.
THEY EXIST TO BE EXPLOITED. NONE WILL TAKE A STAND.
WE WILL RULE THIS WORLD FOR A THOUSAND YEARS BECAUSE THEY DARE NOT EVEN RAISE A VOICE AGAINST US.
THEY ARE WEAK. THEY ARE COWARDS. THEY ARE CATTLE.
THERE IS NO ONE LEFT TO CHALLENGE ME NOW.

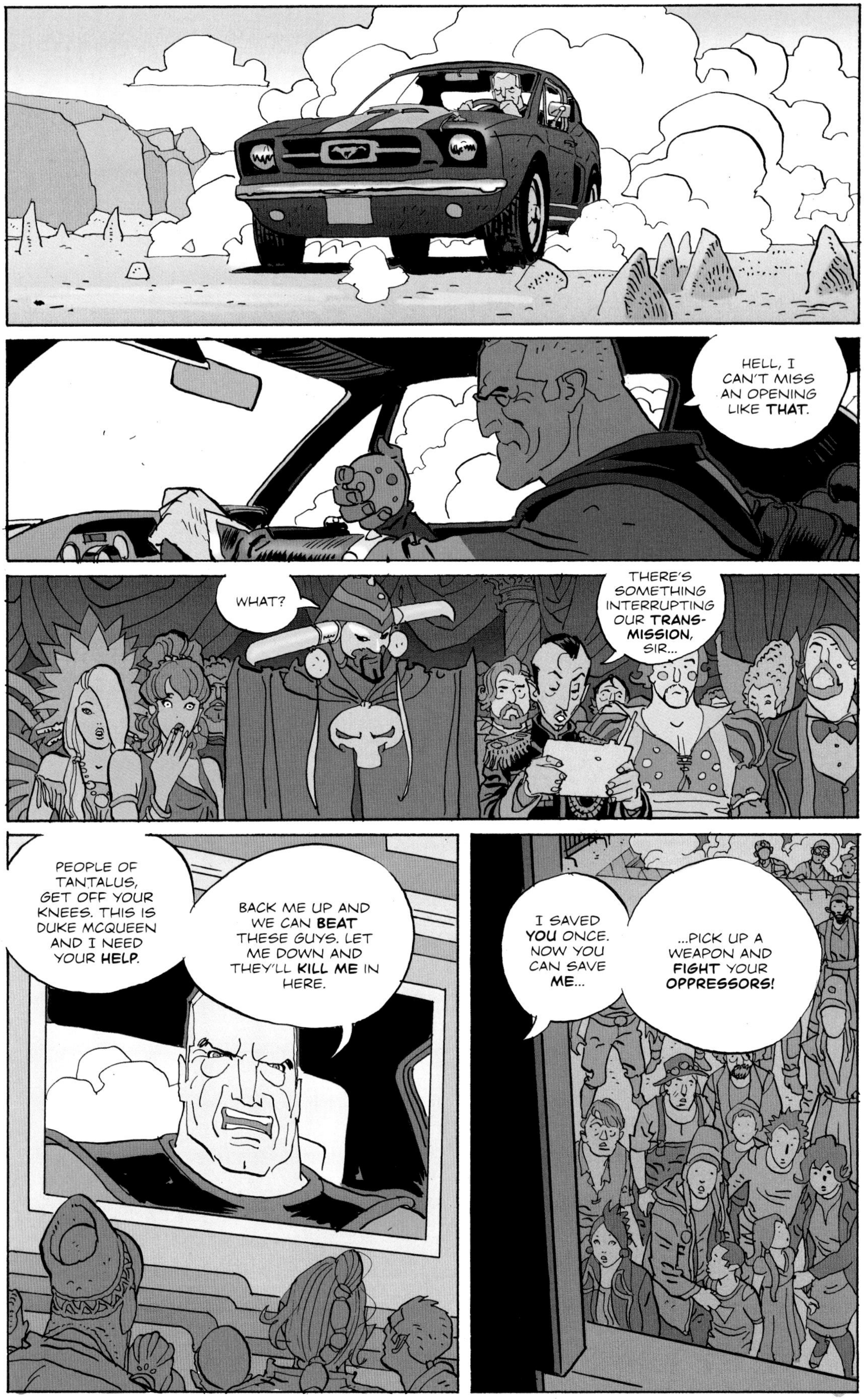
HELL, I CAN'T MISS AN OPENING LIKE **THAT**.
WHAT?
THERE'S SOMETHING INTERRUPTING OUR **TRANSMISSION**, SIR...
PEOPLE OF TANTALUS, GET OFF YOUR KNEES. THIS IS DUKE MCQUEEN AND I NEED YOUR **HELP**.
BACK ME UP AND WE CAN **BEAT** THESE GUYS. LET ME DOWN AND THEY'LL **KILL ME** IN HERE.
I SAVED **YOU** ONCE. NOW YOU CAN SAVE **ME**...
...PICK UP A WEAPON AND **FIGHT** YOUR **OPPRESSORS!**

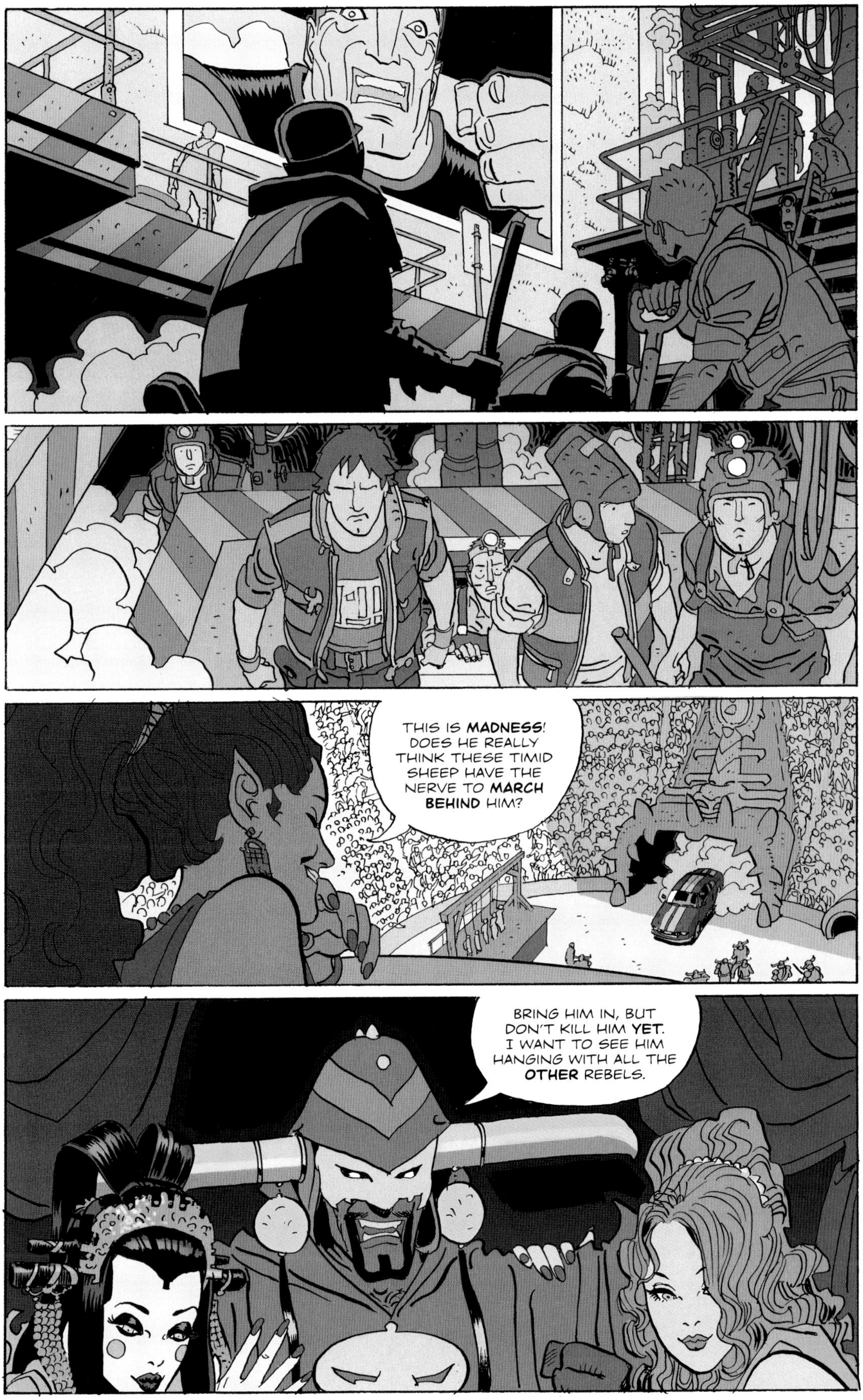
THIS IS **MADNESS**! DOES HE REALLY THINK THESE TIMID SHEEP HAVE THE NERVE TO **MARCH BEHIND** HIM?
BRING HIM IN, BUT DON'T KILL HIM **YET**. I WANT TO SEE HIM HANGING WITH ALL THE **OTHER** REBELS.

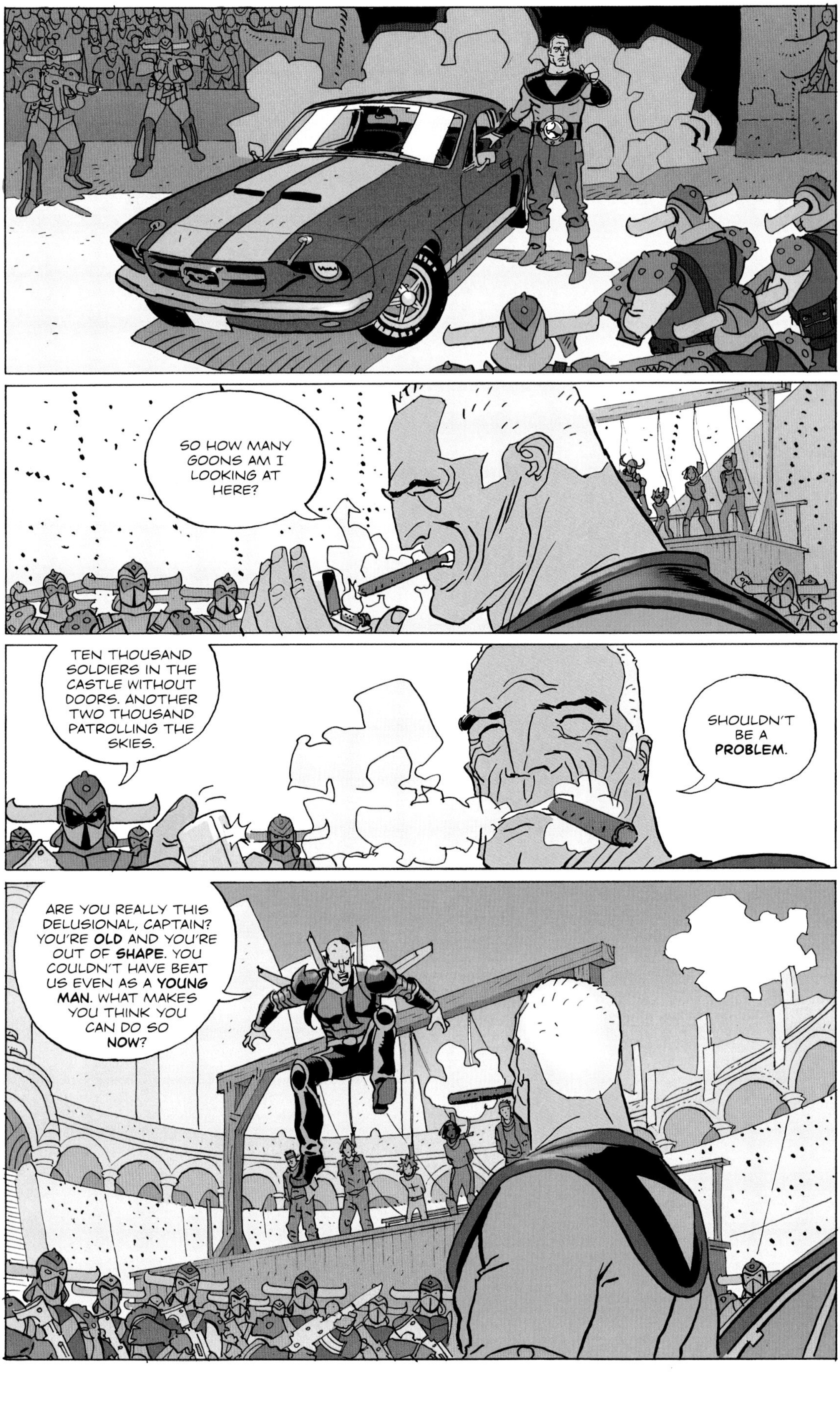
SO HOW MANY GOONS AM I LOOKING AT HERE?
TEN THOUSAND SOLDIERS IN THE CASTLE WITHOUT DOORS. ANOTHER TWO THOUSAND PATROLLING THE SKIES.
SHOULDN'T BE A PROBLEM.
ARE YOU REALLY THIS DELUSIONAL, CAPTAIN? YOU'RE OLD AND YOU'RE OUT OF SHAPE. YOU COULDN'T HAVE BEAT US EVEN AS A YOUNG MAN. WHAT MAKES YOU THINK YOU CAN DO SO NOW?

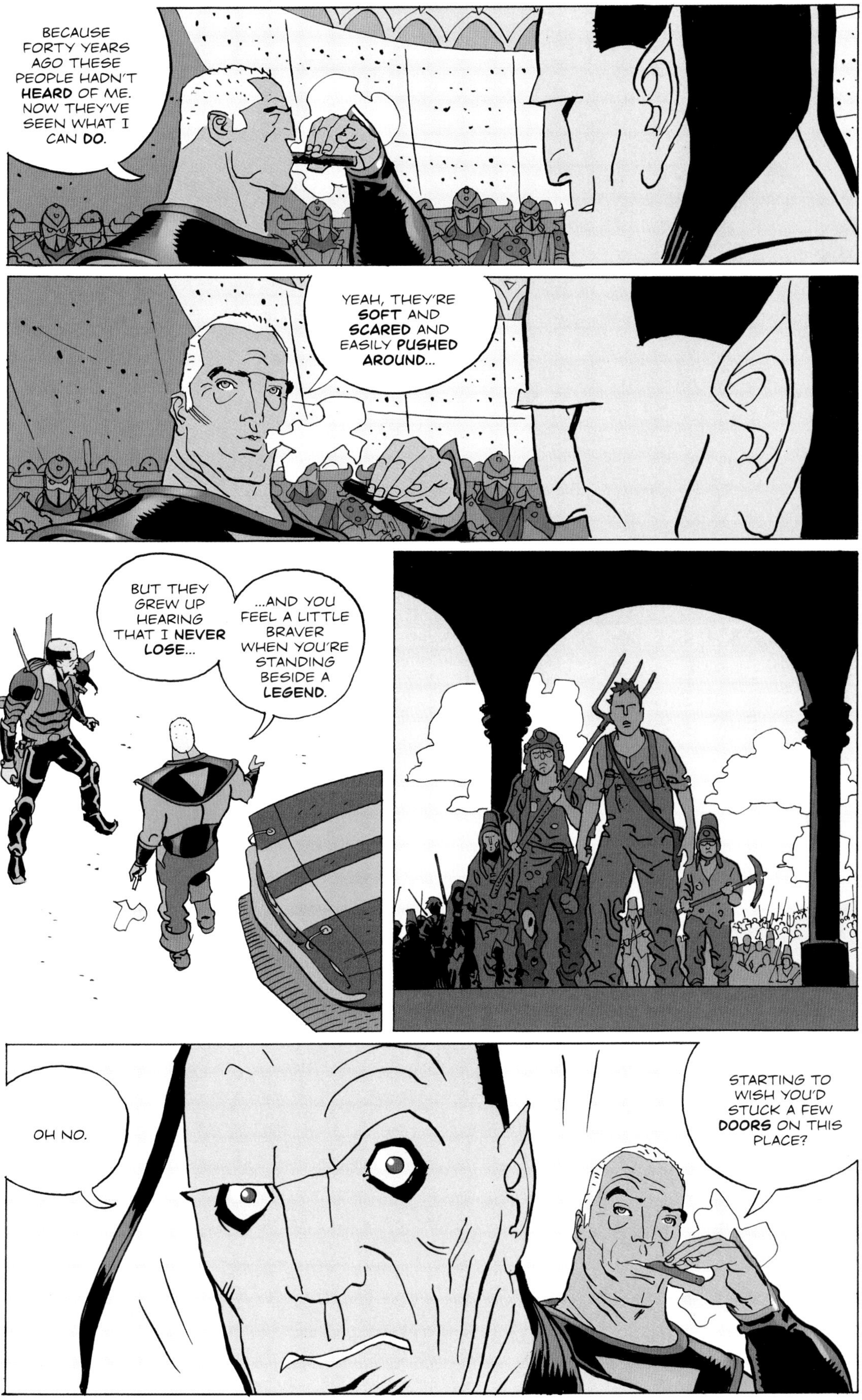
BECAUSE FORTY YEARS AGO THESE PEOPLE HADN'T HEARD OF ME. NOW THEY'VE SEEN WHAT I CAN DO.
YEAH, THEY'RE SOFT AND SCARED AND EASILY PUSHED AROUND...
BUT THEY GREW UP HEARING THAT I NEVER LOSE...
...AND YOU FEEL A LITTLE BRAVER WHEN YOU'RE STANDING BESIDE A LEGEND.
OH NO.
STARTING TO WISH YOU'D STUCK A FEW DOORS ON THIS PLACE?

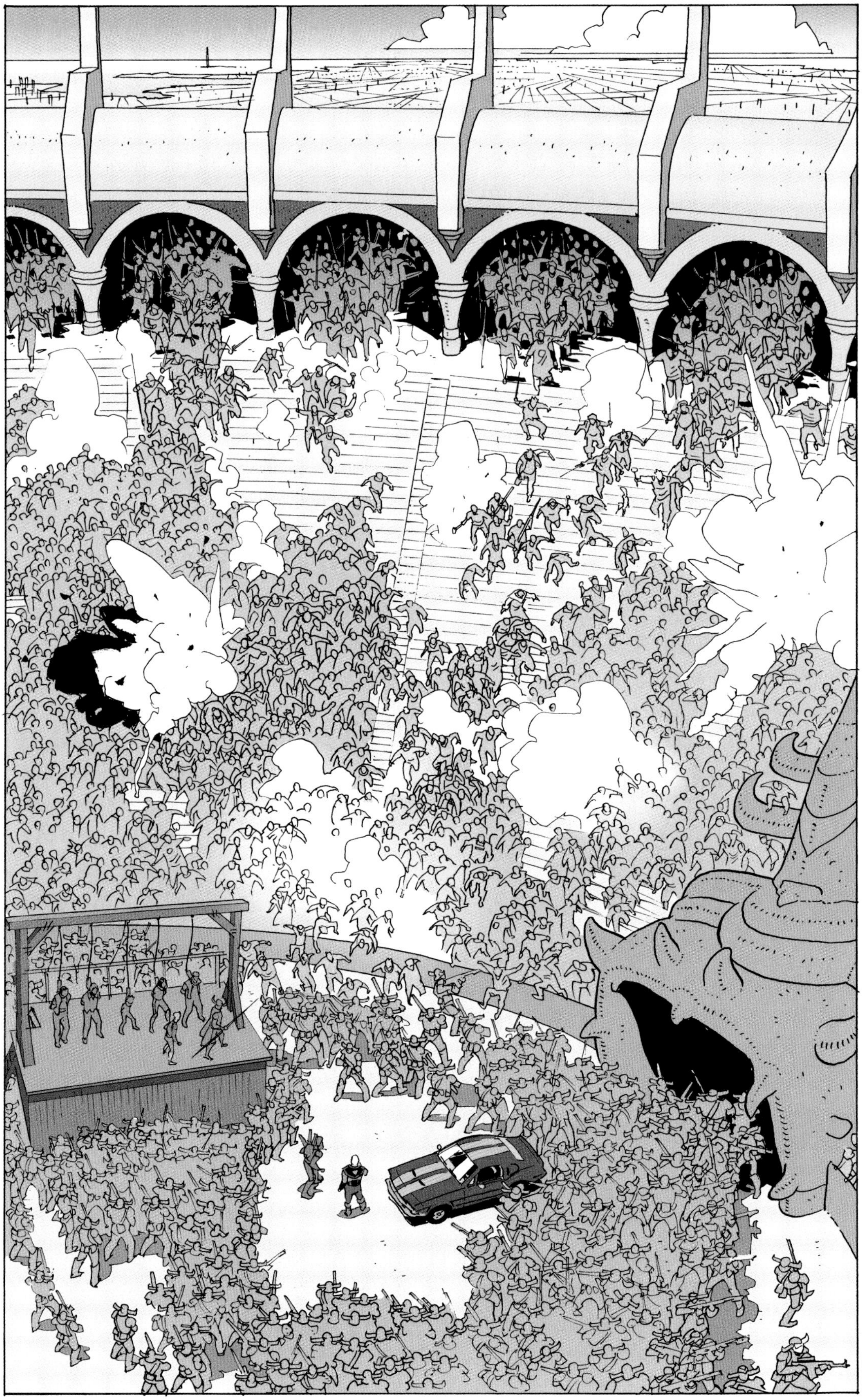

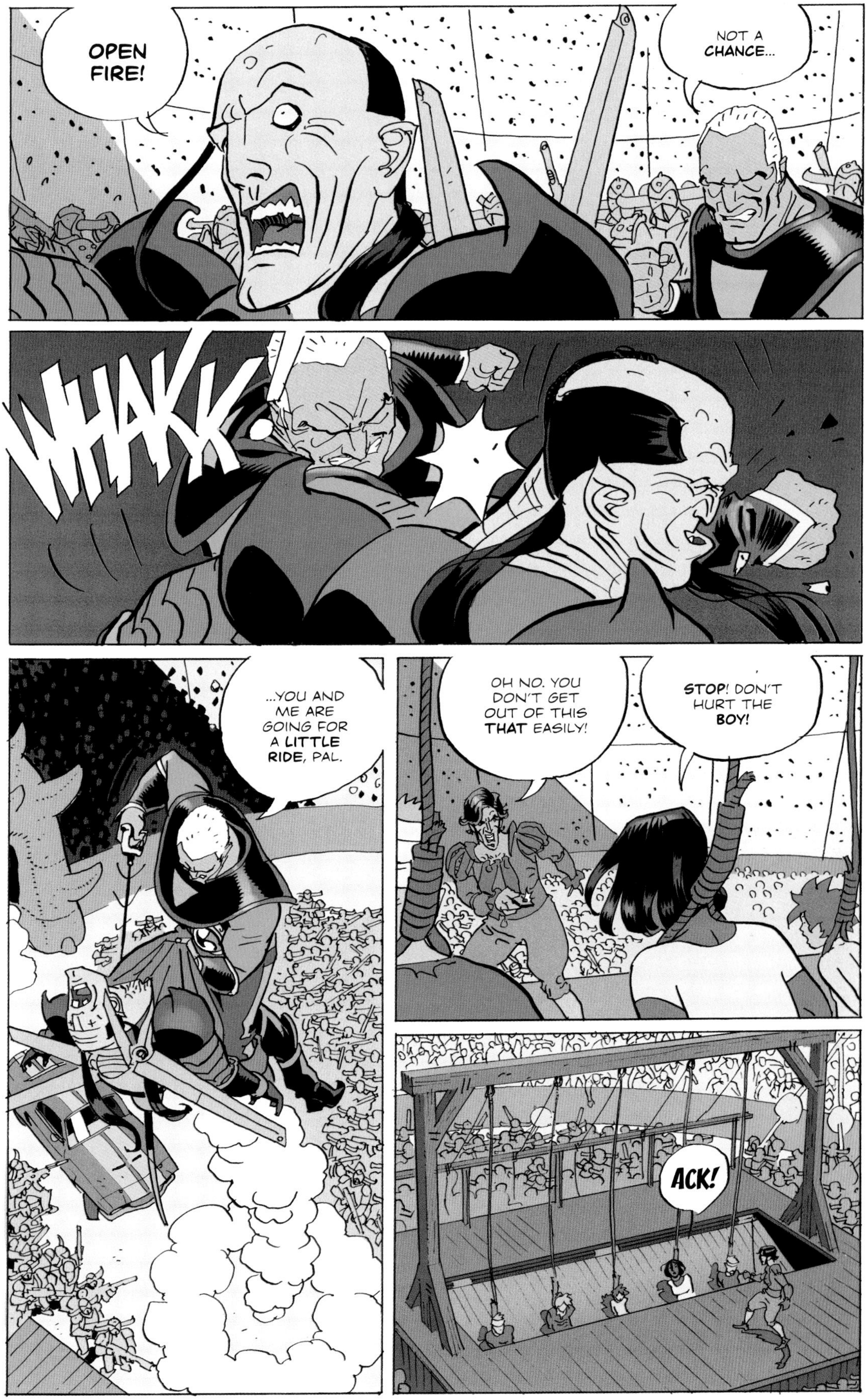
OPEN FIRE!
NOT A CHANCE...
WHAKK
...YOU AND ME ARE GOING FOR A LITTLE RIDE, PAL.
OH NO. YOU DON'T GET OUT OF THIS THAT EASILY!
STOP! DON'T HURT THE BOY!
ACK!

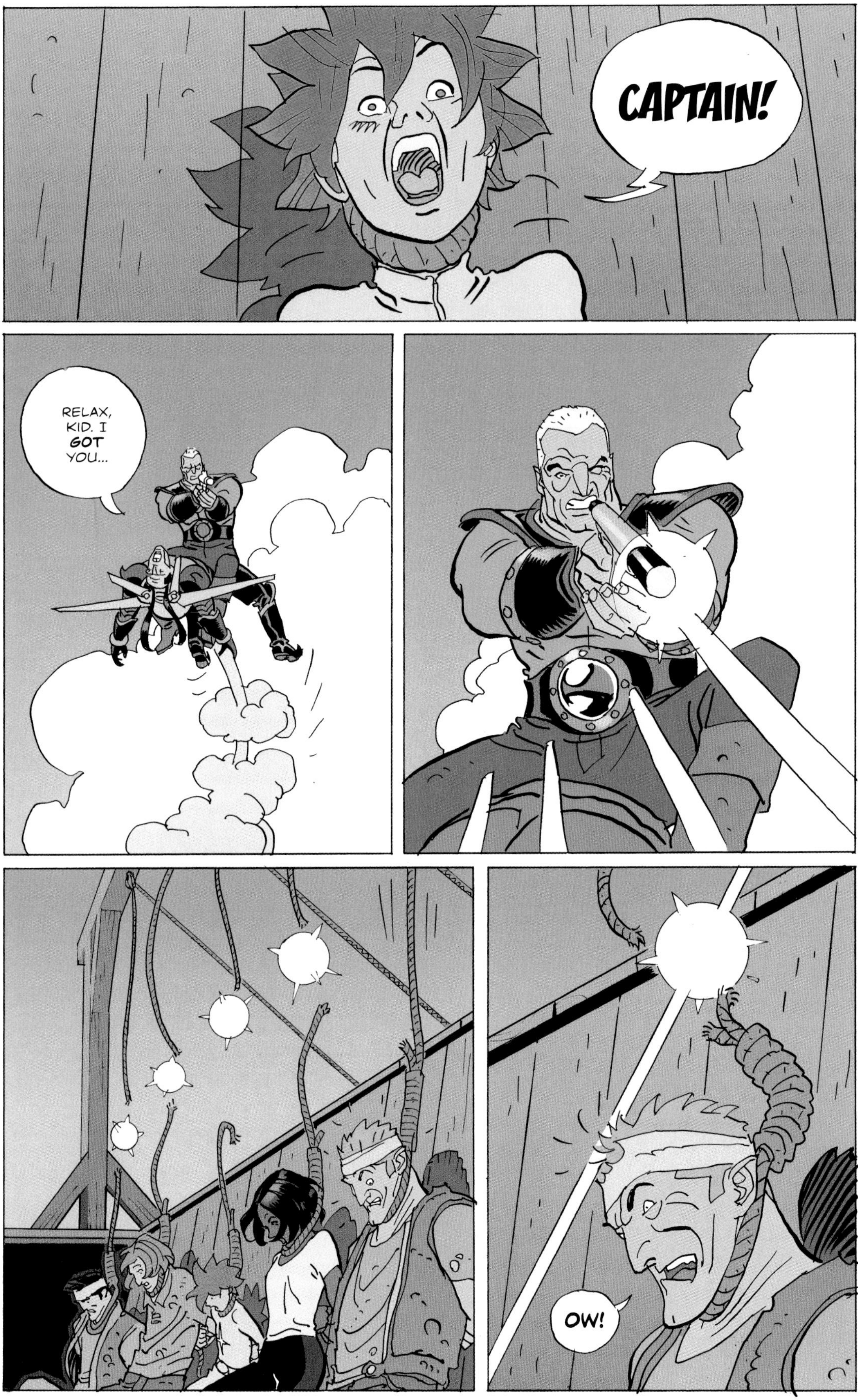
CAPTAIN!
RELAX, KID. I GOT YOU...
OW!

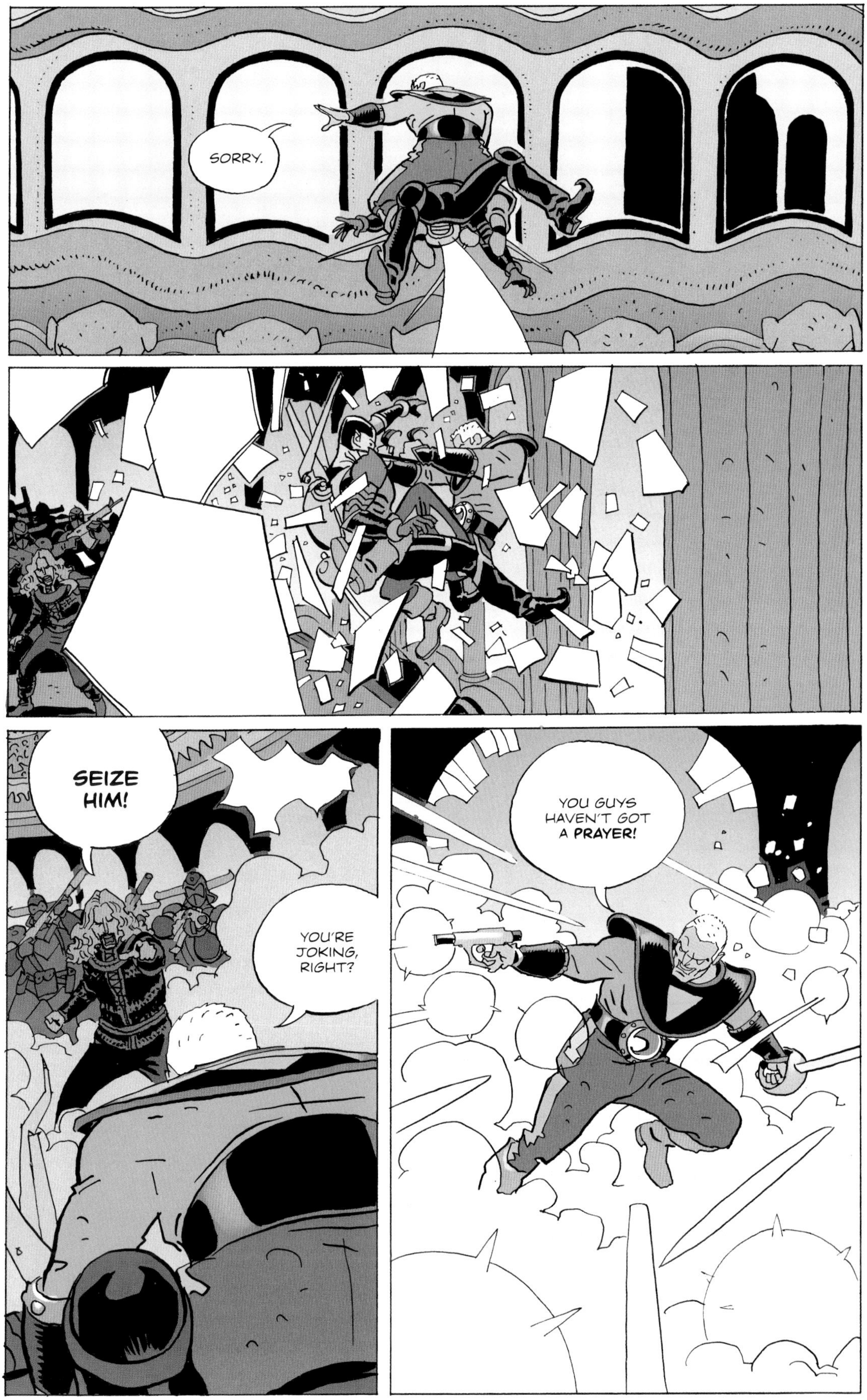

SORRY.
SEIZE HIM!
YOU'RE JOKING, RIGHT?
YOU GUYS HAVEN'T GOT A **PRAYER!**

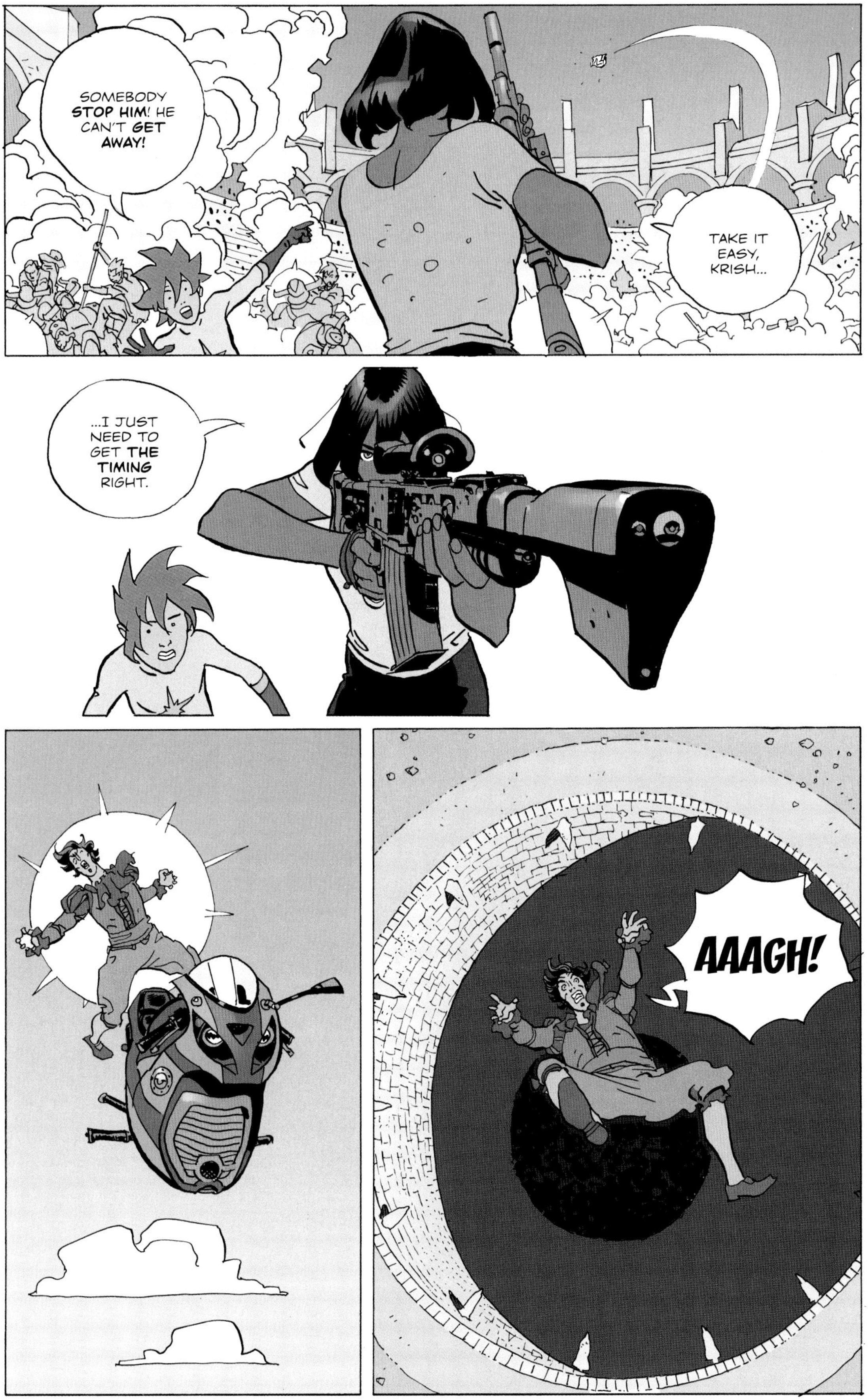
SOMEBODY STOP HIM! HE CAN'T GET AWAY!
TAKE IT EASY, KRISH...
...I JUST NEED TO GET THE TIMING RIGHT.
AAAGH!

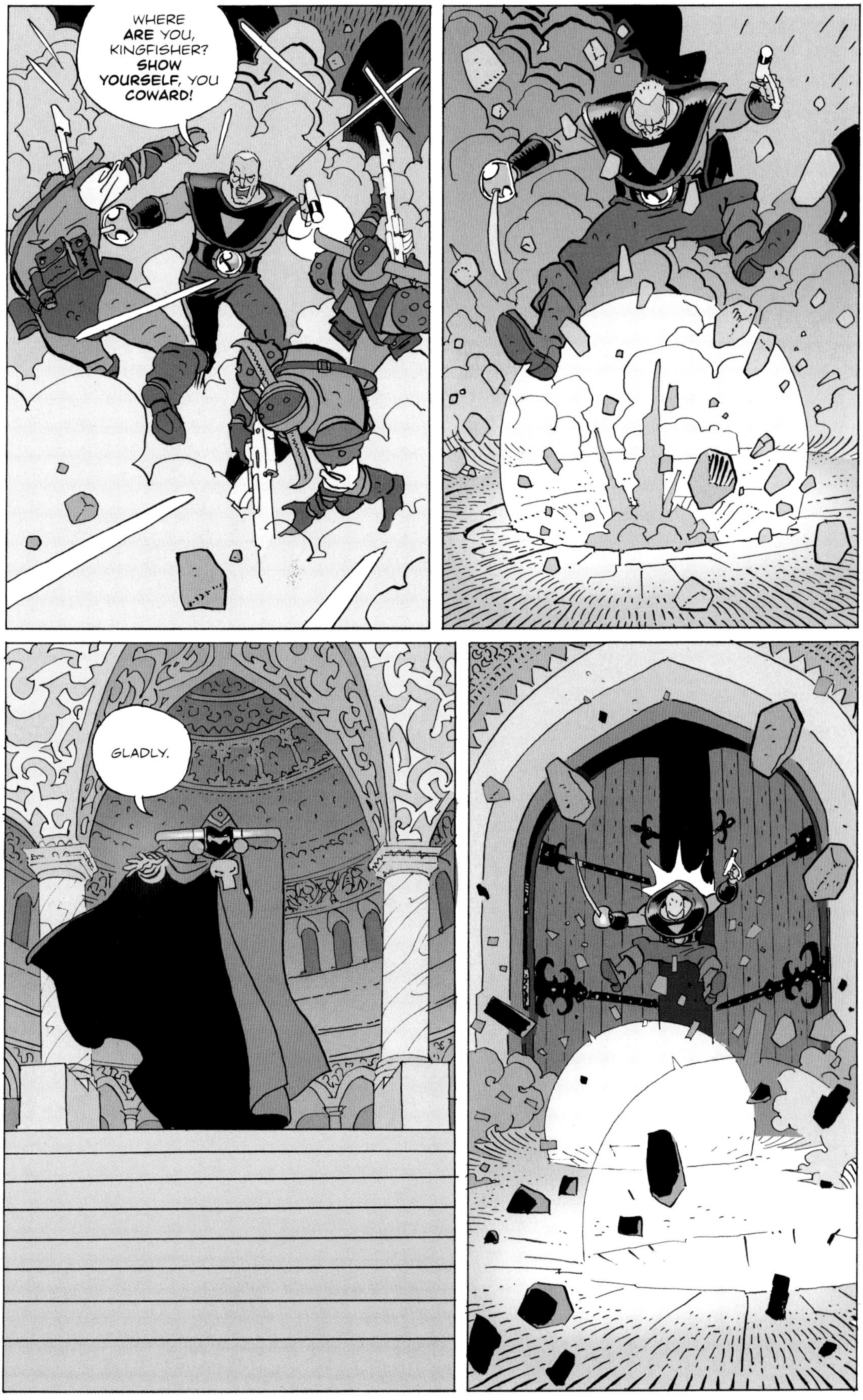
WHERE **ARE** YOU, KINGFISHER? **SHOW YOURSELF**, YOU **COWARD!**
GLADLY.

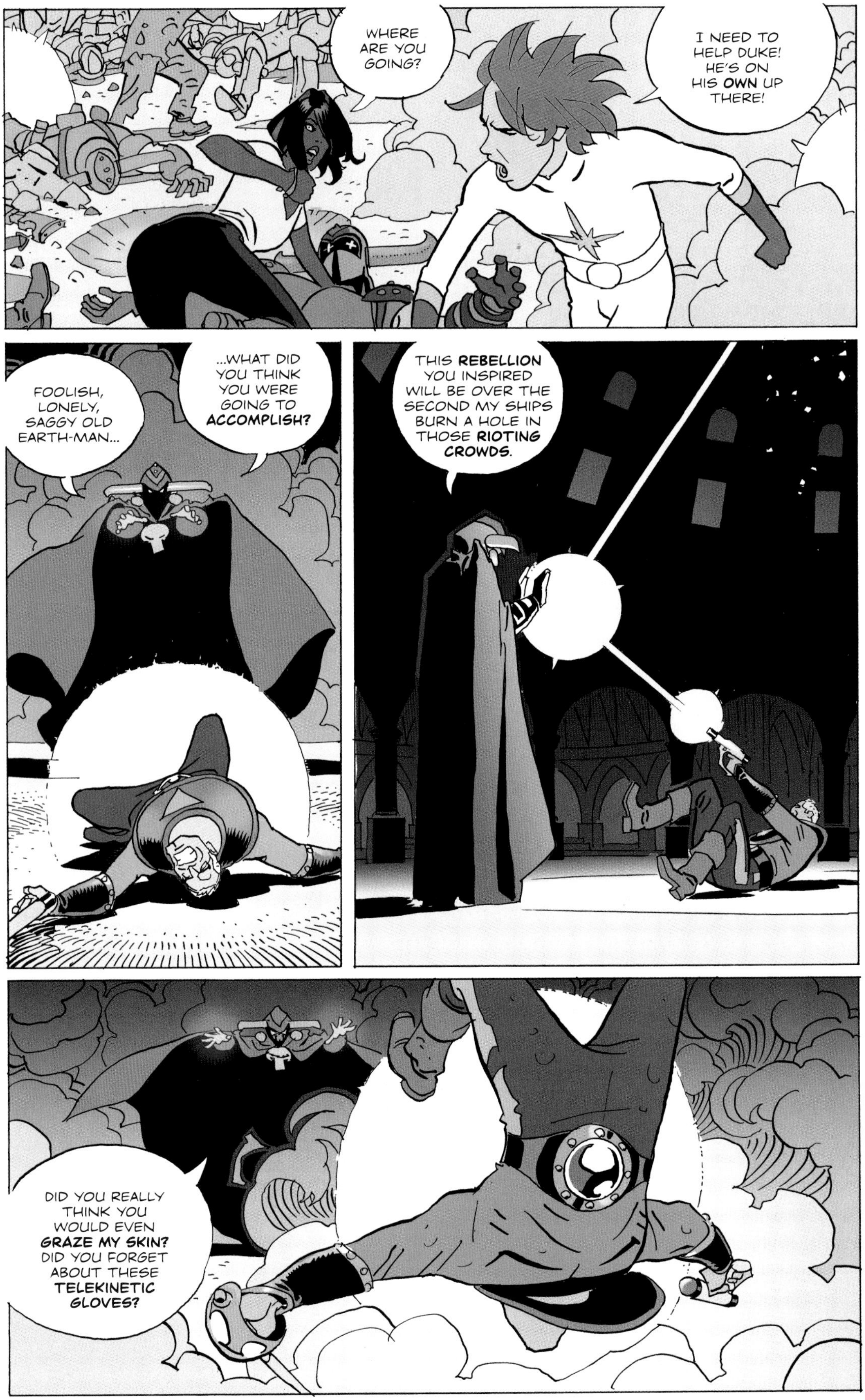
WHERE ARE YOU GOING?
I NEED TO HELP DUKE! HE'S ON HIS **OWN** UP THERE!
FOOLISH, LONELY, SAGGY OLD EARTH-MAN...
...WHAT DID YOU THINK YOU WERE GOING TO **ACCOMPLISH?**
THIS **REBELLION** YOU INSPIRED WILL BE OVER THE SECOND MY SHIPS BURN A HOLE IN THOSE **RIOTING CROWDS**.
DID YOU REALLY THINK YOU WOULD EVEN **GRAZE MY SKIN?** DID YOU FORGET ABOUT THESE **TELEKINETIC GLOVES?**

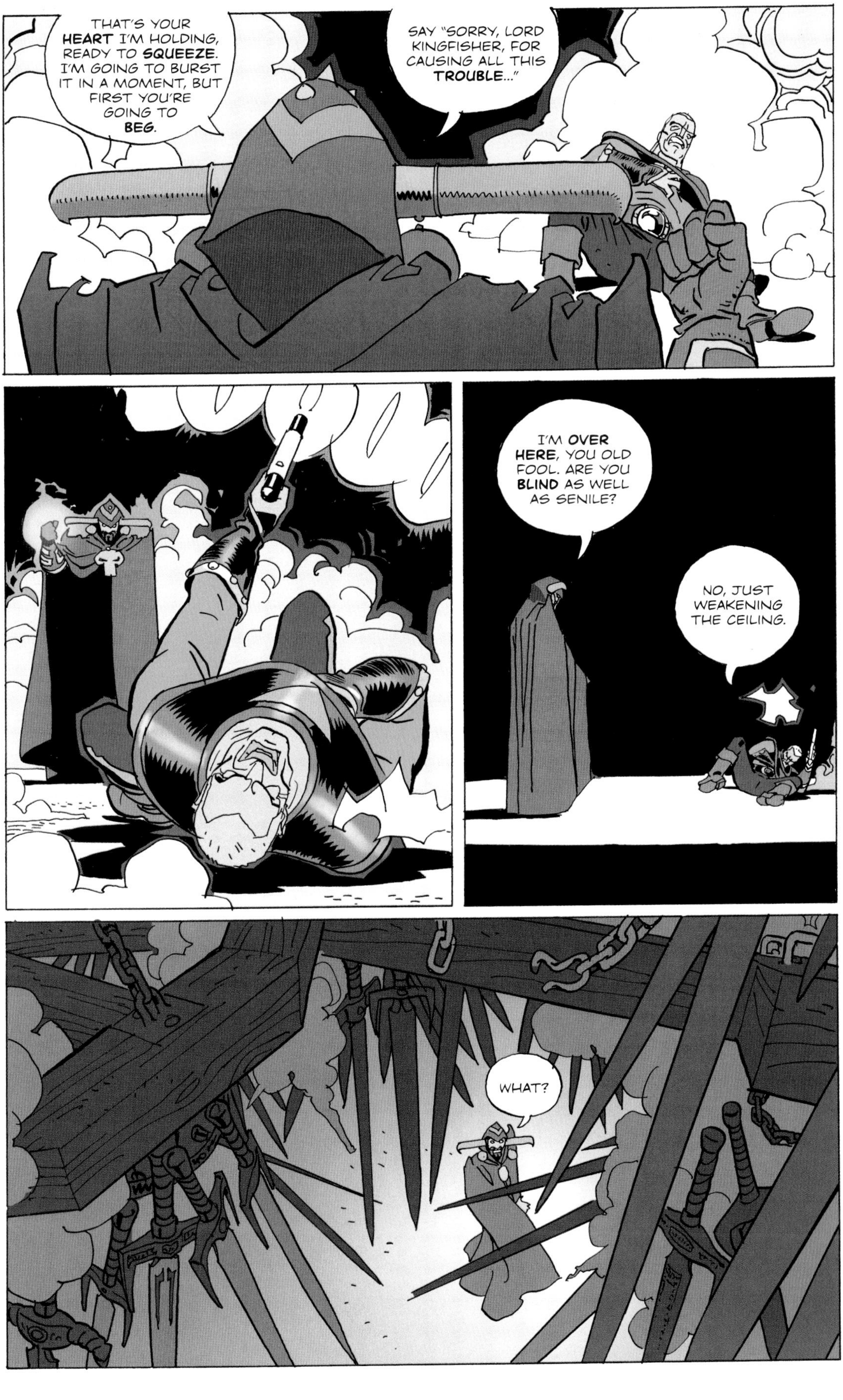
THAT'S YOUR HEART I'M HOLDING, READY TO SQUEEZE. I'M GOING TO BURST IT IN A MOMENT, BUT FIRST YOU'RE GOING TO BEG.
SAY "SORRY, LORD KINGFISHER, FOR CAUSING ALL THIS TROUBLE..."
I'M OVER HERE, YOU OLD FOOL. ARE YOU BLIND AS WELL AS SENILE?
NO, JUST WEAKENING THE CEILING.
WHAT?

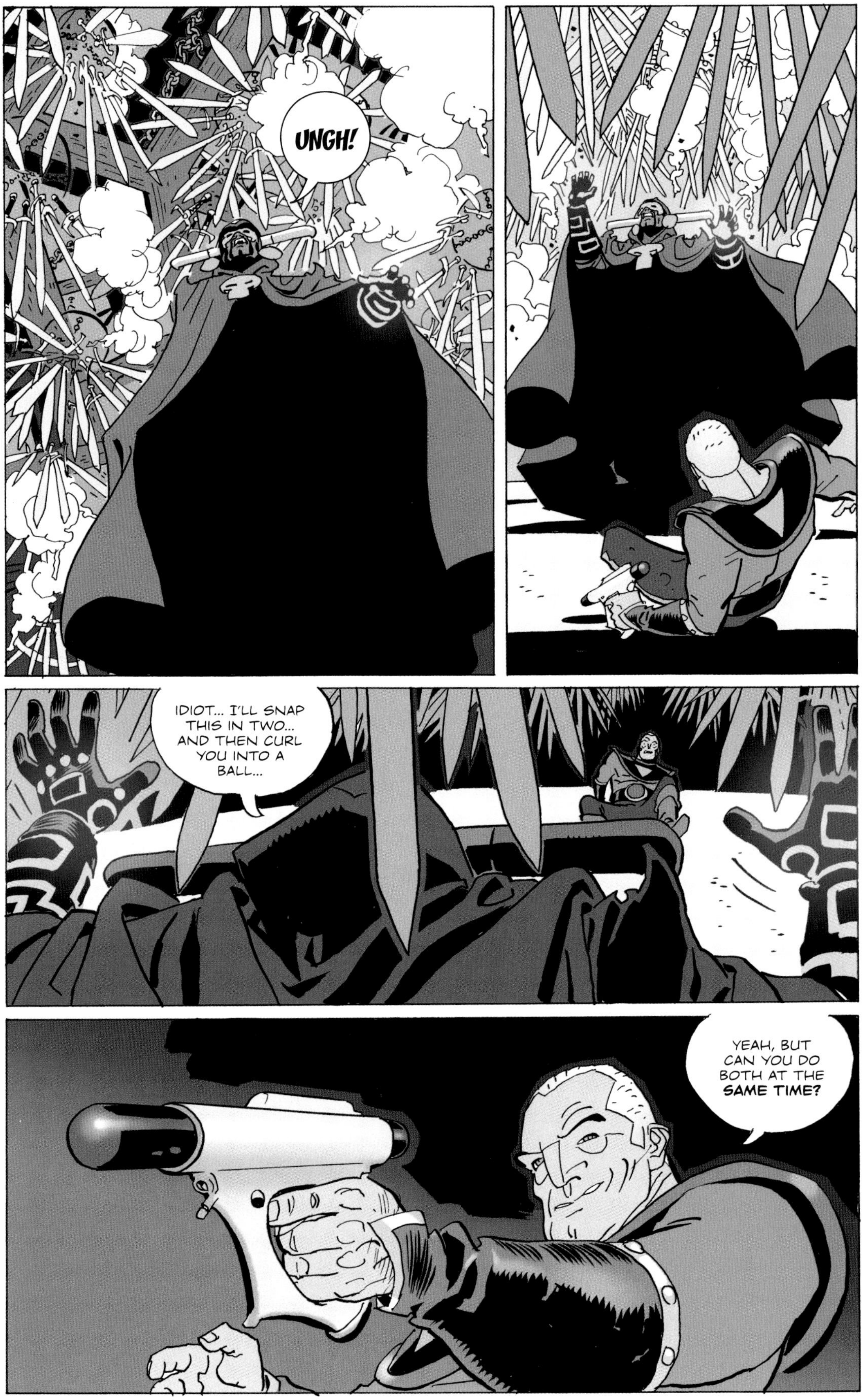
UNGH!
IDIOT... I'LL SNAP THIS IN TWO... AND THEN CURL YOU INTO A BALL...
YEAH, BUT CAN YOU DO BOTH AT THE **SAME TIME?**

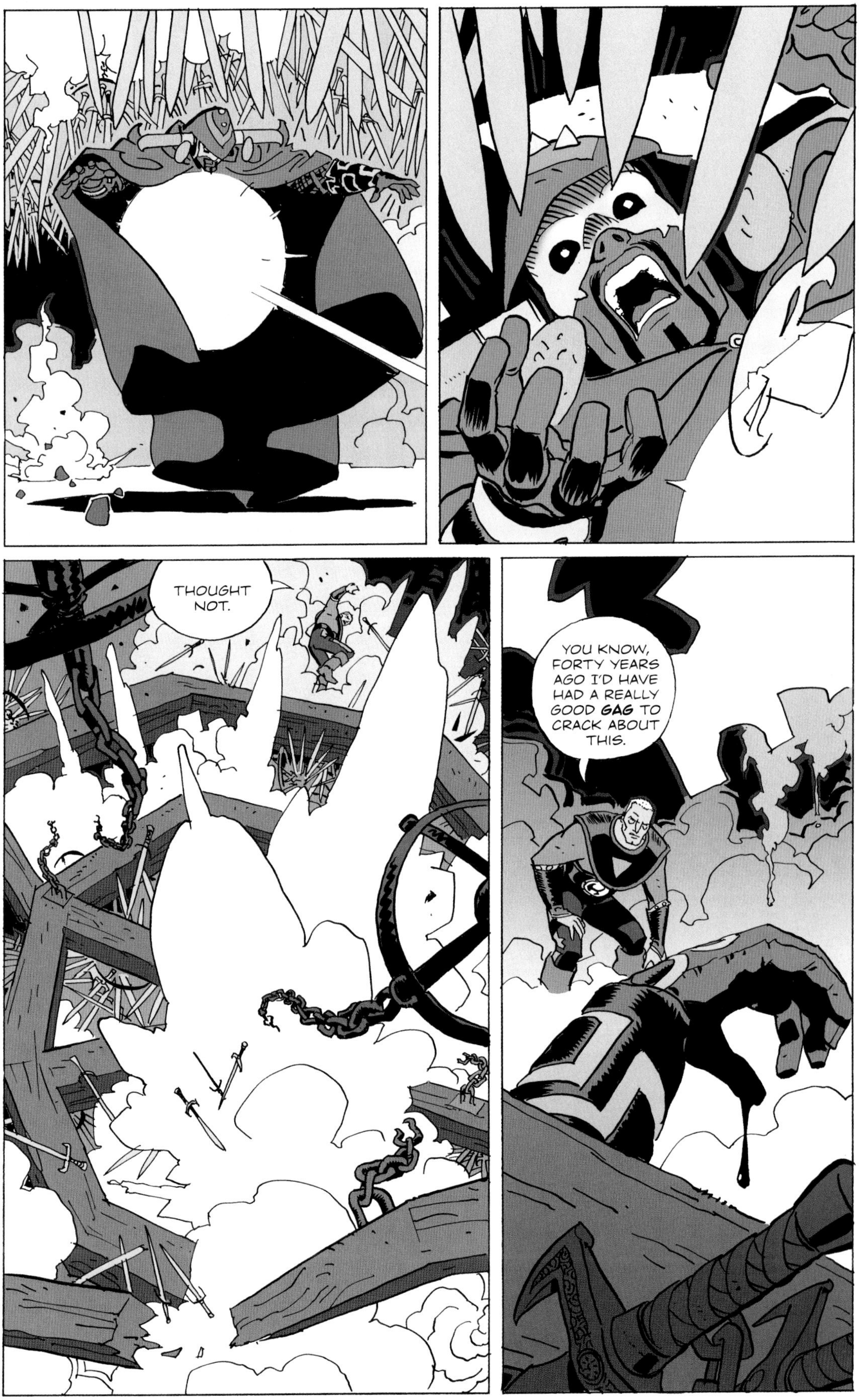
THOUGHT NOT.
YOU KNOW, FORTY YEARS AGO I'D HAVE HAD A REALLY GOOD **GAG** TO CRACK ABOUT THIS.

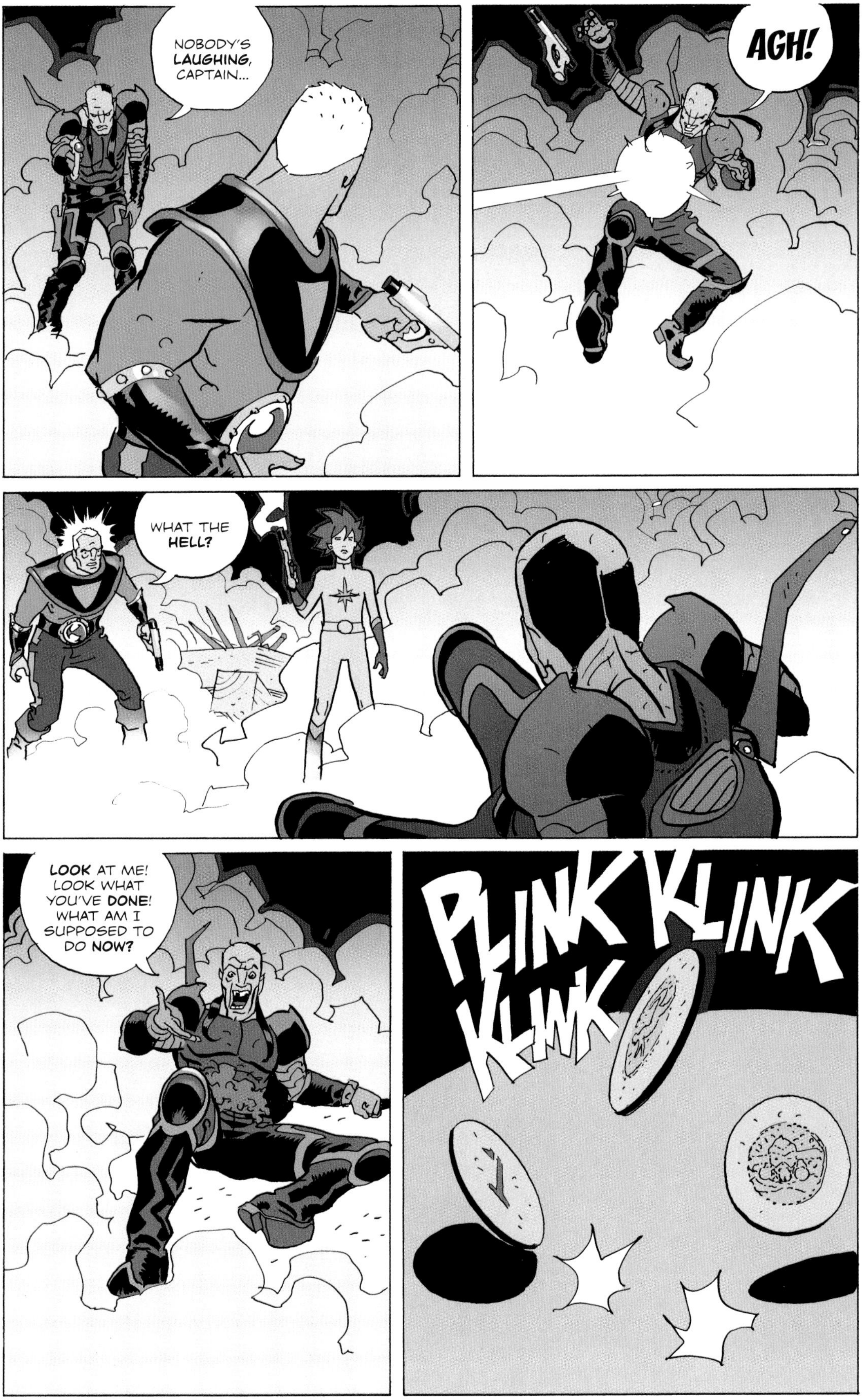
NOBODY'S LAUGHING, CAPTAIN...
AGH!
WHAT THE HELL?
LOOK AT ME! LOOK WHAT YOU'VE DONE! WHAT AM I SUPPOSED TO DO NOW?
PLINK KLINK
KLINK

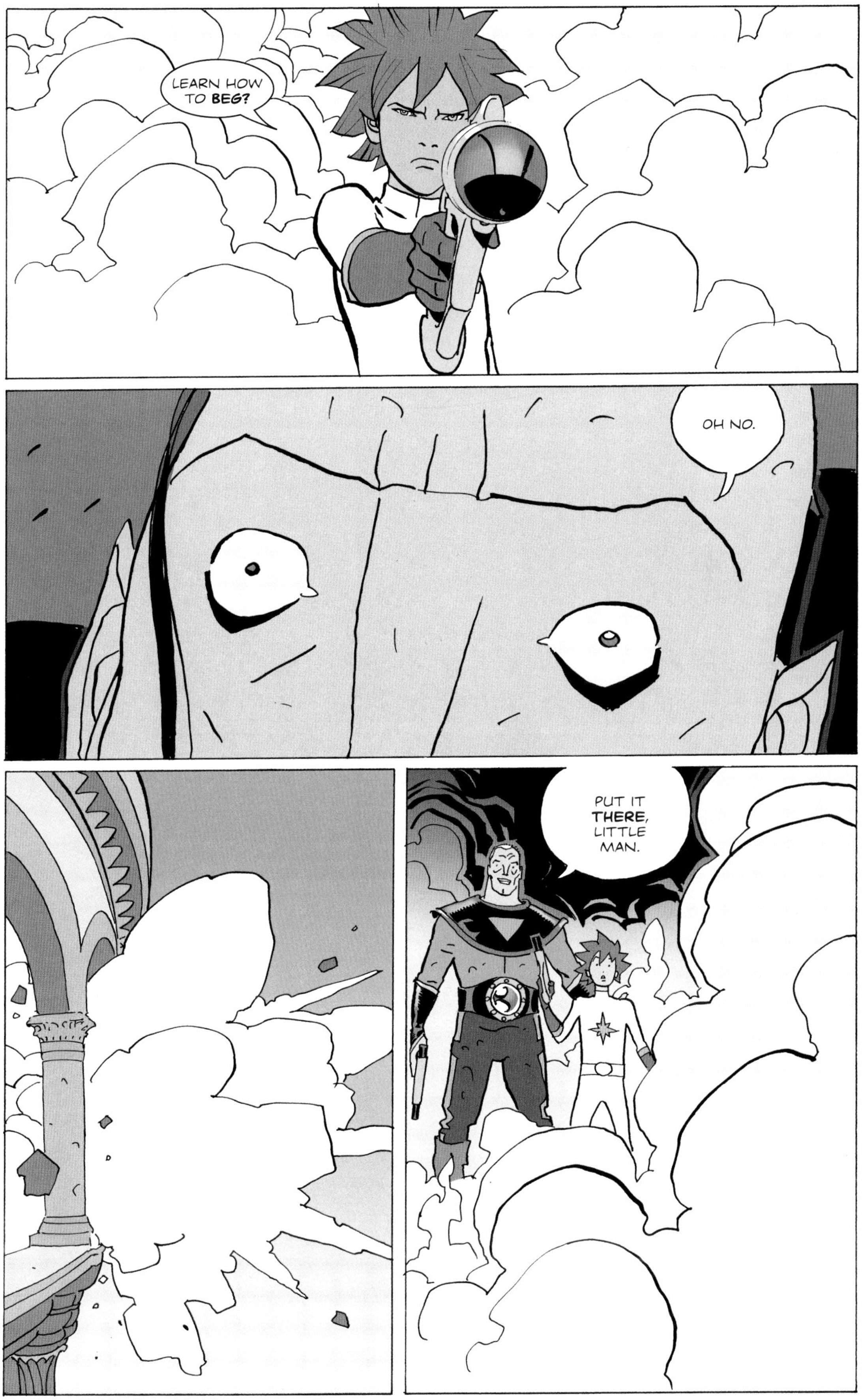
LEARN HOW TO **BEG?**
OH NO.
PUT IT **THERE,** LITTLE MAN.

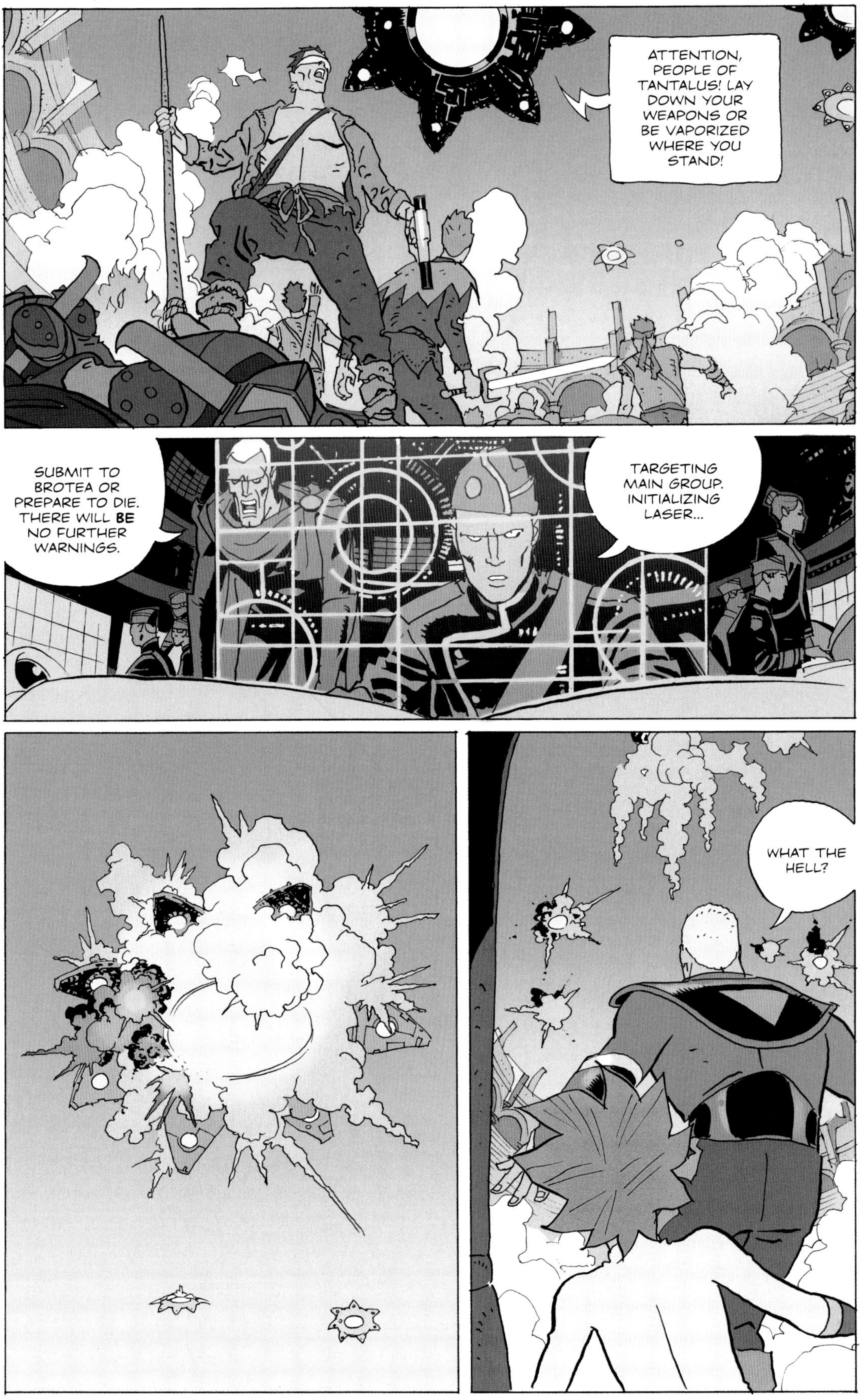
ATTENTION, PEOPLE OF TANTALUS! LAY DOWN YOUR WEAPONS OR BE VAPORIZED WHERE YOU STAND!
SUBMIT TO BROTEA OR PREPARE TO DIE. THERE WILL **BE** NO FURTHER WARNINGS.
TARGETING MAIN GROUP. INITIALIZING LASER...
WHAT THE HELL?

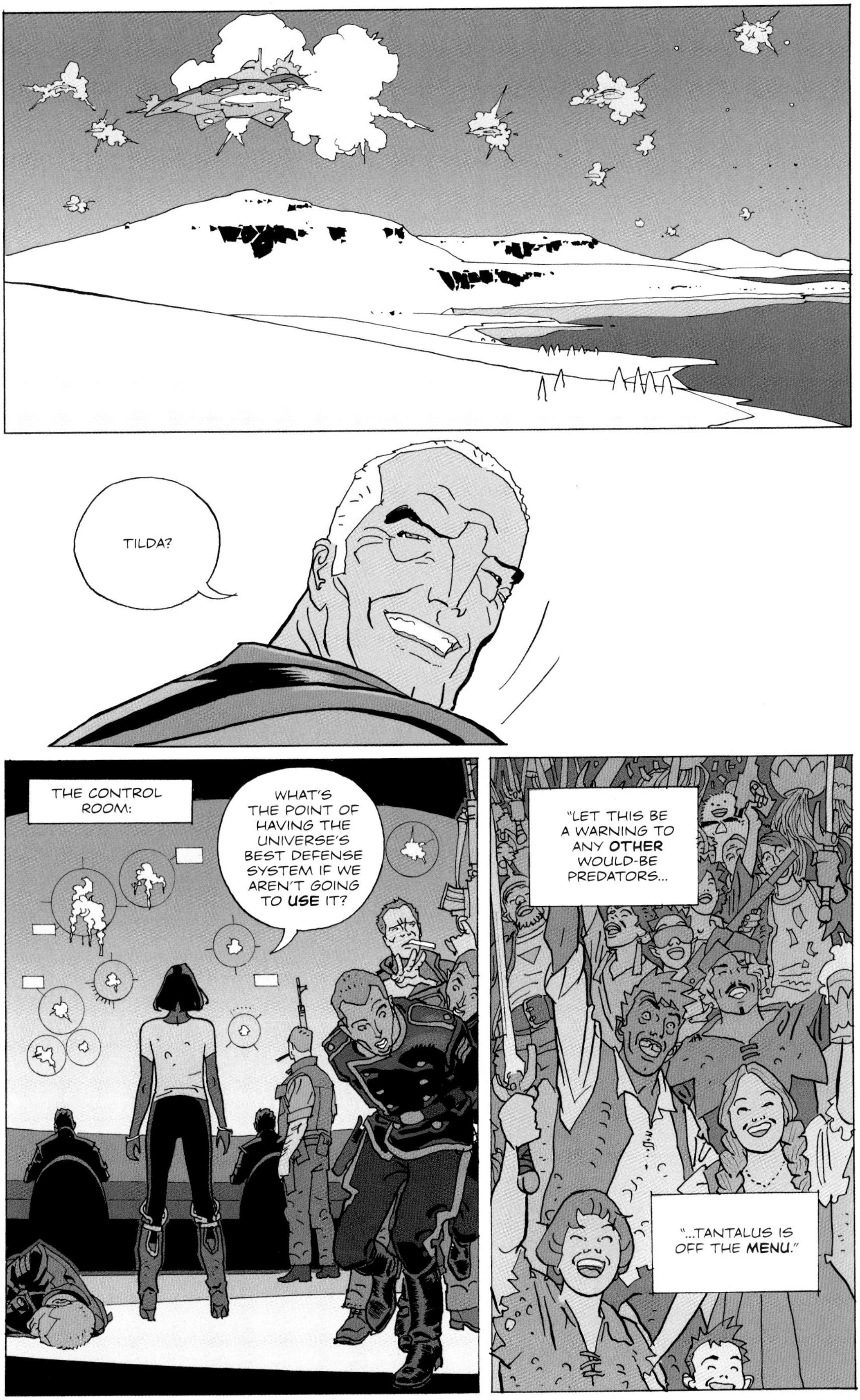
TILDA?
THE CONTROL ROOM:
WHAT'S THE POINT OF HAVING THE UNIVERSE'S BEST DEFENSE SYSTEM IF WE AREN'T GOING TO USE IT?
"LET THIS BE A WARNING TO ANY OTHER WOULD-BE PREDATORS...
"...TANTALUS IS OFF THE MENU."

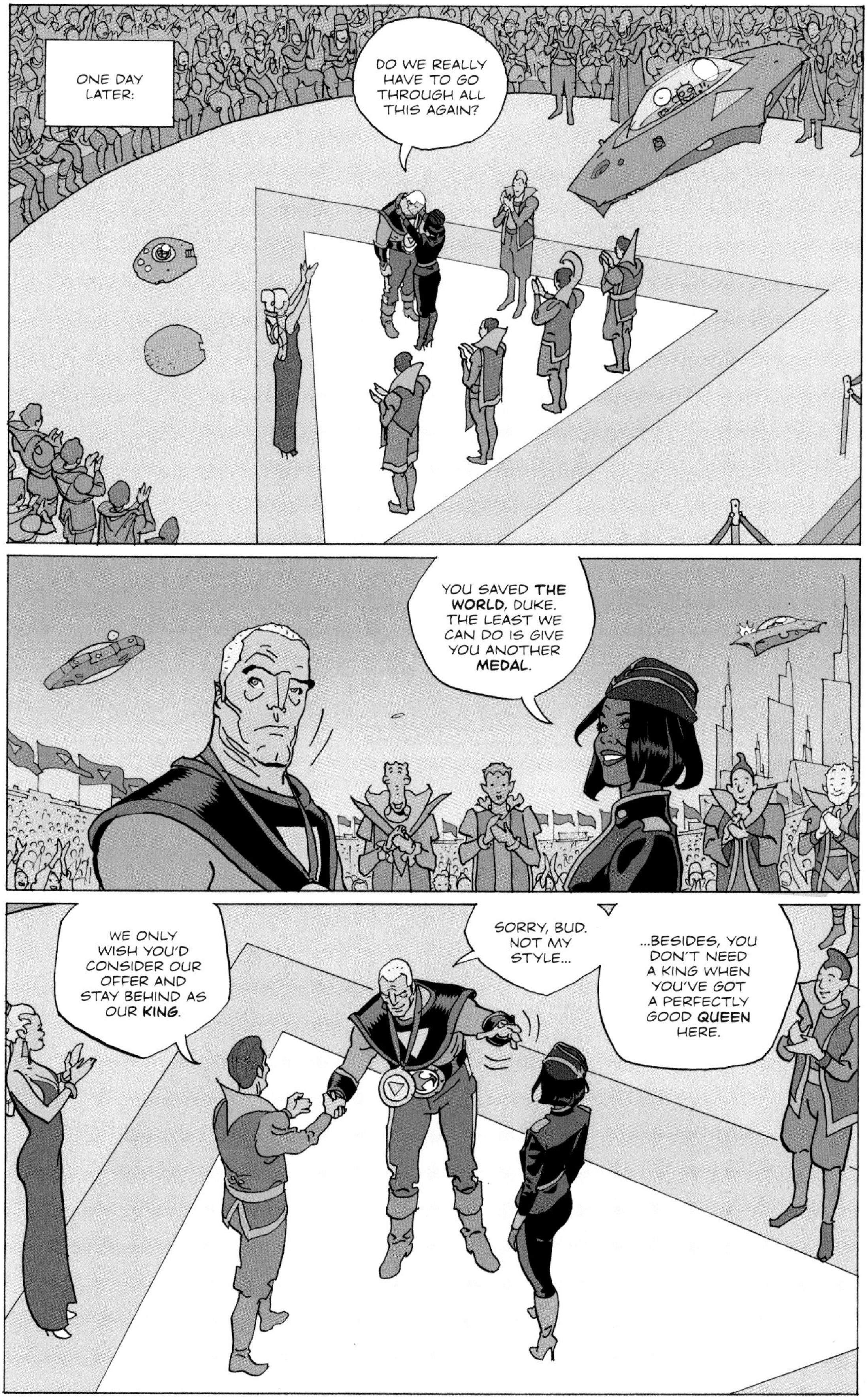
ONE DAY LATER:
DO WE REALLY HAVE TO GO THROUGH ALL THIS AGAIN?
YOU SAVED **THE WORLD**, DUKE. THE LEAST WE CAN DO IS GIVE YOU ANOTHER **MEDAL**.
WE ONLY WISH YOU'D CONSIDER OUR OFFER AND STAY BEHIND AS OUR **KING**.
SORRY, BUD. NOT MY STYLE...
...BESIDES, YOU DON'T NEED A KING WHEN YOU'VE GOT A PERFECTLY GOOD **QUEEN** HERE.

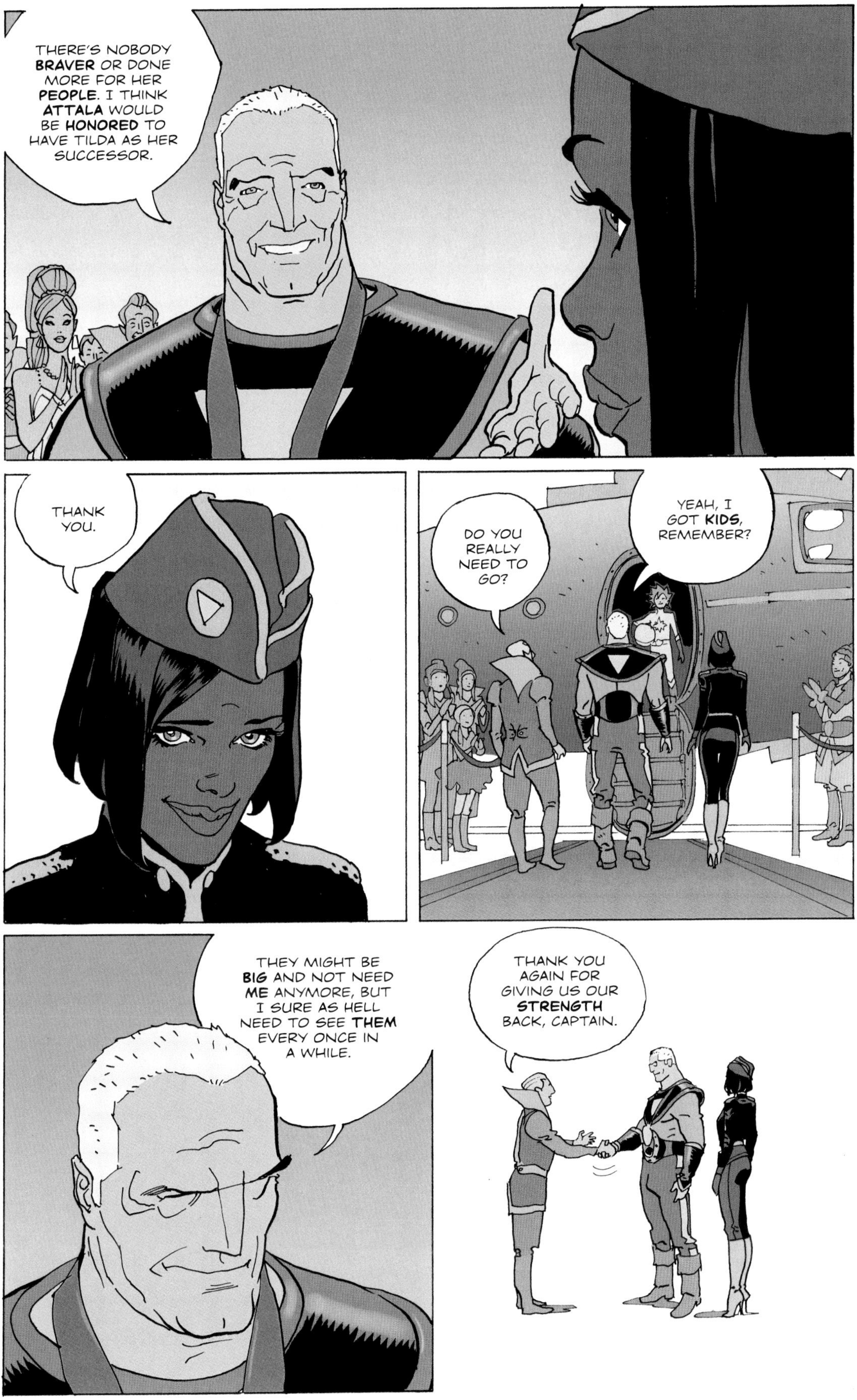
THERE'S NOBODY BRAVER OR DONE MORE FOR HER PEOPLE. I THINK ATTALA WOULD BE HONORED TO HAVE TILDA AS HER SUCCESSOR.
THANK YOU.
DO YOU REALLY NEED TO GO?
YEAH, I GOT KIDS, REMEMBER?
THEY MIGHT BE BIG AND NOT NEED ME ANYMORE, BUT I SURE AS HELL NEED TO SEE THEM EVERY ONCE IN A WHILE.
THANK YOU AGAIN FOR GIVING US OUR STRENGTH BACK, CAPTAIN.

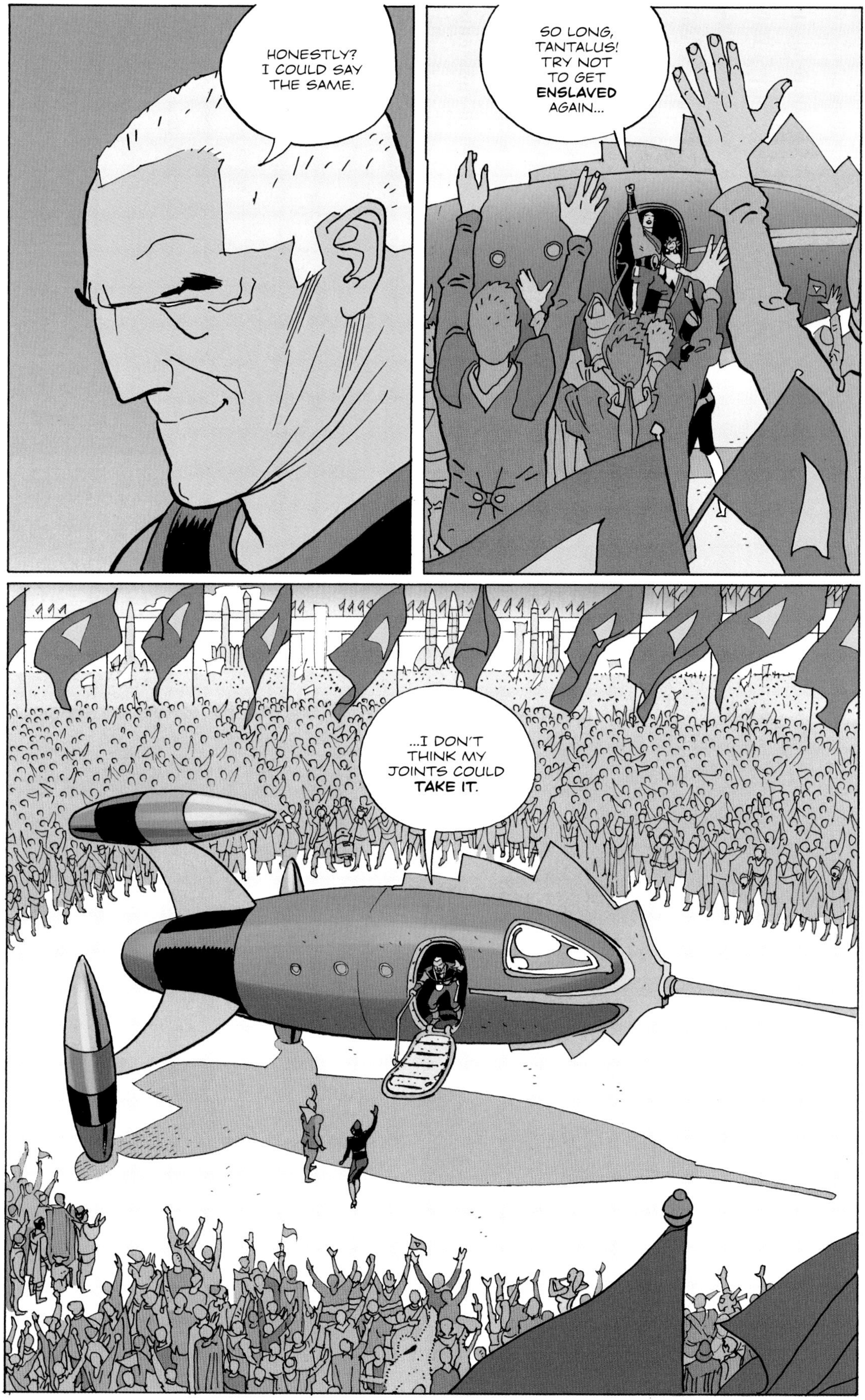
HONESTLY? I COULD SAY THE SAME.
SO LONG, TANTALUS! TRY NOT TO GET **ENSLAVED** AGAIN...
...I DON'T THINK MY JOINTS COULD **TAKE IT**.

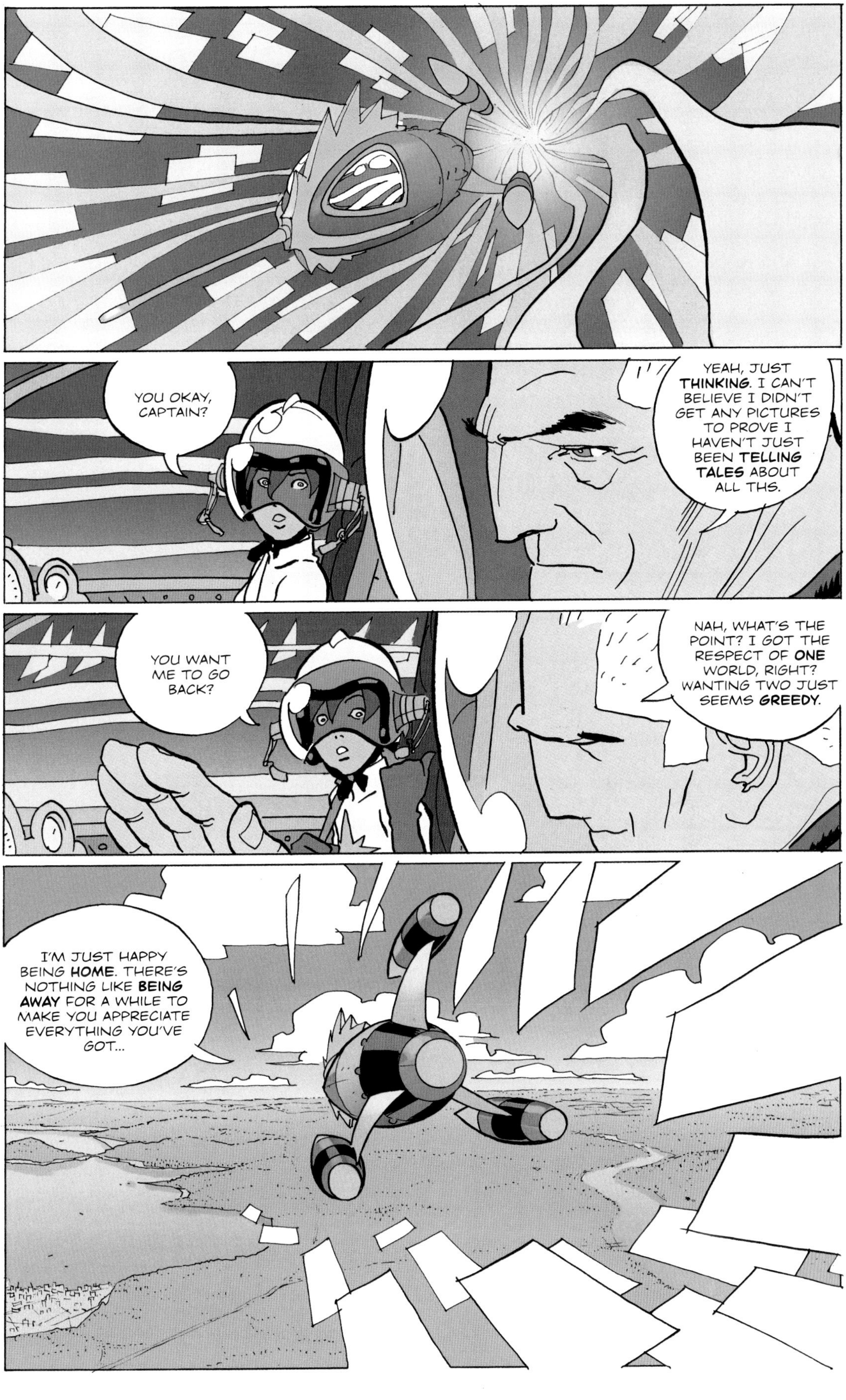
YOU OKAY, CAPTAIN?
YEAH, JUST **THINKING**. I CAN'T BELIEVE I DIDN'T GET ANY PICTURES TO PROVE I HAVEN'T JUST BEEN **TELLING TALES** ABOUT ALL THS.
YOU WANT ME TO GO BACK?
NAH, WHAT'S THE POINT? I GOT THE RESPECT OF **ONE** WORLD, RIGHT? WANTING TWO JUST SEEMS **GREEDY**.
I'M JUST HAPPY BEING **HOME**. THERE'S NOTHING LIKE **BEING AWAY** FOR A WHILE TO MAKE YOU APPRECIATE EVERYTHING YOU'VE GOT...

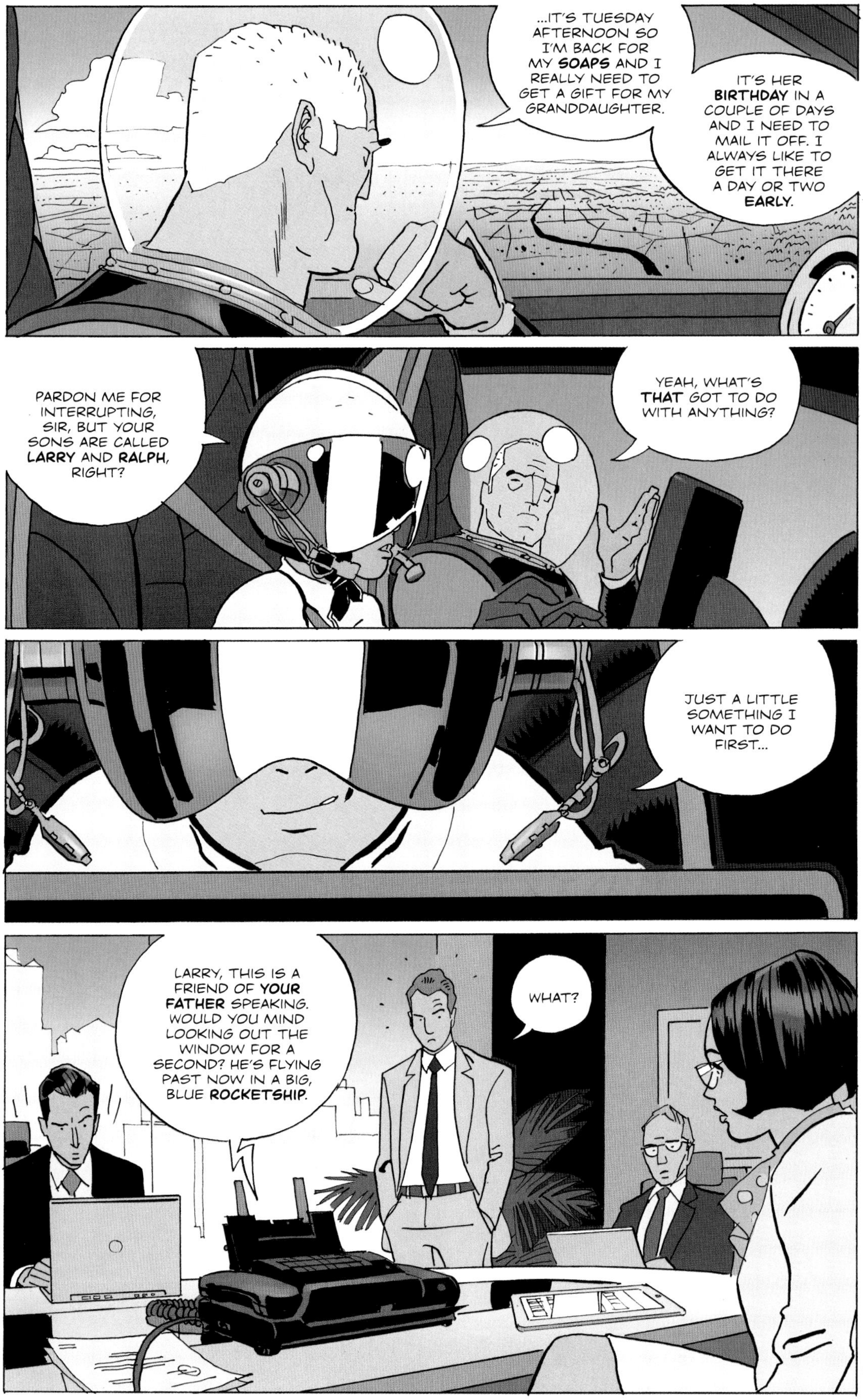
...IT'S TUESDAY AFTERNOON SO I'M BACK FOR MY **SOAPS** AND I REALLY NEED TO GET A GIFT FOR MY GRANDDAUGHTER.
IT'S HER **BIRTHDAY** IN A COUPLE OF DAYS AND I NEED TO MAIL IT OFF. I ALWAYS LIKE TO GET IT THERE A DAY OR TWO **EARLY**.
PARDON ME FOR INTERRUPTING, SIR, BUT YOUR SONS ARE CALLED **LARRY** AND **RALPH**, RIGHT?
YEAH, WHAT'S **THAT** GOT TO DO WITH ANYTHING?
JUST A LITTLE SOMETHING I WANT TO DO FIRST...
LARRY, THIS IS A FRIEND OF **YOUR FATHER** SPEAKING. WOULD YOU MIND LOOKING OUT THE WINDOW FOR A SECOND? HE'S FLYING PAST NOW IN A BIG, BLUE **ROCKETSHIP**.
WHAT?

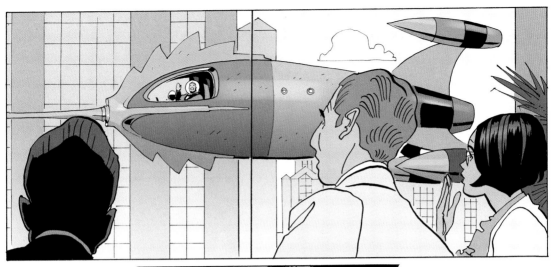

RALPH, ARE YOU AT HOME WITH YOUR CHILDREN? GOOD. TAKE THEM OUT INTO THE GARDEN AND KEEP YOUR EYES ON THE SKY, PLEASE.

KID, THIS IS NUTS. WE CAN'T JUST GO FLYING THROUGH A RESIDENTIAL AREA...

DADDY, WHAT WAS **THAT**?

I THINK THAT WAS YOUR **GRANDPA**, HONEY.

HA! YOU KNOW HOW **CRAZY** THIS IS GOING TO DRIVE PEOPLE?

SO LET'S GIVE THEM SOMETHING TO **REALLY** TALK ABOUT...

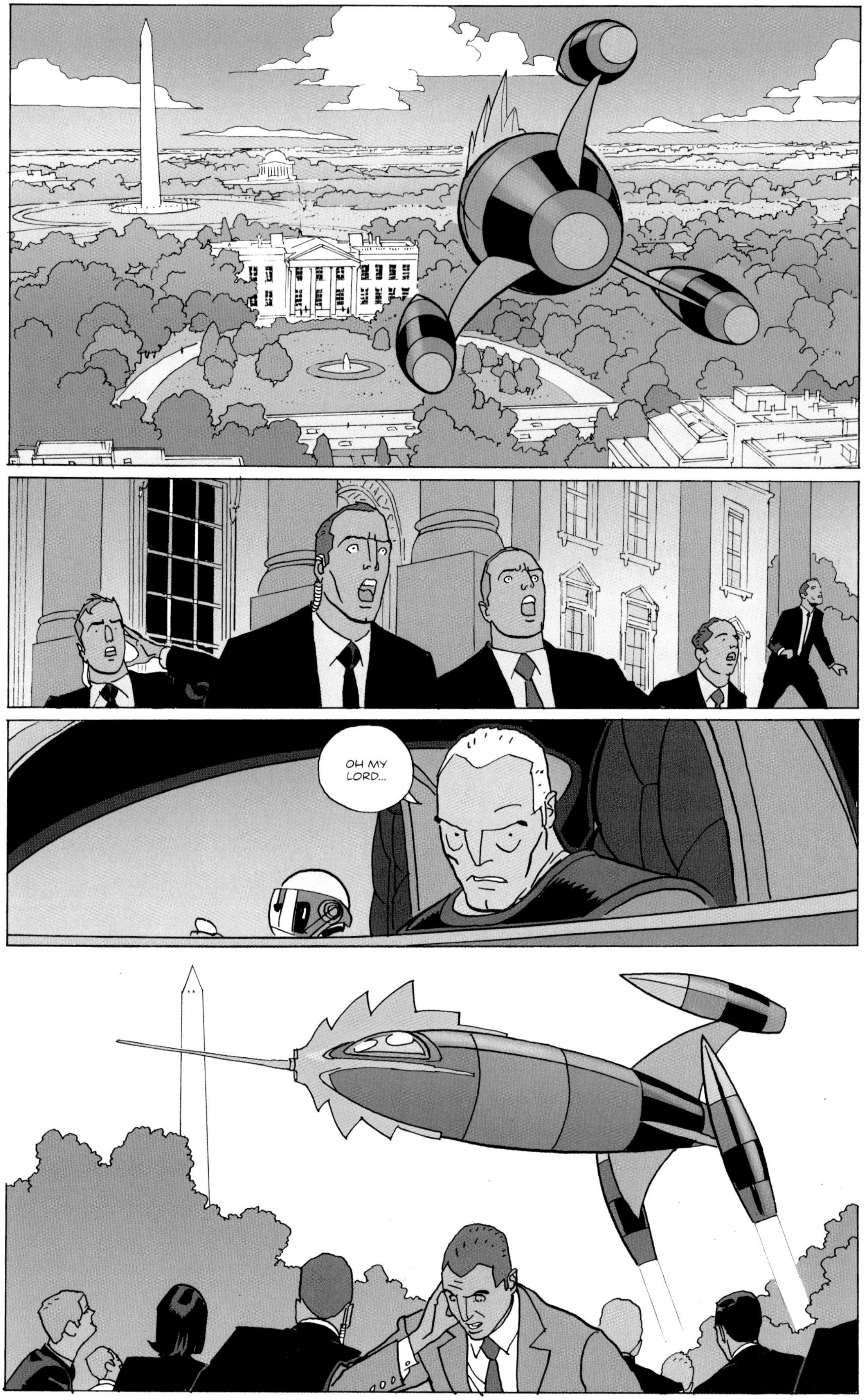
OH MY LORD...

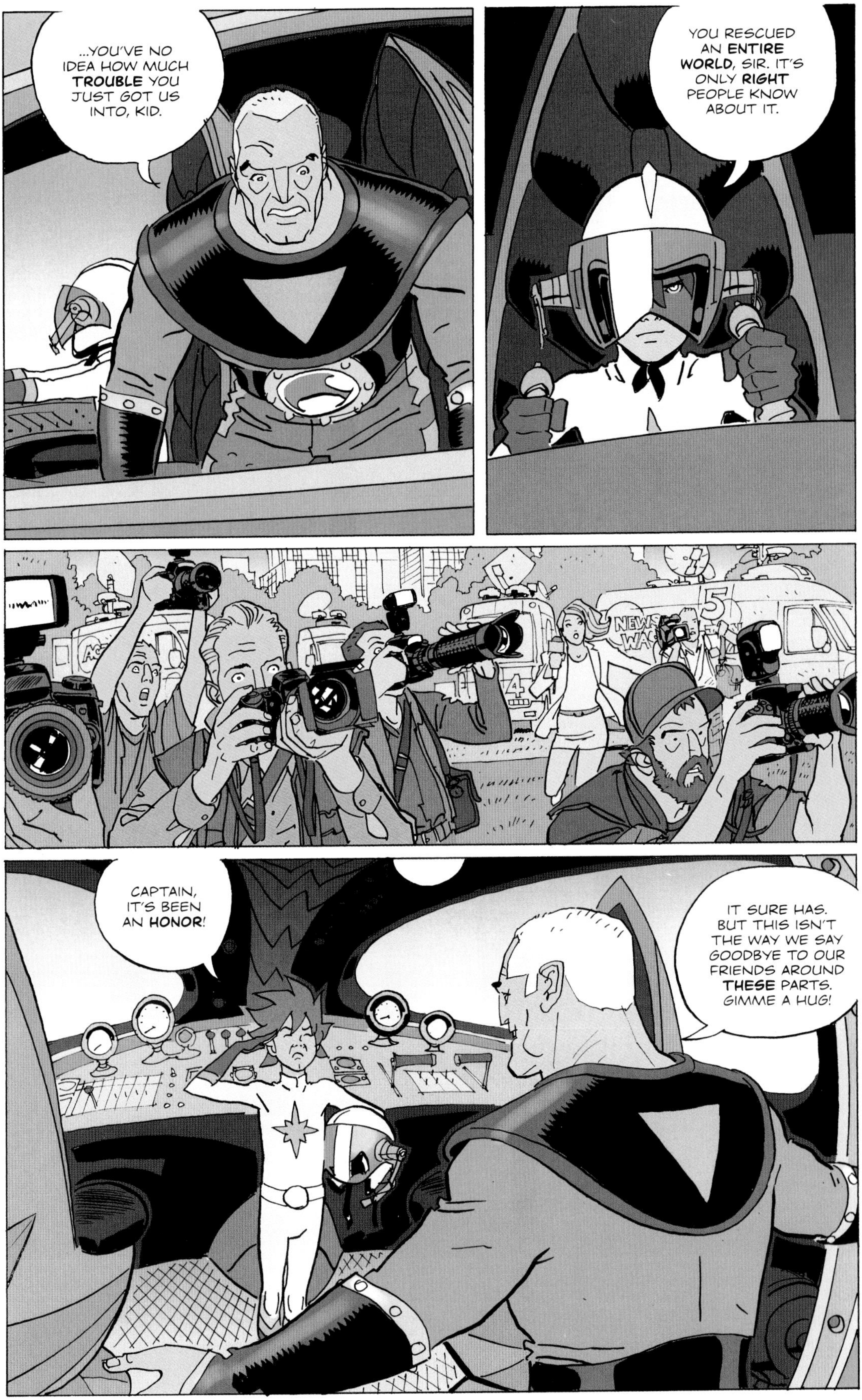
...YOU'VE NO IDEA HOW MUCH **TROUBLE** YOU JUST GOT US INTO, KID.
YOU RESCUED AN **ENTIRE WORLD**, SIR. IT'S ONLY **RIGHT** PEOPLE KNOW ABOUT IT.
NEWS WA
5
4
CAPTAIN, IT'S BEEN AN **HONOR**!
IT SURE HAS. BUT THIS ISN'T THE WAY WE SAY GOODBYE TO OUR FRIENDS AROUND **THESE** PARTS. GIMME A HUG!

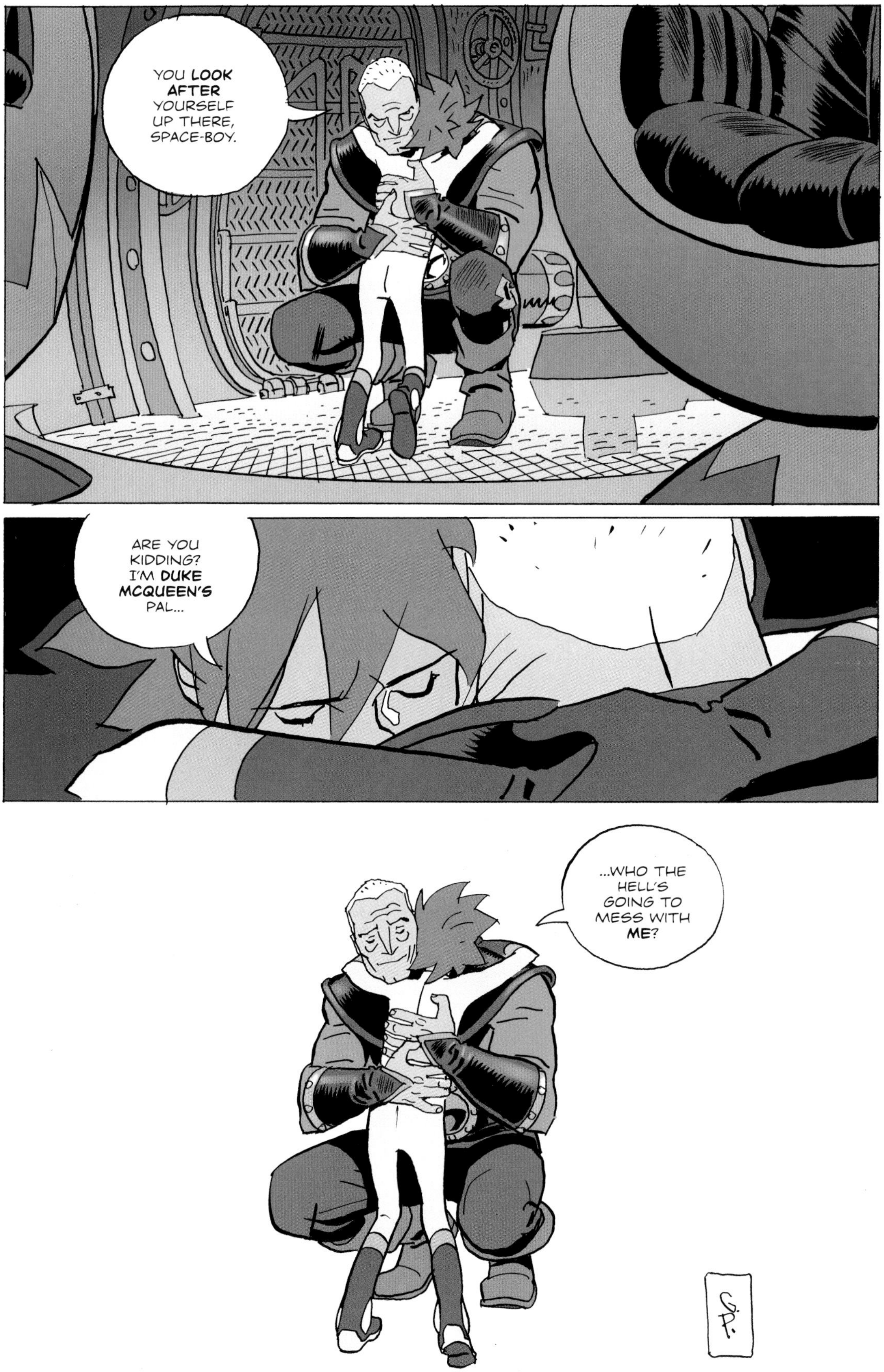
YOU LOOK AFTER YOURSELF UP THERE, SPACE-BOY.
ARE YOU KIDDING? I'M DUKE MCQUEEN'S PAL...
...WHO THE HELL'S GOING TO MESS WITH ME?

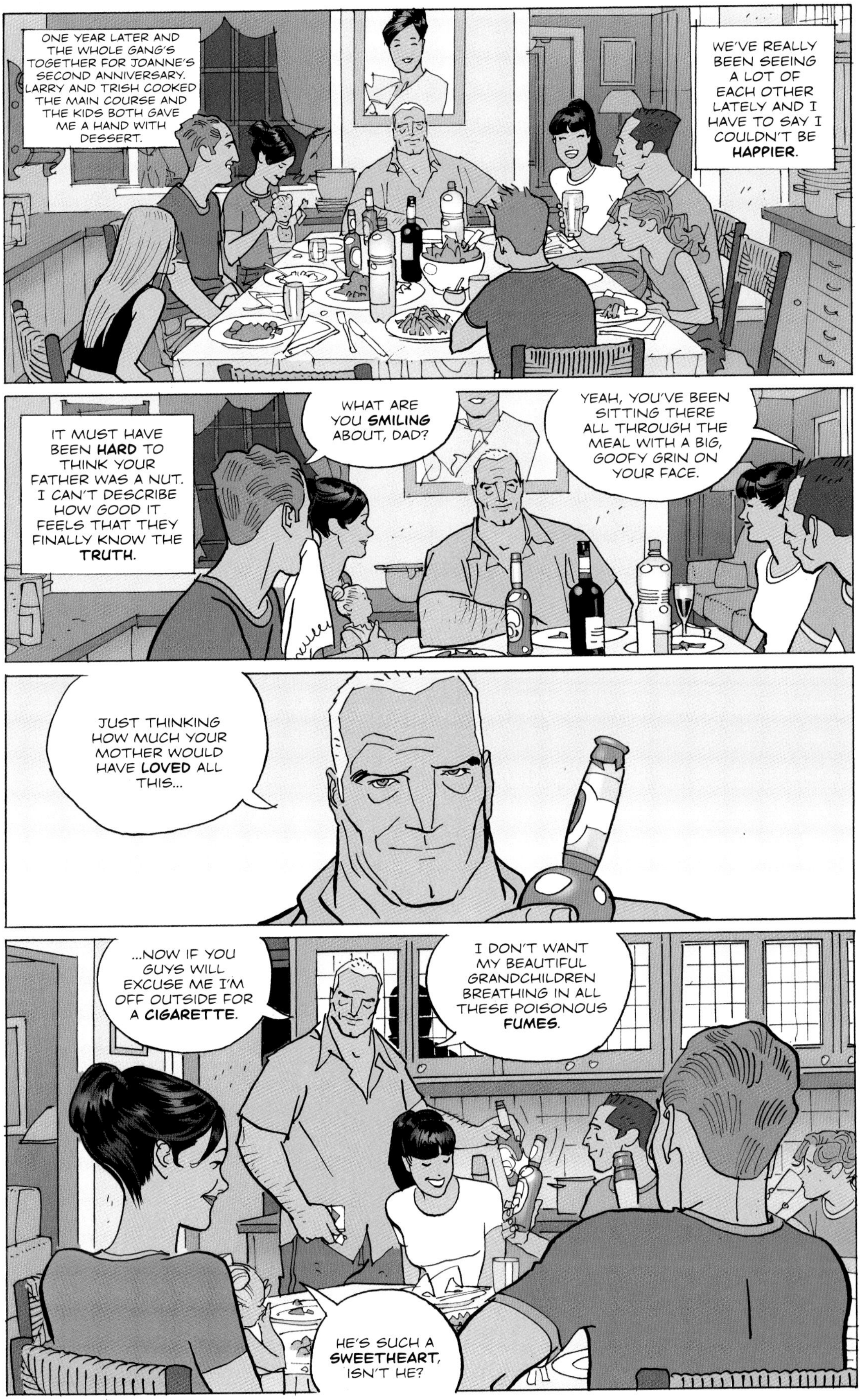
ONE YEAR LATER AND THE WHOLE GANG'S TOGETHER FOR JOANNE'S SECOND ANNIVERSARY. LARRY AND TRISH COOKED THE MAIN COURSE AND THE KIDS BOTH GAVE ME A HAND WITH DESSERT.
WE'VE REALLY BEEN SEEING A LOT OF EACH OTHER LATELY AND I HAVE TO SAY I COULDN'T BE **HAPPIER**.
IT MUST HAVE BEEN **HARD** TO THINK YOUR FATHER WAS A NUT. I CAN'T DESCRIBE HOW GOOD IT FEELS THAT THEY FINALLY KNOW THE **TRUTH**.
WHAT ARE YOU **SMILING** ABOUT, DAD?
YEAH, YOU'VE BEEN SITTING THERE ALL THROUGH THE MEAL WITH A BIG, GOOFY GRIN ON YOUR FACE.
JUST THINKING HOW MUCH YOUR MOTHER WOULD HAVE **LOVED** ALL THIS...
...NOW IF YOU GUYS WILL EXCUSE ME I'M OFF OUTSIDE FOR A **CIGARETTE**.
I DON'T WANT MY BEAUTIFUL GRANDCHILDREN BREATHING IN ALL THESE POISONOUS **FUMES**.
HE'S SUCH A **SWEETHEART**, ISN'T HE?

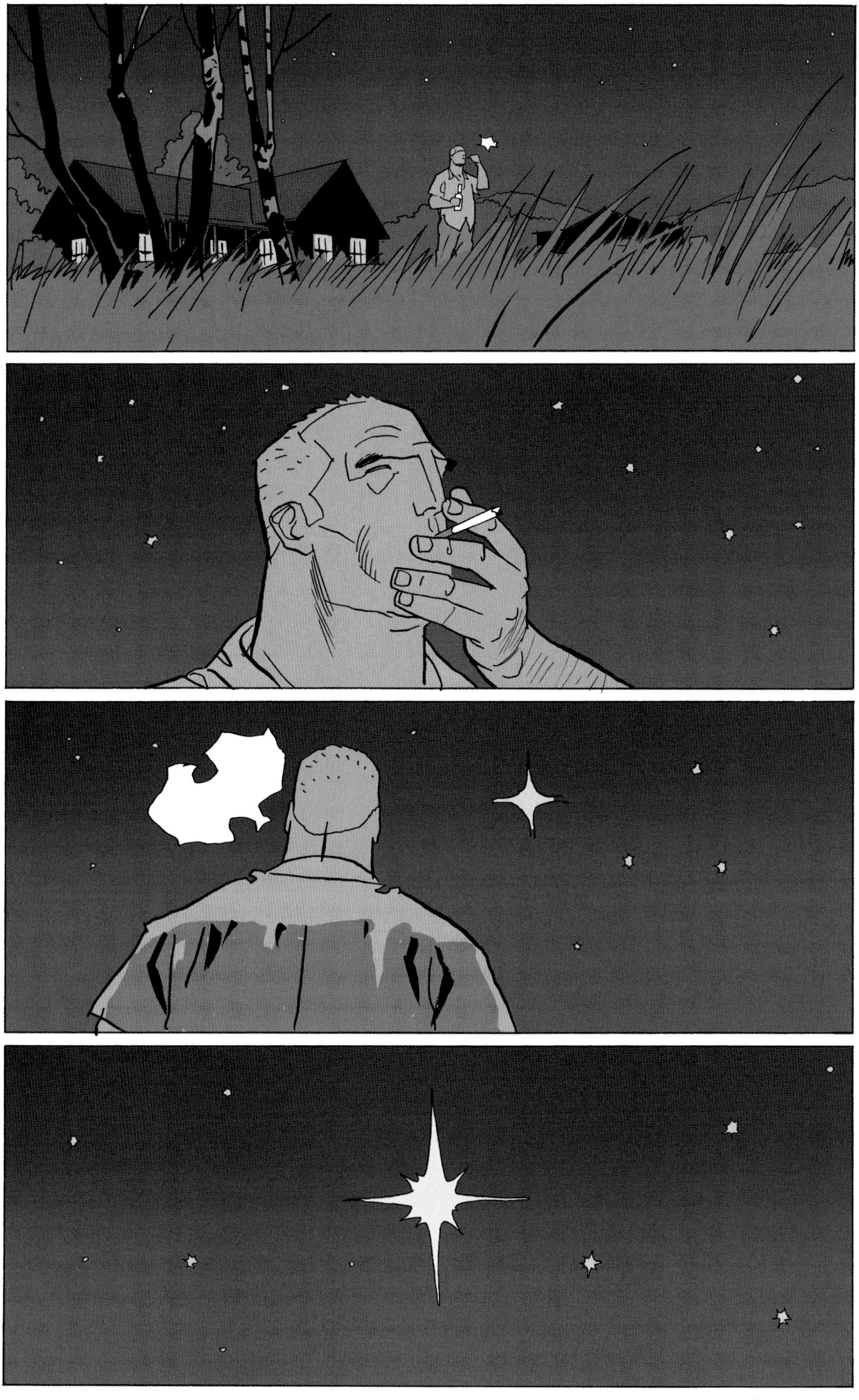

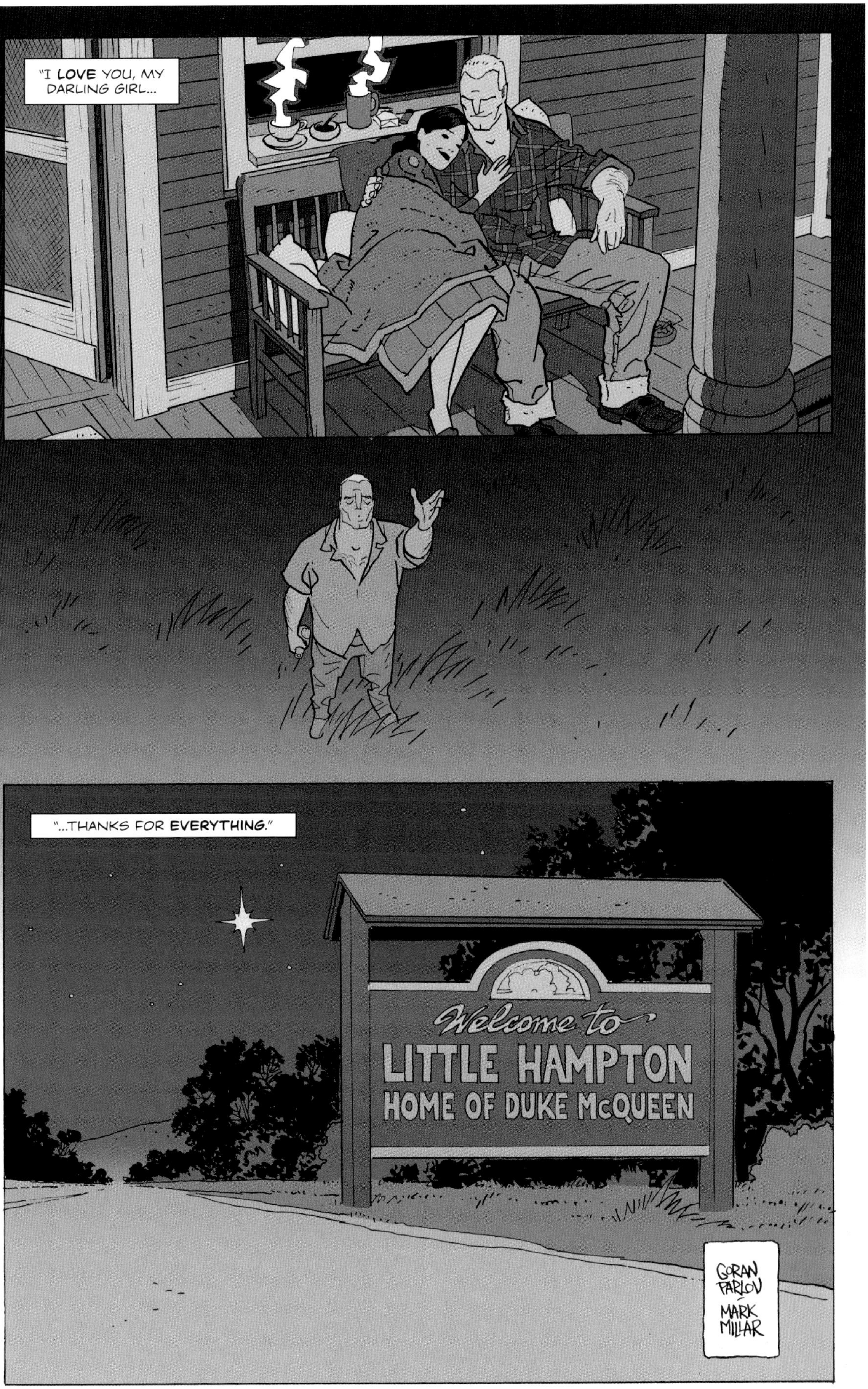
"I LOVE YOU, MY DARLING GIRL...
"...THANKS FOR EVERYTHING."
Welcome to
LITTLE HAMPTON
HOME OF DUKE McQUEEN
GORAN PARLOV
MARK MILLAR

END

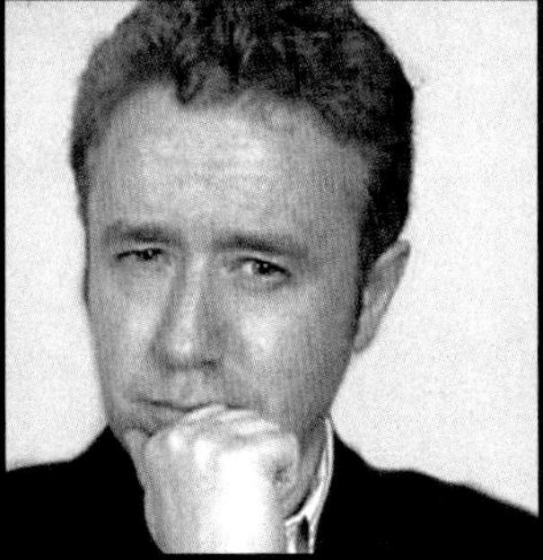

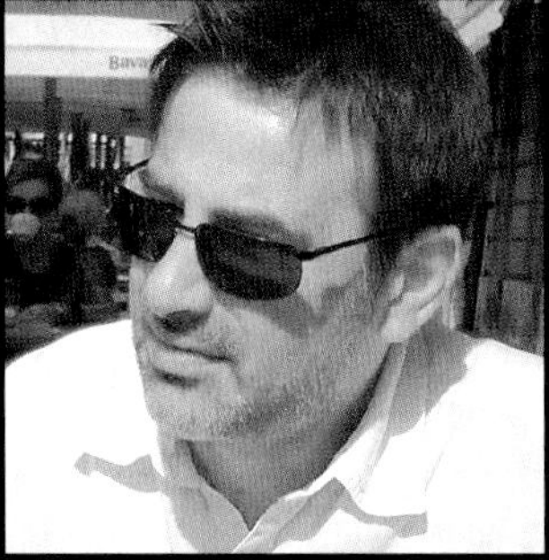

MARK MILLAR is the *New York Times* best-selling writer of *Wanted*, the *Kick-Ass* series, *The Secret Service*, *Jupiter's Legacy*, *Nemesis*, *Superior*, *Super Crooks*, *American Jesus*, *MPH*, *Starlight*, and *Chrononauts*. *Wanted*, *Kick-Ass*, *Kick-Ass 2*, and *The Secret Service* (as *Kingsman: The Secret Service*) have been adapted into feature films, and *Nemesis*, *Superior*, *Starlight*, *War Heroes*, and *Chrononauts* are in development at major studios.

His DC Comics work includes the seminal *Superman: Red Son*, and at Marvel Comics he created *The Ultimates* – selected by *Time* magazine as the comic book of the decade, *Wolverine: Old Man Logan*, and *Civil War* – the industry's biggest-selling superhero series in almost two decades.

Mark has been an Executive Producer on all his movie adaptations and is currently creative consultant to Fox Studios on their Marvel slate of movies. His autobiography, *Genius*, will be published next year.

GORAN PARLOV was born in Pula, Croatia. After graduating from the Art Academy in Zagreb, Goran moved to Italy, where he began his career as a comic book artist. His first published work was for Italy's *Sergio Bonelli Editore*, which included art for *Tex* – one of the most popular characters in Italian comics. Other assignments included the *Nick Raider* and *Magico Vento* series.

Goran began working for the American market in the early 2000s, with credits including *Outlaw Nation* and *Y: The Last Man* for Vertigo; *Terminator 3* for Beckett Comics; and *Black Widow*, *The Punisher: MAX*, and *Fury: MAX* for Marvel.

After living in Milan for almost a decade, Goran returned to Croatia, where he now resides in Zagreb. This is his first collaboration with Mark Millar.

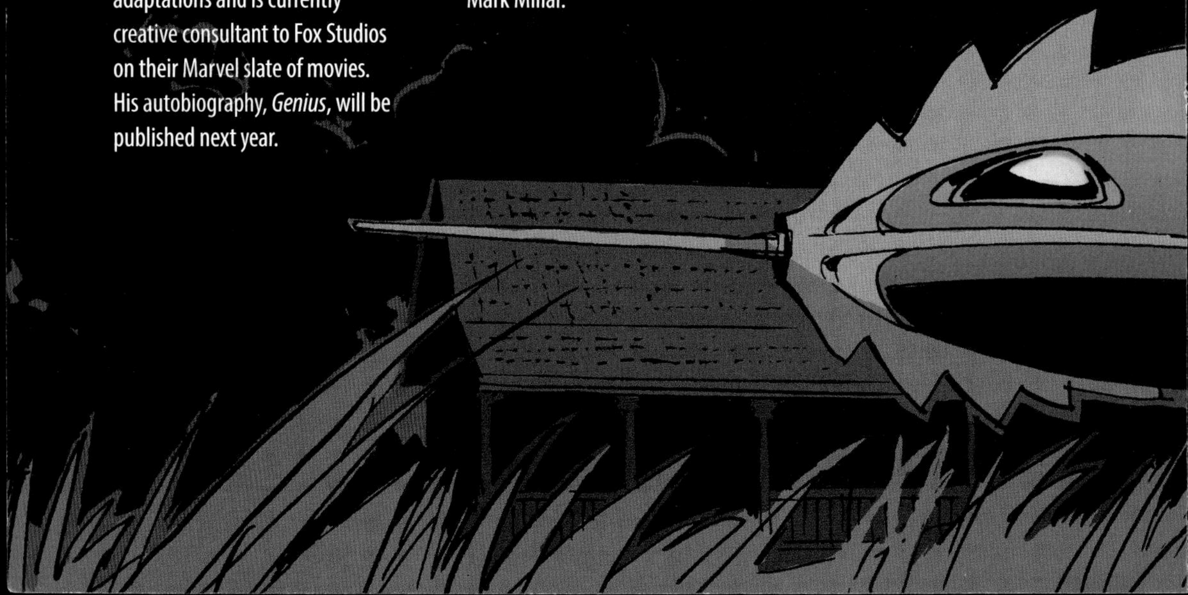

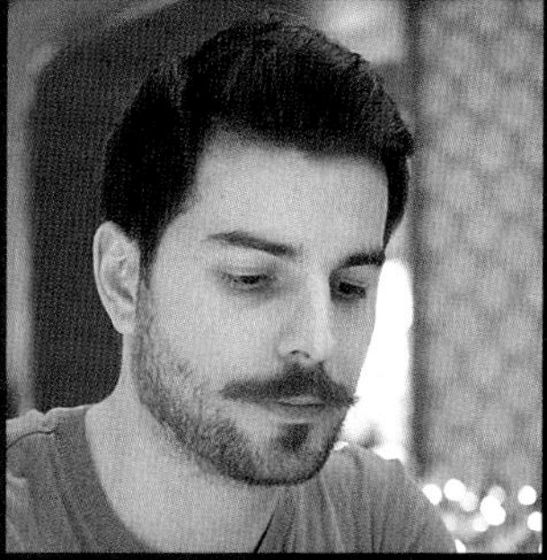

IVE SVORCINA was born in 1986 on a small island in the Adriatic Sea, Croatia. Being self-taught, he somehow managed to start his professional career in 2006, and since then he has worked for such publishers as Marvel, Delcourt, Image Comics, and smaller publishers in Croatia.

Notable achievements include getting kicked out of the computer science college and getting nominated for an Eisner award for his work on *Thor*.

Currently he resides in Zagreb, thinking about moving somewhere warmer and sunnier.

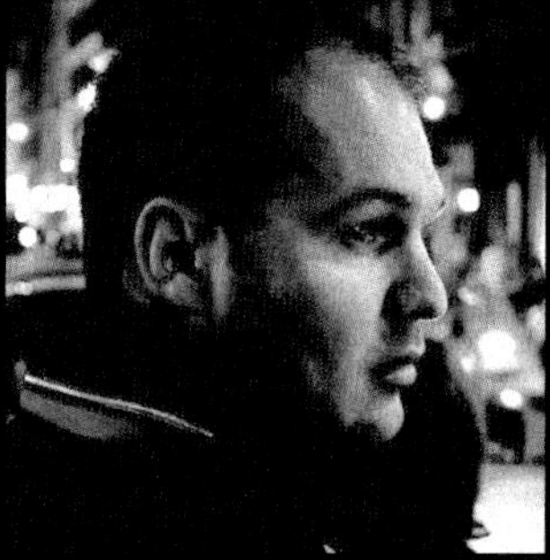

MARKO ŠUNJIĆ was born in 1975 in Split, Croatia. After graduating from the University of Zagreb's Department of Mathematics, he started working as a software developer.

Since comics are his greatest passion, Marko founded Croatia's biggest comic website, www.stripovi.com, in 2001.

Five years later, he established Fibra Publishing House, which publishes Croatian translations of some of the world's best comics. He is very proud of his editions, which include titles like *Sandman*, *Watchmen*, *Maus*, *The Incal*, and many others.

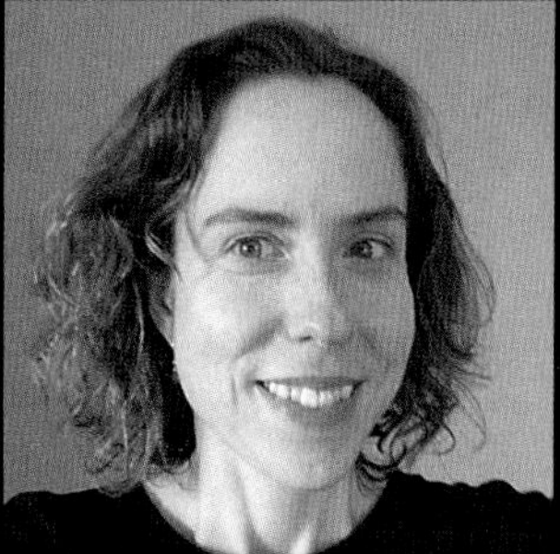

NICOLE BOOSE began her comics career as an assistant editor for Harris Comics' *Vampirella*, before joining the editorial staff at Marvel Comics. There, she edited titles including *Cable & Deadpool*, *Invincible Iron Man*, and Stephen King's *Dark Tower* adaptations, and oversaw Marvel's line of custom comic publications.

Since 2008, Nicole has worked as a freelance editor and consultant in the comics industry, with editorial credits that include the Millarworld titles *Superior*, *Super Crooks*, *Jupiter's Legacy*, *MPH*, *Starlight*, and *Chrononauts*. Nicole is also Communications Manager for Comics Experience, an online school and community for comic creators.

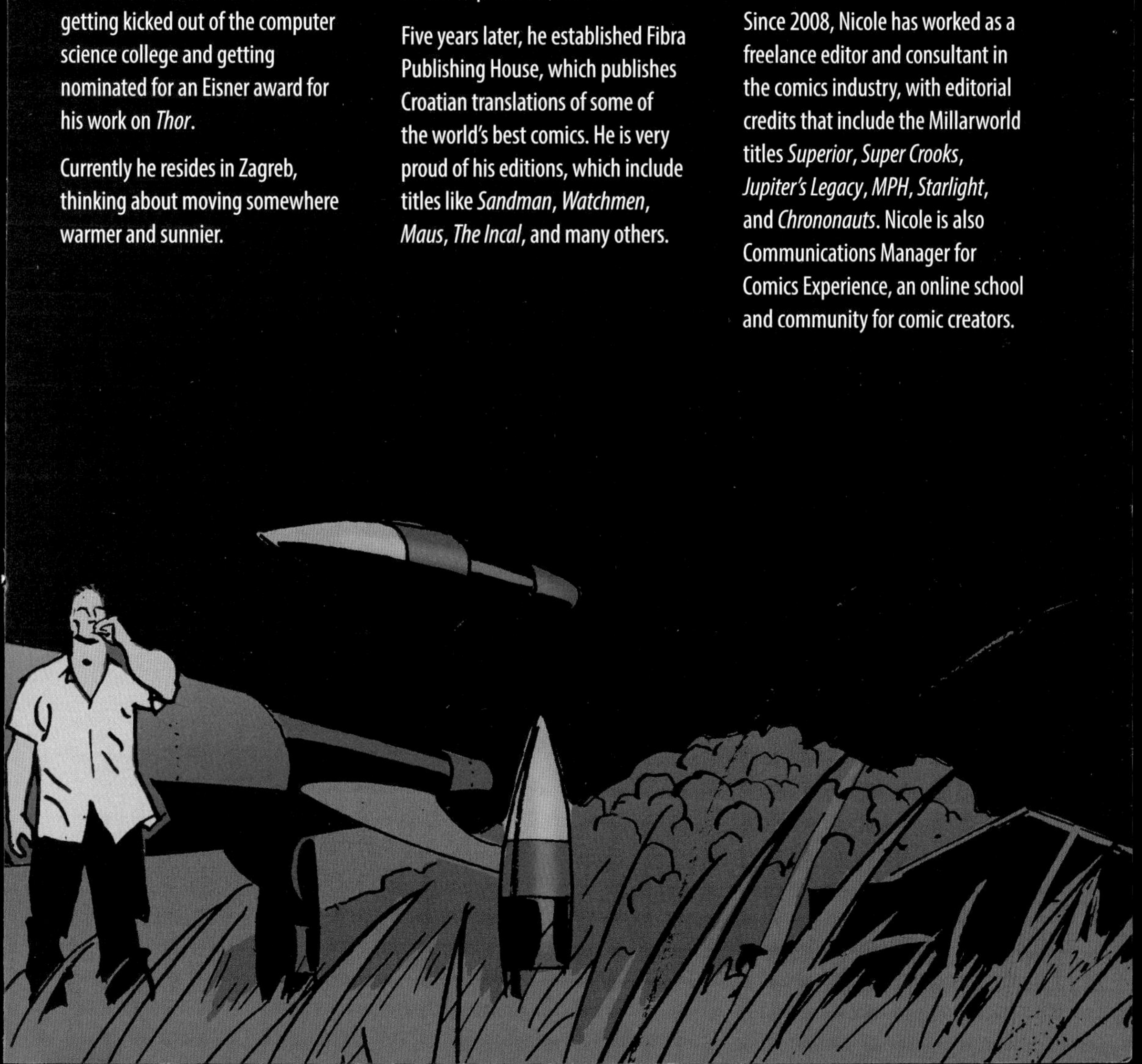

VARIANT COVER GALLERY

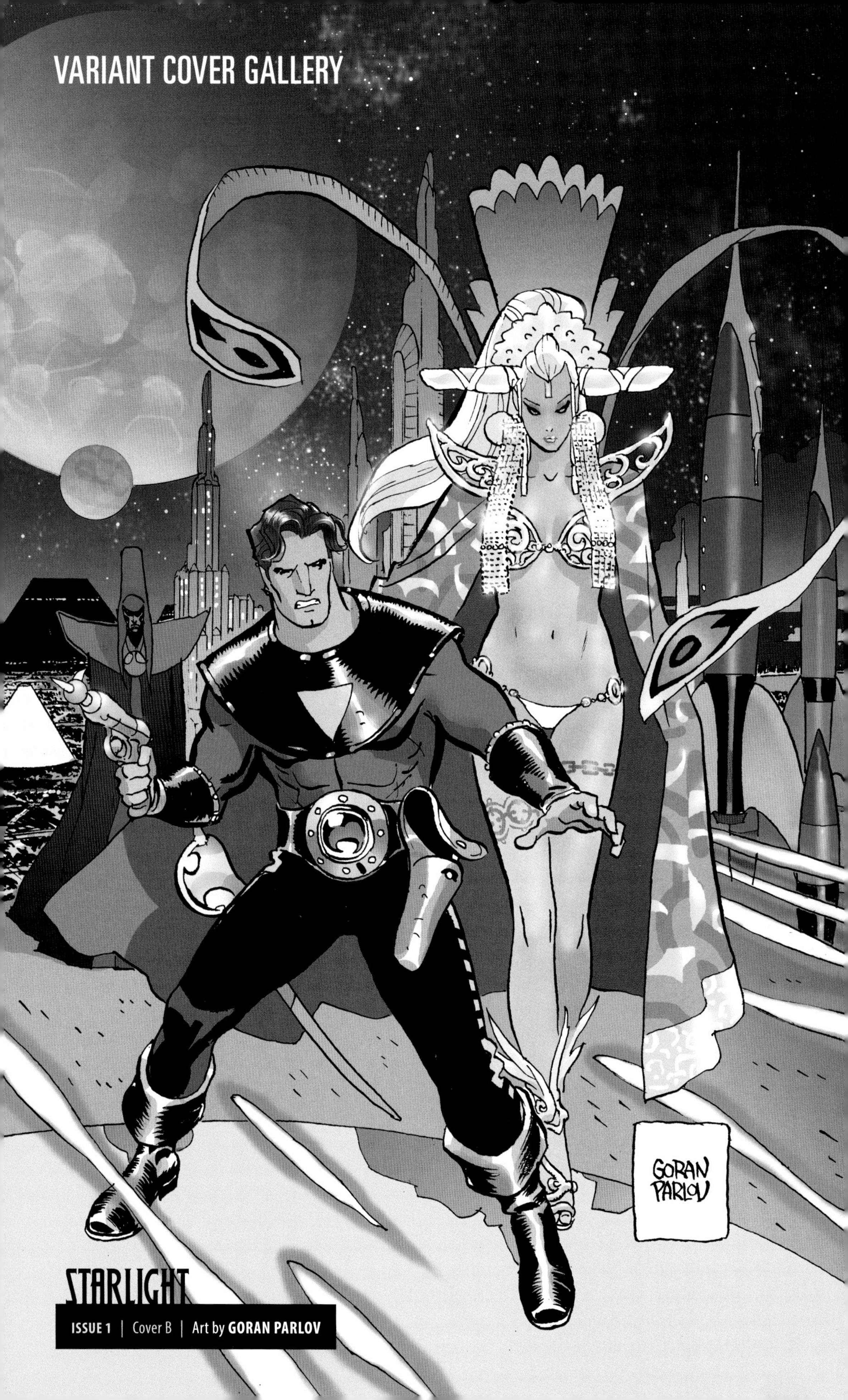
GORAN
PARLOV

STARLIGHT

ISSUE 1 | Cover B | Art by **GORAN PARLOV**

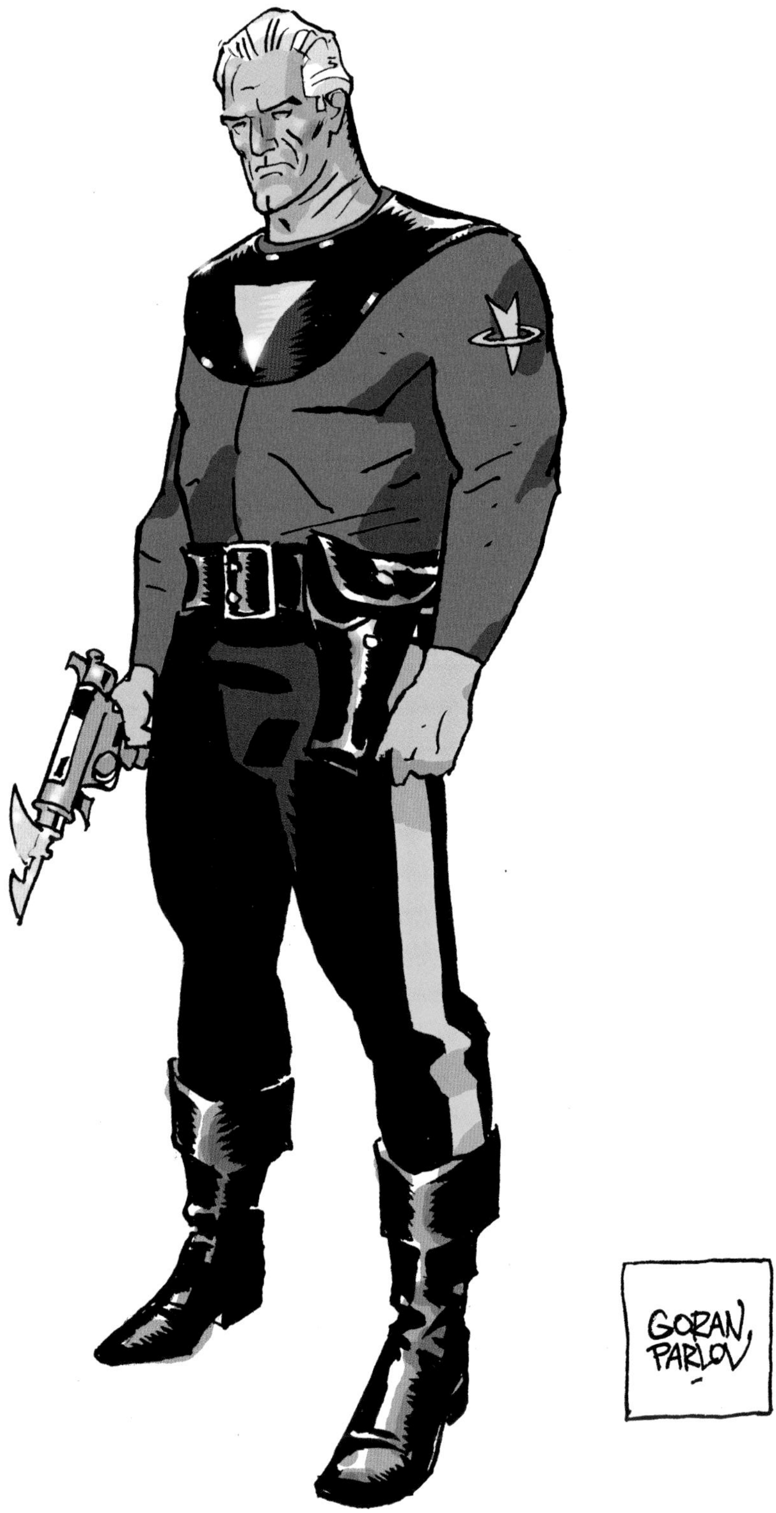
GORAN PARLOV

STARLIGHT

ISSUE 1 | Cover C | Art by **GORAN PARLOV**

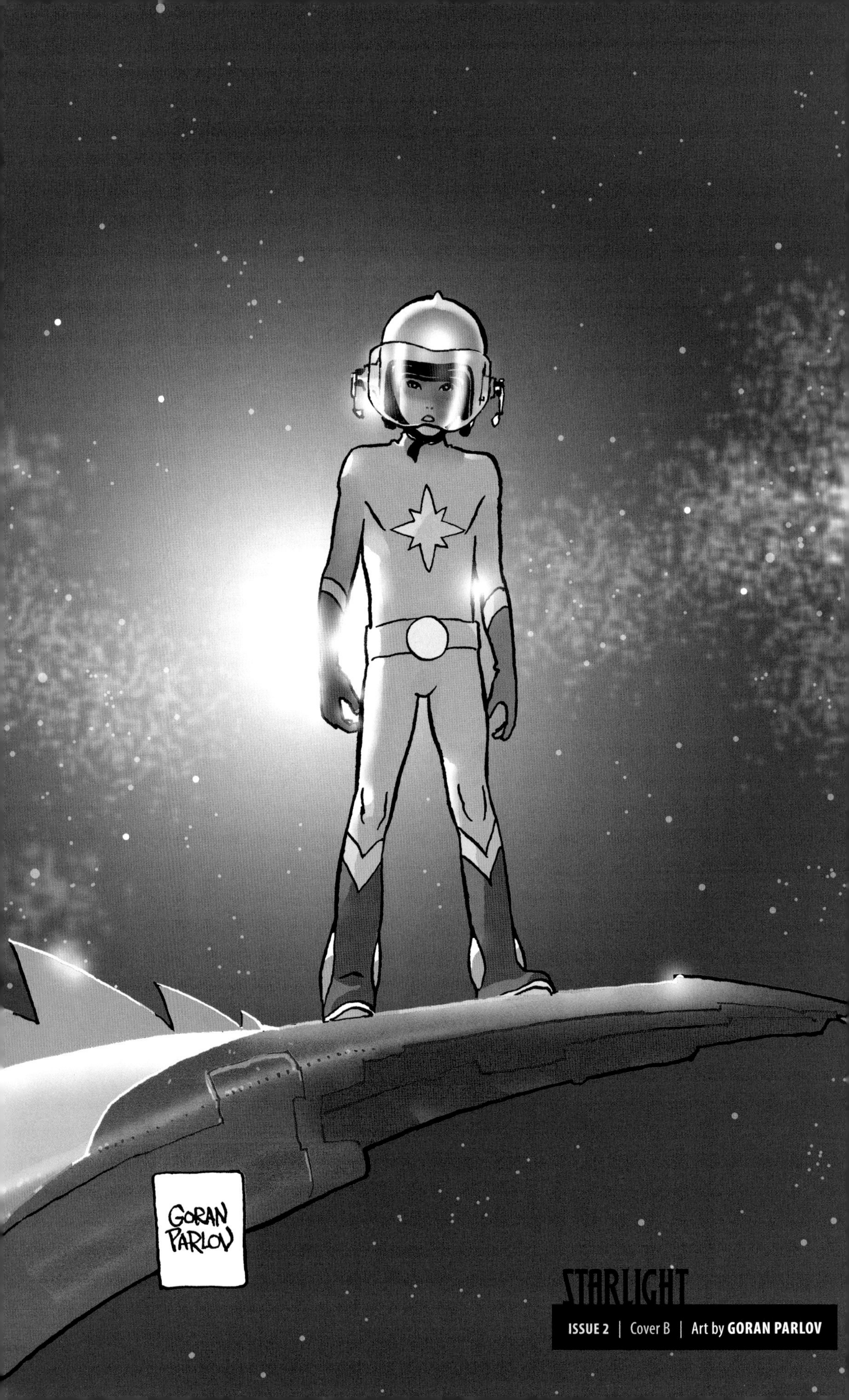
GORAN PARLOV

STARLIGHT

ISSUE 2 | Cover B | Art by **GORAN PARLOV**

STARLIGHT

ISSUE 3 | Cover B | Art by **GORAN PARLOV**

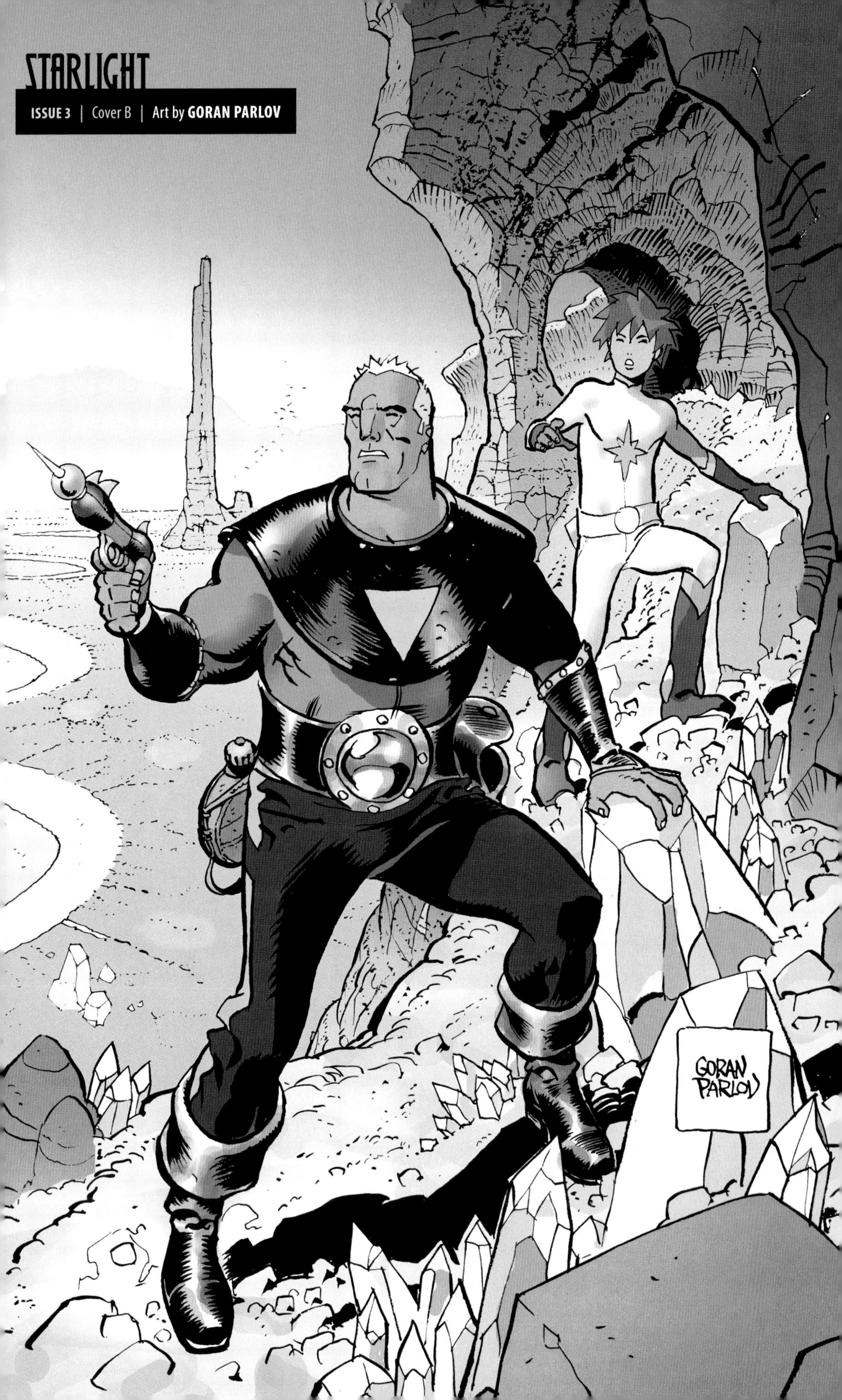
GORAN PARLOV

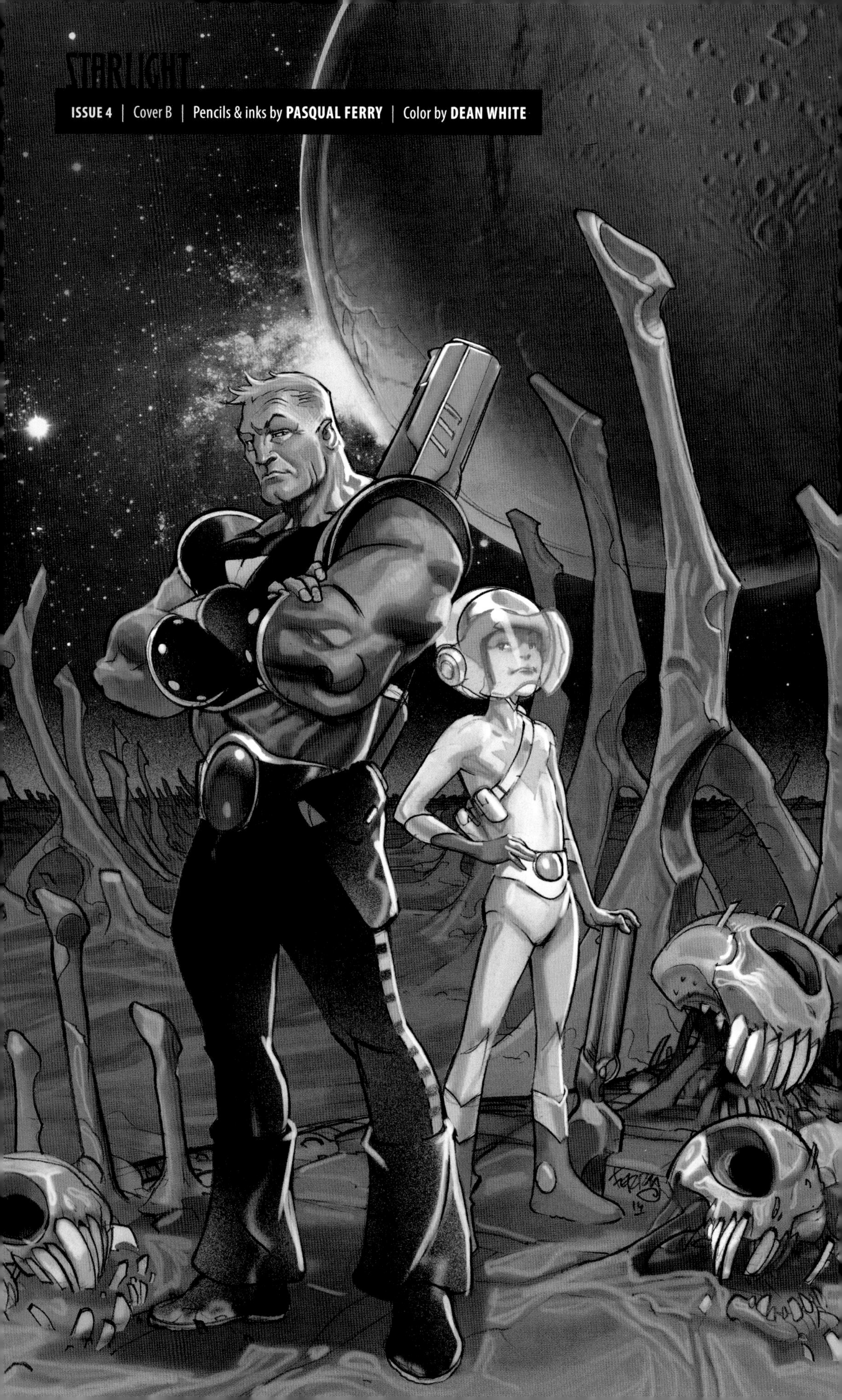

STARLIGHT

ISSUE 4 | Cover B | Pencils & inks by **PASQUAL FERRY** | Color by **DEAN WHITE**

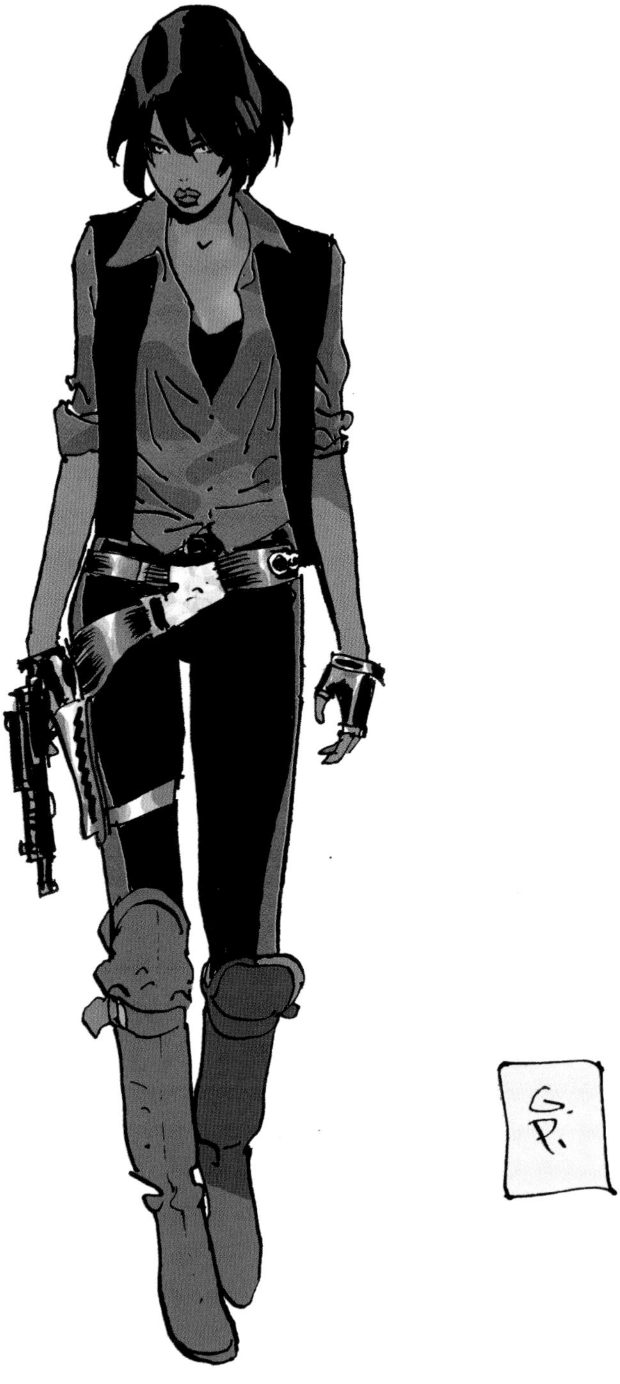
G.
P.

STARLIGHT

ISSUE 4 | Cover C | Art by **GORAN PARLOV**

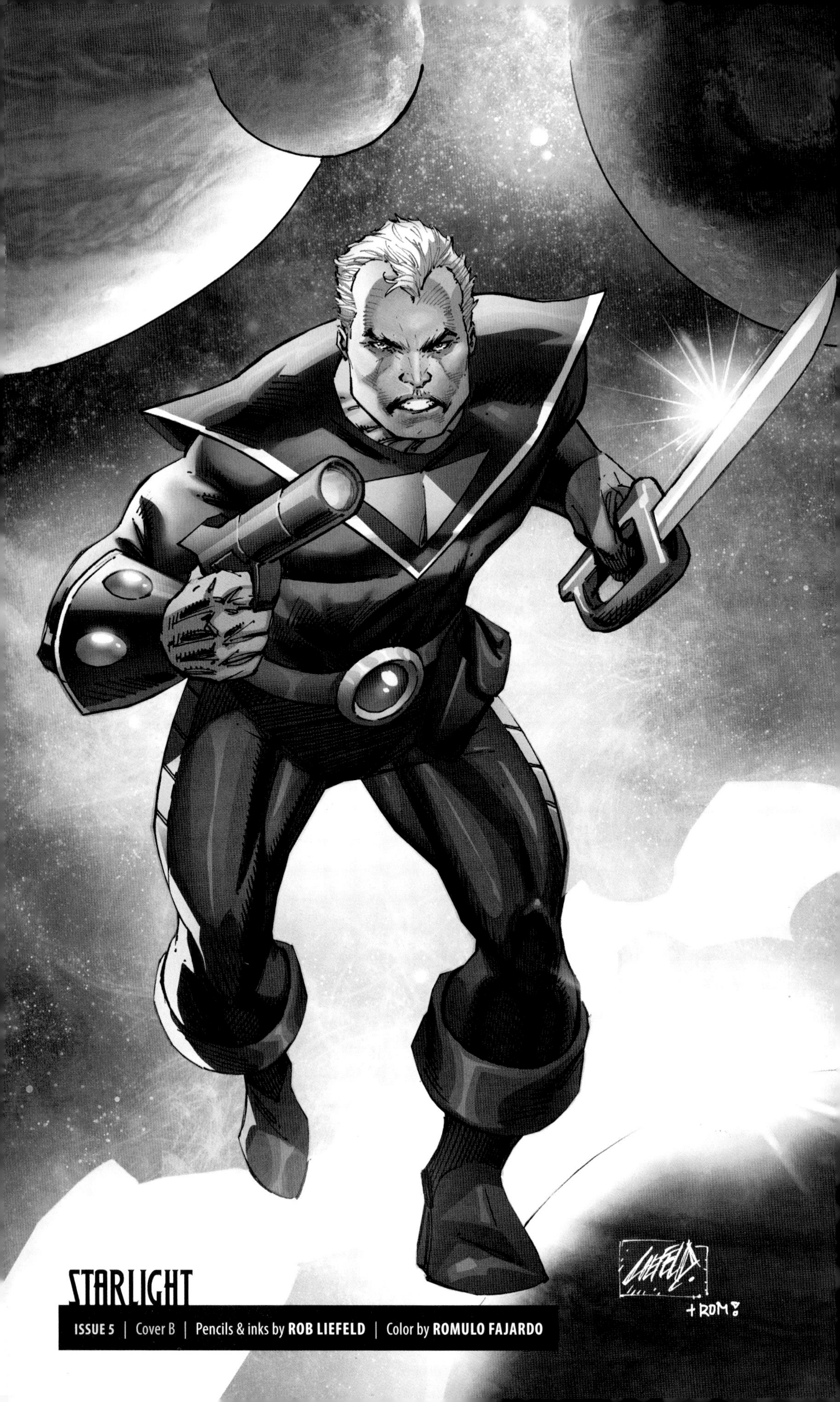
LIEFELD
+ROM!

STARLIGHT

ISSUE 5 | Cover B | Pencils & inks by **ROB LIEFELD** | Color by **ROMULO FAJARDO**

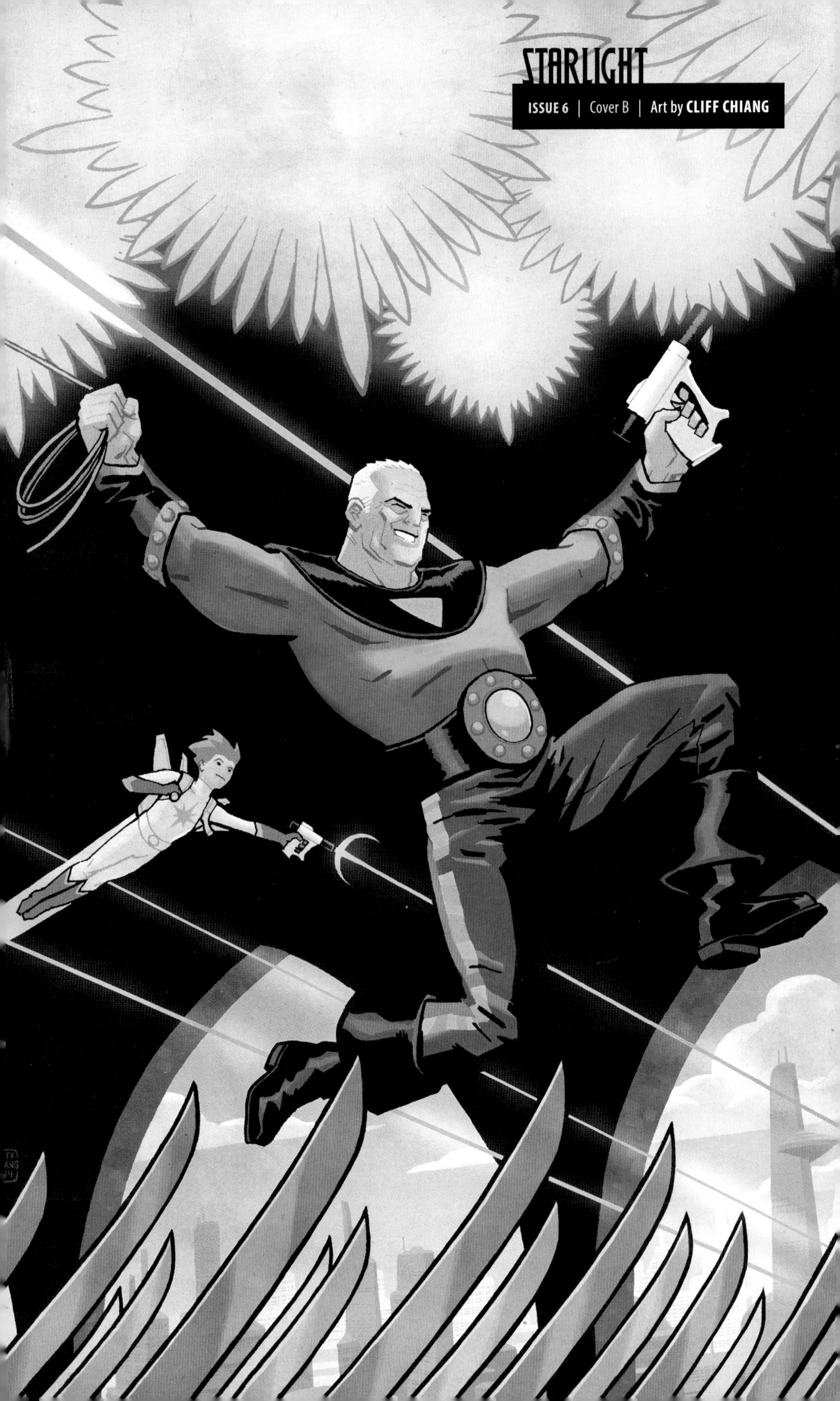

STARLIGHT

ISSUE 6 | Cover B | Art by CLIFF CHIANG

MILLARWORLD

THE COLLECTION CHECKLIST

KICK-ASS
MARK MILLAR
JOHN ROMITA JR.

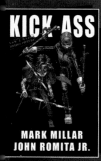

KICK-ASS
Art by John Romita Jr.

- [ ] Kick-Ass #1-8

HIT-GIRL
MARK MILLAR
JOHN ROMITA JR.

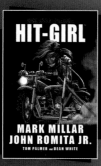

HIT-GIRL
Art by John Romita Jr.

- [ ] Hit-Girl #1-5

KICK-ASS 2
MARK MILLAR
JOHN ROMITA JR.

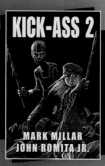

KICK-ASS 2
Art by John Romita Jr.

- [ ] Kick-Ass 2 #1-7

KICK-ASS 3
MARK MILLAR
JOHN ROMITA JR.

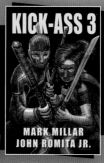

KICK-ASS 3
Art by John Romita Jr.

- [ ] Kick-Ass 3 #1-8

MILLAR MURPHY
CHRONONAUTS
#1

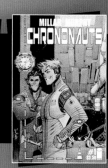

CHRONONAUTS
Art by Sean Gordon Murphy

- [ ] Chrononauts #1-4

MARK MILLAR DUNCAN FEGREDO
MPH

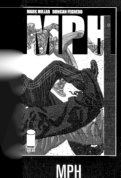

MPH
Art by Duncan Fegredo

- [ ] MPH #1-5

MARK MILLAR GORAN PARLOV
STARLIGHT

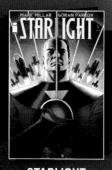

STARLIGHT
Art by Goran Parlov

- [ ] Starlight #1-6

MARK MILLAR DAVE GIBBONS MATTHEW VAUGHN
KINGSMAN
THE SECRET SERVICE

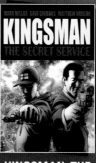

KINGSMAN: THE SECRET SERVICE
Art by Dave Gibbons

- [ ] The Secret Service #1-6

MARK MILLAR · WILFREDO TORRES
JUPITER'S CIRCLE

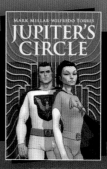

JUPITER'S CIRCLE
Art by Wilfredo Torres

- [ ] Jupiter's Circle #1-5

MARK MILLAR · FRANK QUITELY
JUPITER'S LEGACY

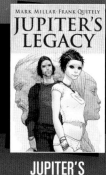

JUPITER'S LEGACY
Art by Frank Quitely

- [ ] Jupiter's Legacy #1-5

MARK MILLAR LEINIL YU
SUPER CROOKS
THE HEIST

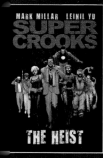

SUPER CROOKS
Art by Leinil Yu

- [ ] Super Crooks #1-4

MARK MILLAR & LEINIL YU
SUPERIOR
FROM THE WRITER OF KICK-ASS

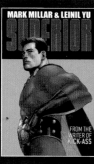

SUPERIOR
Art by Leinil Yu

- [ ] Superior #1-7

MILLAR & McNIVEN'S
NEMESIS

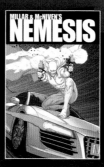

NEMESIS
Art by Steve McNiven

- [ ] Nemesis #1-4

WANTED
MARK MILLAR • JG JONES • PAUL MOUNTS
UNIVERSAL PICTURES

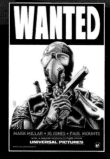

WANTED
Art by JG Jones

- [ ] Wanted #1-6

AMERICAN JESUS
BOOK ONE : CHOSEN
MARK MILLAR ✦ PETER GROSS

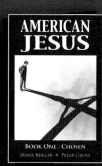

AMERICAN JESUS
Art by Peter Gross

- [ ] American Jesus #1-3